Comparative Ethnic and Race Relations

Race and empire in British politics

This book discusses British thought on race and racial differences in the latter phases of empire from the 1890s to the early 1960s. It focuses on the role of racial ideas in British society and politics and looks at the decline in Victorian ideas of white Anglo-Saxon racial solidarity.

The impact of anthropology is shown to have had a major role in shifting the focus on race in British ruling-class circles from a classical and humanistic imperialism towards a more objective study of ethnic and cultural groups by the 1930s and 1940s. As the empire turned into a Commonwealth, liberal ideas on race relations helped shape the post-war rise of 'race relations' sociology that grew up around the Edinburgh School of Anthropology and the Institute of Race Relations.

Drawing on extensive government documents, private papers, newspapers, magazines and interviews, this book breaks new ground in the analysis both of racial discourse in twentieth-century British politics and of the changing conception of race amongst anthropologists, sociologists and the professional intelligentsia. The book will be of interest to those interested in the evolution of racial ideas as well as specialists in contemporary race relations.

PAUL RICH lives in Warwick and is Associate Fellow in the Department of Politics at the University of Warwick. He has written extensively on British and South African politics and literature and is the author of *White Power and the Liberal Conscience: Racial Segregation and South-African liberalism, 1921–1960* (1984) and joint editor of *Race, Government and Politics in Britain* (1986). His study of English nationalism *Ruined Eden: Landscape, Nation and People in English Culture* is due to be published next year. He is currently working on British and American relations with South Africa between 1939 and 1976.

Comparative ethnic and race relations

Published for the Centre for Research in Ethnic Relations at the University of Warwick

Senior Editor
Professor John Rex *Associate Director & Research Professor of Ethnic Relations, University of Warwick*

Editors
Muhammed Anwar, *University of Warwick*
Mr Malcolm Cross *Principal Research Fellow, University of Warwick*

This series has been formed to publish works of original theory, empirical research, and texts on the problems of racially mixed societies. It is based on the work of the Centre for Research in Ethnic Relations, a Designated Research Centre of the Economic and Social Research Council, and the main centre for the study of race relations in Britain.

The series will continue to draw on the work produced at the Centre, though the editors encourage manuscripts from scholars whose work has been associated with the Centre, or whose research lies in similar fields. Future titles will concentrate on anti-racist issues in education, on the organisation and political demands of ethnic minorities, on migration patterns, changes in immigration policies in relation to migrants and refugees, and on questions relating to employment, welfare and urban restructuring as these affect minority communities.

The books will appeal to an international readership of scholars, students and professionals concerned with racial issues, across a wide range of disciplines (such as sociology, anthropology, social policy, politics, economics, education and law), as well as among professional social administrators, teachers, government officials, health service workers and others.

Other books in this series:
Michael Banton: *Racial and ethnic competition*
Tomas Hammar (ed.): *European immigration policy*
Roger Hewitt: *White talk black talk: inter-racial friendships and communication amongst adolescents*
Richard Jenkins: *Racism and recruitment: managers, organisations and equal opportunity in the labour market*
Richard Jenkins and John Solomos (eds.): *Racism and equal opportunity policies in the 1980s*
Frank Reeves: *British racial discourse*
John Rex and David Mason (eds.): *Theories of race and ethnic relations*
Paul Rich: *Race and empire in British politics*
Robin Ward and Richard Jenkins (eds.): *Ethnic communities in business*
John Solomos: *Black youth, racism and the state: the politics of ideology and policy*

Imperial Welcome. Cartoon by Low; reproduced by kind permission of London Express Newspapers

Race and Empire in British Politics

PAUL B. RICH

Department of Politics, University of Bristol

Second edition

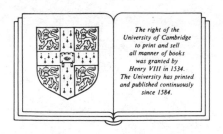

The right of the
University of Cambridge
to print and sell
all manner of books
was granted by
Henry VIII in 1534.
The University has printed
and published continuously
since 1584.

CAMBRIDGE UNIVERSITY PRESS

Cambridge
New York   Port Chester
Melbourne   Sydney

Published by the Press Syndicate of the University of Cambridge
The Pitt Building, Trumpington Street, Cambridge CB2 1RP
40 West 20th Street, New York, NY 10011, USA
10 Stamford Road, Oakleigh, Melbourne 3166, Australia

First published 1986
Second edition published 1990

Printed in Great Britain at the University Press, Cambridge

British Library cataloguing in publication data

Rich, Paul B.
Race and empire in British politics. – (Comparative
ethnic and race relations series)
1. Great Britain – Race relations 2. Great
Britain – Politics and government – 20th century
I. Title   II. Series
305.8'00941   DA125.A1

Library of Congress cataloguing in publication data

Rich, Paul B. 1950–
Race and empire in British politics.
(Comparative ethnic and race relations series)
Bibliography: p.
Includes index.
1. Racism – Great Britain – History. 2. Great Britain –
Colonies – Race relations. 3. Great Britain – Colonies –
Emigration and immigration. 4. Great Britain – Race
relations. 5. Commonwealth of Nations – History.
I. Title. II. Series.
DA125.A1R52   1986   305.8'00941   86-2588

ISBN 0 521 38958 5

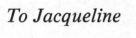
To Jacqueline

Contents

Preface

The research for this work was completed while I was a Research Associate at the Research Unit on Ethnic Relations at the University of Aston in Birmingham between May 1980 and early 1984. Since the field of race relations and ethnicity is a predominantly sociological and anthropological one, it was my keen wish to give the area an increasing historical focus. From previous work on South African liberalism, published in my book, *White Power and the Liberal Conscience: Racial Segregation and South African Liberalism, 1921–1960* (Manchester University Press, 1984), I have realised the significance and potentiality of intellectual history as a means of unravelling modes of intellectual inquiry and situating the seemingly fixed and proven patterns of thought that come to define an area of academic research and analysis. Perhaps for this very reason it is often a method treated with suspicion by many British social scientists and historians, both on the right and the left of the political spectrum. However, if this book clarifies and illuminates both a certain tradition of thinking on race and race relations in British intellectual life and the linkage between imperial race thinking and more recent phases of inquiry on the subject, then the work will have achieved its intended objective.

Until recently, the British field of race and ethnic research has been both limited and parochial in its scope. Though there was a promising pattern of research developing in the 1960s centred around the journal *Race*, events in the late 1960s and early 1970s around the Campaign Against Racial Discrimination and the Institute of Race Relations have left the area highly politicised, and contentious. This work has been written with the intention of avoiding these disputes except where they affect directly the problem of historical interpretation. The main task that confronts researchers in this field is less one of intellectual pyrotechnics and endless debates over sociological theorising and nomenclature, but hard and detailed empirical research into an area that is rich in sources.

In the process of working on this study I have inevitably a large number of people to thank both for putting me on to certain historical sources, but also for helping in the clarification of terms of meaning. In particular, I would like to thank Michael Banton, Michael Biddiss, John Halliday, Colin Holmes, Jeffrey Green, Zig Layton-Henry, David Dabydeen, Robin Cohen, Malcolm Cross, Michael Lee, Chris Saunders and John Stone for various helpful comments and suggestions while this book was being written. Heather Lynn, librarian at the Centre for Research in Ethnic Relations, has been of great assistance in obtaining large numbers of old and rare books on inter-library loan as too have the staff of the University of Warwick library. Finally I would like to thank Rose Goodwin for patiently and excellently typing the manuscript.

March 1989   PAUL B. RICH

Abbreviations

CARD	Campaign Against Racial Discrimination
CBMS	Central Board of Missionary Societies
CRA	Congo Reform Association
CSSRC	Colonial Social Science Research Council
ILP	Independent Labour Party
ITUC-NW	International Trade Union Congress of Negro Workers
IRR	Institute of Race Relations
JRAI	Journal of the Royal Anthropological Institute
JUMPR	Joint Unit for Minority Policy Research
LAI	League Against Imperialism
LCP	League of Coloured Peoples
LCSS	London Council of Social Service
MRC	Medical Research Council
NAACP	National Association for the Advancement of Coloured People
NCCL	National Council for Civil Liberties
NCSS	National Council of Social Service
NUS	National Union of Seamen
PEP	Political and Economic Planning
RAI	Royal Anthropological Institute
RIIA	Royal Institute of International Affairs
SAIRR	South African Institute of Race Relations
SAS	Scottish Anthropological Society
WASU	West African Students' Union
WISC	West Indian Standing Conference

Introduction

This work looks at British racial thought and the last phase of empire from the 1890s to the early 1960s. It focuses upon a period of rapid and dramatic transformation in British power as the empire it controlled changed from being the largest and grandest of European nineteenth-century capitalist imperialisms, controlling a quarter of the world's population, into a largely symbolic and ceremonial 'Commonwealth of Nations'. This decline in imperial power, however, was not accompanied by an equal and concomitant decline in racial ideas and ideologies for the advent of black immigration to Britain in the 1940s and 1950s led to a new phase of racial tension and hostility in British politics that culminated in rioting in such cities as Bristol, Liverpool and London (Brixton) in 1980 and 1981. For many observers, the more recent phase in domestic racial tensions are an inextricable inheritance of the British imperial past. The very withdrawal from empire has been seen as exaggerating many features endemic to an imperial tradition based upon notions of white, or more particularly Anglo-Saxon, racial supremacy which has now retreated inwards towards the black ethnic minorities in Britain itself and sought to marginalise them in inner-city wards as a new colonised under-class.[1]

Furthermore, the imperial past of Britain has been seen by scholars of race relations as bequeathing a distinct ideology of 'conservative imperialism' which has interacted with rival ideologies of 'liberal individualism' and 'international socialism'.[2] This imperial tradition is seen as an ideological construct divorced from an understanding of political power and the configurations of historical change, and the theory of history engrained within it has not been sharply spelt out. The objective of this work is thus to establish the nature and meaning of the imperial tradition in its last major phase. It looks in particular at the tradition of political ideas established around the race concept from the imperial context and seeks to establish how far this legacy of race thinking affected British cities at the time of the commencement of an internal pattern of race relations on colour

1

lines, from the inter-war years in such cities as Liverpool and Cardiff, and nationally after 1945.

Considerable attention has thus been paid in this study to the nature and role of ideas about race and empire during a period of rapid political change. The focus has thus been upon the political dimensions of race rather than upon an all-embracing sociological theory which contains the danger of imprisoning race thinking within a deterministic ideological teleology linked to social structure. While the sociological explanation of knowledge contains numerous insights into the manner in which thought is produced and generated within a particular matrix of social structures, it leads ultimately to the supersession of politics as an independent activity rooted in its own traditions of thought and behaviour.[3] The importance, therefore, of analysing race thinking as part of British intellectual history lies in the critical examination of historicist theories of 'racist' ideology, which have been so prevalent in the sociological literature on race and which subordinate past history to contemporary political interests.[4] While the race thinking of previous generations in Britain has bequeathed a legacy for more contemporary politics, it is still essential to understand their thinking on their own terms. There has been a tendency in a large body of the historiography of race in Europe to subordinate all discussion to the experience of National Socialism and the intellectual and ideological origins of the Final Solution. This mode of historical inquiry, however, overlooks the different world in which thinkers of race lived during the nineteenth and early twentieth centuries and imposes upon them motives and objectives defined in contemporary terms.[5]

This problem of historical analysis emerges particularly in the case of the term 'racism', which has come to be used very generally in recent historical writings on race and racial thinking. In one sense, the saliency of 'race' in a society presupposes the existence also of 'racism' for, as Pierre van den Berghe has pointed out, 'without racism physical characteristics are devoid of social significance'.[6] 'Racism' in this general context means any form of belief system that rationalises and justifies the assumption that one human group is inferior to another, and is thus operational at the level of social attitudes. This perspective, which has been strongly visible in much social science writing since the early 1940s and the appearance of Ruth Benedict's *Race and Racism*, has not satisfied some sociologists concerned with linking manifestly 'racist' attitudes to underlying social structures.[7] The problem, however, for historians is substantially a different one to that facing the student of contemporary society and social behaviour for the 'facts' of social structures from the past are by no means given, but come down through the prism of documents and records that have themselves been interpreted and selected by human minds. Thus, as Marc Bloch so ably reminded historical scholars: 'in the last analysis, it is human consciousness which is the subject matter of history. The interrelations, confusions and infections of human consciousness are for history, reality itself.'[8]

The onus on historians, therefore, is less the easy task of passing judgement on past actions than in seeking to understand human behaviour in the particular social context in which it is being studied. History has, as Bloch remarked, a need to renounce its 'false angelic airs' for historians can no more play God than sociologists.[9] At the same time, this greater humility towards the subject matter of the past can lead to the avoidance of the 'presentist' dilemmas defined by the American historian Carl Becker in 1912 as meaning 'the imperative command that knowledge shall serve purpose, and learning be applied to the solution of the problems of human life'.[10] This divorces historical scholarship completely from present-day questions and problems, and in fact the cleavage is by no means so stark as some conservative historiography would like to imagine, for there is a general demonstration effect derived from studying the past which does affect present-day political behaviour. But the linkage is tenuous and indirect and there is no necessary reason even why those who remember their past may not still be condemned to repeat it.

Sooner or later, indeed, historians will need to develop a wider and more systematic theory of 'racism' in Western history and culture anchored in a commonly agreed periodisation of its growth and development. Contemporary historiography employs a very catholic use of the term, reading back far into Western history a racist discourse that is more recognisably modern in its meaning.[11] Though Christine Bolt has rooted the work in the nineteenth-century anthropological discourse on race and the notion of hostility based simply on colour, it is clear that the term has even more modern origins.[12] The word 'racism' really only emerges into popular usage *entre deux guerres* and in reaction especially to National Socialism in Germany. In 1938, Magnus Hirschfeld's posthumous *Racism*, which examined Nazi racial theory and underlined what was seen as a doctrine of 'race war', was published in English.[13] The book reflected a changing climate of intellectual and scholarly attitudes towards race in the 1930s (which is examined more fully in Chapter Four) and the evolving meaning of a word which had hitherto been generally synonymous with 'nation' in British liberal discourse. Informed opinion in Britain had in fact traditionally had a weak understanding of the nature of 'nationalism', and in colonial areas like South Africa, furthermore, 'race' was generally meant to refer to the two white groups of British and Afrikaners.

The aetiology of the word 'racism' is not without meaning and significance, for historical study has traditionally failed to generate a vocabulary of its own (unlike the social sciences) and has been generally dependent upon a more popular use of words and meanings. In the case of 'racism', though, the meaning has to a considerable degree been superimposed via committees of experts, who have been seen by some sociologists as the natural bodies to deal with the 'problems' arising from race in the wake of the Second World War.[14] If 'racism', however, becomes linked to an a priori theory of social causation in Western societies stemming from a theory of capitalist expansion since the fifteenth and sixteenth centuries and its eventual development into overseas imperialism and slavery, then the term cannot be taken simply at face value but needs extensive and critical historical testing. No theory or term in history is sacrosanct and can only survive rigorous testing against the evidence available. This problem emerges in the recent study of Peter Fryer on the history of black people in Britain. Here the term 'racism' is given a teleological and historicist quality once it has been separated from an earlier phase of 'race prejudice', which was less systematic and was symptomatic of a more isolated and parochial British community in the era before the seventeenth century. Once, however, the overseas connection is established via the slave trade, then the economic conditions are said to have been available for the generation of racist ideology based on the oral tradition of the slave plantocracy in Barbados. Via word of mouth, this racist tradition became implanted in British society and culture as a relatively systematic ideology, and its eventual emergence into a full-blown pseudo-scientific ideology in the nineteenth century was thus more or less inevitable, given the theory, for 'in time [racism] acquires a pseudo-scientific veneer that glosses over its irrationalities and enables it to claim intellectual respectability. And it is transmitted largely through the printed word.'[15]

The weakness with Fryer's analysis of racism is its fatalistic quality and his failure to distinguish between the more extreme and systematic views of the Caribbean slave plantocracy and the more flexible attitudes that were generally manifest in British society itself, where the black population outside the capital in the seventeenth and eighteenth centuries was infinitesimal. Indeed, as Anthony Barker has shown in a study of British attitudes to the negro in the period of the slave trade, black races before the 1770s were judged inferior more through their cultural attributes and the traditional associations within Christian culture of blackness with evil than on any theory of innate racial inferiority.[16] Furthermore, when a more systematic racism did begin to emerge in the 1770s on the basis of works like Edward Long's *History of Jamaica*, it was not an inevitable result of the notion of a 'Great Chain of Being' in European culture, which a number of scholars have used to explain the emergence of European racist thought. The Chain of Being notion was an essentially static one and a number of philosophers had difficulty in applying it in practice, preferring instead to argue for a more empirically based subtle gradation of species. The crucial distinction was between man and brute animal and between reason and instinct, and Long's extremism drove him to deny this by arguing for the infertility of the offspring of the union of blacks and whites, an observation that is clearly contradicted by the mixed unions of the black population in English society at this time.[17] The prevalence of Long's views, therefore, is questionable, despite the importance placed on his work by a number of historians.[18] His assertion that Africans mated with apes, for example, was likely to have been undermined by the more popular images of black sexual debauchery and the promiscuity of black women with white men, while school textbooks generally preferred to ignore the sexual dimension altogether and to focus on blacks as culturally backward in a manner similar to other non-African peoples.[19]

Thus the link between formalised racist ideology in Britain and the economic interests of the slave plantocracy must be considered tenuous at best. Additional sources must be looked for to explain the fostering of racism in the period *after* the abolition in 1807 of the slave trade and the emergence, by the middle years of the nineteenth century, of newer modes of imperial expansion that had their economic base in interests different to those of the slave plantocracy. This Victorian context is the focus of Chapter One of this study, which looks at the debate on race in terms of the evolution of an expanding liberal middle class that, like its eighteenth-century forebears, was sceptical of too great an emphasis on dogmatic and extreme theories.

Much of the emphasis of this study is thus on the body of central, informed thought that by the twentieth century had come to be called 'middle opinion'. Its general ethos was one of faith in slow, governmental reform and belief in the progressive evolution of scientific rationality.[20] It was thus a typical example of what Noel Annan has noted as the 'curious strength of positivism' in English thought, though it could be gripped by more systematic social theories on occasions, as with liberal idealism towards the century's end.[21] The central argument of this study is that British middle opinion acted as a crucial cushion against the more general extension of systematic racist doctrines in the nineteenth and twentieth centuries, whilst at the same time still continuing much of the earlier cultural provincialism on the issue of race which was to continue into the era of black immigration to Britain in the period since the Second World War. Some of this provincialism can be ascribed to the more general weakness of British thought on nationalism in the nineteenth and early twentieth centuries, for, while periodic fits of nationalist fervour gripped the public mood in Britain, the country for the most part escaped the great age of nineteenth-century nation-building in Europe. The English Channel thus acted as a crucial ideological and intellectual barrier on matters of race well into the twentieth century. Though debate on races and 'inter-racial contact' had begun to flourish in the imperial context by the last quarter of the nineteenth century, it tended to be conducted amongst small circles of informed specialists who had an eye to influencing imperial policy rather than wider English public opinion.

This relative isolation and provincialism of English thought on race in the nineteenth century thus partly explains the remarkable survival of 'neo-Victorian' ideas on race and its linkage to geographical and cultural theories of group differences.[22] This study, therefore, of the pattern of thought on race between the 1890s and the 1960s in Britain reveals certain wider features of English social and political thought as a whole at this time, and its generally insular and incremental quality. The value of intellectual history as an academic enterprise is thus that it can be a vital means of clarifying and complementing other historical subject areas such as social history, especially if the focus is upon important moments of *change* in thought.[23] To this extent, intellectual history as a distinct area of historical research and writing is indelibly shaped by the revolution in European social thought in the nineteenth century arising from the concept of *social dynamics* in the writings of Comte, Marx and Spencer. Intellectual history thus represents a considerable expansion and development of an older tradition of 'history of ideas' which, as Leonard Krieger has argued, 'refers to a category of literature in which articulate concepts have themselves been the primary historical agents, with the personal bearers and external relations adduced as conditions of them'[24] Intellectual history is concerned not simply with articulate and formal patterns of thought, but also with the less systematised and articulate thinking which makes up a wider climate of thinking within a society at a particular point in time. As a field it is thus a vital component part of a socio-historical understanding of a society's nature and functioning, but, unlike much sociological faith in the possibility of a 'science' of social processes, whether of the Marxist or structural functional sort, it is characterised by a general loss of faith in the inherent lawfulness of human nature and behaviour.[25] Intellectual history thus insists on the basic autonomy of human ideas and beliefs from social scientific 'structures' and is important in revealing the contingent nature of sociological beliefs themselves. As Quentin Skinner has remarked: 'to discover from the history of thought that there are in fact no . . . timeless concepts, but only the various different concepts which have gone with various different societies, is to discover a general truth not only about the past but about ourselves as well'.[26]

This has been the underlying premise in this work, which has sought to unravel the key traditions of belief on race in British society during a period of considerable social and political change which includes three important wars – the Anglo-Boer War of 1899–1902, the First World War (1914–18) and the Second World War (1939–45). During this period the notion of the British Empire began to change in establishment discourse at least into that of a 'Commonwealth'. The first phase, leading up to the First World War, is discussed in Chapter 1, which looks at the manner in which Victorian racial ideas developed under the umbrella of an Anglo-Saxonist racial ideology until 1905–6 and the re-emergence of liberalism in British politics. Thereafter, as Chapter 2 shows, a tradition of cultural relativism towards different races became established by Mary Kingsley's acolytes, though it eventually became bogged down in the racism of E. D. Morel in the aftermath of the First World War on the issue of the use of French troops in the occupied Rhineland.

While mainstream liberals hoped for international equality and the brotherhood of races before the First World War, establishment-oriented circles sought to liberalise imperialism from above through the Commonwealth concept. This is examined in Chapter 3, especially in terms of the racial ideas of those groups such as the Rhodes Trust and the Round Table which were instrumental in first promoting the Commonwealth concept before and after the First World War. One important aspect of this reformulation was the loss of historical self-confidence in comparison to the Victorians and the shift towards a benevolent notion of British imperial 'trusteeship'. With the weakening of older historical certainties there also emerged a growing reliance on British institutions, especially parliament and the monarchy, whose stature in some measure increased internally while external British power and influence waned.

Given this strength of the dominant establishment ideology, Chapter 4 looks at the efforts by the political left to develop an alternative concept to Empire–Commonwealth in the inter-war years. It focuses on efforts by such figures as Norman Leys, Sydney Olivier and Leonard Barnes to attack British colonial policy for its connivance with white-settler power in the colonial setting, especially in East and Southern Africa. Some of the criticisms of British imperialism made by an earlier generation of liberals before the First World War were developed in socialist circles in the 1920s and 1930s, most notably among a group of black *émigré* intellectuals which included George Padmore, Jomo Kenyatta and I. T. A. Wallace-Johnstone. The British left, though, remained remarkably unmoved by the nature of colonial racism and still reacted to colonial issues in a humanitarian and moralistic manner more typical of their Victorian forebears. The black Pan-Africanist cause enjoyed only a short-lived influence on British left-wing opinion, reaching its apogee at the 1945 Manchester Pan-African Congress, and by the end of the Second World

War the British left had been substantially accommodated to the modernisation of colonial government through the colonial development and
welfare programme.

The failure of this more general political challenge in Britain to the dominant Empire–Commonwealth ideology made the discussions within the
intelligentsia on the nature and meaning of race all the more important in the
inter-war years. From Victorian times, race had an important place in
debates in anthropological and scientific circles and had long been
associated with ideas of 'scientific racism' based upon notions of biological
hierarchies between racial types analogous to those between different
biological species. The advent of Darwinian ideas from the 1870s onwards
in many respects reinforced these notions and there continued to be periodic
debates about the origins of races and whether they took the form of
monogenesis – evolution from a single racial stock – or *polygenesis* – evolution from originally different racial stocks. Chapter 5 discusses the
continuation of these debates in sociological and anthropological circles in
the twentieth century and argues that the small coterie of professional
scholars in this field had a particular importance in a society such as Britain,
for they were conveyors of new ideas from both Europe and the United
States into an insular culture where many of the Victorian notions of race
survived in popular discourse. In the first half of the twentieth century, the
social sciences were first starting to obtain professional status in British
universities, so the debate was conducted by an amalgam of both gentleman
amateurs in the older tradition and more professional scholars like A. C.
Haddon and Julian Huxley, who, by the 1930s and the advent of National
Socialism in Germany, were instrumental in helping shift mainstream and
middle opinion from the older racial ideology, especially with the
emergence of studies in genetics.

This debate, though, did not work solely in a liberal direction for there
was a strong conservative counterattack on race which viewed racial groups
as characterised by different hereditarian traits. These views, which
survived in circles of eugenists as well as in physical anthropology well into
the 1930s, had some impact on the early discussions on internal British race
relations in the seaport towns in the inter-war years. Chapter 6 looks at the
response by some sections of the administration as well as the police to the
emergence of small communities of blacks, mostly seamen, in such seaports
as Cardiff and Liverpool in the 1920s and 1930s and the growth of fears
regarding the 'miscegenation' between these blacks and local white women
with the resulting 'social problem' of 'half-caste' children. In the case of
Liverpool especially, eugenic ideas on 'half-castes' continued to have a
considerable impact well into the 1930s, for they reinforced the campaign
by the National Union of Seamen to restrict the immigration of black

seamen into Britain so that jobs on British ships could be reserved for white, British seamen.

A more professional approach to the study of immigration began to emerge, however, through the Liverpool University School of Social Science in the late 1930s, and by the Second World War a new optimism began to be engendered by hopes for a more welfare-orientated society which would absorb earlier racial conflicts. The war itself, though, introduced a new racial dimension into British politics both in the imperial and domestic arenas. Chapter 7 looks at the shift towards ideas of colonial development and welfare programmes in the colonies in the 1930s and 1940s with the publication of Lord Hailey's *African Survey* in 1938, which led to a more unified and imperial view of 'race relations'. The pursuit of a strategy of guided social engineering in British colonies became especially important after the outbreak of war when the resources and manpower from the colonies became vital in the war against Germany and Japan. The arrival of some 17,000 black American troops in Britain by the end of 1942 produced a new race relations situation in Britain and there was a renewed impetus, especially from the Colonial Office, for the British government to pursue a clear liberal policy and resist any segregation of these black GIs, despite the fact that the American army had itself not yet been completely desegregated. The presence of black students in Britain had taken an added significance by the war years and the Colonial Office stepped into the arena of welfare provision for these students, which had formerly been conducted informally through voluntary and philanthropic agencies. The result was, for a period, a close political alliance between black students, organised through the West African Students' Union (WASU) and the Colonial Office.

Indeed, the story of race in British politics by the time of renewed black immigration to Britain after 1948 is one of successful cooptation and control as part of an overall plan of colonial economic development and slow diffusion of political power to groups of 'moderate' and amenable nationalist opinion. The black workers from the West Indies imported into Britain during the war years had been seen as part of these overall aims, for the skills they acquired were seen as useful back in the colonies from which they had come. There was no ready acceptance that they were likely to settle permanently in Britain. By the late 1940s, however, it began to dawn on civil servants and politicians that the wave of immigration from the West Indies and from South Asia was likely to be permanent and that new policies would have to be devised accordingly. Chapter 8 looks at the discussions in governing circles, in the period after the arrival of the *Empire Windrush* in 1948, of the kind of responses the government should make in order to guide and control this new race relations situation in British society. The imposition of controls was considered but was at this stage rejected through fear of outraging nationalist opinion in the colonies. The government instead sought to dissuade the immigrants from going to the seaports and increasing the size of the black communities there and encouraged them to move to inland cities and towns where they could more easily find jobs and be 'absorbed' into British society through dispersal. This strategy the government tried to pursue during the 1950s by tapping the resources of various voluntary bodies on a local basis in order to fulfil the ideal of 'assimilation' of the immigrants into British society. There was a remarkable continuity in Victorian paternalist ideas as the voluntary bodies sought to establish a more formal pattern of social relations between the dominant white society and the black minority communities. This became especially pressing after the disturbances at Notting Dale and Nottingham in the summer of 1958 and efforts in some localities were stepped up to provide a forum for inter-racial 'harmony' through International Friendship Councils.

These efforts at containing the growing domestic pattern of race relations in Britain through more indirect methods began to break down by the late 1950s in the face of growing racial hostility and calls for control on Commonwealth immigration, which culminated in the passing of the first act of restriction, the 1962 Commonwealth Immigrants Act. The central conclusion of this is, however, that, while it was possible to establish some continuity in both imperial ideas and policy in the field of race and colonial development, the tradition was by no means absolute. Imperialism as an ideology gripped the public mood as a sense of national mission only for a relatively brief period in British history, in the 1880s and 1890s. Before then, British imperial power had tended to be exerted informally through methods that fell short, in many cases, of full-scale colonisation, though the argument that the middle years of the century were characterised only by a 'free trade imperialism' eschewing annexation is overstated. After the high point of imperial ardour, with the growing loss of faith in the whole enterprise after the Anglo-Boer War, the whole system increasingly needed a new set of psychological buttresses to prop it up. The actual 'decline', though, of the empire from the end of the First World War onwards was by no means a simple and unilinear process. This 'decline' was interrupted by a fit of revival at the end of the Second World War at the time of the defeat of fascism. The post-war colonial development and welfare programme under the aegis of the Commonwealth represented a renewed spurt to the imperial enterprise that only began to run out of steam by the late 1950s as the cost of the project and changing political demands following the emergence of international criticism of imperialism compelled its abandonment.[27] Suez was the last fling of a beast irreparably doomed by the passage of events.

The loss of empire came as a profound psychological shock to a society that had grown used to having colonial possessions, despite its ignorance of their nature and extent. The sense of imperial mission and 'trusteeship' and governance over 'backward races' extended, however, only to the colonial sphere and became difficult to reapply back within the imperial metropolis itself once a series of black communities, with links back to former colonial possessions, had begun to emerge in its midst. A break thus began to occur in British thought and attitudes towards race in the course of the 1960s with the final withdrawal from empire and the establishment of a new state-organised system of management of domestic race relations, combined with strict immigration control. The nature of this political hiatus in British race relations is briefly examined in the concluding chapter of this work. If the earlier phase of domestic race relations, from 1948 to 1969, had been partly shaped by the legacy of a patrician imperial benevolence, the phase after that reflects a polarised mode of internal social control. Thus the Scarman Report can possibly be seen as reflecting a new mode of domestic colonialism now divorced from the former tradition of imperial paternalism and benevolence. Without the former set of informal restraints on state power exercised by the old liberal imperialism, the harsher aspects of imposed colonial rule now stand out in their nakedness. This is the final legacy of an experience of running a world empire in which the rhetoric of benign imperial intentions at the centre was not matched by colonial rule itself at the local level.

1

Empire and Anglo-Saxonism

Race thinking in Britain in the late nineteenth and early twentieth centuries was strongly shaped by the twin experiences of imperial expansion overseas and industrial growth and class conflict at home. Victorian racialism represented a complex amalgam of competing ideologies and interests and developed a set of stereotypes towards blacks that portrayed them as both savage and bestial figures who needed to be controlled at all costs and as passive and helpless beings in need of missionary care and protection. During the middle years of the nineteenth century the former tended to predominate at the expense of the latter as the evangelical anti-slavery impulse that had achieved the abolition of slavery in the 1830s began to give way to a more virulently racist hostility. There thus developed the stereotype of the lazy and indolent negro, whom Thomas Carlyle lambasted in 1849 in his *'Occasional Discourse on the Nigger Question'* as the 'Quashee' working for mere pumpkins. This image of blacks was born in part from a rising racial consciousness in Western Europe during the first half of the nineteenth century combined with a material concern for the release of increasing supplies of labour to service the needs of colonial expansion. It was, furthermore, a 'teleological racism', as Philip Curtin has termed it, which emphasised the need for colonial governments to drive out black peasants and tribesmen into the labour market, so conveniently linking the ideal of a colonial *mission civilisatrice* with the requirement of instilling nineteenth-century labour disciplines into non-Western societies.[1] 'If Quashee will not honestly aid in bringing out these sugars, cinnamons and nobler products of the West Indian Islands *for the benefit of all mankind*', Carlyle wrote, 'then I say neither will the Powers permit Quashee to continue growing pumpkins there for his own lazy benefit; but will shear him out, by and by, like a lazy gourd overshadowing rich ground; him and all that partake with him – perhaps in a very terrible manner'[2] (emphasis added).

This was not a view shared by all the mid-Victorian intelligentsia for

12

some liberals saw the abolition of slavery as a blessing and confidently hoped that free trade would stimulate a prosperous West Indian peasantry.[3] However, the Carlylean view was reinforced in the late 1860s and 1870s after the 1865 Governor Eyre controversy split the Victorian intelligentsia[4] and the rise of anthropological and 'scientific' racism, such as that of Robert Knox, author of *The Races of Man* (1859), enhanced the claims of a British racial superiority over black and brown races.[5] The theory of anatomical race differences, which had a protracted impact on British racial thought until at least the Second World War, tended to undermine the earlier belief in human quality – a view forthrightly stated in the early nineteenth century by Thomas Macaulay and John Dougan.[6] Liberal ideas on race thus received little support within the intelligentsia when it was most needed in the critical period of the 1860s and 1870s before the last phase of imperial expansion into Africa.

Combined with this scientific racism, though, was a more romantic tradition of British racial mission which, by the latter part of the century, became increasingly linked to overseas British imperialism. This racial ideal was defined especially in terms of notions of common Anglo-Saxon racial origins in the colonies of white settlement and the belief that British parliamentary liberties were a product of Anglo-Saxon tribal institutions which had been carried down through the centuries and underlay the British imperial mission to spread freedom and justice to other, more backward parts of the world.[7] This Anglo-Saxon racial ideal led some imperial advocates to stress the common ties of 'blood' with the United States, and so making it a natural ally for Britain as rival European powers like France and Germany had begun to challenge British imperial pre-eminence by the 1880s. 'The enforcement of the Pax Britannica throughout the British Empire', wrote the prominent lawyer and scholar A. V. Dicey in 1897, 'and the maintenance of civilized order throughout the length and breadth of the United States . . . is the main service which the Anglo-Saxon race renders to civilisation'.[8]

The eclipse of Celticism

This racial Anglo-Saxonism became in some respects a natural accompaniment of British overseas imperialism since it was an ideology that both embodied a view of the historical past as well as stressing the common racial make-up of the white British colonies of settlement.[9] It developed, though, in the wake of a debate about the nature of the British 'national character' in the mid-years of the nineteenth century in which some Victorian intellectuals had championed alternative ideals of a more plural British nation including the 'Celtic' peoples in Scotland, Ireland and Wales.

There was, indeed, no ethnographic consensus in the mid-Victorian period on the make-up of the British population and some scholars of English history stressed the role of Celtic 'survivals' throughout the period of the Anglo-Saxon invasions following the withdrawal of the Romans in the fifth century AD. These ideas became especially popularised by Matthew Arnold in *The Study of Celtic Literature*, which was 'a major effort to determine the Celtic component of the English national character'.[10]

Arnold's work was not written to defend oppressed nationalities as such, but rather to stress the polyglot nature of the British nation and the diversity of cultures that were available to rejuvenate what he saw as the chief obstacle to the fostering of a healthy national cultural tradition: the philistinism of the English middle classes. The 'Celtic element' in the 'English nation' Arnold saw as essentially sentimental, with characteristics of 'wishful regret' and 'passionate melancholy'. This Celtic element checked the 'steadying Saxon temperament', so that the national make-up of the English led them to having 'middle place' between the Germans on the one hand and the Welsh on the other:

> their religion has the external form and apparatus of a rationalism, so far this Germanic nature carries them; but long before they got to science, their feeling, their better elements catch them, and turn their religion all towards piety and unction.[11]

It was thus absurd to believe that British overseas expansion could be nothing but Anglo-Saxon in its character:

> we ride one force of our nature to death; we will be nothing but Anglo-Saxons in the old world or in the New; and when our race has built Bold Street, Liverpool, and pronounced it very good, is hurried across the Atlantic, and builds Nashville and Jacksonville, and Milledgeville and thinks it is fulfilling the designs of Providence in an incomparable manner. But true Anglo-Saxons, simply and sweetly rooted in German nature, we are not and cannot be; all we have accomplished by our onesidedness is to blunt and confuse the national basis of ourselves altogether, and to become something eccentric, unattractive and unharmonious.[12]

In comparison with this vision of a more plurally based conception of 'Englishness', the apostles of the 'Teutonic' conception of English national origin, such as Charles Kingsley and Anthony Froude, tended to assert a single racial base for Britain. This was more easy to apply on the imperial plane than the more complex and ambiguous pluralist notion. It was essential in terms of an ideology of racial improvement in colonies of white settlement, which were conceptualised in the imperial imagination as essentially rural and pastoral abodes for the regeneration of a race that was undergoing deterioration in the imperial metropolis itself as cities and industrial conglomerations destroyed the old idea of England as a green landscape. Froude, for example, in his classic work *Oceana* in 1886, doubted that the grandchildren of those who had migrated to the cities could be other than 'sickly, poor and stunted wretches whom no school teaching, however excellent, could save from physical decrepitude'. Overseas colonies, however, represented the saving grace for 'the English race', which might now 'for ages renew its mighty youth, bring forth as many millions as it would, and would still have means to breed and rear them strong as the best which she had produced in her early prime'.[13]

The meaning of 'race' in British imperialism

This single idea of 'race' thus took over in imperial discourse and tended to embody both a biological and a eugenic conception of promoting race fitness as well as a historical view of its own past based upon ideas of spreading 'Anglo-Saxon' civilisation to other parts of the globe. Charles Dilke, in *Greater Britain* in 1868, had seen this in terms of an extension of Britain onto an international basis,[14] though by 1885 Froude expressed a more sober assessment of colonial nationalism by recognising that the empire would need to be more federally organised into a 'commonwealth' of Oceana which would be 'held together by common blood, common interest, and a common pride in the great position which unity can secure'.[15]

In this imperial racial vision, the Celtic dimension was usually ignored or overridden. Dilke, for example, when confronted by the huge Irish presence in New York, dismissed it as an irrelevance for 'the humblest township of New England reflects more truly the America of the past, the most chaotic village of Nebraska portrays more fully the hopes and tendencies of the America of the present, than do this huge state and city'.[16] The brutalising imagery of Victorian cartoonists led to an image of the Irish, especially, as linked to the slumland underworld of Victorian towns and cities, and this tended to be transposed onto the imperial plane to reinforce the idea of Anglo-Saxon racial superiority. In America, one reviewer in the *Edinburgh Review* wrote: 'the Anglo-Saxon is everywhere the more successful pioneer and backwoodsman. The Irish are certainly not to be found among the hunters and squatters who prepare the forest for the husbandmen of more settled civilised habits' and living in their 'miserable abodes' in New York the Irish tended to live in spots 'as isolated as if they were in the heart of Hindustan.' Overall, the racial supremacy of Anglo-Saxons was assured in the USA for 'though they may not break down Celtic individuality, they will control and modify its tendencies'.[17] Thus, by linking the Irish and more generally 'the Celts' with the city underworld, the proponents of Anglo-Saxonism and Teutonism could easily use the historical model of the Anglo-Saxon village as the yardstick by which to judge village societies in the imperial context.

By the last three decades of the nineteenth century, the comparative method was dominated by the figure of Sir Henry Maine, who established the essential terms of debate among both legal historians and scholars of comparative institutions. In *Village Communities in East and West*, Maine applied the notion of Edward A. Freeman that Teutonic society could be located as a 'survival' in the cantons of Switzerland of the villages of rural India. The Indian 'village community' Maine saw as resembling the 'Teutonic township' since it was united by the same features of patriarchal kinship and the joint peasant ownership of land.[18] It was this ideal-type model of the Indian village community which Maine saw as being progressively undermined by the commercial cash nexus introduced by British imperial rule and the erection of a superstructure of parasitical zamindari landlords.[19] The argument was carried a stage further by more radical critics, such as H. M. Hyndman in *The Bankruptcy of India* in 1886, who stressed the 'steady prosperity and marvellous continuity' of the Indian village communities which had been the 'unit of early Aryan civilis-ation, as the *gens* was the unit of the social system in the Gentile organisa-tion of savagery and barbarism'.[20] It was the increasing threat to the 'complete organism' by nineteenth-century British industrialism which motivated Hyndman to launch a strident attack on the Raj, but within the essential vocabulary and paradigm of savagery–barbarism–civilisation. Maine had thus helped make this intellectually respectable through comparing the Teutonic racial myth with that of the mythology of Aryan racial origins in North India. The latter had become fairly generally accepted on the basis of linguistic criteria established by comparative philologists between 1850 and 1870, a study that was frequently seen as a successful *science des origines*.[21]

Until the 1880s, Teutonic racism occupied a fairly prominent place in the Victorian discourse on race and race differences and acted as an important intellectual anchoring-point in the comparative study of social and political institutions at a time when the notion of a British empire was gaining sharper political and ideological focus. The advocates of Teutonism, however, such as Freeman, were mainly concerned with developing an awareness of racial identity among European 'Teutonic' or 'Aryan' nations such as the English, and the 'Low Dutch'. These national identities were associated with liberal political ideals such as freedom and the rule of law, but had a generally limited application in the colonial context. Freeman opposed the cause of imperial federation, seeing it as a pathway to Indian numerical domination through sheer size of population, and the 'liberal racialist' ideal tended to be eclipsed in the mounting wave of popular enthusiasm for imperial expansion in the last two decades of the century.[22] Furthermore, the idea of Teutonism was based on a historical mode of reasoning through which its exponents hoped to establish its 'scientific' credibility. It tended, though, to be rather narrowly focused on mythological links with the forests of North Germany, where English liberties were seen to have their origins. It failed to provide the ideological buttress with the colonies of white settlement and with the United States which the more general term 'Anglo-Saxon' embraced, and thus tended to become eclipsed in political discourse in the last two decades of the century. Freeman, for example, propounded in 1877 a theory of racial differences based on the 'doctrine of survivals' that avoided anatomical and anthropological criteria, which were then becoming increasingly fashionable, and looked to language differences centred on the idea of a 'community of blood'. Whilst admitting that it was impossible to prove the actual existence of this 'community of blood', Freeman saw the train of survivals acting through the male line of succession, which could be established, he believed, through historical study. It was only by such means that the 'howling wilderness of scientific uncertainty' could be avoided[23] and a historical 'science' be established which rejected sociological study in favour of the 'fascinating process by which we learn to trace out the way in which a belief, a word, a legend, we might add a grammatical form, survives in this or that phrase or custom, whose origin has long been forgotten and which, without a knowledge of that origin, seems utterly meaningless'.[24]

Freeman's historical method, however, was generally too abstruse and obscure for an era that has been defined by Carlton Hayes as the 'generation of materialism'.[25] It seemed increasingly out of tune with a mood that favoured both the ethos of industrialism and of more concrete scientific research. The growing use of photography as a mode of illustration in the press and later the emergence of the cinema by the early years of the twentieth century necessitated a more visual presentation of the race theme and its popularisation to an audience that was becoming increasingly literate. The Teutonic notion thus generally survived as a junior partner in the British discourse on race and as more of a buttress to the appeal to imperial grandeur than as a particularly significant device for scientific classification. Freeman, for instance, saw three high peaks in European and 'Aryan' history in the empires of Greece, Rome and the Teuton and in 'this mighty drama' it was these 'three races' which 'stand forth before all others, as those to whom, each in its own way, the mission has been given to be the rulers and the teachers of the world'.[26]

The focus thus increasingly shifted towards an anthropometric investigation of race differences, which had the advantage of being able to claim a 'scientific' legitimacy on the basis of statistical and quantitative classification. Anthropological disputes about the number and form of racial 'types' had been legion throughout the century, but the notion of the existence of such types had been given some reinforcement by the mid-1880s when anthropologists in Britain reached a general agreement on the cephalic index in 1886. Furthermore, the shift away from the earlier anthropological interest in skull shape towards anthropometrical measurements of the entire human skeleton seemed to reinforce the scientific claim, especially when Francis Galton, the renowned Victorian traveller, statistician and founder of eugenics, became president of the Anthropological Institute between 1885 and 1889. In 1884 Galton measured 9,000 people at the International Health Exhibition in South Kensington, and the anthropological interest in race in the imperial context was reinforced at an Anthropological Conference on Native Races in British Possessions held in 1887 at the time of Queen Victoria's Golden Jubilee.[27] Anthropometry in Britain was fostered at a time when it was seen internationally as legitimating claims of national identity, such as in Germany after the victory against France in the Franco-Prussian War of 1870 and in Italy after its unification under Cavour.[28] The measurement of human types reinforced visible phenotypical differences that could be made patent through photographic illustrations, and by the late 1890s a spate of popular works began to appear, with lavish detail, to illustrate the nature and diversity of human races and the implicit superiority of the white Anglo-Saxon races and civilisation. *The Living Races of Mankind*, jointly edited by H. N. Hutchinson, J. W. Gregory and R. Hydeken, for example, appeared in 1900 in 18 fortnightly parts with some 600 illustrations described as being 'from life'. The necessity for understanding such racial diversity arose, the authors argued, from the growing commercial challenges to British imperial influence:

> We have begun to realise that the most promising fields of enterprise for our ever-increasing community, the most profitable markets for our wares, may some day be found in places which are now the darkest corners of the earth, and that the half-clothed savage, just emerging from the brute condition, is a human being capable of being educated, in the near future, into a customer for British trade and a contributor to the world's wealth.[29]

As anthropometric investigation became linked to empire, it tended to buttress an existing commonsense racism which reinforced 'the English gentleman's sense of his racial superiority' and of his being part of 'an enlightened intelligentsia in a largely barbarian England'.[30] The imperial theme stressed especially the cultural backwardness of the black race compared to their strong physical ability. The 'muscular development' of black races, the authors of *The Living Races of Mankind* pointed out, was 'good' and when it came to the question of work which 'depends only on muscle they excell the average European; but in anything requiring judgment they are easily beaten. The nervous system is not very sensitive, and the appreciation of pain is dull. Operations can be conducted without anaesthetic.'[31] This racial image reinforced the well-entrenched Carlylean stereotype of the markedly dull, but physically fit black man who needed to be coerced into work. By the end of the Edwardian period, though, there were growing signs of a more subtle anthropological analysis of different black societies and cultures as the cultural relativism of Mary Kingsley and her school began to impress itself on British debates on race – a theme discussed more fully in the next chapter. It began to shape a more diverse description of different racial types, such as those of Sir Harry Johnston's *The Negro in the New World* in 1910. This still, however, linked the negro race with primitiveness along with the Bushman (San) and the Australian Aborigine and gave illustrations of the 'Caucasian type' as an 'Anglo-Saxon American' and an 'Englishman'.[32]

This greater flexibility in the analysis of racial distinctions was partly born of a growing anxiety felt in some circles by the 1890s of the fitness of white settlers to stand up to competition from cheap black and brown and yellow labour in the tropics. Indeed, at the same time as popular imperial euphoria was reaching its climax through the jingoist yellow press, some writers on empire began to question the ultimate permanence of colonial rule. In 1894 Charles Pearson, a prominent Australian politician in the state of Victoria, wrote, in *National Life and Character*, of the likelihood of an expanding black and yellow belt in the tropical areas of the globe which he thought would reduce the role of white men to a merely supervisory one centred on the introduction of Western industrial methods to agricultural societies.[33] In a similar vein, Benjamin Kidd wrote in 1898 in *The Control of the Tropics* of a growing inter-imperial rivalry in the tropical regions for trade and markets. This rivalry was seen as mainly for indirect colonial control since Kidd rejected the idea of acclimatisation by white men to tropical climates, which he saw as suitable only for black races of inferior intellectual and cultural attainment. If white men went to such regions they risked, in the absence of continual cultural contacts with their temperate northern culture, being reduced to the level of those black races with whom they had made their 'unnatural home'.[34]

These were more pessimistic images of inter-racial contact born of Western imperial expansion. A more sophisticated analysis that was not burdened by deterministic geographical and climatic explanations of race differences had begun to emerge by the Anglo-Boer War of 1899–1902. The Victorian liberal scholar, diplomat, traveller and politician, James Bryce, was especially important in widening the terms of Victorian debate into a more twentieth-century conception of 'inter-racial relations'. Though Bryce was of the same generation of academic liberals who had grown to maturity in the period of agitation for political reform in the 1860s, he outlived his contemporaries and developed the Victorian method of comparative history further in the direction of comparative sociology.

Bryce's thought on race in the global context of inter-imperial rivalries was significant for a number of reasons, not least that it emerged in part out of an earlier debate on the relationship of race and nationality in Britain itself. This stemmed from the split in the Liberal Party over home rule for Ireland in 1886 and the defection of Joseph Chamberlain and the Liberal Unionist bloc to the Conservatives, keeping the Liberals effectively out of the government for most of the next twenty years. Attacking the Home Rule policy of Gladstone, the Liberal politician and amateur ethnologist, Sir John Lubbock, wrote to *The Times* arguing that there was no such thing as four distinct nationalities in Britain of England, Scotland, Ireland and Wales, as Gladstone had maintained, but a racial division along lines worked out by John Beddoe in his *The Races of Britain* (1885). These divisions included a Saxon division that covered most of east England, the east of Ireland and Scotland, and a Celtic division that comprised most of west Ireland and west Scotland together with Wales and Cornwall. To promote Home Rule would mean promoting racial antagonisms, which would only 'add to our political difficulties and tend to weaken the British Empire'.[35] Lubbock's argument reflected the shift in Liberal thought from Arnold's earlier plea to recognise Celtic radical differences as part of his ideal of a plural British national make-up.

Bryce's reply to Lubbock contained some echoes of the earlier Arnold argument for he accused Lubbock of confusing races with nationalities. 'A nationality', he urged, 'may be made up of any number of races, because race is only one of several elements which go to create a nationality.'[36] Gladstone's case was reasonable to Bryce if it involved recognising the 'opinions' of each of the four surviving nationalities in Britain:

An Englishman has but one patriotism, because England and the United Kingdom are to him practically the same thing. A Scotchman has two, but he is sensible of no opposition between them. He is none the less loyal to the United Kingdom because he is also loyal to Scotland. And he believes the day may come when the same may be true of an Irishman.[37]

Bryce clearly considered that multiple nationalisms in Britain did not inhibit the idea of a wider United Kingdom patriotism, which could at the same time be fostered in the imperial context. He made no plea for a transformation of the British national identity like Arnold and by and large sought a more tolerant recognition of the status quo in which Welsh, Scots and Irish had dual allegiances to their own sub-nations as well as to the wider Great Britain. This reflected a Victorian liberal view on the evolved state of the British *nation*, which could be intrinsically distinguished from more 'backward' *races*. Bryce drew out these comparisons after extensive travelling in both America and South Africa, and in *The American Commonwealth* (1888) and *Impressions of South Africa* (1895) he viewed the advance of the American negro into citizenship within the structures of Southern segregation with some optimism.[38] He also saw the development of distinct agrarian African communities such as the Basuto in Southern Africa as a model for wider harmonious contacts between the 'advanced' white race and the 'backward' African one.[39] As a historically minded observer, he brought into his analysis of inter-racial relations a broad vision of historical patterns and one scholar, John Stone, has compared him to Max Weber in his broad understanding of the relationship between race relations and the structure of power in society, which he saw in its social and political as well as its economic dimensions.[40] The point about race for Bryce was that it involved the element of relationships as opposed to the discrete study of races *per se*, which had generally preoccupied his Victorian contemporaries, especially the anthropologists. Implicit within this was a recognition of the economic forces within the nineteenth-century imperial world which had brought all hitherto separate races and societies into a single global system. The analogy he used here to explain this new process was from the more familiar Victorian class system. 'It is hardly too much to say', he said in his important Romanes lecture at the University of Oxford in 1902, *The Relations of the Advanced and the Backward Races of Mankind*, 'that for economic purposes all mankind is fast becoming one people, in which the hitherto backward nations are taking a place analogous to that which the unskilled workers have held in each one of the civilised nations.'[41] This vocabulary of 'advanced' and 'backward' nations/races was a frequent device used by the Victorians to understand the international plane since it extended the discourse of British class politics and the debate over the family into the realm of inter-state relations. The Victorian notion of 'advanced' and 'backward' had been initially applied to the question of individual and family behaviour as a biological metaphor derived from Darwinian notions of 'fitness'. When it came to the question of the global realm of racial and national relationships the same metaphor seemed equally appropriate and was to dominate the discussion of race relations until at least the inter-war years.[42] Bryce saw this process being manifested when different 'races' came into contact which differed in physical, or military or mental capacity. The result was one of four different possibilities:

> Either the weaker race dies out before the stronger, or it is absorbed into the stronger, the latter remaining practically unaffected, or the two become commingled into something different from what either was before, or, finally, the two continue to dwell together unmixed, each preserving a character of its own.[43]

This offered up alternatives in terms of extermination or genocide, dominant assimilation, two-way assimilation or a 'melting pot', or a model of social pluralism.[44] Bryce considered that one of the interesting features of these alternatives was the prevalence throughout history of 'extinction' or 'absorption' for 'more than half of the tribes or peoples that existed when authentic history begins would seem to have vanished'.[45] History appeared as a process of race struggle in which the 'stronger races' would be 'factors in history for some generations or centuries to come'[46] and though doubtful of the ability of 'exclusive race aristocracies' to survive by restrictions on intermarriage with other races, Bryce nevertheless considered that the 'aversion to colour reaches its maximum among the Teutons'.[47]

Bryce relied ultimately upon a cultural rather than an economic explanation for differing problems of inter-racial behaviour and this had an important legacy for racial thought in Britain, for Bryce's lecture appears to have been widely read – it was, for example, one of the first essays on race that Norman Leys, as a medical doctor in East Africa, read with profit.[48] Bryce's thinking on the relations of 'superior' and 'subject' races was probably especially shaped by the model of imperial rule in India, which he likened closely to the Roman Empire.[49] In an essay in 1901, he justified the British Raj as a Roman-style despotism because 'no other sort of government would suit a vast population of different races and tongues, divided by religious animosities of Hindus and Mussulmans, and with no sort of experience of self-government on a scale larger than a Village Council'.[50] Nevertheless, the relationships between the 'conquering' and 'conquered' races in the Roman and British Indian examples were, he admitted, different in that the Roman case led to a 'fusion of the peoples' while the Raj made such a fusion impossible. Unlike the Roman case, climate led to a different pattern of race relations for 'the English race becomes so enfeebled in the second generation without respite under the Indian sun that it would probably die out, at least in the plains, in the third or fourth'. Furthermore, the added factor of colour prevented any fusion in the Indian situation, given especially 'the hauteur of the English and the sense of social incompatibility which both elements feel'.[51] Bryce's analysis of race relations underlined a more popular sense of racial separateness in the Indian imperial context in the latter years of the nineteenth century.

Bryce's use of the Roman imperial model (in contrast to Greek Hellenism of earlier Victorians) to rationalise the despotism of the late Victorian Raj was a key to his understanding of racial relationships. The allusion to Rome was a convenient ideological ploy in late Victorian imperial thought for it was 'made to serve as a heuristic reinforcement, a magnificent historical reference in a historically conscious age'.[52] If history for Bryce had been a history of race struggle between 'advanced' and 'backward' races, then the quintessence of rule by an 'advanced' race was that of the British in India, for here was an enlightened despotism which was supported by the mass of the Indian population with only 'a few intelligent men, educated in European ideas' complaining of the despotism of the Anglo-Indian bureaucracy.[53] Britain, Bryce argued, was as safe from rebellion in India as was imperial Rome, and the only possibility of this happening would be when caste and religious divisions broke down in Indian society. The possibility of this lay in 'a future which is still far distant',[54] though the idea haunted some imperialists and underlay some of Kipling's Indian stories, such as *The Strange Ride of Morrowbie Jukes*.

Bryce's thought on race relations was thus dominated by a strong faith in the British imperial mission, though this began to be undermined by the Anglo-Boer War. In early 1900 he recognised the need 'to concentrate all the forces of the best and finest liberalism in demonstrating the needlessness and iniquity of this war, and in trying to unite liberals in demanding fair terms of peace for the Boers'. By seeking to strike a 'heavy blow' at 'jingoism in general',[55] Bryce aligned himself with pro-Boer opinion in a faction separate from 'liberal imperialists' such as Rosebery, Asquith and Grey, who supported the general aims of British imperialism in South Africa. The experience of the war also led Bryce to adopt in the following years a less imperialistic view of race and race relations. In 1904 he gave the opening address at the founding of the British Sociological Society and began to shift to some extent from his earlier emphasis upon classical historical analogies in favour of contemporary comparative sociological analysis. In 1915, in a lecture on *Race Sentiment as a Factor in History*, Bryce began emphasising the historically contingent nature of 'racial feeling', which he considered now to date only from the French Revolution, rather than being an endemic feature throughout all human history.[56] Furthermore, in the light of the war, this racial feeling was now seen as a dangerous component in nationalism and the fomenting of 'international hatreds'.[57] Foreseeing a time when competition between races would lead to only some six or seven races being left, Bryce saw 'race consciousness' becoming increasingly intense, for 'race sentiment, taken alone, has never been a cause of war; it has merely aggravated other grounds of emnity: and even now it is not so much itself a motive or self-assertion as a particular form of national unity'.[58] There was also the possibility, Bryce thought, that at the end of the war class conflict would displace national rivalries, though in the main he looked with great pessimism at the 'popular sentiment' which had goaded on national leaders into war and a 'racial quarrel' that had 'lit up a war on a scale vaster than the world has seen before'.[59]

Bryce's pessimism was not simply the gloomy assessment of a Liberal elder statesman, but the reflection of a breakdown in the nineteenth-century international order in which the market model of liberal capitalism had been applied to international relations. The nineteenth-century conception of the bourgeois nation-state had assumed an ultimate harmony of interests between rival nationalisms through the beneficent workings of a free trade system. The emergence of a more popular 'social nationalism', however, had undermined this model of the world order, just as it had undermined the domestic model of bourgeois politics within the nation-state through the rise of trade unions and labour parties.[60] 'It is . . . pretty clear to anyone who marks the influence of nationalism during the last fifty years', Dicey wrote to Bryce after reading his *Essays and Addresses* in 1918, 'that a sentiment which seemed to Mazzini and Cavour almost wholly good, contains in it a good deal of possible evil, and that at best nationalism which was presented as the basis of moral unity may also well be the reason of disunity.'[61] A challenge had thus been made to the essential moral legitimacy of the older bourgeois view of nationalism and the nation-state, and though at the end of the war there was a new effort in the study and analysis of the new phase of 'international relations', especially in the Royal Institute of International Affairs formed at Chatham House in 1919, there was a certain fear and dislike of the more modern phase of nationalism in British governing circles.

The demise of the Anglo-Saxonist ideal

As the more evolved model of the bourgeois nation had fallen into question, so had the area of more backward 'races' fallen into doubt too. Even before the war, the employment of Anglo-Saxonist racial ideology had fallen into decline as the appeal to imperial race patriotism became increasingly unpopular in the wake of the Anglo-Boer War. There was probably never a complete consensus on the exact meaning of the term, for in the colonial context its use had sometimes occurred alongside a critique of some aspects of imperial policy. The Australian George E. Boxall, in *The Anglo-Saxon: A Study in Evolution* (1902), for example, had challenged the classical view of imperial culture presented by writers such as Froude and Bryce. 'The sole object of the English system of education', he complained in an attack on the Oxford tradition of *literae humaniores* and classical scholarship, 'seems to be to subordinate the Anglo-Saxon intellect to the Greek and Latin, to cramp the mind of the superior race down to the intellectual level of the inferior race'.[62] Indeed the 'craze for Greek learning' in England helped explain why education there was 'at a lower ebb' than in 'other Teutonic countries'.[63]

This argument was in tune with the mood for 'national efficiency' after the Anglo-Boer War which some liberal imperialists such as Lord Rosebery had interpreted in terms of a need for more scientific education in order to compete with rival empires such as Germany.[64] The high point of Anglo-Saxonist solidarity between Britain and the United States had been between the Venezuela Boundary dispute of 1895–6 and 1905, when the Japanese victory against Russia appeared to end for the foreseeable future any significant Russian threat to British and American interests in Asia and the Pacific.[65] Resting largely on a common illusion in both Britain and America of a collective racial superiority over other peoples, the cult of Anglo-Saxonism lived on in the public mind to surface on occasions of internal political crisis, such as that following the end of the First World War.[66] By 1905, however, the appeal of Anglo-Saxonism had begun to flag with the loss of popular enthusiasm for the expansionist imperialism of the 1880s and 1890s. It tended to be increasingly espoused by groups on the political right as part of a campaign for national conscription and increased defence expenditure to meet the growing military challenge from Germany. Major Stewart L. Murray, for example, in *The Peace of the Anglo-Saxon*, linked Anglo-Saxonism to a Social Darwinist vision of perpetual 'struggle for existence among nations'[67] which had been exemplified by the recent Russo-Japanese War. Attacking the Liberal Pro-Boers and Campbell-Bannerman's slogan of 'methods of barbarism' in the Boer War, Murray employed Anglo-Saxonism in an appeal to national unity behind the imperial ideal and as 'the best-known term to denote that mix of Celtic, Saxon, Norse, and Norman blood which now flows in the united stream in the veins of the Anglo-Saxon peoples'.[68] The 'spirit of nationality' he thought had awoken 'latest and slowest among the great Anglo-Saxon race',[69] but it had now revealed itself as 'a great blood brotherhood of nations, with a great mission in the world and a great part to play in the further evolution of humanity'.[70]

The ideal of a 'great blood brotherhood' continued to exist in an attenuated form in the minds of many prominent politicians and public figures in Britain, America and the English colonies of white settlement in the years up to and after the First World War. In the wake of the Boer War, the imperial mission, which adventurers like Cecil Rhodes had espoused in former years, began to meet public opprobrium. Imperialism seemed linked to British bullying of smaller nations, and even Rudyard Kipling had warned in his 'Recessional' in 1897 of the dangers of national arrogance:

> If, drunk with power, we loose
>   Wild tongues that have not Thee in awe,
> Such boastings as the Gentiles use,
>   Or lesser breeds without the Law –
> Lord God of Hosts, be with us yet,
> Lest we forget — lest we forget!

Thus, the appeal to a common Anglo-Saxon racial solidarity could not ultimately mask over a crisis of imperial faith. The Liberal victory in the 1906 general election did signal the arrival of new avenues of thought on the question of 'inter-racial relations', though one still heavily shaped by the idea of at least a common cultural superiority of the 'blood brotherhood' of English-speaking nations. This superiority, however, as the next chapter shows, was increasingly depicted in relative rather than absolute terms, and a growing sensitivity to the anthropological study of non-Western and non-white societies began to undermine many of the simplicities of Victorian racial theory.

2

Mary Kingsley and the emergence of cultural relativism

The problem of India

The re-emergence of liberalism in British politics after the Anglo-Boer War tended to focus thinking on race in the arena of Africa and the Caribbean rather than India, which was seen as a sub-continent with a culture increasingly impervious and resistant to missionary ideas of religious proselytisation. Though it had been the hope of utilitarian thinkers that Western market processes could radically transform Indian society in the first half of the nineteenth century and reinforce the ideal of westernising Indian culture and society in accordance with Macaulay's Minute of 1835, the Mutiny in 1857 had come as a profound shock to British self-confidence. The abolition of Company rule in 1858 and the eventual proclamation of the Queen as Empress of India in 1876 did little to assuage this feeling of estrangement from the customs and mores of an agrarian society of such a vaste nature. The industrialisation in Britain during the nineteenth century and the lurch into further imperial expansion from the 1880s onwards tended to reinforce the feeling of growing racial and cultural differences between the British caste of ruling sahibs and the mass of apparently backward Indian peasantry, who appeared to many observers to have declined from a former state of relative civilisation and grandeur. By the 1890s, the belief in an inherently racial divide between British and Indian culture was shared even by relatively progressive observers such as a correspondent of the Fabian, Graham Wallas, who wrote in 1892 of her profound shock on seeing at first hand the state of rural India. 'The real fact is', she declared, 'that these men are a different species of animals to ourselves – their physical and mental constitution are extraordinarily different ... their physical constitution is feeble and weedy and often disgustingly sensual. Their character is fawning and grovelling to superiors, bullying to inferiors, mean and deceptive to equals. Their general level of character does not show as much reason as ordinary European children and is much more full of spite and meanness.'[1]

27

This belief in Western cultural superiority over India would become progressively attenuated in the light of growing political nationalism by the early twentieth century, especially in the wake of the partition of Bengal in 1905 and the resulting Indian boycott of British goods.[2] However, for a number of liberal imperialists there seemed few obvious paths by which to initiate major societal transformation in the absence of any flourishing peasantry in most parts of the sub-continent. The main focus of criticism was the steady erosion of the authority of the zamindari landlords through the introduction of market forces into the rural economy, which was seen as undermining a crucial prop of British imperial authority. 'Land cannot be treated like ordinary private property', wrote one such critic in the *Westminster Review* in 1909 in the wake of the Bengal agitation: 'for every landholder is really a public trustee and should give an account of his stewardship. England is at last re-discovering this brutal truth.'[3]

Some critics on the left went further and saw the common 'Aryan' race of Britain and India as producing political conflicts readily recognisable in European terms. Keir Hardie, for example, was shocked by the extent of the 'colour line' in the sub-continent, especially as the Indian people were 'of the same Aryan stock as ourselves':

> Take a gathering of Indians. Remove their graceful picturesque costumes, and clothe them in coat and trousers, wash the sun out of their skins, and then a stranger suddenly let down into the midst of them would have difficult in saying whether he was in Manchester or Madras. This fact has a very important bearing upon the question of how far the Indian people can be trusted with the right of self-government.[4]

This, however, was to judge the state of India entirely by the standards of the West and still made no concession to the autonomy of Indian culture on its own terms. Most British observers of India had great difficulty in making such an imaginative leap, for Indian culture they saw in essentially static terms and as being ultimately dependent on the guidance of the Raj. Kipling's portrayal of the Swami in *Kim* epitomised this dilemma for, while he was seen as manifesting deep wisdom and insight derived from the continent's rich religious and cultural tradition, he was dependent upon the young sahib, Kim, dressed up as an Indian beggar, to make his way around the modern Westernised veneer imposed on the traditional India. Though written from the highly Eurocentric view of the British imperial intruders, the novel ironically reflected a basic dilemma that confronted the Indian nationalist movement in its search for a strategy to mobilise the Indian masses to overthrow British rule. While a Western-educated intelligentsia had emerged in Bengal, its progressive reformist constitutionalism looked unable to acquire a mass base and it was only Gandhi who was able eventually to synthesise this progressive reformism with a traditional appeal to a past golden age of *Ramraj* when India had been perfect. Indian history from the Mutiny in 1857 to ultimate Independence in 1947 thus probably did have an essential unity, with only the period since 1947 representing a progressive emancipation from the Victorian era.[5]

The reformers in Britain tended to sense this dilemma and thus had great difficulty in being able to understand the dynamics of Indian social and political development on its own terms. Most missionaries had, by the turn of the century, despaired of being able to penetrate Hindu religious customs and inject modes of Western thought[6] and there was a general sense that the two 'minds' of East and West were intrinsically incompatible. 'Wherever the Western mind considers the whole problem of the country inductively', wrote one writer in the *Nineteenth Century*, reflecting the general dominance of empiricism and positivism in English social thought, 'the Eastern mind, as a rule – and especially where the idealism is keenest – starts with the large ideal; and the problem becomes for it that of bringing the ideal down into ... the apparently antagonistic conditions of today'.[7]

Liberals thus had great difficulty in understanding the cohesion of Indian culture and felt more at home in the apparently more manageable colonial societies of the Afro-Caribbean, where missionary teaching had produced an educated class which were more likely to be able to help steer these societies in a Western direction. In the light of the doubts in the 1890s on the long-term durability of colonial rule in tropical areas, this issue became especially pressing and, in the absence of strong anthropological guidance at this stage, the emergence of a new cultural relativism on inter-racial relations amongst liberals tended to emerge from less academic circles. One such early exponent of the new liberal thought on the issue was the traveller and amateur ethnologist, Mary Kingsley.

The Kingsleyite School

Mary Kingsley was not the first to espouse the idea of the separate cultural worth of African societies compared with those of Europe for in some respects this ideal developed out of the romantic tradition of the 'noble savage' of the eighteenth and early nineteenth centuries.[8] It had also been part of the early Pan-Africanist tradition of political thought and Edward Wilmott Blyden had propounded the idea of generating an indigenous African cultural revival rooted in Islam. In England as early as 1881 Joseph Renner Maxwell cautioned an audience in a lecture at St Jude's Institute in London not to 'make the West African proletariat fancy that he is still

savage because he eats his native foofoo and palaver sauce – a very palat-
able and relishable dish I assure you; but convince him that the essential
principles of civilisation require him to eat it in a decent and respectable
manner'. Furthermore, it was 'not necessary that the tradition and
ceremonies of civilisation be in all places one and utterly alike, but may be
changed according to diversities of countries, times and men's manners, so
that nothing can be done to infringe its spirit'.[9]

This notion of cultural relativism was, however, propounded by a black
man from West Africa before a relatively small audience at a time when the
Scramble for Africa was just about to commence. Isolated and with no
organised pressure group to take up his case, Maxwell's solitary call went
unheeded in Victorian imperial England of the 1880s, and by 1892 his
theme had become a far more disillusioned one. In *The Negro Question: Or
Hints for the Physical Improvement of the Negro Race* Maxwell declared
the negro race to be physically ugly for 'his woolly pat is not so becoming as
the flaxen hair of the Anglo-Saxon'.[10] Effectively internalising the dominant Anglo-Saxonist racial ideology of the period, Maxwell now sought to
turn it against the black race in Africa by advocating its social and moral
improvement through 'miscegenation' with whites. Given that 'great minds
like Carlyle, Freeman and Froude' had been 'unable to conquer their
prejudices against the Negro, what are we to expect from the millions of
minor intelligences?'[11] Though confessing that in the three years he had
been at Oxford he had not once been insulted on account of his colour,
nevertheless the black race had 'no history but that of suffering' and it was
better that it disappeared altogether than that it continue 'the laughing stock
of the world'.[12] General Booth's plea in his work *In Darkest England* in
1890 for the settlement overseas of 100,000 poor women Maxwell
considered a means for the regeneration of African societies through intermarriage and the introduction of 'European civilisation' into the continent.
'The most advanced African tribe is more or less still barbarian', he
concluded, 'compared with the races of Europe and Asia'.[13]

The development of Maxwell's thought at least reflected the racialisation
of political discourse in Britain in the 1880s as well as demonstrating the
destruction of an early plea for cultural relativism through a feeling of
cultural despair. The tradition probably did not die out even among the
small African community itself in England at this time, though accounts of
racial hostility exhibited by ordinary working people towards Africans in
Britain indicated that British society was profoundly discriminatory in the
way it treated blacks in its midst and gave them little cause for self-
confidence in the period before the First World War.[14]

Mary Kingsley's writings, *Travels in West Africa* (1897) and *West
African Studies* (1899), were thus of importance in rejuvenating the

cultural relativist ideal at the high point of imperial enthusiasm and went on to have a significant impact on political and anthropological thought in the years after the Anglo-Boer War, in which she died prematurely in Cape Town as a nurse in 1900.

Her ideas were in many respects unsystematised, and much of her writing was done to advance the West African trading interests. Nevertheless, she recognised the separate cultural worth and identity of African societies and saw that the missionary ideas of Christian proselytisation and the Colonial Office policy of direct rule tended towards the destruction of African social and political institutions. To this extent, as Bernard Porter has pointed out, Mary Kingsley was one of the first English social anthropologists as well as an early propagator of the concept of 'indirect rule'.[15] Furthermore, she was important in shifting attention away from India and Asian societies towards Africa and the study of black races.

Much of Mary Kingsley's thinking on race was shaped by the Victorian climate of polygenism and a hierarchy of racial fitness, with the white Anglo-Saxon at the top. There was also, though, a strong emphasis in her writing on the distinct fitness of African societies, in contrast to the teleological racism of Carlyle and the high tide of Victorian racial thought. Confessing that she hated 'the humbug in England's policy towards weaker races for the sake of all the misery on white and black it brings',[16] Mary Kingsley likened the state of the 'backward' West African societies to those of thirteenth-century Europe. However, this did not necessarily imply the need for the old civilising mission concept of raising up such African societies so that they would eventually come to parallel European ones, for with the application of 'science' there was no reason why a different sort of 'humanitarianism' could not ensure their own separate cultural path of development:

> If you will try Science, all the evils of the clash between the two culture periods could be avoided, and you could assist these West Africans in their thirteenth century to rise into the nineteenth-century state without their having the hard fight for it that you yourself had. This would be a grand humanitarian bit of work; by doing it you would raise a monument before God to the honour of England such as no nation has ever yet raised to Him on earth.[17]

In some respects she was a defender of the old Gladstonian free trade liberalism, represented in West Africa by such traders as John Holt and Sir George Goldie, who were suspicious of the new imperialism of the 1890s and wished to be free to pursue their own activities outside Colonial Office control.[18] The high tide of commercial enthusiasm for imperial expansion into West Africa had been in the 1880s and early 1890s during a period of economic recession and fear of rivalries from other European powers with interests in the area. The appointment of Joseph Chamberlain as Colonial Secretary in 1895 had paradoxically seen the waning of this enthusiasm for further capital investment in the African colonies.[19] Thus Mary Kingsley was a woman who united the otherwise divided West African groups behind a policy rooted in many of the ideals of the era of free trade imperialism before the imperial high tide of the 1890s. There were, though, additional features to her arguments which had an important impact on the liberal critics of imperial policy after the turn of the century.

Mary Kingsley particularly stressed the importance of the study of African societies and customs and their difference from those of India, a society she considered dominated by religion:

> the true negro is, I believe, by far the better man than the Asiatic; he is physically superior, and he is more like an Englishman than the Asiatic; he is a logical practical man, with feelings that are a credit to him, and are particularly strong in the direction of property; he has a way of thinking he has rights, whether he likes to use them or not, and will fight for them when he is driven to it. Fight you for a religious idea the African will not. He is not the stuff you make martyrs out of, nor does he desire to shake off the shackles of the flesh and swoon into Nirvana.[20]

There were accordingly dangers from half-educating the African in Western cultural ways and producing a semi-educated black leadership cut off from its cultural roots:

> I am aware that there is now in West Africa a handful of Africans who have mastered white culture, who know it too well to misunderstand the inner spirit of it, who are men too true to have let it cut them off in either sympathy or love from Africa . . . That handful of African men are now fighting a hard enough fight to prevent the distracted, uninformed Africans from riding against what so looks like white treachery, though it is only white want of knowledge; and also against those 'water flies' who are neither Africans nor Europeans, but who are the curse of the Coast – the men who mislead the white man and betray the black.[21]

This view was not so very different from the racial Pan-Africanism of the scholar and Ambassador at St James for Liberia, Edward Wilmott Blyden. Mary Kingsley met Blyden in London in 1898, and, though he did not share her view of the low contribution of Africa to world civilisation, he certainly agreed with her vision of a racially pure negro race reclaiming a united

African continent for its own distinct culture, based, however, on Islam as opposed to Christianity.[22]

Mary Kingsley's criticism of Colonial Office amateurism in West Africa led to *The African Society* being founded in her memory in 1901 to encourage the scientific study of African societies and cultures. Blyden was one of the vice-presidents and Mary Kingsley's ideas were partly responsible for encouraging the small anthropological community centred around the Anthropological Institute to start abandoning their rather esoteric interest in the relics of the African past and begin moving towards the study of change in contemporary African cultures as part of the study of colonial administration.[23] Mary Kingsley was not alone in this, for black Africans and West Indians were also beginning to make a direct impact upon opinion in Britain at this time, too. The same year as Mary Kingsley's death, 1900, the first Pan-African Conference was held in London, mainly through the activities of the African Association, formed in 1897 by the Trinidadian, Henry Sylvester Williams.[24] Though its deliberations on African culture and history and its hostility to European notions of racial supremacy were mostly ignored by the British press, W. T. Stead's *Review of Reviews* gave it considerable attention. In August the jingoist magazine published an article, 'The Revolt against the Paleface', in which it confessed that the notion that black men had rights was a new notion to most British people. It regretted that Mary Kingsley was not still alive to attend the conference, seeing her as 'the only Paleface who could make the Black Man intelligible in Europe'. It considered that 'it may be right on the principle of the Golden Rule to subject our black brothers to Mr Carlyle's beneficent whip', but nevertheless felt that it could not be right 'to shoot him wholesale or hang him retail if he refuses to abandon practices disturbing whitemen'. While 'justice and fair play' need not necessarily involve the recognition of equality between black and white, they still implied an absence of oppression through murder and torture.[25]

Mary Kingsley's ideas were important for crystallising many conceptions felt by liberals on race at a time when the nature of British imperial control was itself beginning to come under question in the light of the experiences of the Anglo-Boer War. Her ideas even left a strong impression on Rudyard Kipling, who was impressed by her 'utter fearlessness' and 'the controlled power that seemed to give her natural command of the situation'. Her 'even, disinterested tones', furthermore, he felt were 'in precise key with the Victorian atmosphere and surroundings' though 'the matter of her discourse was heathen and adventurous'.[26] This ability to blunt potential opposition from the imperial lobby was crucial in that Mary Kingsley's ideas were able to spread in English society before the First World War and define a debate in which blacks participated as well.

The debate on imperialism

One of the first major works to reflect Mary Kingsley's ideas was the book *Imperialism* (1902) by J. A. Hobson, which mounted a strong attack on British imperial policy in South Africa based upon an underconsumptionist theory that imperial expansionism was partly induced by the diversion of capital investment away from the domestic market into overseas and colonial markets, where there were higher rates of return. Hobson also added a racial dimension to this thesis when he warned that the continuation of imperial control would necessitate the increasing use of black troops, which were better fitted to tropical climates, rather than the eugenically unfit British stock coming from the overcrowded cities of Britain. 'In the last resort', he argued, 'war is determined neither by generalship nor superiority of weapons, but by those elements of brute endurance which are incompatible with the life of industrial towns'.[27] It was thus a 'fatuous attempt', echoing the popular panic regarding the general physical 'unfitness' of British military manpower, to try to 'convert ineffective slum dwellers and weedy city clerks into tough military materials'. The Victorian ideal of seeking new colonial possessions as a new pastoral terrain for race rejuvenation rebounded back on the mother country if it meant a call on ever larger numbers of indigenous men to fight colonial wars. The solution lay in the imperial mother country divesting herself of this military responsibility by accepting that in tropical climates black troops were better suited to fight than white men.[28]

There was much in this that reflected the ideas of Benjamin Kidd on the unsuitability of tropical societies for white settlement. Hobson, though, envisioned a dark time ahead 'when the horrors of our eighteenth-century struggle with France in North America and India may be revived upon a gigantic scale, and Africa and Asia may furnish huge cock-pits for the struggles of black and yellow armies representing the imperialists' rivalries in Christendom'. Such a 'debacle of Western Civilization'[29] was a logical consequence of the general imperialist tendency towards war and militarism, which he identified with the Boer War of 1899–1902.[30] This was a view that met with some sympathy in the liberal and radical circles of Britain at the time, for much of the moral impetus behind the liberal critique of imperialism stemmed from an anti-war sentiment. 'Under the reign of imperialism', the liberal philosopher, Leonard Hobhouse, wrote in *Democracy and Reaction*, 'the temple of Janus is never closed. Blood never ceases to run.'[31]

Hobson's book, however, was written at a time when the bulk of public opinion had been mobilised behind the British war effort in South Africa and liberalism was very much on the defensive. Hobson privately admitted to Gilbert Murray that there was a 'genuinely moral enthusiasm' behind the war, stimulated by imperial propagandists like Rudyard Kipling, which had been 'recognised and utilised by the self-seeking interests which really direct the course of imperialism'. The main objective behind his book in fact lay 'more in fortifying friends than in convincing enemies',[32] indicating that Hobson's liberal anti-imperialism had an uncertain public face and a defensive political morality that was strongly dependent upon wider political changes which he felt to be outside the liberals' influence.

The emergence, however, of the issue of forced labour in the Belgian Congo in the years after the Anglo-Boer War came as a welcome chance for liberal critics of imperialism in Britain both to mobilise their cause and to develop some of the criticisms of colonial policy mounted by Mary Kingsley before her death. Since 1885, when the Treaty of Berlin had partitioned a number of African colonial territories amongst the European imperial powers, the Congo 'Free State' had been under the personal control of King Leopold of Belgium. This was initially welcomed by humanitarian groups all over Europe as providing both a much needed structure of political authority as well as opening up the territory to commercial interests. By the 1890s, however, reports began to seep out of 'Congo atrocities' involving the use of forced labour by rubber traders, who had secured a monopoly concession from King Leopold despite the promises made in 1885. The humanitarian groups in England, though led by the Anti-Slavery Society, avoided getting too closely involved in the issue (beyond making appeals to Chambers of Commerce), since by 1900 there was a feeling that Britain had lost its authority to initiate a case against Leopold due to its own poor moral standing in the war in South Africa.[33]

This political vacuum in reformist circles encouraged the new liberalism that was considerably revitalised in the light of Mary Kingsley's writings and propaganda of the late 1890s. Foremost in this new crusade for reform in the Congo and the removal of King Leopold's control was a former shipping clerk of the Liverpool shipping line, Elder Dempsters, Edward Dene Morel. Of part French extraction and deeply influenced by a long family association with Quakerism, Morel had an unquestioned Anglophile faith in the superior moral strength of the British nation.[34] He also had a strongly ideological conception of liberalism in contrast to the more pragmatic form displayed by the anti-slavery lobby. This was reinforced by Mary Kingsley's writings, which generally had a profound influence both on his view of Africa and his subsequent career.[35]

Morel's importance lay especially in his fiery journalistic style, which appealed to the West African commercial interests seeking a change in colonial policy, and the new anthropological opinion stimulated by Mary Kingsley, anxious for the 'protection' of African societies from European imperialism. It was a representative of the latter, Mrs Alice Stopford Green

– the founder of the Africa Society in Mary Kingsley's memory – who put Morel in touch with the influential London African lobby[36] and, with these new links, Morel was able to found the Congo Reform Association in 1904.

Over the following years, the CRA had considerable impact on racial thought in Britain for it both popularised many of the polygenist ideas of Mary Kingsley as well as widening the original political alliance forged with West African commerical interests to other sections of colonial opinion from Southern Africa that might be described as 'liberal segregationist'. The role of the African traveller, artist and former colonial administrator, Sir Harry Johnston, was particularly crucial in this respect for he had connections with Pro-Boer opinion, such as Sir Charles Dilke and W.T. Stead, which could enhance the political effectiveness of the campaign, especially as the Labour Party under Ramsey Macdonald showed a marked disinclination to take up its cause.[37] Johnston urged Morel to see the moral issues that the CRA was concerning itself with as applying to the whole of 'negro Africa', though excluding areas where white settlement was climatically possible since otherwise they would confuse 'public intelligence'.[38] Extending the issue onto a continental-wide scale tended to foster the image of a 'black Africa' which ran the risk both of political and moral corruption through miscegenation and of the disruption of African social and cultural life as a result of imperial penetration.

The ideology of the CRA thus reflected the polygenism of Kingsley and Hobson and the *racial* conception of African political and moral well-being. In a book, *Red Rubber*, published in 1906, Johnston and Morel warned that failure to secure reform in the Congo risked widespread African resistance to European imperial hegemony in Africa. There was a threat of a united black revolt to overthrow what Johnston termed 'the new civilisation we are trying to implant'[39] and Morel warned that 'any day may see the rise of an intelligent native corporal with a brain above his fellows, some bastard Arab blood in his veins perhaps, who will make a bold bid for empire against the officials of the absentee landlord'.[40] Mary Kingsley's argument for the need to preserve African cultures and ensure their own form of evolution from their 'thirteenth-century' status thus became developed into a new paternalist ideology emphasising the need to insulate black African society from 'harmful' influences from the West. The military aspects of the Congo rubber monopoly worried Morel and Johnston particularly, for it was through the influence of modern weaponry and warfare that such an African revolt could start. 'The presence of a lawless, marauding soldiery ever increasing in numbers', Morel wrote, 'and only held in nominal discipline by the conferring of full freedom to loot and rape, is a menace.'[41]

The significance of Kingsleyite ideas in Morel's thought lay in their combining a set of 'scientific' claims derived from Darwinian evolutionary biology with a more traditional philanthropic concern to 'protect' African societies from Western imperial penetration. This could, on occasions, degenerate into a somewhat hysterical moralism that threatened to get increasingly out of touch with more conventional political processes. While Morel initially favoured a relatively pragmatic approach that could exert influence on the Foreign Office under Sir Edward Grey, this soon gave way to a more wide-ranging attack on European power politics as a whole, especially after 1909, when Morel declared in an unofficial report to the Foreign Office that there was extensive corruption in French official circles.[42] By 1912 he was arguing that 'a compromise on fundamentals would but postpone the evil day'[43] and began a more fundamental critique of European politics as a consequence of the failure of the CRA to shift Foreign Office policy to any significant extent. The British Liberal government, however, increasingly moved towards recognising the annexation of the Congo territory by the Belgian Parliament, and when this eventually occurred in 1912 the usefulness of the CRA was virtually at an end. The organisation was finally wound up in 1913. Nevertheless, Morel's concern for what he termed the 'fate of millions of helpless people in Africa'[44] lived on into the years after the First World War, especially through the activities of the Anti-Slavery Society.

Later phases of Kingsleyism

The advent of world war in 1914 led to a radicalisation of political thought on the left as many of the assumptions of European cultural superiority became finally destroyed in the mud and blood of Flanders. There was, though, a striking tenacity of many of the Kingsleyite ideas on race. Despite the original hostility by liberals such as Hobson and Morel to the jingoistic aspects of British imperialism, the notion of 'protecting' African societies from Western penetration survived in much liberal political thinking.

One important body, for example, that had now come to adapt itself to the Kingsleyite critique of British colonial policy was the Anti-Slavery Society. While originally one of the Victorian humanitarian organisations to which Mary Kingsley had been opposed, the merger of the Society with the Aborigines Protection Society led to a former colleague of E. D. Morel in the CRA, the Rev. John Harris, becoming its secretary in 1909. Harris had originally been a missionary in the Upper Congo between 1898 and 1905 before working for the CRA, and the experience there of seeing the effects of the forced labour by the rubber monopolists left with him a strong conviction of the need to regenerate African societies through peasant agriculture.

Harris became one of the most important long-term followers of the Kingsleyite school, for he remained active in anti-slavery circles until his death in 1940 and was a strong advocate of colonial development in West Africa on the basis of African land holding and the promotion of cash crops such as cocoa and palm oil as opposed to the more exploitative trade in rubber. Unlike the more idealistic Morel, he tried to cultivate relationships with the Colonial Office and saw his base in the Anti-Slavery Society as a means of acting as a mediator between the emerging African Westernised middle class in West Africa and the colonial administration. In his book, *Dawn in Darkest Africa* (1914), he warned of the dangers of mounting 'race prejudice' amongst the white administrative and trading class in West Africa which could upset the commercial relationship between Britain and her West African colonies and of the widening of the 'gulf' between the younger African intelligentsia and the 'noble-minded officials and ex-officials in the government'.[45]

Harris was astute enough to recognise that there was a rising African demand for a Western education in Britain and that growing numbers of chiefs and African dignatories were anxious for their sons to get educated in the 'mother country'. This was in part a product of a transformation in social relations in West Africa between 1880 and the turn of the century as European colonial monopolies destroyed the old class of African merchants and traders and the cash economy expanded. Africans thus sought Western education in an increasingly competitive society in which racial discrimination was becoming rampant. From his intermediary position, Harris realised that it was essential for this educational demand to be guided and channelled if it was not to produce a new class of bitter and alienated African leaders who had had the experience, whilst being students in Britain, of suffering racial ostracism from the indifferent and ignorant British public. Educated Africans at this time ran the risk of being mocked at and treated with contempt by even the poorest of the English working class and thus were likely to suffer a considerable incongruity of social status at their most formative intellectual stage.[46] Harris thus urged philanthropic interests to begin undertaking a welfare role for African students in Britain, though he also pointed out that the Colonial Office should be involved in this, too.[47] Over the following decades, Harris developed this welfare role in Britain in the 1920s and 1930s, though it eventually ended disastrously as he lost the confidence of the body that came to represent West African student opinion in Britain, Ladipo Solanke's *West African Students Union* (WASU), a development we discuss in Chapter 7.

Harris remained a strong paternalist in his dealings with Africans and in some respects his Kingsleyism was an intellectual gloss on a more fundamental nostalgia for an older Africa, based upon simple African tribesmen, a dark African wilderness and individualistic, self-reliant white traders, which was rapidly vanishing. As his knowledge of Africa widened, he took up other issues such as African land rights in the settler colonies in East and Southern Africa. His Victorian liberal background, though, led him to misunderstand the central imperatives behind the segregationist ideology in South Africa and in 1913 he supported the South African Natives Land Act on the grounds that it entailed a *separation* of African and white land holdings as opposed to a complete segregation of the races.[48] In this he differed considerably from the more radical critics of white segregationism in Africa such as Sydney Olivier and Norman Leys, though these divisions did not become clear until the 1920s. In 1919 Olivier supplied a warm preface to Harris's book, *Africa: Slave or Free?*[49]

Harris's ambiguity towards white segregationism, however, led him to fall out increasingly with educated African opinion, especially after the 1914 deputation to Britain by the South African Native National Congress (later the African National Congress) to protest against the Natives Land Act. Harris helped to arrange a financial loan for the deputation, but was subsequently angered by the unwillingness or inability of the African delegation to repay it and developed an increasing distrust of African financial honesty.[50] This would prove crucial in his later welfare work for Africans in Europe during and after the First World War, and he came increasingly to believe that Africans and blacks generally were not suited to live in an industrial society like Britain, though by 1919 he had moved to a position supportive of black industrial workers' rights in South Africa, blaming the colour bar in the gold mines entirely on the restrictive self-interest of the white workers organised via the Mine Workers' Union.[51]

At a time when many sections of the British left were indifferent to the questions of colour and race, Harris was an important figure in generating public concern in Britain over black rights in the colonial setting. He particularly attacked a 'Mrs X' in 1919 (who appears to resemble closely Beatrice Webb) for her concern with domestic social reform in Britain, whilst completely ignoring the exploitation of black workers that went on in colonial plantations. Such socialists Harris considered should be attacked for their 'stagnant complacency'. There were 'thoughtless hundreds [of them], content to draw dividends and make no inquiries so long as the injustices [were] beyond their immediate ken', and he was keen that 'intellectuals' should as far as possible influence the Labour Party's thinking on colonial policy and develop it in a liberal direction.[52]

With the outbreak of war in 1914, Harris got involved in welfare work for the increasing number of blacks who were coming to Europe as part of the war effort. It soon became apparent that numbers of blacks would be needed to perform menial tasks behind the Allied lines, though as far as possible it was intended that they should not be directly involved in the fighting. Consequently a 'Native Labour Contingent' was formed, with numbers of blacks from South Africa and the protectorate territories being sent to Britain. Harris became secretary of the 'Committee for the Welfare of Africans in Europe', which raised funds for recreational facilities which could 'protect' Africans from European cultural influences. The committee represented many of the traditional humanitarian and welfare bodies in Britain and was chaired by the Earl of Selborne, though it came under the strong influence of South African segregationist ideas via the commander of the Native Labour Contingent Colonel S. B. Pritchard, a former Secretary of Native Affairs of the South African Native Affairs Department. The committee tried to insulate the Africans in the Labour Contingent from out-side influences and to provide sufficient recreational amusement to occupy unfilled time.[53] The fund-raising to provide warm clothing for the Africans in the winter months of the war, for example, reinforced Victorian ideas of race differences being based on climate. H. C. Sloley, a former resident commissioner from Lesotho and one of the organisers of the Native Labour Contingent, wrote, for example, that black Africans were really not fitted for life in Europe:

> I do not know that the industrial employment of Africans in Europe has ever been seriously proposed, except in the present instance, as a military measure to deal with a temporary necessity . . . their experience in this country under social conditions differing so widely from those of South Africa, has inevitably unfitted them to take their places usefully and contentedly *in their natural environment.*[54] (emphasis added)

This segregationism was frequently echoed by the activists on the local committees that raised the funds for the Welfare Committee's operations. Support was obtained from such cities as Bristol, Edinburgh, Sheffield, Hull, Manchester, Leeds and Eastbourne, while the Union Castle Shipping Company and a brewery gave contributions. The chairman of the Edinburgh committee declared that the 'loyalty' exhibited by the Africans of the Native Labour Contingent necessitated 'public opinion' showing its appreciation 'by seeing to it that everything possible is done to safeguard the natives from the dangers of Europe'.[55] In the case of Glasgow an appeal was launched for funds to provide recreational and welfare amenities for 300 African men, which would be supervised by chaplains who were 'picked men of great experience in dealing with African natives'.[56]

It was in this context of welfare for the Native Labour Contingent that Harris approached the question of race in the peace settlement at the end of the war. This issue for Harris represented a chance to enforce and elaborate the 'colonial charter' of the Treaty of Berlin in 1885, which had established the principle of free trade and African welfare. His campaigns before and after the Treaty of Versailles thus contributed to the development of the notion of 'colonial trusteeship' as opposed to international government of colonies.[57] Harris's enthusiasm for British colonial trusteeship was reinforced by a continuing Kingsleyite view on the separateness of African cultures and the need to insulate them from contact with imperialism. He thus urged the 'screening-off' of black races from this contact, especially in 'the early stages of development' and the setting-aside of at least a portion of every colony for exclusive 'native' use. Only administrators, missionaries and merchants would be allowed into these zones and their presence would be mainly concerned with assisting the tribes in administration. The guiding idea was to be 'service to backward races'.[58]

A similar manifestation of this benevolent segregationism was in the campaigning of E. D. Morel on the question of the employment by France of black colonial troops in the Rhineland when she occupied it from Germany in 1920 after the latter's default on the repayment of reparations. Morel's thinking revealed many of the contradictions and ambiguities inherent within the liberal criticism of imperialism and its linkage to a model of African peasant proprietorship as a means of escaping the perceived ills of proletarianisation under settler capitalism. In a pamphlet, *Africa and the Peace of Europe*, in 1917, Morel envisaged a 'partnership' between the 'European working man' and the African peasant, with the former engaged in the manufacture of the raw materials furnished by the latter and then supplying the finished products to a burgeoning African market that was placed under international control. The scheme was a means of further 'protecting' African societies from European industrialism, especially in colonies in East and Central Africa, whilst also appealing to the moral instincts of the European working class to help in the development of African peasant production. It was essential, he felt, to secure the 'preservation of African rights in the soil of Africa' for in the 'African opportunity to dispose of these products to the best advantage of the African, is concentrated the very essence of the struggle which Democracy is waging in Europe against capitalism. The working classes of Europe can only remain indifferent to the claims of the producing classes of Africa to their own detriment.'[59] Morel thus reformulated the Kingsleyite vision of African cultural relativism for an increasingly radical labour movement in Britain during and after the First World War.

This benevolent form of racial segregation helped shape the climate of opinion in English progressive circles at the time of the campaign after 1920 against the black French troops on the Rhine. Morel saw the Versailles Peace Treaty of 1919 as favouring French militarism, which he had come to hate ever since the Congo campaign in the years before 1912.[60] There was undoubtedly some individual fanaticism in the way Morel pursued the campaign between 1920 and 1922, when the troops were finally withdrawn. Morel carried considerable political weight in radical anti-war circles and he received, at least for a time, some support from sections of the liberal press, such as the *Labour Leader* (for the ILP) and the *Daily Herald*, as well as the Liberal *Nation*. Many British radical and humanitarian groups saw the importation of the troops into Germany and the resulting allegations of the raping of German women and girls after the establishment of brothels there as reinforcing the need for the geographical and cultural insulation of Africans from the West. As a consequence, Mary Kingsley's ideas on race differences, which had been worked out in the comparative gentility of late Victorian Britain and spoken at relatively elite gatherings of 'African experts', began to be generalised into a more popular racist ideology. Morel, for example, wrote in the *Daily Herald* that such 'outrages' on the Rhine were the 'barbaric incarnation of a policy laid down by the Treaty of Versailles' intended to 'reduce to the lowest depths of despair and humiliation a whole people'.[61]

Morel saw the issue as illustrating the point that African social and cultural mores such as polygamy should be insulated from European contact. 'The African race', he wrote, 'is the most developed sexually of any. These levies are recruited from tribes in a primitive state of development. They have not, of course, their women with them. Sexually they are unrestrained and unrestrainable.'[62] There was a strong element of ideological continuity with Morel's pre-war views of African societies and they were echoed in the Liberal journal, *The Nation*, where H. W. Massingham complained of 'the parading of the coloured troops in the time-honoured shrines of German state patriotism' and 'the lordship of half-savage soldiers over the culture and civism of the Rhine'.[63] While employing language not as extreme as Morel's, Massingham undoubtedly reflected a fairly common strain of hostility to racial 'miscegenation' in the 1920s in liberal circles, which was later expressed in the British context in hostility to liaisons between black seamen and white women in seaport towns. This issue was especially seen as likely to lead to a social 'problem' of 'half-caste' children.[64]

The issue demonstrated the lack of clarity and consistency in the thinking at this time over race in liberal and radical circles in Britain. This can partly be ascribed to the wider failure of liberal groups by the time of the First World War to have evolved a coherent ideology of anti-imperialism in which a critique of race could have been developed. Bernard Porter has argued that the achievement of the liberal critics of British imperialism 'added up to something far short of a rival *Weltanschauung* to the

Victorians; they were too diffuse and tentative – a few discordant notes scattered about the score which might jar a little on the ear, but which had not yet been brought together to make an alternative melody'.[65] The reasons for this intellectual failure undoubtedly lay in the inability of the liberals to find a strong or adequate enough alternative morality to the ethics of British imperialism. Despite the move by such intellectuals as L.T. Hobhouse, J.A. Hobson and Graham Wallas towards a 'new liberalism' which emphasised a more collectivist and organic plane of political action,[66] most liberal thinking was burdened by a more eclectic positivism, which has been as such an important feature of British intellectual life. This positivism left the liberals ill-equipped to tackle the dominant morality of the British establishment reflected in Rudyard Kipling's notion of the law.[67] This in many ways acted as a surrogate English version of a social theory which on the Continent was developed via Weber and Durkheim into a cohesive sociology.[68] Sociological analysis thus failed to develop beyond its limited empirical role in British intellectual life before at least the late 1920s.[69] J. A. Hobson, one of the most important of the anti imperial liberal critics, privately confessed to being unable to come to terms with Kipling's defence of the 'moral' enthusiasm in Britain for the Anglo-Boer War, despite the fact that it was a morality which could falsify the 'facts' of British imperialism. Likewise, on the question of race differences, Hobson had difficulty in moving out of the Victorian paradigm of 'higher' and 'lower' races, resorting continually back to the classical model of individual rights. He wrote to Gilbert Murray:

> In theory it is not necessary to show a separate gain to the 'lower' race taken under the trust of the civilised world. It is the same question as that of individual rights. There are no natural inherent rights of individuals or nations: the good of 'the whole' must of course be the standard. But as in the politics of a state it is an important measure of practical government that the individual should be regarded as a valuable end in himself, so with the nationality.[70]

The liberals needed a new vocabulary with which to discuss race in terms of modern biology so that they could be freed from the older Victorian hierarchical concept of race differences whilst also moving beyond the nineteenth-century conception of nationalism as an extension of bourgeois individualism. While this had partly been initiated through Mary Kingsley's notion of a cultural relativism, it still did not allow for an understanding of the changing power *relation* behind 'inter-racial contacts'. The discussion, however, at the 1911 Universal Races Congress was a landmark in the era before the First World War in that some liberals recognised the global nature of this phenomenon.

The 1911 Universal Races Congress

The Kingsleyite view of race differences reflected the survival of polygenism in late Victorian thought and its general tendency to accommodate itself to the older Victorian conception of a hierarchy of races dominated by white Anglo-Saxons. The tenacity of this view indicated that some of the older Victorian debate between polygenists and monogenists was not completely over despite its temporary suspension with the impact of Darwinism in the 1870s.[71] In the Edwardian period, therefore, a slow reaction began to take place in favour of a revived monogenism, and one important stimulus to this was the growing interest by the international peace movement in race issues. This movement had grown up in the wake of the 1899 Hague Conference on War and it was Felix Adler, Professor of Political and Social Studies at Columbia University, who first suggested an international congress on race at an International Union of Ethical Societies at Eisenach in 1906.[72] The idea was given added impetus after a Moral Education Congress held in London in 1908 at which 23 governments were represented.[73] As a result, a German Jew, Gustav Spiller, resident in London, started organising a race congress in 1909 with the ultimate purpose of discussing 'the larger racial issues in the light of modern knowledge and modern conscience, with a view to encouraging a good understanding, friendly feelings and co-operation among all races and nations'. 'Political aspects', however, were to be 'subordinated to this comprehensive end.'[74]

The general nature of these objectives tended to incur the disapproval of the British humanitarian lobby and the Anti-Slavery Society refused to involve itself in the scheme, considering it too ambitious and unlikely to advance the Society's own interests.[75] This tended to enhance the scheme's generally ethical nature, divorced as it was from any organised body or pressure group, and reinforced the idea that general education on race differences could both heighten the moral conscience on the issue and decrease the likelihood of race being manipulated in the service of national self-interest and political power. Whilst confessing that 'the racial question is one of the great sores of the world', Spiller had a considerable degree of optimism in the capacity for the ethical improvement of nation-states' policies, especially in the English-speaking world.[76] His efforts at getting the issue discussed marked a strategy difference to previous efforts of the liberal anti-imperial lobby at the time of the Anglo-Boer War. Furthermore, those efforts in Britain to have race debated in a 'scientific' context had been generally unsuccessful since the founding of the Sociological Society in 1904 had resulted in the race debate becoming bogged down in a discussion on the nature and limits of eugenics.[77] Thus the idea of the Universal Races

Congress, with its liberal, if rather naive, New World pedigree, represented a new development on the race issue for the English liberals who attended its sessions at the University of London between 26 July and 29 July 1911.

The ideological significance of the Congress lay especially in its developing a comparative view of race relations. It marked a renewed attempt to relate race to a liberal theory of international relations based upon growing international structures of inter-state cooperation. There was a fairly widespread opinion that a new code of conduct of some kind was needed to regulate the relationship between different racial groups in the international context. Shortly before the Congress opened, Harry Johnston, who by this time had broken with Morel on the Congo reform issue, rebuked the ideologists of white race supremacy in an article supporting the Congress and its objectives, which he felt had triumphed over 'British apathy and . . . the dislike in certain quarters of discussing any "racial questions"'.[78] While still maintaining that there was a supreme white race in Europe, America and the colonies of white settlement, Johnston attacked the polygenist advocates of permanent black racial inferiority. 'Emphatically, there is but one *species* of man living on the earth at the present day', he wrote, 'and the utmost rank which can be given to his divergent types is that of the difference of one sub-species or variety from another. This statement is proved by the complete fertility between all known types of existing Man, and that continued fertility, again, of their mixed descendants. There are no human mules.'[79] This strong support for monogenism was echoed by the organisers of the Congress. Spiller in particular welcomed the arguments of the Frenchman, Jean Finot, against the racial determinism of Gobineau and his successors in Europe.[80] There was no such thing as pure races, Finot reported in the *Review of Reviews*, and it was the brain which shaped human life. With a strong element of neo-Lamarckianism which emphasised the inheritance of acquired characteristics, Finot argued for the creation of new national types through the influence of new environmental conditions:

> Nothing could be more illusory than the physiological distinctions established among humans. It is our brain which shapes our life. Under the influence of external physiological conditions we are transformed and adapted to the current type. Immigrants become absorbed physiologically and mentally to the dominant type. Many races have contributed to the development of the German race.[81]

This led to an exploding of the Victorian view of a hierarchy between 'advanced' and 'backward' races for the intermixture of different races meant that there were no 'pure' races. Furthermore, the notion of 'advancement' could now be linked to the degree to which the nation was an intermixture of different racial groups. 'The more advanced a people', Finot argued in his important study, *Race Prejudice*, in 1906, 'and the greater its vitality, so much the more intermixed with others it is found to be.'[82] Those nations like the United States, France and Britain which were 'at the van of civilisation' were so because they all possessed 'heterogeneous' blood. The conclusion was thus that with no 'pure' races, patriotism could no longer be 'a brutal instinct of blood' and there was a need for 'the obvious and absolute fraternity of the inhabitants of the same country, together with the possibility and the necessity of advancing towards its political and social realisation'.[83]

This view did not dispose of the idea of separate races, but it assumed that, through the right kind of machinery, proper kinds of 'relations' could be established between different races and nations in the pursuit of the wider goal of world peace. It was this latter question which occupied a large part of the Congress's deliberations. Harry Johnston wrote of the need for a 'common inter-racial religion' which could underpin these relationships[84] and Spiller proposed 'an impartial investigator' who could 'look upon the various important peoples of the world as, to all intents and purposes, essentially equals in intellect, enterprise, morality and physique'.[85] Racial equality should also be taught, he suggested, in schools, especially in geography and history and there was an onus on sociologists and anthropologists to point out the 'fundamental fallacy' behind 'static' rather than 'dynamic' views of race.[86]

The differences between Johnston and Spiller indicated varying opinions towards the question of 'inter-racial relations': was it to be on some form of religious basis, as Johnston suggested or, as Spiller implied in his statement outlining the objectives of the 1911 Congress, 'in the light of science and the modern conscience'? Generally, the latter view prevailed at the Congress and was reflected in the contribution of the Bostonian, Edwin D. Mead, who argued for an 'international organisation for inter-racial goodwill' modelled to some extent on the Congo Reform Association, which had been established in both Britain and the United States. An international association of such national bodies, furthermore, could be held each year as the National Peace Congresses in the same countries, thus linking the race issue to the issue of world peace.[87] He urged another congress three years hence and the Congress resolved before it ended its deliberations to establish a permanent secretariat and to hold further conferences at least every four years.[88]

Yet the general idealism of the Congress masked over a more vacuous conception behind their idea of promoting an international association to promote inter-racial goodwill. The Congress did not succeed in obtaining a positive response from established political opinion and it was uncertain where future political alliances could be made to translate at least some of the ideas expressed in the Congress into a political reality. The discussion revealed that the Victorian monogenism–polygenism debate was by no means dead and *The Times* focused on what it saw as 'trifling matters' at the Congress, for example the question 'as to whether the first parents of the delegates hung by the tail from one tree or many trees' and the difficulties of relating the Congress's idealism to anthropological facts.[89] The general lack of agreement at the Congress also brought an attack from the former governor of Jamaica and prominent Fabian socialist, Sydney Olivier, who wrote that 'there have been so many interpretations of real manifestos of friendly enthusiasm and such a chaotic discontinuity of anything approaching enlightening discussion of any subject' that the Congress could not be considered a success.[90]

Overall, while it is possible to share the view of Michael Biddiss that the Congress did mark the development of an increasingly enlightened discussion of race by 'characters of courage striving through whatever muddle to be more humane than the generality of men or even the generality of intellectuals in an age addicted consciously or otherwise to racist norms and modes of explanation',[91] its deliberations manifested some limitations. The grandiose objectives of the Congress and its benign faith in the power of reason and 'conscience' to alter national states' policies towards the ideal of a universal brotherhood of man, in which colour became irrelevant, were very much part of a liberal political creed which had not yet been radically undermined by the experience of the First World War. The Congress lacked clear political insight into the nature of the issues it was seeking to confront and this led to it producing no strong political message. Though a second conference was announced, to be held in Honolulu, by 1913 there was a lack of funds to hold it. A meeting was planned for Paris in 1915, but was never held due to the First World War.[92] The optimism of the Universal Race Congress's enthusiastic proponents ended in 1914, and when attention to internation action on race issues was renewed after the war, a different climate of opinion was manifest.

The objective of the 1911 Congress was rooted in incorporating race relations into a nation-state system modelled on that of Europe over the previous century. Its ethos was thus still one of nineteenth-century liberalism in that it saw the emergent black states – some of whose spokesmen were present – as fitting into this basic system. By 1918, however, this liberalism had been considerably shaken by a rising nationalism. Moreover, race itself was being increasingly linked to a specifically colour-conscious nationalism in many parts of colonial Africa and the Far East in the immediate post-war period. Some of this nationalism represented a growth among colonial political elites – as in the National Congress of British West Africa – of Pan-African ideas previously espoused by such figures as Edward Wilmott Blyden and Duse Mohammed Ali, whose paper, *The African Times and Orient Review*, was established in 1912 in the wake of the Universal Races Congress to act as its 'unofficial mouthpiece'.[93]

Mohammed hoped the 1911 Congress would initiate a series of conferences which would raise the question of 'colour prejudice' in the British empire. Though professing a strong faith in the British imperial mission, his book, *In the Land of the Pharaohs* (1912), attacked the notion of 'Oriental incapacity', which he found in so much contemporary British writing. 'I have patiently awaited the demise of colour prejudice for many years', he wrote, 'and I have a rather large spade in readiness herewith to expedite its interment; but I greatly fear its tale of years is likely to wrest the laurels from the heavy brow of Methuselah, establishing for itself a long-distance record which no human agency will ever take away.'[94] Many black people in Britain still hoped, though, that racial prejudice would eventually die away and they distinguished the less systematised colour prejudice there from the more virulent racial hostility encountered in the colonial setting. There seemed to some African leaders a growing need to raise this issue in London itself as the heart of the British empire and to assert the independent cultural and historical traditions of Asian and African societies within the imperial context.

The *African Times and Orient Review* thus initially kept up links with the ethical opinion that had been forged at the 1911 Universal Races Congress, though growing nationalism eventually took the paper in a more radical direction. In 1913 one article by Dr Stanton Coite, president of the West London Ethical Society, asserted Seeley's 'fundamental doctrine' of 'the Higher Patriotism, the idealistic spirit of Nationality'.[95] The paper, however, became increasingly critical of white settler power in East and Southern Africa, and Cuba was upheld as a model of inter-racial harmony since it had freed itself to some extent from imperialism. In October 1913 Marcus Garvey wrote of the West Indies as a 'mirror of civilisation', prophesying the founding of an empire there 'on which the sun shall shine as ceremoniously as it shines on the Empire in the North today'.[96]

Black nationalism tended to form only a temporary alliance with the liberals in the Universal Races Congress, and the advent of the First World War acted as a shock which drove a wedge through it. The Victorian conception of state power as formed from large imperial conglomerates, within which liberal principles of liberty and parliamentary democracy were to be allowed to flourish, received a central body blow with the transformation of the European political order in 1918. By this time, the mood of black political opinion in Britain had begun to change from the more conciliatory position at the time of the 1911 Congress. F. E. M. Hercules, of the Society of Peoples of African Origin, wrote in the *African Telegraph* of his disillusionment with the internationalist and universalist ideals of the pre-war period when he had been 'grasping blindly for a "something" that would transcend mere nationality, searching after the elusive "something" in humanity that would help men to meet in common and to remain linked without being narrowed by petty considerations of political frontiers or geopolitical barriers'. The experience of living in Britain itself helped to shatter such ideals for Hercules, for in a society which he found racked by 'barriers' and 'prejudices' and which had a 'caste system as rigid as any practised by the Hindoos' he felt driven back to 'the refuge of my own people'.[97] From the long-term perspective, therefore, it is difficult to accept the notion that the Universal Races Congress contributed to the Pan-Africanist tradition.[98]

The universalist creed of the Victorian liberal tradition was considerably shaken by the war and the emergence of colonial nationalism eroded much of the earlier faith in the power of reason to ensure a growing 'unity' between different 'races' in a single world order. The ideal survived in a truncated form to put in renewed appearances periodically in British politics, such as in the early 1930s when a short-lived Joint Council was formed in London to promote 'understanding' between white and black, and again in the 1950s with the Racial Unity movement (see pp. 177-82). By the inter-war years the idealistic pre-war liberal internationalist tradition moved some way away from its earlier preoccupation with race issues and became increasingly concerned with the League of Nations and the campaign to outlaw war. As a consequence, the field of 'inter-racial relations' failed to develop in the same manner as that of international relations, which gained the authoritative backing of the Royal Institute of International Affairs at Chatham House. In one sense, this reflected a more general phenomenon in global politics – that race issues failed to define in any significant sense the totality of global power politics and remained only one sub-branch of a much more complex set of inter-state relations comprising economic, strategic and political dimensions.[99] For this reason, later hopes after the Second World War that 'race relations' could be developed as a subject area on lines similar to international relations were somewhat ill conceived. Race issues remained the preserve of a minority idealist tradition of political thought that was increasingly marginalised in the post-1945 period by the emergence of a hard headed school of political realism that found the appeal to racial solidarity transcending nation-states somewhat utopian and out of tune with the general tenor of international politics.

3

The Commonwealth ideal and the problem of racial segregation

The cultural relativism of the emergent liberal anthropology in Britain remained a generally limited and partial critique of imperial policy for it accrued from the less rigidly defined social structures of colonial West Africa. As Kingsleyite ideas became applied in other African societies they tended to be accommodated to the more coherent ideologies of racial segregation that grew up to buttress white colonial settlement in East and Central Africa in the years before and after the First World War. Cultural relativism remained ultimately blunted in the face of white settler power and became overlain by a more sophisticated political ideal of empire management in the form of the conception of a British 'Commonwealth of Nations'. The nineteenth-century debate on imperial race relations was thus in considerable measure perpetuated within the Commonwealth tradition of political discourse. 'The Commonwealth' as an ideal became linked with a new middle position in political debate between the advocates of global racial segregation on the one hand and the radical critics of imperialism on the other. The Commonwealth school imbibed some of the teachings of the cultural relativists and extended them on the imperial plane into a set of pragmatic policies that, as far as possible, sought mediation and brokerage between rival schools of colonial policy at the local level. This pragmatism, and ultimately political opportunism, proved politically successful until at least the advent of the Second World War, as this chapter seeks to show, though thereafter the demise of British global power induced a crisis in Commonwealth ideology that was never satisfactorily resolved in the years after 1945.

The challenge of segregation

The rise of segregationism in the United States was increasingly worrying a number of the liberal and radical critics of empire by the early years of the century and represented a major challenge to the universalist ideals of

50

Victorian liberal imperialism. For some imperial enthusiasts the segregationist creed represented a potentially new mode of developing imperial control in the wake of the decline of the faith in a common Anglo-Saxon racial solidarity. As the 'highest stage of white supremacy', segregationism as a political ideology did not necessarily have to be linked to an overtly racist political creed such as Anglo-Saxonism, for, as John Cell has pointed out, it has exhibited throughout the twentieth century a remarkable toughness and adaptability to different cultural and political circumstances. Indeed, it was frequently reformulated in new ideological terms to stay in accord with changing climates of opinion and so appear a respectable solution to an ongoing 'race problem'. This was often necessary in order to convince popular audiences that areas where white and 'Anglo-Saxon' populations dwelt, such as the American South, Southern Africa and to some extent Queensland in Australia, could remain under white rule despite pessimistic predictions that the advancing black population rate and the climatic unsuitability of tropical areas for whites meant that this rule was inevitably doomed.[1]

The key area of contention was the birthplace of the segregationist creed itself, the American South, though the British imperial debate tended to shift towards the South African domain after the attainment of Union there in 1910. It was in the South that Jim Crow segregation had advanced in the 1870s and 1880s, especially after the withdrawal of Federal troops in 1877 and the progressive nullification of the Civil Rights Act of 1875, culminating in the Supreme Court decision in 1896 in *Plessy* v *Ferguson* that legislation was 'powerless to eradicate racial instincts' and that separate facilities for blacks and whites in education could be equal.[2] Segregation was to some extent produced by a change in the balance of political power in Southern society and was additionally fortified by the high tide of racial Anglo-Saxonism in the United States, which stemmed from a new expansionist imperialism epitomised by the war against Spain in 1898.[3] It also appeared eminently reasonable even to mainstream thinkers on race in the light of 'scientific' theories of the anthropometric and eugenic superiority of white Anglo-Saxons not only over black people, but also over brown, yellow and southern European peoples.[4]

To a number of British race experts the Southern drift into segregation appeared an absurdity that was ultimately doomed to failure. The black West Indian writer, Theophilus E. S. Scholes, in *The British Empire and Alliances* in 1899, portrayed the political ascendancy of the whites in the South as already failing and praised the British empire for having been 'wise enough and *self-contained enough*, not to attempt to wreck this "train of nature", but to allow it to go on in its own way'. The Americans, he argued, had 'adopted the opposite course, hence the commotions and "Babel" of the South'[5] (emphasis added). Like other writers such as W. P. Livingstone and Sydney Oliver, Scholes upheld the West Indies as the suitable ideal model for British policy makers to pursue in the sphere of colonial race relations for 'in respect of loyalty, Jamaica represents the whole British West Indies, and the British West Indies are British subjects of the African race within the Empire'.[6]

By the early twentieth century, however, a reaction had begun to set in against the liberal espousal of the West Indian model for it had always implied, even to the most enthusiastic Victorian advocates of Anglo-Saxon racial domination, a certain degree of inter-racial mixing and 'miscegenation'. Anthony Trollope, in 1859, had envisaged a new mixed race inhabiting the West Indian islands 'fitted by nature for their burning sun, in whose blood shall be mixed some portion of Northern energy, and which shall owe its physical prowess to African progenitors – a race that shall be no more ashamed of the name of negro than we are of the same of Saxon?'.[7] Even Grant Allen, in a novel, *In All Shades*, in 1886, that was later attacked by Olivier for prophesying race war, saw the visibly white Anglo-Saxon colonists in the West Indies as frequently having coloured ancestry. Furthermore, their ultimate control over the potentially rebellious black peasantry Allen depicted as resting not simply on race *per se* but on superior civilisation, which would see the whites through in the absence of overwhelming military superiority.[8] This consideration by and large comforted those pessimistic theorists of the climatic unsuitability of tropical areas to white settlement in the 1880s and 1890s who saw the West Indies as an example of social *devolution* and a reversal of the more general Victorian faith in social advance and progress. A benevolent despotism on the Indian pattern, argued a reviewer of Anthony Froude's book, *The West Indies*, in the *Edinburgh Review* in 1888, was 'impossible without the support of an adequate military or police force, sufficient to compel obedience if the law of the land be resisted, and that is precisely what does not exist, and cannot exist, in the British West Indies'.[9] The imagined rebellion in Trinidad in Allen's *In All Shades* was only pre-empted by the magistrate, Edward Hawthorne, promising to take up the blacks' grievance and resigning his judgeship to petition the Colonial Office in London on needed reforms.

The weakness of British military and imperial power in the Caribbean thus nullified the hopes of those advocates of its alleged racial harmony, and the Southern model of segregation had a contrasting appeal to advocates of British imperial consolidation in the years before the First World War. In 1910, the noted theatre critic and translator of Ibsen's plays into English, William Archer, published a strong defence of Southern segregationism in his book, *Through Afro-America: an English Reading of the Race*

Problem, and bitterly attacked Olivier's championing of the West Indies in contrast to the polarised model of Jim Crow segregation. The Southern States, Archer wrote, were 'the great crucible in which this experiment in inter-racial chemistry is working itself out'.[10] Jim Crowism represented a 'legitimate measure of defence against constant discomfort' for it was 'the crowding, the swamping, the submerging of the white race by the blacks, that the South cannot reasonably be expected to endure'.[11] Given that in the South 'one person in every four is physically indistinguishable from an African savage', it would be an 'extravagance of paradox' to maintain that this was a 'positively desirable condition', preferable to that of a country which represents a 'normal uniformity of complexion'. England would not be a 'more desirable place of residence' if one quarter of its population was so 'transmuted', and Archer vehemently resisted those early exponents of a multi-racial society since 'a monochromic civilization' was 'on the face of it preferable to such a piebald civilization as at present exists in the Southern States'.[12]

Archer's segregationism had a strong appeal for the interests campaigning for political unification in South Africa and the organ of the Closer Union movement there, *The State*, published two articles by Archer on 'Black and White in the Southern States of America', where he argued that without territorial segregation 'the black nation' in America 'would be a hampering, extraneous element in the body politics, like a bullet encysted in the human frame. It might lie there for years without setting up inflammation or gangrene, and causing no more than occasional twinges of pain, but it certainly could not contribute to the health efficiency or comfort of the organism.'[13] Amalgamation of the races was 'a thousand leagues remote from the sphere of practical politics'[14] and segregation thus the most rational and practical scheme of political and social engineering in an age which still believed in a science of political processes.

This plea for the Southern model of segregation at the time of South African Union came, nevertheless, when a number of liberal critics were beginning to doubt the long-term ability of the white settler colonists there to maintain white rule. 'Deliberately to set out upon a new career as a civilised nation with a definition of civilisation which takes as the criterion race and colour, not individual character and attainments', wrote J. A. Hobson in *The Crisis of Liberalism*, 'is nothing less than to sow a crop of dark and dangerous problems for the future.'[15] Southern segregationism as a model of white rule thus tended to fortify an indigenous tradition of local British imperial control in Southern Africa which had been increasingly interacting with local white settler power in the benign faith that the somewhat attenuated values of the late nineteenth-century Cape liberal tradition could be extended northwards into a Southern African *Pax Capensis*.[16] This hope progressively declined in the years after Union as the internal logic of South African segregationism became manifest, though by this time the British government had absolved itself of any responsibility for intervening in the Union government's internal affairs.[17] The political legacy of the attainment of Union, however, left a long-lasting legacy on the emergence of the Commonwealth conception as many of those involved in achieving it went on to exert considerable political influence in Britain through the Round Table movement.

The Commonwealth and the Round Table

The 'Commonwealth' as an intrinsically pacific conception increased in stature as a key anchoring notion behind the British imperial purpose in the years after the Anglo-Boer War. Following the short-lived outburst of martial enthusiasm for military conquest of the Boer Republics, a reaction set in against empire as an ethical ideal for, 'having begun its career as a description of the politics of Napoleon III, by 1900 it had become a word signifying an arrogant and bullying form of British nationalism'.[18] This re-evaluation particularly occurred in intellectual and cultural bodies which sought to temper imperial ideals with liberal principles. Henry Wilson, for example, writing in the journal of the Ruskin Society, called for 'a sane and moderate imperialism' in which the British empire became part of 'the gradual process which has been going on all over the world since the dawn of history' whereby smaller states were absorbed into larger ones. This meant a rejection of the ideal of purity of race, for all the great powers were based upon a composite number of races.[19] With the establishment of the Union of South Africa in 1910, there seemed to be a working model on hand for a wider notion of imperial consolidation and unification and there was growing use of the term 'imperial commonwealth' to describe the empire of white settlement. Hopes were thus revived for the establishment of a more united empire of 'Greater Britain' and the eventual attainment of the nineteenth-century imperial designs of Dilke, Froude and Seeley.[20]

The group of people who were most influential in disseminating this conception of Commonwealth in the years after 1910 was the Round Table movement, formed by a number of members of the former staff of Alfred Milner, in South Africa after 1902. The 'Milner Kindergarten', consisting of such figures as Lionel Curtis, Geoffrey Dawson, Leo Amery, Philip Kerr (Lord Lothian) and Robert Brand, managed to exert considerable influence on British political debate despite its relatively marginal position inside the establishment and the absence of strong institutional support. As a body of 'eccentrics and seers, whose prestige was never commensurate with their power',[21] the Round Table operated in some degree outside the main structures of establishment conservatism and inertia and was able to generate sufficiently radical political ideas on the evolution of British imperialism as to neutralise much of the liberal critique that began to be mounted after the First World War in Labour and anti-colonial circles. One of the ways in which this was done was through the development of a blunted form of multi-racialism which had the advantage of blurring the differences between the policies on race developed in different parts of the Empire– Commonwealth and forestalling a major debate on races and race differences in Britain until the Second World War.

Thus, while the Round Table did come to see the development of the empire in terms of the evolution of a 'multi-racial Commonwealth'[22] this was largely because of its brokerage role between different sections of opinion within the British establishment. It especially sought to neutralise conflict between the champions of white settlement in Africa and those who argued for the advancement of India to dominion status.

The initial experience of the group, though, came in South Africa after 1902, when ideas of racial segregation began to be developed to rationalise separate white and black territorial spheres. The function of this ideology of 'possessory segregation' has been a matter of some debate among historians, some of whom have seen it as the ideological rationalisation of a system of economic exploitation of the African working class in the mines by means of the employment of a subsistence base in the pre-capitalist reserve economies. With the institutionalisation of the migrant labour system between the African 'reserves' and the 'white' urban areas, it became possible for the mine-owners to pay wages below the level of subsistence necessary for the reproduction of labour power, as occurred in societies dominated by a single mode of production.[23] Alongside this economic explanation for racial segregation in South Africa, however, there were additional ideological features in terms of the building-up of a local white nationalism which could be sufficiently strong to resist the perceived 'black peril' of African political activism. The process of rapid proletarianisation on the Witwatersrand and at Kimberley had already led to a partial breakdown of more traditional modes of social control through tribal chiefs, and alternative communities were springing up which frequently lay outside the direct control of the local white colonial apparatus. Some of these were 'Ethiopian' or 'Zionist' churches which had developed in the 1890s and early 1900s and which were seen by the white settlers as a contributing cause of the Bambata Rebellion in Natal in 1906–7.[24] The fears of a united black uprising led by American-educated black preachers exerted a powerful hold on the white settler imagination in South Africa in the early years of the century and were graphically depicted by the novelist, John Buchan, who had served briefly in the Milner Kindergarten between

1901 and 1903, in his popular story, *Prester John*, published in 1910.[25] Moreover, with an upsurge of white fears of attacks by black servants on white women in the cities, especially Johannesburg, during this period, the notion of a 'black peril' gained widespread currency not only in South Africa but in British discussions of race, too. In a debate on South Africa in 1906, for example, Winston Churchill, the new Liberal Under Secretary of State for the Colonies, told the House of Commons of the danger to white rule in South Africa from the 'Ethiopian movement' and the African Methodist Episcopal Church. There was, he said, a 'gulf which separates the African negro from the immemorial civilisation of India and China', and the 'Black Peril' was 'the one bond of union between the European races which live in the country' for it was 'surely as grim a problem as any mind could be forced to face'.[26] Black resistance to white rule in South Africa was generally seen by 1910 as potentially far more threatening than anything in the West Indies.

The development of racial segregation in South Africa undoubtedly owed much to internal imperatives within that society as the older tradition of Victorian liberalism in the Cape Colony broke down before a much wider white nationalism in the years before Union in 1910. The term was first used there in 1903 by a Cape liberal lawyer, Richard Rose-Innes, to rationalise a policy of establishing 'native reserves' in order to induce a ready supply of black labour for the mines and farms.[27] The American model of segregation which had grown up in the South in the 1880s and 1890s in order to entrench white economic and political supremacy after the failure of Reconstruction, shaped some thinking on the issue, especially via the experiments in 'industrial training' on the land at Booker T. Washington's Tuskegee Institute and at the Hampton Institute in Virginia. This form of rural training and education impressed many British observers of American race relations since it appeared to be resisting full black proletarianisation and instead kept up peasant links with the land.[28] It was also championed by a number of white 'race experts' in South Africa and acted as a model for the first black 'inter-state native college', opened at Fort Hare in the Eastern Cape in 1915. Rural educational training, as Buchan had envisaged it in *Prester John*, was an obvious political answer to white fears of a united black rebellion. Segregationism thus acted as a modernising ideology, which could direct thinking towards a certain degree of social engineering in African society in order to direct black political energies towards the reserves and weaken links with the metropolitan and 'detribalising' culture of the cities.

The segregationist model in South Africa appealed to some of the members of the Milner Kindergarten who shifted away from the urban system of compounds. Some liberals in Britain, like Gilbert Murray, feared the compound system would extend to British colonies as a mode of social control since the system 'offers such opportunities for the fraud which is normal in contracts between whites and blacks, and does its work of gradual demoralization so insidiously, and with so little shock to public feeling, that he may expect it to spread and flourish in other continents'.[29] The Kindergarten, however, saw the issue in 'racial' terms. Leo Amery, for example, wrote as early as 1900 on the desirability of establishing separate political insitutions for the Africans in South Africa, especially on the Basutoland model which had so impressed observers like James Bryce before the war. Amery considered that 'the whole future of the native question will probably lead to a sort of caste system' with a 'gradual equalisation and intercourse' in political, business and educational spheres, but no fusion between the races.[30] Over the next few years a debate developed on the Witwatersrand on the nature of racial segregation and a number of 'race experts' there began to develop a distinct model of race relations between 'white' urban areas and black pastoral reserves. This 'territorial' or 'possessory' segregation was a more fluid ideology than the Indian caste model, though fears of pollution through interaction with different races strongly characterised South African racism, leading eventually to the first law outlawing inter-racial sexual liaisons, in 1927.[31] Lionel Curtis, one of the most significant intellectuals within the Milner Kindergarten and later the Round Table group, wrote in a paper to the Fortnightly Club in Johannesburg in 1906 (which came together to discuss Closer Union) of the need for segregation in order to entrench white rule in South Africa. The point was to prevent South Africa needing a fall back on British troops 'for the suppression of native disorder' and this meant engendering in the minds of the whites 'a sense of responsibility even greater than that which is followed by the Indian bureaucracy'. Curtis thus rejected the Cape policy of incorporating educated blacks under the banner of a 'white civilisation' and favoured instead 'the gradual separation of the whites and blacks into their respective territories'.[32] 'I am picturing a state of affairs', he continued, 'in which the native is free to move about South Africa but has been led to fix his home in native territory and to find himself in the position of an uitlander when he goes outside it. These territories could then be administered by the South African Government by means of a highly organised Civil Service, very much as India is administered by the Imperial Gov't.'[33]

Curtis saw South Africa as representing a fascinating laboratory for experimenting with new models of imperial government and where some of the experience derived from the Indian empire could be reapplied in the context of growing white self-government. As early as 1900, as town clerk of Johannesburg, he saw the country as 'a school of citizenship with all the inconveniences and delays that appertain thereto' rather than as 'an

efficient administration superimposed over a people'.[34] The appeal of
segregation lay in its providing the ideological base for the orderly
withdrawal of British administrative control and the easing of race relations
after a period of acute racial hostility, especially on the Witwatersrand and
in Natal. The wider applicability of this to the rest of the empire seemed also
obvious in view of the diversity of races within it. Rejecting the liberal
imperialist view that the purpose of the empire was an evolutionary civilising
mission whereby 'the lower races' were given the same laws, rights and
institutions as 'the highest', Curtis sought to apply the segregationist model
to the empire as a whole. The objective should be 'the maintenance of laws,
rights and institutions natural to each level of civilisation' and the best
policy likely to effect this 'will be one that aims in all parts of the Empire at
the segregation of each race and civilisation in territories of their own.
Within these territories each race can be accorded such powers of self-
government as they can exercise without detriment to themselves or to other
members of the Empire. Such higher powers of government as the lower
races cannot be trusted to exercise should be exercised for them by the
white community best situated to secure the best government.' While such a
policy was best secured by the segregation of different races in the South
African context, Curtis also saw the South African model as 'a microcosm'
of the imperial race relations dilemma.[35]

These considerations, prompted by South African Union, became
especially important in the years after 1910 when the question arose of the
incorporation of India into the imperial conference system.[36] The Milner
Kindergarten never quite shared Milner's own dogmatic racial patriotism
even while its members were based in South Africa reorganising the
administration of the Transvaal after the Anglo-Boer War. The experience
of working in South African colonial administration between 1901 and
1908 led them towards a vision of the empire as an integrated entity and one
to be considered from an international perspective.[37] When they returned to
England in 1908–9 and began to establish the Round Table movement for
wider imperial consolidation, they began to address the question of the 'two
empires' of the Indian Raj on the one hand, and the colonies of white settlement on the other.[38] The Round Table favoured a federal imperial parliament with 110 representatives from Britain and 79 from the dominions, and
Curtis had, according to Lord Hailey, already been persuaded by Sir W.
Morris of the Indian civil service that Indian self-government was the only
intelligible goal for British policy.[39] By 1912 some Round Table members
moved towards the idea of allowing India some seats in the envisaged
parliament. Philip Kerr saw this as the key question facing the British
empire at this particular stage in history. 'If we manage to create in India a
self-governing, responsible dominion', he told the Round Table in Canada,

'and if India, when it is responsible and self-governing, elects to remain within the British Empire, we shall have solved the greatest difficulty which presents itself in the world today.' The future progress of the world thus hinged on 'whether there is to be a long renewal of the world-old feud between east and west, black and white, or whether we can find a system based on mutual give and take which will enable them to live in peace and goodwill together'. By a 'reconstruction of the constitutional edifice of the empire', Kerr believed it possible that the British empire could demonstrate a way of resolving international racial cleavages and so have 'proved to the world that there is some other way than war by which disputes between nations and disputes between black, yellow and white can be settled'.[40]

This vision of a new imperial order based upon the representation of India in a federal imperial parliament grew out of the recognition of a new and politically significant Indian middle class and fear of a possible future race war in India and the Asian empire. In 1912 the *Round Table* journal noted the emergence of a Western-educated Indian elite, and an 'intelligent and comparatively civilised white race', settled mostly in the north of India, ruling over a 'subject race of dark complexion and inferior attainments'.[41] It was highly fallacious to compare British rule in India to that of Africa, for India was 'full of highly educated, thoughtful and competent people . . . It has numberless country gentlemen exactly like the country gentlemen of England' and a professional middle class which was making increasing demands to have a say in public policy.[42] This view reflected a general concern in British governing circles at the time at the critical position of India within the empire, and a number of liberals, like Gilbert Murray, were becoming harshly critical of the way Kipling had 'used his great powers to stir up in the minds of hundreds of thousands of Englishmen a blind and savage contempt for the Bengali'.[43] There was an especial worry regarding the ignorance of the British public about India and an awareness of the need to awaken them to the critical stage reached in imperial relationships and thus achieve imperial consolidation both politically and economically.[44] The problem regarding the incorporation of India, however, lay not simply in terms of finding an acceptable political package for the educated Indian intelligentsia but also of resolving the issue of Indian emigration to the colonies of white settlement. In some of these colonies Indian indentured labour had been especially imported from at least the middle of the nineteenth century, as in the case of the Natal sugar plantations; while in Australia and New Zealand, there had been the importation of Indian and Polynesian labour, though immigration controls had been imposed in the early years of the twentieth century. The imperial lobby in Britain presented no united front to oppose the implementation of these controls, reflecting the weakness of the imperial centre to local colonial and settler designs to create white 'Anglo-Saxon' states.[45] As the Royal Colonial Institute's journal, *United Empire*, argued in 1921, for example, 'the objections of British-born subjects to unrestricted intercourse with Asiatics are sound . . . the ideal of a white community cannot be realised if the colour question is ignored, nor can the western standards of living and wages be maintained in competition with cheap oriental labour'.[46] During the First World War one-and-a-quarter million Indians were sent overseas and all indentured labourers in British colonies were only finally freed on 1 January 1920, known as 'India's Independence Day'. Abolition of the system only came after a considerable period of pressure from the Indian political leadership under Gandhi in South Africa, humanitarian reform movements in Britain and white commercial and labour interests in Natal and Australia fearful of Asiatic competition. While even the British viceroy in India, Lord Curzon, had come to recognise the injustices of indentured labour by 1901, in South Africa, Curtis, as head of the Asiatic Department in the Transvaal, went one step further and helped organise the importation of Chinese labour. Though this labour was eventually withdrawn by 1909 after the issue had aroused vocal and often racist opposition at the 1906 general election in Britain, the issue of Indian indentured labour remained a festering sore in the evolution of the Commonwealth. In November 1915, Curtis wrote to the new Indian viceroy, Lord Chelmsford, of the need for 'equality of rights' between the two parts of the Commonwealth, but failed to tackle the indentured labour system head on, and indeed continued to oppose the settlement of Indians in the dominions and white colonies.[47]

The reformulation of the imperialist notion into the Commonwealth ideal during the First World War by Curtis and the Round Table group stemmed from the growing weakness in the earlier tradition of Milnerite racial patriotism, which had been linked to the case for tariff reform before the outbreak of hostilities.[48] The perceptive American political scientist, George Louis Beer, traced this in 1915 to the decline of the Roman idea of *imperium* in the British imperial ideal, for the British Empire was 'in a satiated state and its imperial type of nationalism does not, as is unfortunately too often the case when nationalism is restricted to a narrow field, imply hostility towards other nationalities, but merely a desire to preserve inviolate that political civilization which English-speaking peoples rightly or wrongly, but unquestionably sincerely, cherish as their priceless birthright'.[49] The observation was considerably reinforced over the following years by the growing participation in Round Table activities of the classical scholar, Alfred Zimmern, who was actively involved in the Workers Educational Association.[50] Zimmern was the author of *The Greek Commonwealth*, which first appeared in 1911, and saw the Hellenic civilisation of the Greeks as not only laying the basis of European political thought but also acting as a model of a large-scale civilised community which transcended local and national differences.[51] This enthusiasm for the values of Greek civilisation represented a reaction away from the more authoritarian model of imperial Rome so favoured by late nineteenth-century British imperial enthusiasts. Zimmern interpreted the goals of the British empire in uncompromisingly liberal terms and, with the outbreak of war with Germany in 1914, distinguished between the state-controlled Prussian system of German *Kultur*, which had laid the basis for German 'militarism', and the British ideal of civilisation as the enforcement of the rule of law and the spreading of free political institutions.[52] This also linked British imperial goals to more universal ones: 'The qualities that go to the making of free and ordered institutions are not national and universal. They are no monopoly of Great Britain. They are free to be the attributes of any race or any race nation. They belong to civilised humanity as a whole. They are part of the higher life of the human race.'[53]

This ideal of the British empire accorded closely with the evolving views of Lionel Curtis, who became the first Beit lecturer in imperial history at Oxford in 1912 and together with the Oxford Branch of the Round Table, consisting of Reginald Coupland, Keith Feiling and Harold Pritchard, began a series of imperial studies. Curtis saw the purpose of the British 'Commonwealth' in terms of a liberal Hegelianism that owed much to his former tutor at Oxford, Edward A. Freeman, and the conception of T. H. Green that will and not force lay at the basis of the state. The Hegelian notion of a British imperial 'mission' thus reinforced a more general feeling in the Round Table group that Britain was 'especially fitted', as Reginald Coupland termed it in a talk at the Oxford Ralegh Club, for easing relations with 'coloured races' since 300 of the 800 million inhabitants of the empire were Indians and hence 'fellow subjects'.[54]

This view reinforced the Round Table claim that India should gain dominion status. It was also an important factor in Curtis's conception of the Commonwealth. In 1915 the first part of his report on this for the Round Table was published as *The Project of the Commonwealth* and was followed the next year by *The Commonwealth of Nations*. Here Curtis developed the notion that the British empire determined 'by peaceful methods of law the relations of a large number of races and communities' and 'in this sense' it was 'a state'.[55] From Freeman's *History of Federal Government in Greece and Rome* he developed the notion that the British Commonwealth was structured around a pattern of evolutionary law that made it intrinsically different to Eastern despotism: 'Here is a form of society essentially capable of adapting its framework to changing conditions. It is a progressive society, one in which men can adapt themselves to conditions as they find them, and so dominate circumstances instead of being dominated by them.'[56]

Curtis saw this pattern of pragmatic evolutionism in English history from the time of the ancient Saxon moot, and so tried to apply Victorian Whig notions of English history to the wider 'state' of the Commonwealth.[57] This emphasis upon continuous historical change reflected, though, a more critical reappraisal of British power in a changing international order, which Curtis still saw to some extent in racial terms. 'Now that the empty parts of the world have all been opened to settlement', he wrote, 'their populations will continue to increase by leaps and bounds, and in any case the inhabitants of these little islands must represent a steadily dwindling proportion of the white race, that is to say, of the young family of the world.'[58] He did not thus feel it necessary to assert an intrinsically English racial superiority and thus distanced himself from the contemporary school of racial anthropology. 'It would be difficult', he argued, 'to point to qualities inherent in the English which distinguished them above their neighbours on the continent.' The English success in empire building had to be ascribed 'to the respective merits not of breed but of institutions':

> In the course of the last few thousand years the people of Europe have distinguished themselves from those of Asia, Africa, America and Oceana by their higher capacity for adaptation. Nowhere had this capacity such free play as in these islands protected by the English Channel, with the result that it developed there a society which differed specifically from that of the continent. The English had advanced further than the other nations of Europe in replacing the personal authority of rulers by laws based on the experience of those who obeyed them and subject to revision in the light of future experience.[59]

This redefined the Victorian imperial purpose away from the biological theories of races of the anthropologists, for it was thus not so much the British 'race' *per se* which had built the Empire–Commonwealth but British institutions, as Curtis reminded his readers: 'destiny has placed on the shoulders of this Commonwealth an overwhelming share of the duty imposed on Europe – that of controlling its relations with races more backward than its own'. The liberal Anglican conception of duty was an important factor in Curtis's thought and fortified the conception that the British still had a mission to spread freedom and responsible government around the world.[60]

Curtis's belief in the inherent beneficence of English institutions also led him to view the role of the United States in the international relationships between races as somewhat limited. America had 'never advanced beyond the conception of a national commonwealth' and the absence of an imperial tradition he saw as making her unfit to deal with any wider race relations. 'The presence of the negro in their midst has taught them that a mixture in one country of an advanced with a backward race is in itself the greatest menace to liberty' and the cardinal principle of the system had thus been to refuse American blacks full citizenship rights. 'To the question, have the majority of mankind who are not Europeans to be initiated in the mysteries of freedom', Curtis concluded,'[the Americans] have never felt themselves called upon to provide an answer.'[61]

This restatement of the goals of the British Empire–Commonwealth thus not only sought to screen out the appeal of alternative American models of race relations, such as the segregationism of the South favoured by some 'race experts' like William Archer, but also neutralised to some extent the more universalist claims of the liberal internationalists as they had been espoused at the 1911 Universal Races Congress. J. A. Hobson, in a review of Curtis's *The Commonwealth of Nations* in the *Manchester Guardian*, charged that it really went no further than the country's German opponents for it sought 'to extend her Kultur into a world Kultur' of British people.[62] As Curtis was then in India, Zimmern counterattacked against Hobson's charge, saying that the British Commonwealth ideal really embraced the liberalism of the Victorians: 'The whole position is that liberty and self-government are good for all men, white or dark; and this, as I understand it, is simply the old liberal doctrine of the Victorian era. The word 'Kultur' is misleading because it confuses what is national with what is civic and universal.'[63]

Hobson retorted that this argument assumed that Britain 'had developed a special genius for government' and that 'the Anglo-Saxon idea' was thus of universal validity. It also led to the assumption that the present emphasis upon liberty and self-government constituted the basic motive behind British colonial and imperial policy, which was 'an error of psychology' which 'naturally brings upon us from other nations the charge of pharisanism and hyprocracy [*sic*]'.[64] Zimmern, though, appealed to the theme of political pragmatism ultimately underlying the Commonwealth ideal as he saw it. 'If you asked me to agree to the surrender of British liberty for a mess of pottage of an unprincipled internationalism', he wrote back to Hobson, 'I should think as much a moral duty to resist you as the "objectors" do resist the recruiting officers.'[65]

Curtis's belief in the inherent beneficence of English institutions also led the moral purpose of the British imperial ideal in an era of rapid change in European and global power politics. Zimmern's hope, though, that the Commonwealth could be a means to 'solve the problem of British imperial government on decent lines' and 'reverse Turgot's epigram and create an attractive force comparable to XIXth century nationalism which will bring in ripe fruit from neighbouring trees'[66] was an ideal that was not fulfilled in the post-war world order, since it ultimately conflicted with the liberal

nationalism that underpinned the 1919 Versailles Treaty. The Commonwealth effectively came to define the aims of British imperial government in
the 1920s more through default than design as the rise of American
isolationism led to the refusal of the United States to join the League of
Nations and no other international organisation had as powerful a political
appeal. By 1919 some sections of opinion on the left in Britain began taking
up the Commonwealth ideal as part of a wider campaign to support the
nationalist claims in India, Egypt and other parts of the empire. The
envisaged 'Commonwealth of Nations' was seen by the *Daily Herald*, for
example, in Tennysonian terms as 'the Federation of the World'.[67]

The 1923 Imperial Conference, however, marked the end of any effective
attempts at imperial centralisation and though Curtis and some of the
Round Table idealists continued to hope for moves in this direction, the
reality of colonial and dominion nationalism ensured that the appeal of the
'Commonwealth' lay essentially in moral terms and as a rhetorical device
that obscured the realities of political negotiation.[68] Zimmern still hoped
that Commonwealth policies would not represent 'the result of a bargain, or
simply a common interest, but a common philosophy of empire'.[69] This
reflected to some extent the humanistic idealism that was rampant in the
upper class in Britain in the inter-war years and the domination of classical
educational ideals over those of the more mercantilist view of imperialism
as a means of entrenching British economic power in the dominion and
colonial context.[70] Certainly the centrifugal forces within the empire were
recognised by some observers in the early 1920s, but their hopes for action
to sustain a British *Lebensraum* in the dominions went substantially
unheeded. One writer in the *Nineteenth Century*, for example, saw the aim
of imperial unity as the fostering of capital investment in 'British territory' in
order to plan for a future in which Britain itself would be increasingly eclipsed
by the colonies of white settlement: 'Today the Mother Country leads far
ahead with her massed civilisation, her developed wealth, her preponderant
manpower.' However,

> every year the importance and value of this estate will gravitate
> more and more to the Dominions and possessions beyond the seas.
> When, a century hence, Canada has her seventy millions, New
> Zealand her five millions, Australia her fifty millions and South
> Africa her twenty-five millions of white people, with all the wealth
> and prestige there implied, the potency and significance of the
> Empire will be better implied, the potency and significance of the
> Empire will be better understood.[71]

The same year, Lord Milner's widow published in *The Times* 'the credo'
of her late husband, which expressed his longer-term hopes for imperial

unity and its acceptance by British public opinion. The central objective of the imperial enthusiasts he saw as getting over 'the dangerous interval during which Imperialism, which for long appealed only to the far-seeing few, should become the accepted faith of the whole nation'. The defensive view of imperialism as essentially a holding operation before public opinion came to see the light, revealed a deeper unease in Milner's mind that really it was not publicly accepted and thus reflected a deep anxiety about the future of the imperial 'faith' in empire. His belief drew a strong chord of support from some sections of the establishment in the 1920s, especially Geoffrey Dawson, the editor of *The Times*.[72] However, Milner's belief in imperialism was really a hang-over from a previous period and indicated how far he had moved away from the Commonwealth ideal which inspired the Round Table group and whose internationalism he came to distrust.[73] For the most part, the mainstream of establishment opinion had moved towards accepting the Commonwealth ideal by the mid-1920s as a new and non-militaristic stage in British imperialism. 'The empire, as we know it', declared Stanley Baldwin in 1924, 'is different from any that has existed hitherto; for it has not been the creation of conquering armies, although armies have played their part, but our Empire arose from the bone and sinew of our people'.[74] This popularised the notion of empire as a product of English history and culture, a theme close to Baldwin's heart as he continually played on the theme of England and patriotism in opposition to socialism and class conflict, in the early 1920s.[75]

This became embodied in the Empire Exhibition at Wembley in 1924, which, despite the scorn poured upon it by the liberal intelligentsia, nevertheless acted as a strong reinforcement of the imperial ethos in a period of growing national decline.[76] The monarchy, too, acted as a strongly imperial symbol as it entered a new phase of grandeur and ritual. As David Cannadine has recently pointed out, the British monarchy increased in public esteem during the course of the twentieth century at the same time as its actual political influence declined. This was partly as a detraction from economic and social problems in Britain itself and partly as a consequence of the decline of Britain in international power politics. As some compensation, though, the monarchy came to symbolise imperial continuity in a world order that became increasingly insecure.[77] It thus reinforced the growing legitimacy of the Commonwealth concept in official discourse, which by the time of the Second World War could stand, as Lord Bledisloe stated in his Empire Day message in 1943, for 'bold adventure, love of liberty and justice, and spiritual ideals'.[78] This liberal conception of Empire–Commonwealth carried on into the post-war years under the Labour government, too. In 1946 a government pamphlet for schools, *Britain and the Colonies*, argued that 'even the critics of empire now begin to appreciate that the maintenance and strengthening of the British Commonwealth is no sinister imperialism in the worst sense, and that all of us who have a common loyalty to the Throne are honestly trying to create a better world not only for ourselves but for mankind generally'.[79] Such was the altruistic justification for the Commonwealth in the changing climate of politics in the late 1940s and 1950s, and in 1953 the new queen, Elizabeth II, was crowned not as the ruler of 'The British Dominions beyond the Sea' but as 'Head of the Commonwealth'.[80]

The eclipse of segregation

The development of the Commonwealth ideal did much to attenuate the appeal of segregationism in British political discourse on race. Even before the end of the First World War, the segregationist William Arthur saw India in terms other than those of race. In *India and the Future* in 1917, he refuted those writers and opinion formers who had seen Indians as 'niggers' and saw them instead as 'sunburnt whitemen'. Colour, indeed, was 'an accident in India' and while it marked a 'radical difference' in Africa and the American South it was almost irrelevant in India beyond the 'slight negroid infusion' in the southern part of the country.[81] This thus distinguished and separated India from other parts of the Empire and restricted the segregationist appeal:

> In moving among negroes, one has constantly to avoid – perhaps to struggle against – a sense of their fundamental, inherent, ineradicable inferiority. Whatever may be their amiable and even admirable qualities, one cannot resist the conviction that they are some degrees nearer the brute; nor can one wonder at their proved incapacity to evolve for themselves any approach to civilisation. In moving among Indians, on the other hand, what is constantly borne in upon one is a sense of their fundamental equality, and a vague wonder as to how they happen to have such a position of apparent, and to some extent real, inferiority.[83]

This 'inferiority' Archer ascribed not to 'low development' as with black Africans but to a civilisation that had 'fallen': 'you cannot but feel nearer to barbarism than in any other country that makes the slightest pretence to civilisation'.[84] This feeling of the cultural barbarism of Indian life was fairly common amongst British reformers and philanthropists. It was strongly present in Beatrice Webb's description of India on her tour there in 1912 and was linked to the more general Fabian distaste for administrative inefficiency. She did not, though, doubt that there *could* be cases of considerable administrative rationality for she was especially impressed by the Japanese imperial administration in Korea. There was thus more of an ethnocentric distaste for Indian cultural backwardness than a racialist dismissal of permanent Indian inferiority.[85]

In the wake of the Montagu–Chelmsford reforms, therefore, and the postwar nationalism in India, a general shift in British attitudes to India had occurred in which political reforms and the ultimate attainment of dominion status were seen as crucial if the Empire–Commonwealth was to be maintained. 'To shake the allegiance of India to the British Commonwealth', wrote Basil Matthews in his popular book, *The Clash of Colour* (1924), 'is to shake the entire fabric of which India is – in population – by far the greatest part'.[86]

This still left open the question of policy towards blacks in the African and West Indian context, but by the 1920s the pre-war interest by a number of 'race experts' in the Tuskegee model of industrial training in the American South had become generalised onto the imperial plane. The generality of the industrial-training model allowed the issue of racial segregation *per se* to be suspended, at least for the present, by an emphasis upon the economic development of black peasant agriculture and the imparting of the necessary educational skills. As Kenneth King has pointed out, this approach ensured that 'the premises were thus apparently shifted from racial differences to Negro needs as defined by comparative statistics'.[87] This was the underlying theme of the Phelps-Stokes Commission Report on education in Africa in 1922, in which the South African educationist, C. T. Loram, and the West African, Dr J. E. K. Aggrey, played a prominent role. Industrial-training ideas derived from the Tuskegee model began to shape British colonial policy in Africa and also to define the emergent subject area of 'race relations'.[88] One of the Commission's participants, Thomas Jesse Jones, a Welsh sociologist who taught at Hampton Institute in Virginia, broadcast on the race theme to the British public on the radio in 1931. Championing the work of colonial administrators, settlers and missionaries, Jones ignored the ideological issues involved by appealing to his audience in the Home Counties to avoid 'sentimentality and suspicion towards those actually on the job on the fringes of Empire'. What was needed was 'an intelligent balance of the principles and ideals of the home people, on the one hand, and the realities, the experience and the ideals of the colonial workers on the other'.[89]

The issues surrounding segregationism thus tended to become subordinated to a more general question of 'race relations' in the Commonwealth and the promotion of more static and less evolutionary social research shaped by the Chicago School of American sociology. Despite Curtis's earlier belief in 1916 that the American model of race relations did not need to shape the liberal idealism of the Commonwealth, in practice, political problems confronting liberal researchers and intellectuals at the local level forced them into a systemic sociological analysis, as with the founding of the South African Institute of Race Relations in 1929 with money from the Phelps-Stokes and Carnegie Foundation funds.[90] This greater sociological sophistication, however, helped to weaken the fears of a global racial clash that had surfaced in British political discourse in the wake of the First World War as a consequence of numerous nationalist agitations in the colonial setting. The hardening of racial attitudes had been seen even amongst prominent liberals such as James Bryce, who, in 1921, had called for strict immigration controls and the avoidance of mixed racial liaisons:

> the growth of a mixed race produced by the mix of persons of white and persons of colour raises difficult political as well as social problems. This mixed race might in some countries prove inferior to both of the present stocks, and the troubles that have arisen in several countries suggest that it at present is safer to discourage the entrance of any large numbers of Africans or South Eastern Asiatics into countries now inhabited by white men only.[91]

By the late 1920s, the advocates of global segregation had tended to become a minority on the margins of British political debate as the theme of the Commonwealth, the political advancement of India and the management of 'race relations' in Africa and the West Indies gained the centre stage. Though the eugenists continued to dwell on the miscegenation issue – Major Leonard Darwin, President of the Eugenics Education Society wrote to the dominion premiers at the 1923 Imperial Conference warning that 'interbreeding between widely divergent races' could result in the 'production of types inferior to both parent stocks'[92] – the championing of racial segregation progressively declined as a viable global political strategy. J.W. Gregory, the professor of geology at the University of Glasgow, sought to keep the issue alive through works like *The Menace of Colour* (1925) and *Race as a Political Factor* (1931),[93] in which segregation was presented as a global strategy to ensure world peace, for 'sympathetic intercourse between selected individuals, combined with the segregation of each race as a whole, may be expected to lead to a happier and more peaceful world than the jarring friction inevitable when dissimilar people meet in competition for their daily bread'.[94] Ethical opinion, however, was divided over such views, especially after Gregory gave the Conway Memorial Lecture at the South Place Ethical Society in 1931 with the strong support of Sir Arthur Keith, the curator of the Hunterian Library at the Royal College of Surgeons. The Ethical movement, by the early 1930s, was becoming embarrassed by the segregationist issue and a special committee of the

South Place Ethical Society in July of 1931 led to calls for the disbandment of the Conway Memorial Committee, which had invited Gregory. The American black singer, Paul Robeson, was one of the suggested names to give the next lecture, though eventually Harold Laski was chosen to talk on 'Nationalism and the Future of Civilisation'.[95]

South Africa, in fact, became the one state within the Commonwealth to take up the eugenic pleas against 'miscegenation' with its 1927 Immorality Act outlawing sexual relationships between blacks and whites, though a large number of states in the USA had similar laws at this time too. It was still the hope of the former South African premier, Jan Smuts, in a series of lectures at the newly opened Rhodes House in Oxford in 1929, that British imperial policy could promote a *Lebensraum* in its colonial territories in East and Central Africa as part of a policy of establishing a new white race fitted for the African tropical environment. It was, he argued, distinctly possible that 'a new human type may in time arise under the unusual climatic conditions of Eastern Africa . . . the human laboratory of Africa may yet produce strange results, and time alone can show whether or not the experiment was worthwhile in the interests of humanity'.[96] Despite the active support of the Colonial Office under Lord Milner and then Leo Amery in the 1920s for the white settler states in Africa, the collapse of Wall Street in 1929 effectively postponed indefinitely such a gigantic strategy of biological social engineering. In a critique of Smuts's lectures, the missionary, J. H. Oldham, refuted the idea that there could be a white 'civilisation' in Eastern Africa in the same sense as in Europe and America and argued that the main creative forces in Africa came not from white settlement but from the sale of its tropical products. What was needed, therefore, was the development of African mineral and agricultural resources and the 'effective imperial organisation of scientific resources'.[97]

Oldham's plea both hearkened back to the cultural relativism of Mary Kingsley as well as taking up an increasingly popular ideal of the inter-war years – that of harnessing scientific expertise to imperial development. It set the tone of the discussion in the early 1930s on African colonial development and the thinking behind the *African Survey*, published by Lord Hailey in 1938, in which the biologist, Julian Huxley, was involved.[98] Eventually this passed into the conventional wisdom of government with the passing of the 1940 Colonial Development and Welfare Act. By thus appearing as a moderate political ideal wedded to longer strategies of colonial economic development, the Commonwealth concept by the late 1930s and the outbreak of war had effectively pre-empted the more radical critics of imperialism on the left who had hoped optimistically at the end of the First World War that the edifice of empire would be demolished completely.

4

The widening critique of empire

The critics of British imperialism who emerged in the inter-war years developed many of the themes in the pre-1914 liberal tradition which were exemplified by the 1911 Universal Races Congress. The experience of the First World War drove some British opponents of empire beyond a merely ethical conception of promoting a universal 'racial' harmony towards a sociological, and in many cases socialist, analysis of the social structures that underpinned the operation of imperial rule. With a weakening of much of the imperial self-confidence during the war, a small number of influential propagandists emerged into public life in the early 1920s seeking to tackle more directly the issues surrounding racial discimination and economic exploitation in the colonial sphere, especially Africa. Some saw the holding of the Pan-African Congress in London in 1920 – attended by W. E. B. Du Bois from the United States – as bringing home the immediacy of racial issues in the wake of acute racial conflict in both America and parts of the British colonial empire at the end of the war. 'The time has come', wrote Norman Angell to John Harris of the Anti-Slavery Society, 'to revise the old assumptions regarding the necessary social or intellectual inferiority of the coloured', since what was now required was 'a pronouncement against the colour line as a basis of social differentiation'.[1]

The liberal analysis of British imperialism

Many of the figures attached to the anti-imperial circle in Britain were drawn from the professional middle classes and lived on the margins of establishment power and authority. Some, like Sydney Olivier and Leonard Barnes, had worked in the Colonial Office and seen the operation of colonial policy at first hand. Others, such as Norman Leys (a medical doctor) and W. McGregor Ross (a director of public works), saw enough at first hand in the case of land settlement policy in Kenya to feel a deep sense of moral outrage with the working of empire to engage in writing and lobbying for a change in policy. Few of the British liberals, though, developed any coherent ideological base for their anti-imperialism before the Second World War and it remained for outsiders on the far left, such as George Padmore and the League Against Imperialism, to begin a more Marxist analysis of British imperialism and call for a radical policy for imperial dismantlement. But such voices remained, until the late 1940s, isolated and with few allies as the main body of anti-imperial opinion remained dominated by the liberal critics struggling to free themselves from the establishment's clutches through ties of education and social class. As Leonard Barnes later recollected, the establishment of Britain appeared to act 'as a kind of highwayman who holds up the private citizen at pistol point shouting *Your Integrity* or *Your Life*'.[2]

One of the more basic ideological problems confronting these critics lay in penetrating the operation of racial segregation as it had been developed in the Southern United States and later institutionalised in the Southern African context. By the turn of the century, liberals such as J. A. Hobson were far more pessimistic regarding black American progress than James Bryce, in *The American Commonwealth*, had been in the 1880s when the negro was seen as 'growing into citizenhood'.[3] The triumph of segregation in the South from the 1890s onwards appeared to threaten the rest of American democracy, with little or no chance of organised resistance to reverse this. Writing in 1903 only eight years after Booker T. Washington's Atlanta Address and some six years before the foundation of the NAACP, Hobson's analysis reflected a deep pessimism at the chances of altering or reversing the segregationist tide. The American victory over Spain appeared to have confirmed the imperial spirit in the North, which could well spill over into the treatment of American blacks. 'It must at least be accounted a possibility of the future', Hobson concluded, 'that this idea of permanently subject people may so transform American civilisation that upon a servile basis of negro and mean white labour may be erected a commercial and professional aristocracy, consisting of higher and more dignified grades of white Teutonic and Celtic Americans, with the real powers of political and industrial government vested in the hands of a small able oligarchy of millionaires'. In this situation the 'negro problem' was 'a test question for the American character'.[4]

Hobson's gloomy outlook for American democracy at a period of segregationist triumph reflected the fact that the United States did not contain any significant prospects for a major ideological alternative to segregationism in this period. Some British observers of race issues tended to look rather to the West Indies at this time, where any Creole leanings to nationalism in the nineteenth century had given way to the desire to own property. An ordered pattern of social evolution seemed to many observers to be in progress without any formal racial segregation. W. P. Livingstone, for example, in a book entitled *Black Jamaica: a Study in Evolution*, argued, with some indebtedness to Benjamin Kidd's *Social Evolution* and *The Control of the Tropics*, that an evolutionary process was occurring in Jamaican race relations, which he dated from the Morant Bay disturbances of 1865 when the black race on the island 'made its real start on the path of progress'.[5] Though 'the position of all . . . classes is governed by the caste of colour', this was by no means rigid and the society was 'established on a system of mutual tolerance, which, however, has its well-understood limitations'. Overall, the negroes continued to be 'the most abiding people in the empire', which was partly due to 'the pacific element in the tropical character' and also 'to an acquired respect for the law and authority of the white'.[6] Given this seemingly problem-free model of race relations, it was not surprising that some authorities on 'the native problem', such as Sir Harry Johnston, considered that 'when a little better and more modern education is diffused throughout the British West Indies we shall probably see in them the most happily governed section of the British Empire, which is inhabited by a diversity of human races'.[7]

A more perceptive analyst in comparative race relations, Sydney Olivier, however, saw in the essentially free peasant base to the West Indies colonial system the key to understanding a more harmonious pattern of inter-racial contact, and came gradually to see through the segregationist ideology employed in the South African context. A positivist and an early Fabian, Olivier worked in the Colonial Office from 1882, becoming governor of Jamaica from 1907 to 1913. Unlike many liberal writers on race in the late nineteenth and early twentieth centuries, Olivier was significant in that he progressively freed himself from many Victorian notions of race differences he had imbibed in his upbringing. In the first edition of his book, *White Capital and Coloured Labour*, published by the Independent Labour Party in 1906, he saw the 'cause and moulding force of race' as 'local environment'.[8] Though 'the organon, or logic, of inter-racial intercourse' was 'still rudimentary', its basic methods were 'no mystery' for they were based, as most Victorians believed, on those used when 'dealing with children'.[9] In essence, Olivier believed that the Fabian creed of positivism and scientific rationality could be applied to colonial race relations just as it could to government in the imperial mother country. His interest in this sphere was somewhat unusual, though, for most Fabians manifested a marked disinterest in colonial questions at this time and tended, indeed, positively to support British imperialism, as in George Bernard Shaw's pamphlet in 1900, *Fabianism and the Empire*.

This Victorian legacy in Olivier's thought led him to conclude that different 'races' had great difficulty in understanding each other for 'each pure race' was 'constitutionally unfitted for understanding or even imagining the existence of much that enters into the life of each of all other races and may be either the most sacred or most commonplace thing in that life'.[10] Olivier was already familiar with the writings of Mary Kingsley on West Africa and was especially impressed by the 'fine direct sympathy' and 'the insight of the plain woman of genius' when she analysed the 'psychology' of the people of West Africa. It was possible 'quite seriously' to take Africans as 'rational beings to be weighed in the same scales as the white races'.[11] The implication of this was that it was possible for different races to live in a harmonious manner in what would now be termed a 'plural society', and Olivier developed the Jamaican social model to illustrate the theme that a colour–class society could function as a stable social entity compared to a society racially polarised between white and black as in the American South or South Africa:

> A community of white or black alone is in far greater danger of remaining, so far as the unofficial classes are concerned, a community of employers and serfs, concessionaires and tributaries, with, at best, a bureaucracy to keep the peace between them. The graded mixed class in Jamaica helps to make an organic whole of the community and saves it from this distinct cleavage.[12]

Olivier thus attacked the 'negrophobes' who argued for 'race exclusiveness' as in the United States and pointed out that the 'wholesome and hopeful equilibrium' which had been established in 'mixed communities' was due to an absence of any theory of race discrimination.[13] Such an 'equilibrium' Olivier began to doubt in societies where capitalism was proletarianising black peasants. 'The European wage proletariat and its standards of industrial virtue', he argued, 'were only created by long evolution arising out of private landlordism and the pressure of climate and poverty. So long as the African has access to land, and is saved from poverty by the simplicity of his needs and the ease of meeting them, so long the capitalist employer is sure to find his labour unmanageable under the "free wage system".' Much of this permeation of African cultural values was derived from the then influential work of Dudley Kidd, which Olivier later repudiated.[14] There was, though, an awareness that this African resistance to proletarianisation would break down in settler colonial territories like South Africa if Africans were deprived of access to land. Olivier's analysis of the 1905 Report of the Commission on Native Affairs in South Africa, chaired by Godfrey Lagden, led to his doubts about the traditional Victorian 'civilising mission' over 'backward races', which he admitted was mainly impelled by 'the economic motive'.[15] This 'civilisation' which whites were bringing to the African continent Olivier considered a mere disguise for individual 'self-seeking and violence' which was organised on the basis of 'social injustice and corporate class interests'. Moreover, the very 'process' of this civilisation amounted to the freeing of the individual 'from the appearance and consciousness of personal responsibility, whilst infinitely enhancing the emoluments of organised selfishness'.[16]

It was the idea of reclaiming individual responsibility for social actions which the liberal critics increasingly emphasised in the colonial context over the following years. Norman Leys, for example, felt a sense of bewilderment on leaving the University of Glasgow in 1899 and championed the cause of black and yellow people as providing 'something to make them stand up to the circumstances of the new civilisation that I suppose is coming to them'.[17] He became disgusted by the operation of Portuguese colonialism in Mozambique and outraged by the land-grabbing in the Kenya colony, and began criticising the current authorities on British colonial policy in East Africa, such as Sir Harry Johnston, for failing to condemn the colonial administrators there.[18] On his return to Britain in 1919 he sought the mobilisation of political support against colonial interests in East Africa and tried, unsuccessfully, to spark a Fabian interest in colonial affairs.[19] The establishment of the Labour Party Imperial Advisory Committee in 1918 acted as a kind of forum for the analysis and discussion of imperial matters, though it was the complaint of some critics like Barnes that, while its recommendations were seldom rejected outright, the party headquarters 'paid little positive attention to them, subconsciously assuming, I imagine, with the rest of the country that the colonial situation was internationally unimportant'.[20] Leys, however, pressured not simply the Labour Party and its Imperial Advisory Committee but tried to mobilise a humanitarian conscience via missionary bodies like the International Missionary Council and C. P. Scott, editor of the *Manchester Guardian*. It became clear, furthermore, that a strategy of simply relying on lobbying and pressurising the Colonial Office was not going to change matters at an early date. Following his return to Britain in 1922, Leys began to collaborate with McGregor Ross in publishing tracts and book-length analyses of white settler colonialism in East Africa in order to influence and inform British public opinion and hopefully awaken a philanthropic conscience on the issue. The acerbic book, *Kenya*, was thus published by Leys in 1924 while in 1927 Ross published the more moderately toned *Kenya from Within*. Both men thus undoubtedly helped end a vacuum in thought on the left in Britain at this time on colonial matters and to develop a humanitarian concern at the extension of economic exploitation by capitalist and white settler interests in British African colonies.[21]

Both Leys and Olivier stressed that the Colonial Office had in a number of ways abandoned the imperial civilising mission of the nineteenth century in favour of collaboration with the white settler interests. 'The European colony in Kenya'. Leys wrote, 'did not create [the] theory of domination by a racial minority. It is implicit in the conceptions of the dominant school of political thought of the last generation. And in Kenya its emergence was inevitable, after the policy was entered upon of endowing Europeans with all the arable land in the country except what Africans needed to grow their own food upon.'[22] Like Morel and Olivier, Leys believed in fostering a self-sufficient African peasant agriculture protected from white commerical interests and also helped to shift colonial policy in the direction of development and welfare.[23]

He saw no absolute racial divide in Africa but a cultural relativism between white and black societies and thus made an impassioned moral attack upon the tenets of racial segregation. 'Advocates of the segregation policy', he wrote, 'never seem able to explain just what kind of future segregation Africans are to look forward to. On one point only they seem all to be agreed. They would all keep Africans strictly under authority. Unfortunately for the adherents of this social theory the whole tendency of African life runs the other way. Christians of the second generation in Africa are always restive under any authority, civil or ecclesiastic, which they have no share in controlling.'[24] This view of the inevitable collapse of segregation overlooked the economic structures and interests behind it and Leys and Ross's campaign against colonial policy in East Africa was weakened by its failure to win any allies from amongst businessmen.[25] This became especially clear when the focus turned towards the heartland of white segregationism in Africa, that of South Africa. For the British left Olivier's ideas on this region became increasingly relevant when he entered the political debate in the late 1920s.

After the First World War, Olivier, from his retirement home at Ramsden in Oxfordshire, increasingly directed his attention to South African segregation whilst also being involved in Labour Party circles as a member of its Imperial Advisory Committee. A firm believer in the League of Nations and the trusteeship system, in *The Anatomy of African Misery* in 1927 he attacked British colonial policy for conniving with South African 'capitalist imperialism'. He dated this from the 1890s when the high commissioner in South Africa, Sir H. B. Loch, tried to have Matabeleland annexed by the British Crown, but was overruled by a Colonial Office that preferred to delegate responsibility to Cecil Rhodes and the British South Africa Company.[26] Having worked in the colonial service, Olivier knew at first hand the essential weakness of British imperialism and its willingness to work in alliance with the white-settler interests in Southern Africa.

This system of white-settler power Olivier explained in terms of a heritage of slavery derived from the Cape, while white racism he saw as an example of an 'Afrikander provincialism' that was in danger of dominating British imperial interests in the whole Southern African region.[27] It was especially important to recognise that territorial segregation, as it had been implemented through the 1913 Natives Land Act, did not mean anything like the full 'segregation' of the different races, for the labour needs of the whites prevented this. With five-ninths of the black population in 1921 already living outside the reserves, such a model he saw as impossible to accomplish and segregation was 'an inappropriate and misleading term' which should 'cease to be used as descriptive of South African native land policy'.[28] The development of 'an entirely self-supporting native peasantry' would 'take many years to accomplish'[29] but was essential if complete social breakdown was not to occur. 'A white aristocratic society' in South Africa which was dependent entirely on servile labour would be 'likely to overtake organised capitalism in Europe through any evolution of the power of the wage-earning classes.'[30]

Olivier's attack on segregationism in South Africa came at an important time politically as many of the precepts that had attracted the Milner Kindergarten and the Round Table group in the period before the First World War began to be undermined. The emergence of Afrikaner nationalism frightened some British imperial spokesmen as it seemed to usher in the spectre of future black revolt.[31] The British government continued to resist South African claims on the three protectorate territories of Bechuanaland, Basutoland and Swaziland, which the Act of Union in 1909 had declared would be eventually incorporated into the Union. Smut's government had only been successful in gaining trusteeship over the former German territory of South West Africa at the Paris Peace Conference of 1919, and as the 1920s progressed the British government's policy towards South Africa became increasingly cautious and by the end of the 1920s the ambitious hopes of the Colonial Secretary, Leo Amery, for a white British dominion from the Limpopo to the Nile were effectively over.[32]

Some enthusiasts within imperialist circles, such as the Royal Colonial Institute, continued to favour the working-out of a joint 'native policy' on segregationist lines by the British and South African governments.[33] This, though, became politically less likely in the course of the 1920s as critics of imperialism in Britain drew attention to the threat of South African segregationism extending into British colonial territories in Central and East Africa.[34] This alarm at South African expansionism was a prominent theme of the opponents of the land settlement policy in Kenya, such as Norman Leys and McGregor Ross, despite the fact that it did not reflect the observations of all imperial observers in Britain itself, who felt, if anything, that South African segregationism was a last-ditch defence of white rule in the face of a mounting tide of African 'race consciousness' which threatened to overwhelm white-settler society.[35] But the liberal critics felt especially impelled to make these warnings due to the general failure of the 1929–31 Labour government to make any significant reversals to Conservative support for the East African white settlers. Leys especially complained that Sydney Webb (Lord Passfield) as Labour's Colonial Secretary was being controlled by the department's civil servants and found himself looking mainly to the ILP faction in parliament for support in his opposition to the recommendations of the Hilton Young Commission on East African Federation.[36]

Indeed, the radical attack on racial segregationism by Leys and Olivier became somewhat blunted in the more general tide of enthusiasm for the Commonwealth in the debate on colonial policy in the Labour Party during the course of the 1920s. The party programme of 1918, *Labour and the New Social Order*, embraced the liberal Commonwealth ideal, wholeheartedly arguing for the maintenance and development of the 'great Commonwealth of all races, all colours, all religions and all degrees of civilization that we call the British Empire' in the direction of 'Local Autonomy and "Home Rule All Round" '.[37] This view was shared by some intellectuals on the party's Advisory Committee on Imperial Affairs, such as Leonard Woolf. In his study, *Empire and Commerce in Africa*, Woolf championed the ideals of the Union of Democratic Control for the 'international trusteeship' of the colonies under the League of Nations.[38] His hopes, though, for this actually occurring were low, for he realised that it would depend upon a massive upsurge of political altruism in European colonial powers still dominated by capitalist political and economic ethics. In an era before the emergence of radical black nationalism, Woolf envisaged the transformation of imperialism solely through political action in the European heartland and failed to imagine this occurring through initiatives within the colonies themselves. As a former Ceylon civil servant until his resignation in 1911, Woolf tended still to see colonial issues through the lens of the imperial administrator, for he wrote that Africa was a 'continent inhabited by a population which belongs almost entirely to non-adult races' and it was 'impossible' for 'Europe' to withdraw from Africa 'and leave these non-adult races to manage their own affairs', since to do so would mean leaving the Africans 'to the more cruel exploitation of irresponsible white men'.[39] Africans were thus envisaged as somewhat passive creatures at the mercy of European capitalism, which could only be reformed from within by an internal process of transformation to socialism. 'The capitalist system in Europe produces the exploitation of Africa', he concluded, 'and the struggle to exploit Africa, politically and economically, will continue as long as the

economic beliefs and desires of Europeans continue to produce the
capitalist system in Europe. The African will never obtain peace and prosperity, and progress until the European ceases to regard Africa as a place in
which he may earn dividends, sell his cotton and gin, obtain land, rubber
and metals, and buy cheap labour.'[40] But Woolf could not see the League 'in
our lifetime' succeeding to the empires in Africa since 'the Western world
has no belief in or desire for its Trusteeship'.[41] With a sense of eventual
historical catastrophe more typical of Victorian thought than that of
enlightened Bloomsbury, he saw 'the old system' continuing 'until its
accumulated evils bring its own destruction', possibly in fact by a revolt of
the colonised: 'the destruction may come, sooner than some people expect,
by a tremendous catastrophe, perhaps a revolt of the "beneficiaries"
against their guardians and benefactors'.[42]

This revealed a marked lack of historical understanding of African
nationalist movements and Woolf's thinking on colonialism evolved only
slowly in the inter-war years as the Labour Party Advisory Committee on
Imperial Affairs, of which he was secretary for nearly thirty years from
1918, gradually came into contact with nationalist political leaders in
Africa and the West Indies. In 1925 a series of British Commonwealth
Labour conferences initiated contacts with colonial and dominion Labour
parties. The following year a British Guiana and West Indies Labour
Conference was attended by a British Labour Party representative, F. O.
Roberts. The resulting report, though, had no obvious impact on the thinking behind the 1926 policy paper, *The Empire in Africa: Labour's Policy*,
drafted by Leonard Woolf and Charles Roden Buxton of the Imperial
Advisory Committee.[43] Here the two guiding principles were 'no economic
exploitation of one class (native) by another class (white man)' and the
securing 'for the native the opportunity of developing, as a free man, the
economic resources of the land for the benefit of the native communities'.[44]
In the next few years further contacts were established with West Indian
leaders which did not lead to any direct influence on the policy of the 1929–31
Labour government, but strengthened its hand when Lord Olivier was
appointed in 1929 by Passfield as the chairman of a commission to investigate the West Indies sugar industry.[45]

By the 1930s, the idea of developing peasant agriculture in the colonies
and taking strong government action to resist the extension of white settler
segregationism began to shape Labour Party thinking on racial and imperial
matters. The 1933 policy document, *The Colonies*, reflected the
experience of government and induced a fair measure of caution in the
party's assessment of the pace that could be made on initiating self-
government. While the West Indies were 'probably already capable of
managing their own affairs', the same could not be said of the African

colonies, where conditions made it 'impossible for them to take over the government of their country on modern lines'.[46] On the other hand, the document developed a fairly extensive analysis of kinds of land policies in Africa, noting the example of 'The African Policy', such as West Africa, Tanganyika and Basutoland, where the African population had rights to the land and where policy was geared to fostering a 'community of agriculturalists and arboriculturalists, and of fostering the growth of large Native industries' and of 'The Capitalist Policy', as in Kenya, where the African population was confined to 'reserves' and where 'our adminis-tration is creating a large and discontented landless proletariat, which is a danger to the country and to the British occupation, and whose working conditions in some respects reproduce or even exaggerate the evils of slavery'.[47]

While policy was still geared in the 1930s to developing 'the Empire' into 'a real Commonwealth of self-governing and Socialist peoples',[48] thinking in Labour circles had not yet come to terms with the idea of a permanent African proletariat in city cultures in East, Central and Southern Africa. The work of the Imperial Advisory Committee had been such as to ensure that Olivier's analysis of segregationism was not confined merely to a Southern African audience.[49]

The consequence was that the West Indies tended to be upheld ·as the *locus classicus* for a free and innovatory peasantry which should be emulated as far as possible elsewhere in the colonial empire. 'As a matter of fact,' Sydney Olivier wrote to Winifred Holtby in 1930, 'beyond missionary and religious influences and help the Jamaican negroes have made their own progress – simply because they had equality of rights, and, since they have been able to get more and more land.'[50] Much of the ethos of this critique of colonial policy was thus directed at the alleged decline in 'public service' in the Colonial Office under pressure from capitalist and white-settler interests, and no alternative model was developed to cope with the strains of new patterns of race relations in an urbanising and industrialising context. The Olivier Report on the sugar industry thus recommended the fostering of smallholdings and the establishment of agricultural schools in the West Indies in order to enhance colonial 'development' there.[51]

This domination of the West Indies peasant model in Labour thinking was reinforced, furthermore, by the fresh research work there in 1934 by the South African economic historian, W. M. Macmillan. After a career inves-tigating the 'poor white' issue in South Africa, followed by historical studies on the liberal missionary, John Philip, and the Cape Coloured population, Macmillan published in 1930, *Complex South Africa*, a pioneering survey of the peasantry of Herschel district in the Eastern Cape and the deterio-ration of its economic base in the face of migrant labour to the

Witwatersrand. The book challenged many of the precepts behind South African segregationist policy and Macmillan himself fell into disfavour with fellow white liberals on the Johannesburg Joint Council on the need to study African poverty in the reserves in relation to the structure of the migrant labour system. With the development of the South African Institute of Race Relations taking a markedly unhistorical approach under the mantle of Anthropology and 'Bantu Studies' in the early 1930s, Macmillan left South Africa in 1932 somewhat embittered and sought fresh pastures of research.[52] Though he was well acqainted with Coupland, Curtis and the Ralegh Club at Oxford, Macmillan's ideas were too radical for him to be involved in the *African Survey* that was to be directed by Malcolm Hailey. In 1934 he toured the West Indies on a grant from the Carnegie Corporation in New York and wrote a critical book in 1935 entitled *Warning from the West Indies*. Here Macmillan doubted the value of smallholdings though he also considered peasant proprietorship essential as 'the only effective means of relieving the glut in the West Indian labour market . . . . The whole-time two or three acre peasant is often enough happy and self-respecting. But he is usually ground down by hard work, and comparatively seldom reaches a really efficient standard of citizenship.'[53] Macmillan thus went on to recommend experiments in collective or communal farming backed up by a Keynesian model of public loans to initiate public works programmes, which he considered far more important for colonial developments than occasional handouts from the Colonial Development Fund.[54] This suggestion for public loans attracted the attention of the Colonial Office and in the wake of the 1937 riots, the Royal Commission on the West Indies, chaired by Lord Moyne, from which Macmillan was himself excluded, went on to suggest a similar measure of planned development through loans aiming not solely at economic growth but also at social welfare.[55]

While Olivier and Macmillan disagreed about the role of peasantries in economic development in the colonial context, both perceived that there was a threat from white segregationism in imperial politics. Macmillan, furthermore, had experience first hand of the American approach to 'race relations' on a visit there in 1934 on his way to the West Indies. Seeing this as a means of depoliticising issues of race, he championed the West Indian social structure in an unpublished article, 'A Student of British Africa looks at America'. 'The educated British West Indian', he wrote, 'with nothing like as good technical education, has more assurance and self-reliance than his brother in the United States'.[56] Macmillan doubted the worth of the 'industrial training' of Hampton and Tuskegee, which emphasised only the practical aspects of education, though acknowledged that there was some value in the American idea of 'Community building'.[57] There was, however, a peculiarly American distrust of issues that were 'political' and 'more and more the emphasis is on Race, and on the study of a new abstraction dubbed "Race Relations" '.[58] This ahistorical way of understanding racial conflicts Macmillan especially condemned in the light of his experience in South Africa in white liberal circles in the 1920s and early 1930s. Despite these reservations, in the wake of the 1940 Colonial Development and Welfare Act, his critique of British colonial policy tended to be increasingly couched in terms of the pace and scale of the policy of 'colonial development' as opposed to the fundamental assumptions behind it. The shift in thinking in British colonial circles in the wake of the Hailey *African Survey* in the late 1930s went some way towards restoring some sort of common debating ground with the liberal critics of empire as the concept of 'Trusteeship' began to gain a positive economic content.[59] Macmillan, from the vantage point of the Labour Party Imperial Advisory Committee and the Advisory Committee on Education in the African Colonies, in the early 1940s acted as an important contributor to this evolving political consensus, despite his personal disappointment at being passed over by the Rhodes Trust for the *African Survey*. In a pamphlet entitled *Democratise the Empire*, in 1941, he continued to warn of South African influence in British colonial policy but also criticised the radical proposal to internationalise British colonial possessions in favour of a 'policy of colonial reform' based on a radical implementation of the colonial development programme. In one respect, these arguments were formulated in terms of a plea for a *restoration* of the tradition of Victorian humanitarian concern with respect to the colonial empire, which, in the light of Olivier's argument, Macmillan saw as having been eclipsed in the early twentieth century by imperial interests centred on Southern Africa. 'The Colonies have learnt', he wrote, 'from our past history that Britain usually has a conscience that can be appealed to, that at the worst of times there have been voices to urge their needs or to expose injustice, and that in time they have been heard. So long as we maintain the democratic tradition we have a great volume of colonial goodwill to support our efforts at reconstruction.'[60]

These somewhat optimistic conclusions were not shared by all critics of colonial policy in the 1930s and 1940s. In contrast to the liberal school of analysts, such as Leys, Macmillan and Olivier, there also began to emerge in Britain a more radical group of critics who doubted the idea of 'democratising' the empire from above and preferred to emphasise the role of black and colonial initiatives in anti-colonial political struggles. In addition, the radicals emphasised the process of proletarianisation incurred by the impact of metropolitan capitalism on rural and peasant societies. While the liberal school for the most part sought to foster, and if need be protect, rural peasant communities from social disintegration, the radicals considered that they failed to observe the emergence of black working-class communities in such societies as the United States and South Africa. Olivier's formative years in the West Indies were before the First World War and he did not link West Indian peasant production to labour emigration to the Panama Canal and the United States, where a process of proletarianisation was under way. Similarly, Leys and McGregor Ross emphasised the need to protect African peasant agriculture from white settler capitalism in Kenya without looking at the political implications of a landless class of squatters and lumpenproletarians around Nairobi which later played a vital part in the emergence of the Mau Mau movement in the 1950s.[61] Macmillan, too, focused upon the destruction of peasant agricul-cure in Herschel in the Eastern Cape before moving to the West Indies, but here, too, he had failed to understand the full significance of the proletarian African culture that was emerging in the slums and townships of the Witwatersrand in the inter-war years and which later played a vital part in African political mobilisation in South Africa in the years after the Second World War.[62] British analysis of race in the colonial sphere at this time thus to a considerable degree lacked an understanding of the changing class dimensions involved and continued to see black societies substantially in rural, pastoral and peasant terms. Despite the evidence of growing trade union organisation amongst black workers, most liberals still saw race in terms of preserving and fostering rural black folkways and remained unaware of the growing political significance of groups of black workers, squatters and urban petty bourgeois journalists and political leaders. The impact of this latter body of radical black opinion was mainly felt in small groups on the left in the 1930s and it was not until the Second World War that the full political implications of Pan-Africanism and Marxist strategies of international working-class collaboration across racial lines began to be fully recognised by wider sections of liberal and informed opinion in Britain.

The left and the radical critique of British imperialism

Radical critics of colonial policy in Britain began to become more vocal in the early 1930s in the wake of the slump in 1929, the collapse of the Labour government in 1931 and the emergence of a more militant Independent Labour Party after its disaffiliation from the Labour Party in 1933. Many of the left-wing radicals began to link class conflict in Britain itself to colonial emancipation in the dependent empire. One notable example was the writer, Leonard Barnes, who has been seen as 'Britain's most formidable critic of Empire in the 1930s'.[63] Barnes's life fitted very much into the generation whose central experience had been that of the trenches in the First World War. Having been wounded in France in 1918, Barnes returned to England to read Classics at Oxford before entering the Colonial Office. Here he dealt with the Ceylon and East African Department and later the West Indies Department, before his friendship with Norman Leys, then practising as a medical doctor in Derbyshire, confirmed his disillusionment with the colonial service. He later recalled in particular Leys's condemnation of the activities of Lionel Curtis, whom he considered 'one of the three wholly evil people I have ever met'.[64]

Between 1925 and 1932 Barnes farmed in Zululand in South Africa and worked as a journalist for South African newspapers. In 1930 he also travelled round the protectorate territories of Basutoland (Lesotho), Bechuanaland (Botswana) and Swaziland as part of an investigation with William and Margaret Ballinger and became familiar with the conditions of African labour reserves which were in the process of being incorporated into the capitalist South African economy centred upon the gold mining of the Witwatersrand. Barnes's two initial books *Caliban in Africa* (1930) and *The New Boer War* (1932) reflected a disillusionment with South African liberalism as a means of achieving internal reform within the South African political system. 'In native policy', he wrote, 'the mild accents of liberalism have long been rendered inaudible by the clamour which ceaselessly clangs through the three northern provinces for a white South Africa at any price.'[65] Unlike Sydney Olivier, however, Barnes did not place any great faith in rejuvenating African peasant agriculture for he realised that an irreversible process of proletarianisation had been initiated. 'In the conditions now obtaining in the Union', he argued, 'the plough which is to prepare the field of native life for the crop of civilisation should be fashioned out of native industrial organisation in some form or other. And industrial organisation must begin among those classes which have been permanently urbanised.'[66] The peasantry were still too detached from the 'general economic system the Europeans have imposed' to be able to challenge it head on,[67] while among the urban proletariat, trade union organisation could function 'as a kind of ductless gland in the body politic, profoundly influencing the brain and modifying the temperament of the State with its invisible hormones'.[68] He especially looked to an industrial organiser like William Ballinger, who went to South Africa in 1928 in an effort to reorganise the black International and Commercial Workers Union of Clements Kadalie, to go to the Protectorates to organise the black workers there. [69] This hope, though, became shattered over the succeeding two years as it became clear that the national government of Baldwin and Macdonald was uninterested in fostering any extensive economic and social development programmes in the protectorates that would in any way conflict with the labour needs of the South African mines.[70]

By 1935, Barnes's thinking on British imperialism began to move to a wider and more comprehensive framework. In *The Duty of Empire* (1935), he considered the empire 'a composite jumble, ramshackle in some parts, repressive in others, aimless in most, and beneficial in a few'.[71] Like William Macmillan he became aware of a rising discontent in the West Indies which was demanding a 'more responsible voice in the counsels of government'[72] and stripped away the protective mask of the Commonwealth ideology from the operation of British imperial interests. 'The nature of the Commonwealth', he considered, set up 'essential barriers' for it relied on no 'exclusive principle'. It was in fact little more than 'a kind of proselytising Pan Britannism' and depended ultimately upon an alliance with the dominions, 'the aristocrats of the Empire community', and an inferior status for India.[73] Nevertheless, on its purely political side he did not completely rule out the value of the Commonwealth notion for it embodied 'a useful experiment in building up an international association on a basis of freedom and equality'.[74]

Barnes's ideas undoubtedly had some impact in left-wing circles in Britain during the 1930s. Norman Leys, for instance, saw *The Duty of Empire* as a rallying call for European socialists to tackle the problem of 'mental struggle' for there was 'one thing . . . worse than material poverty', which was 'enslavement of the mind'.[75] Barnes's writing in one respect addressed itself to the general ideological question of the hegemony of imperial ideas and notions in British political thought at a time when imperialism began to be popularly debated, especially after the foundation of the Left Book Club in 1936 and its rapid accumulation of 44,800 members by the following year.[76] In 1939 Barnes brought out the influential study, *Empire or Democracy*, through the Club and attacked the advocates of the Commonwealth conception from the standpoint of a Hobsonian analysis of economic imperialism, which he saw as 'not an isolated phenomenon, but an integral part of the social disasters which are shaking contemporary civilisation to its foundations'[77] He went on to apply a wider analysis of the imperial phenomenon, seeing the rise of German and Japanese expansionism as examples of imperialism in a 'totalitarian phase' based upon the interests of 'finance capital'.[78] Whatever the actual value of such an analysis in terms of the working of international capitalism, Barnes's work was important for stressing the resurgence of racism in German Nazi imperialism and its likely effects on the weaker imperialisms of France and Britain, which he saw as 'snuggling up to Hitler'. While the actual influence of imperial interests on the Chamberlain appeasement policy in the late 1930s has remained a matter of some controversy among historians, the significance of Barnes's writing lay in his recognising that pre-war imperial aims were still alive in some sections of both the British and Nazi establishments. He pointed out the political danger of this at a time of rising political crisis in British governing circles and helped to awaken the Labour Party and the left to the chance of a capitulation by some sections of the establishment to Hitler.[79] In the wake of the Italian invasion and conquest of Abyssinia in 1936 and until the end of 1938, European imperialism did indeed seem to be on the move again, fortified by a strong dose of political authoritarianism and militarism.[80] One of the chief architects of the Commonwealth notion in Britain in the 1930s, Leo Amery, was privately willing to consider negotiating with Hitler on the restoration of former German African colonies, providing, as he wrote to Jan Smuts, they did not represent a 'strategic menace' to British interests. 'I should not only welcome their getting concessions in Angola', he continued, 'but in the Belgium Congo and the French Colonies', as well.[81]

Barnes's writing, therefore, was an important stimulant to left-wing debate in the 1930s on British imperialism and the class basis behind inter-racial contacts, especially those with the emerging black proletariat in the towns of South Africa. His ideas, however, were not necessarily always followed through even in the Loft Book Club, which, while linking racism to imperialism in such works as R. Palme Dutt's *India Today* (1940) and John Burger's (Leo Marquard) *The Black Man's Burden* (1943), began to produce increasingly diverse studies ideologically after 1942, such as A. G. Russell's *Colour, Race and Empire* (1944). This latter work was initially stimulated by the more limited paradigm of 'the colour bar' and, while stressing the economic exploitation in colonies, still placed some emphasis upon the independent influences of 'racial' factors, if only in the form of open-ended questions:

> The negro ... found his way into areas where the climatic con-
> ditions were especially favourable to the virulent activity of disease
> germs, and the consequent heavy mortality among such stocks
> promoted, as a measure of self-preservation, a high fertility rate.
> The overdevelopment of sexual activity has proved inimical to
> intellectual capacity, and it is perhaps in this that we find some
> reason for the intellectual inferiority with which the African is so
> frequently, and *perhaps* so unjustly, stigmatised.[82] (emphasis
> added)

Clearly elements within the British left *did* need educating about race, and alongside the analysis of a writer like Barnes, an important black Pan-Africanist school of writers and intellectuals developed in Britain during the course of the 1930s. Prominent in this group were such figures as Jomo Kenyatta, Ras Makonnen, I. T. A. Wallace-Johnstone and George Padmore, who represented a significant upsurge in black intellectual debate in what has been termed the 'African diaspora'.[83]

This group of radical black writers and propagandists were especially notable for aligning Pan-Africanist political objectives with a Marxist analysis of imperialism and racism. Though they chose to form an alliance with some sections of the British left who were sympathetic to their cause, most notably Fenner Brockway, Reginald Sorensen and the Independent Labour Party, their role as a black intelligentsia ensured an important difference of interests from those of their white comrades. As both radical activists as well as intellectuals, blacks such as Makonnen, Padmore and James chose to reside in the heart of the British imperial metropolis in the belief that this was where their political struggle to mobilise an anti-imperial and working-class consciousness could best be waged. Furthermore, they came to Britain with a paradoxical sense of English fair play and a belief in the essential justice of English liberalism despite all their hatred for imperialism, which Padmore termed 'the worst racket yet invented by man'.[84]

The radical Pan-Africanists were also noteworthy both for their rejection of the moderate, conciliatory methods of black liberals such as Harold Arundel Moody of the League of Coloured Peoples (who will be discussed more fully in Chapter 7) and their disaffection from a strictly Communist Party line. George Padmore, especially, who was originally born as Malcolm Nurse in Trinidad in 1902, worked actively for the Communist Party after 1927 while a student at Fisk University in the United States and helped plan the First International Conference of Negro Workers in Hamburg in July 1930 as a result of discussions in the Communist-dominated League Against Imperialism.[85] In the early 1930s, before he broke from the ITUC-NW, he wrote a number of pamphlets, including *The Life and Struggles of Negro Toilers*, in which he denounced the 'social fascist labour bureaucrats' of the Second International as well as such black trade union leaders as Clements Kadalie and Allison Champion in South Africa.[86] These leaders were accused of trying to delay an intensifying class struggle, which Padmore saw as rapidly growing up as a result of an intensifying world capitalist crisis. 'Social fascist politicians' such as Lord Olivier were also seen as aiding these black 'misleaders' in this class struggle and the real path for Padmore lay in aiding revolts, uprisings and strikes wherever possible in a 'counteroffensive' against 'the imperialists'.[87]

In 1932, before he severed his connections with the Communist International, Padmore began to establish connections with left-wing circles in Britain, especially with C. A. Smith, later chairman of the Independent Labour Party, and the aristocratic rebel, Nancy Cunard. These ties proved of great value after the Comintern changed its line after the Nazi seizure of power in Germany in January 1933 and its disbanding of the ITUC-NW in

August of that year. Though Padmore was formally expelled in February of 1934 he was already collaborating with Nancy Cunard on her anthology, *Negro*, which appeared in the spring of that year. Padmore also began working with a number of radical critics of racism and imperialism, such as W. E. B. Du Bois in the United States, whom he had formerly denounced, and in 1935 he moved permanently to London to work with a number of left-wing bodies, especially the International African Service Bureau, along with T. R. Makonnen, Jomo Kenyatta, C. L. R. James, Peter Abrahams and I. T. A. Wallace-Johnstone.[88]

In various articles at this time, Padmore linked the cases of racial discrimination against blacks in Britain itself to what he perceived as the growing crisis of imperialism internationally. He argued that the British ruling class was deliberately fomenting a 'racial and national chauvinism' in Britain itself in order to deflect British working-class opinion away from an anti-imperial solidarity with black workers in the colonies. British universities were linked to this strategy in so far as they sought finance from the 'British capitalist class' and clandestinely spread race hatred by 'making . . . violent insinuations about the coloured students behind their backs'.[89] Padmore, therefore, would have no truck even with the nominally liberal aims of educational bodies in Britain and moved some way beyond such left-wing critics of imperialism as Norman Leys, Leonard Barnes and Sydney Olivier in refusing to see the issue as solely a 'colonial' one.

Building up allies in this cause in Britain itself, however, proved difficult. The Independent Labour Party was the most sympathetic body on the left, given the Communist Party's hostility to Padmore following his expulsion from the Comintern. The ILP, though, was past its heyday of the early 1920s when its paper, *The New Leader*, had flowered between 1922 and 1926 under the imaginative editorial hand of H. N. Brailsford[90] As one of the main left-wing opponents, though, of the National Government after the defection of Ramsay Macdonald in 1931, the party was to a considerable degree open to new ideas that were being discussed on the left. It was particularly anxious to develop what Fenner Brockway termed a 'revolutionary socialist position'. It sought in particular to do this not through trying to build a mass movement but 'by thought applied to experience, by learning its lessons from mistakes, by discussion, by the study of the history of the movement in other countries, and by a sincere and constructive effort to find the right way'.[91] In this search for 'the right way', Padmore was undoubtedly able to exert a considerable intellectual and ideological influence after the League Against Imperialism moved its offices to London from Hamburg in the summer of 1933, despite his refusal to become a member and his rejection of overtures to stand as an ILP parliamentary candidate. He encouraged the party particularly to avoid the

Communist strategy of a 'popular front', which he criticised as downplaying the struggle for political independence in the colonial setting. In 1937 he secured the support of Stafford Cripps, then in the political wilderness after the disaffiliation of the Socialist League from the Labour Party, in a foreword to his book *Africa and World Peace*. Complaining that 'the problem of imperialism' had never been adequately understood by the British labour movement, Cripps attacked the complacency about the 'sufferings' of 'colonial peoples' and warned that there were more 'pressing dangers' from overseas imperialism than from internal domestic capitalism. Later, though, in 1938 the LAI's journal, *International African Opinion*, attacked Cripps for conceiving of Africans as 'essentially passive recipients of freedom given to them by Europeans . . . . Thinking Africans know that ultimately they will win theirs, arms in hands, or forever remain slaves.'[92]

Cripps, though, was only one major voice from the British left in support of Padmore and the Pan-Africanist cause and for the most part Padmore remained an isolated figure in Britain in the late 1930s and 1940s, acting mainly as an ideological catalyst behind the radical wing of Pan-Africanism. In his novel, *A Wreath for Udomo* (1956), Peter Abrahams presented Padmore in the character of Thomas Lanwood, a totally committed Marxist intellectual more in love with the idea of power than with power itself. While this assessment may have been somewhat wide of the mark, the Lanwood figure was representative of the general ethos of the time, when black radical intellectuals in exile in Britain were devoted more to systems of ideas than to actual concrete political action itself. The Trotskyite, C. L. R. James, also reflected this more general divorce between theoretical and concrete political engagement when, in an essay on the late George Jackson, he saw the generation of radical black activists in the 1960s as moving one stage beyond that of his own generation and of Du Bois in their uniting of intellectual, moral and physical commitments to revolutionary struggle.[93]

In the latter phases of the Second World War, Padmore did begin initiating a radical political engagement in Britain against overseas British imperialism. Early in 1945 a World Trade Union Conference was organised in London which markedly embarrassed British trade union leaders such as Walter Citrine by demonstrating the strength of independent black trade union initiatives in the colonial setting, free from British trade union influence and control.[94] More importantly, though, was the Fifth Pan-African Congress, held at Manchester in October 1945, which rekindled interest in Pan-Africanist political sentiment after a considerable lull following previous Pan-African Conferences held in 1900, 1919, 1923 and 1927 (of which those in 1919 and 1923 had been somewhat improvised).[95] Padmore boasted that more than 14 organisations of Africans and peoples of African descent in Britain were able to participate in the conference and that there were no organisations in the colonial empire with which the Pan-African Federation in Britain had not been in touch. The conference was thus seen as demonstrating the strength of independent black nationalist sentiment, free from ties with indigenous radical movements in Britain itself. To this extent, the movement reinforced the conception of blacks living in Britain as an alien minority whose true abode and focus for political consciousness lay in the colonial context. 'The British Negro', he thus wrote to Du Bois,

> lives away from the British Isles, and those individuals who are here constitute an alien minority, although they are subjects of the same Crown. As a result, when the Negro comes to this country he does not ally himself with the existing political organisations and become a vehicle within his own racial group for the ideologies prevailing among the British political parties. Rather he tends to get together with other Colonial organisations to advocate and propagate his own political aspirations which . . . concentrate on the question of self-determination for the country whence he comes.[96]

The legacy of the Pan-Africanist movement in Britain for British blacks who had come to live permanently in the country was thus somewhat ambiguous. On the one hand, Padmore and his generation undoubtedly went some way beyond much of the paternalism of the British left-wing critics of empire in their stress upon the role of independent black political initiatives to combat British imperial control. On the other hand, the strong nationalist message in this had only an indirect relevance for the emerging black ethnic minority in Britain itself. Certainly Padmore, Nkrumah and others were keen to see black trade union activity develop in Britain, though they realised this could never develop into any mass organisation as in the colonies. Thus, some black community leaders, such as Pastor Ekarte of the African Churches Mission in Liverpool, found Padmore's guidance of value in the 1940s when it came to the question of fighting for higher wages for black seamen employed by such shipping companies as Elder Dempsters.[97] The longer-term legacy for the black immigrants coming to reside in British towns and cities in the 1950s was, however, very minimal. By this time the focus of Pan Africanist ideals had shifted to the African terrain itself as the British colony of Gold Coast became the independent country of Ghana in 1957 under the presidency of Kwame Nkrumah. George Padmore became Nkrumah's adviser on African affairs. In 1958 the First All African Peoples Organisation Conference was held in Accra under George Padmore's ideological guidance and the Afro-Caribbean minority in Britain had to some extent been bypassed by the turn of events in Africa with the withdrawal of the European colonial presence there. Padmore's radical analysis of imperialism left only an indirect legacy on white left-wing sympathisers of the black political cause such as Fenner Brockway, Reginald Sorensen, and the Movement for Colonial Freedom in its campaign in the 1950s for the outlawing of racial discrimination against blacks in jobs, housing and public places.

The radical Pan-Africanist ideology of Padmore, Makonnen and James thus left a remarkably slight imprint on the political thought of the British left towards imperialism. Leonard Barnes, in his book *Soviet Light on the Colonies* (1944) contrasted Soviet policy towards its non-Russian populations in Central Asia with the British model of colonial rule in Africa. This was done in a manner similar to the earlier writings of Padmore, though there was a lingering paternalistic element in his thought which emerged more fully after the Labour victory in the 1945 general election and the reorientation of socialist thought towards the new phenomenon of a Labour colonial policy.[98] Thus, while Padmore had warned of the dangers of regional development programmes in the colonies allowing American capitalism a backdoor into British colonial development programmes,[99] Barnes stressed the need for an enlightened programme *for* colonial peoples in order to match their attainment of 'adult nationhood'. 'It is intrinsically important', he wrote in an article, 'A Policy for Colonial Peoples', in 1945, 'that the psychological health of the colonial peoples should be positively developed, and that persons of some political insight in Britain should help the development in a considered way.'[100] This approach brought Barnes much into line with the post-war development and welfare programme in the colonies engineered by Arthur Creech Jones and the Colonial Office, and while there were warnings of possible fascist resurgences in some parts of the colonial empire, especially in the white-settler societies in Africa, for the most part the British left-wing critics of empire were muted until the early 1950s and the renewal of political opposition to South African apartheid and the creation of the Federation in Central Africa in 1953. Even then, though, there was a strong faith in British left-wing circles in the economic anachronism of white racism and its inherent destruction before the forces of industrialisation, capitalist or otherwise.[101]

The white left in Britain did not experience the blunt edge of racial discrimination in the same manner as their black radical counterparts. Equally, they did not write for the same constituencies, for the radical black nationalists in Britain saw themselves as gatekeepers in the British imperial metropolis for a nationalist audience in different colonies, while the white British left was appealing to a sense of fairness and justice in the British labour movement *on behalf of* black colonial peoples. The white left thus had a much firmer belief in enlightenment optimism at the heart of the European socialist tradition and the rational logic engrained in government policy. The black radicals, on the other hand, were more strongly aware of the need for political struggle and violence to overthrow European colonialism.

This divergence of view continued to prevail until the alliance of the white British left with the black radicals effectively ended with the emergence of independent African states in the late 1950s and 1960s. New ties began slowly to be forged with a more British-orientated black leadership, such as Claudia Jones and the *West Indian Gazette*. The legacy of the previous political alliance resulted, though, in the white radical opponents of imperialism in Britain being to a considerable extent thrown back, in the 1950s, on the tradition of a liberal concern for justice at precisely the time when a 'race relations' issue began to emerge in Britain itself. The hopes of the Pan-Africanist radicals in the 1930s and 1940s of linking an attack on white racism to a wider ideological critique of British imperialism tended to fade with the emergence in the post-war years of a social science discourse on 'race relations' brought back to the metropolis from the colonial periphery. As the next chapter shows, much of this was a product of a growing anthropological and sociological interest in race as part of a 'science of man' that replaced the older tradition of Victorian classical humanism.[102] The development of this professional concern helped to steer mainstream British opinion away from a historical understanding of race and the rise and decline of empires, and replace it with a more traditional liberal moral concern with issues of racial prejudice. By the late 1950s, accordingly, a climate of guilt had tended to prevail as opposed to active political engagement.

5

Sociology, anthropology and race

Thinking on race in Britain in the twentieth century changed only very slowly and hesitantly under the impact of work in the social sciences. Until at least the Second World War the academic status of both sociology and anthropology was shaky and uncertain, as their respective claims to scientific and scholastic respectability were treated sceptically by a conservative educational establishment dominated by a classical humanism and legal positivism in the Oxbridge tradition.[1] By the 1930s anthropology had started to make comparatively greater headway than sociology as the growing interest in colonial development and welfare provided increased opportunities for anthropological research in colonial territories, especially in Africa. It has been argued by Perry Anderson that the structural functional theory at the heart of this anthropological enterprise was the closest that the English intelligentsia got in the first part of the twentieth century to a coherent social theory. Unlike intellectuals in Central Europe, whose thinking was shaped by the sociology of Max Weber, Emile Durkheim and the psychology of Freud and Jung, English social thought, according to this thesis, remained provincial and rested on a narrow empiricism that eschewed grand theory. Only in the colonial periphery of the English-speaking world was there felt to be an urgent need to generate a more coherent social theory. Here the emergence of social anthropology in the inter-war years around Bronislaw Malinowski and the London School of Economics was to have a wide-ranging intellectual importance at the time when sociology and the social sciences in the British metropolis itself remained underdeveloped, and dominated by amateurs who had little formal academic status.[2]

Undoubtedly there was a strong tradition of empiricism and positivism in English social thought, which has sometimes been ascribed to the pattern of English history whereby its revolutionary epoch in the seventeenth century occurred before the advent of capitalist industrialisation.[3] However, the marginalisation of the social sciences in English intellectual culture was also due to their failure to gain institutionalisation in a Victorian milieu that encouraged piecemeal local case studies into poverty and exacerbated the fissuring into different and rival schools of those involved in it. This resulted in a tendency for sociology to produce a small group of charismatic individualists with rival theories and methods and the consequent devaluing of attempts at the creation of a strong and coherent scholastic orthodoxy.[4] This does not mean that the British achievement should be completely underplayed in comparison to those of the Continent or even America, for the advent of philosophical idealism in the late nineteenth century in England had the effect of saving the subject area from complete fragmentation. Stefan Collini has suggested that this idealism, reflected in the work of such figures as Bernard Bosanquet, T. H. Green and L. T. Hobhouse, nullified some of the positivist pretensions in English intellectual life and led to a concentration on the moral cohesion behind communities and the socialisation of their members.[5] Idealism thus contributed to a greater sociological understanding of social processes in late nineteenth- and early twentieth-century Britain and played an important part in the shift from the nineteenth-century emphasis upon individualism towards a collectivist and organic ideology that underpinned both the rise of the 'new liberalism' before the First World War and later the Labour Party's parliamentary socialism.[6] Ultimately, though, idealism had the effect of steering sociological attention away from a close relationship with historical study and tended to limit its understanding of social processes to those of the 'advanced' societies of Europe and North America and the white dominions. A division of labour with the anthropologists thus prevailed until at least the end of the First World War and the developments in theory by Malinowski and his school, whereby anthropology was confined to the study of the 'backward' or primitive societies, which were generally seen to lack any significant history of their own. Overall, the social science work of sociology and anthropology reflected the basic tenets of Victorian evolutionary theory and advanced them into the twentieth century more or less wholesale.[7] Only gradually would this pattern of thought be broken down, first through the application within sociology of a moral critique of 'racism' or 'racialism' and secondly through an academic revolution in anthropology in which the colonial periphery rebelled against the metropolitan centre, a revolution which led to innovatory work in social theory, especially of the inner mechanics of culture, by the end of the Second World War. In this chapter, we propose to look at these two developments in turn and assess their longer-term significance for the later development in the post-war period of work in 'race relations'.

Race and British sociology

British sociology became institutionalised later than its American or European counterparts for the establishment of the British Sociological Society only occurred in 1904 following a public discussion of scholars and public figures at the recently formed London School of Economics and Political Science. A common thread that ran through some of the early thinking on sociology in Britain was that of eugenics as it had been developed by its founder, Francis Galton, as 'the study of agencies under social control that may improve or impair the racial qualities of future generations, either physically or mentally'. The 'scientific' appeal of eugenics, despite the fact that it contained within its objectives social values as opposed to strict scientific knowledge *per se*, was obvious to the early sociologists, who were keen to establish their credentials as serious students of social processes. Victor Branford, one of the chief organisers of the 1904 meeting, considered eugenics was likely to be the 'very crown and summit to which theoretical Sociology must ultimately lead',[8] and James Bryce, in his opening address at the LSE meeting, urged that sociologists turn their attention to 'the doctrine of heredity and . . . its relation to the various races of mankind'.[9]

Eugenics as a mode of social study was not intrinsically linked to a coherent ideology of racial superiority or inferiority. Recent work has established an important reformist wing of the eugenics movement which was linked to a progressivist movement for social reform,[10] while the notion of 'race' that the eugenists employed often referred to the notion of a 'community of culture' rather than being a deterministic doctrine denoting the inferiority of other races.[11] Nevertheless, the early stress within sociological discussion upon eugenic notions for understanding social structures did represent a continuation of previous debates in the late nineteenth century over the relationship between biological laws and the workings of society and the role of independent human consciousness in this. Herbert Spencer had stressed the notion of social progress linked rigidly to a biological evolutionism and the emergence of a revised liberal tradition in the wake of the writings of T. H. Green had led to a counter-school, best reflected in the writings of L. T. Hobhouse, which asserted the autonomous role of the human mind in the devising of social reform.[12]

Thus, while eugenics found a ready audience of social reformers in 1904, such as H. G. Wells and Bernard Shaw, its linkage with sociology did not meet with unanimous approval and Hobhouse, especially, urged the study of both 'stock' and 'environment' for it was open to social reformers to influence the nature of the human environment as well as its heredity since 'we have the accumulation of considerable tradition as to the way in which a given act will affect the social environment' while 'when we come to bring stock into consideration, we are dealing with that which is still very largely unknown'.[13] This cautionary approach was by and large supported even by the followers of eugenics in the society for, as Dudley Kidd warned, its practitioners were only 'distinguished amateurs',[14] while Francis Galton urged that a young society like the British Sociological Society should do nothing to shock its members for there was plenty of work for it to do 'without running amuck against prejudice'.[15] Victor Branford, too, in his enthusiasm for eugenics, saw it as a means of undermining some of the leading campaigners in the anti-aliens agitation, which was currently a dominant issue before the passing of the 1905 Aliens Restriction Act.[16]

By 1908 the eugenics connection with sociology began to decline as a separate Eugenics Society was formed in that year and Hobhouse defeated his other main rival, the eugenist and civics enthusiast, Patrick Geddes, for the first Martin White Professorship of Sociology at the LSE.[17] Under Hobhouse's editorial hand, the Sociological Society's organ, *The Sociological Review*, took an eclectic approach, publishing articles that were supportive of eugenics, but increasingly moving into a position strongly critical of systematic theories of race. This approach was broadly reflective of Hobhouse's own view of sociology that saw it less as a science than as 'a vitalizing principle that runs through all social investigation, nourishing and nourished by it in turn, stimulating inquiry, correlating results, exhibiting the life of the whole in the parts and returning from a study of the parts to a fuller comprehension of the whole'.[18] Such a wide-ranging approach left sociology free from a eugenic takeover on the one hand, but methodologically weak, on the other, and therefore unable to confront racist ideology as it had developed in Europe by the inter-war years under the influence of Continental fascism. The main moral impetus came from a continuation of late nineteenth-century liberalism and the development of interest in race after the 1911 Universal Races Congress.[19]

British sociological discussion on race after 1907–8 tended, therefore, to echo the mainstream liberal position of promoting harmonious relations between 'advanced' and 'backward' races. John M. Robertson, for example, writing on 'The Tutelage of Races' in the *Sociological Review* in 1908, reached the 'sociological conclusion' that 'in so far as any race or nation has to be under the tutelage of another, the slighter the tutelage the better for both. A complete control tends to abuse the ruled and demoralise the ruler.'[20] Furthermore, when the question of the treatment of 'primitive' races arose, like that of 'the Redskins of North America', there was 'no security whatever save in a segregation which shall leave them free to profit by the example of their neighbours without coming under their power'. The case of the withdrawal of Basutoland from control by the Cape Colony was an example 'in which imperial tutelage of a backward race may relatively avail for good as against mere exploitation by a frontier colony.[21] This benevolent segregationism, however, which was so prevalent in the writings of liberal critics of colonialism in the early years of the century,[22] did nothing to assist in the understanding of the mechanics of historical racist thought, epitomised by Houston Stewart Chamberlain's *The Foundations of the Nineteenth Century*. Reviewing the first English edition of this book in 1911, Robertson argued that it reflected 'the besetting sin of German historiography, the explanation of national and social phenomena in terms of themselves'.[23] 'As a contribution to sociology' the book was 'a fiasco',[24] and Chamberlain's 'doctrine' of race Robertson found 'arbitrary' for 'His biology is a mere rod wherewith to beat the undesirable dog and herald the favourite.'[25] While not debunking the idea of 'race' *per se* Robertson's rejection of German historical idealism helped to strengthen the resistance in British sociology to European and American racial theories of history.

Sociological circles in Britain indeed started to raise doubts about the ability of anthropologists to classify accurately different racial 'types' along a spectrum of 'higher' and 'lower' races. Gustav Spiller was an important figure in this respect as he kept up a close relationship with the Sociological Society in the wake of the 1911 Universal Races Congress and in 1926 became a member of the council of the newly formed Institute of Sociology at Le Play House.[26] As early as 1912, Spiller wrote in the *Sociological Review* that 'until anthropologists who have impartially employed the dynamic or experimental method have definitely pronounced that certain races possess exclusively certain permanent or inborn mental and moral characteristics, practical statesmen and reformers need not be alarmed, as the present evidence tends to be in the direction of proving like mental and moral qualities rather than different ones in all races'.[27] This was a somewhat negative reason for rejecting a fixed racial determinism and Spiller maintained an attitude of sceptical positivist detachment on the issue, awaiting conclusive evidence that would either confirm or refute the claims of the biological determinists. The main thrust of his argument, however, shifted the attention of sociologists away from hereditarian factors towards environmental ones and the concept of 'civilisation':

> Really and truly to appreciate the substantial equality of races we must firmly grasp what appears to the author a bedrock fact. Man alone is civilisable, and civilisation represents, broadly speaking, the socially transmitted and socially augmented, adapted and improved inventions and discoveries made by the whole of mankind from the earliest time to today . . . . Consequently, the stage of civilisation – high or low – at any time and place, fixes the

individual's intellectual, moral, and other limits of attainment. The fact that there is scarcely a race, however primitive its culture, some of whose members have not passed through the highest institutions of learning, is striking proof of this contention.[28]

This shift in emphasis from the earlier vocabulary of 'advanced' and 'backward' races towards 'higher' and 'lower' levels of 'civilisation' increasingly defined sociological discourse in Britain in the years after 1911. In 1915 L. T. Hobhouse, G. C. Wheeler and M. Ginsburg published a study on *The Material Culture and Social Institutions of the Simpler Peoples – an Essay in Correlation* which made a rare sociological intrusion into the area of 'simpler' peoples usually dominated by the anthropologists. The study started from the Darwinian assumption that 'the course of social evolution is not unitary' and that 'different races and different communities of the same race have, in fact, whether they started from the same point or not, diverged early, rapidly, and in many different directions at once'. This left the data available divided into two main fields, that of 'the historical record of civilisations' and 'the immense field of contemporary anthropology'.[29] With the data of the latter being substantialy prehistorical, the authors undertook a study of comparative institutions 'as the first step towards the introduction of order into the field of comparative sociology'.[30] There was clearly no simple process of evolutionary institutional change that accompanied 'the growth of civilisation'. Nevertheless, the authors argued for a general form of correlation, confining themselves to 'the less fortunate races which range from the lowest known *Naturmenschen* to the confines of historic civilisation'.[31] In the process of evolution, it was recognised that a process of 'culture contact, direct or indirect',[32] was in fact normal, but for the most part this exercise in 'comparative sociology' represented no methodological advance on the then current understanding of culture within anthropology as derived from Tylor and the nineteenth-century theorists. It reinforced the more general shift to environmental and cultural processes in the explanation of the varying attainments of different 'races', though it still anchored these in a Eurocentric view of world history and the implicit notion of the inherent superiority of 'Western civilisation'.

The First World War did much to dash the assumptions of European cultural superiority in British liberal circles. The attacks on 'colour prejudice' by liberal critics in the post-war years contributed to a widening of the mental maps of sections of the British intelligentsia in the 1920s as new ideas and experiences started to make themselves felt in British social thought. 'Race prejudice between competitive races is intelligible enough', wrote Sydney Olivier in 1922, 'but it is a product of war, of the bronze and the iron ages. Race prejudice in a dominant race is self-justificatory arrogance.'[33] The feeling that race prejudice was in some respects linked to war encouraged the mood of hostility to it in the 1920s as liberals and socialists hoped for a new international order that would end all war. There was thus an attentive audience for German observers of race and the English translation of Friedrich Hertz's *Race and Civilisation* was warmly received by British sociologists in 1928. This book was an important early survey of European race theories from the eighteenth century onwards. These theories, Hertz argued, represented 'a strange mixture, made up of evolutionary thought on the one hand, and, on the other, the assumption of rigid race types and of absolute and fundamental differences between man and man. They are made up, further, of determinism and a moralizing view of history, of mysticism and the most blatant egotism.'[34] Hertz's book also warned of the dangerous political implications behind anthropological race-typing and quoted the French anthropometrist, G. Vacher de Lapouge, who in 1903 had remarked that 'I am conscious that men will slaughter each other by the million in the coming century for the sake of slight differences in skull measurements.'[35] Hertz considered these measurements had no real meaning, for 'the differences between the size of the brain of Negroes and that of white people are . . . no greater and sometimes even smaller than the differences between white men and women, between educated and uneducated'.[36] The 'anthropo-sociological' school of race theorists, such as Gobineau and H. S. Chamberlain, were thus guilty of 'the uncontrollable feeling over reason, the atavistic instinct of primaeval brutish ancestors over reason-controlled will'.[37] This attack also extended to the more recent school of American race theorists of Nordic racial superiority, such as Lothrop Stoddard, Madison Grant and William McDougall, who were accused of propagating the language of 'racialism', a term still comparatively new in British political discourse.

While Hertz's book was of considerable significance in attacking both European and North American race theorists, his understanding of the colonial context tended to be rather second-hand and based somewhat uncritically on the language of 'advanced' and 'backward' races. He considered it distinctly possible that 'backward' races, such as North American blacks, could be incorporated into 'our civilisation', thus tending to link 'Western civilisation' intrinsically with the white race. In the case of the West Indies he referred to W. P. Livingstone's *Black Jamaica: a Study in Evolution* to support the argument that this process of 'incorporation' would even lead to greater physical resemblances between Jamaican blacks and native British people – a view of race not substantially different to the ethnology of such theorists as Sir Arthur Keith.[38] Hertz thus reinforced the view, already fairly strongly held in sociological circles, that British race attitudes and theories, were substantially different to those of the rest of the world due to the strength of its institutions and liberal culture. 'England is certainly the land in which race prejudice plays comparatively the smallest role', he wrote, 'simply because, of all nations, the English show the greatest political maturity, and because in the process of governing a world empire she has had far and away the widest experience of dealing with all kinds of different races.'[39] This rather uncritical admiration of British liberalism was a fairly common trait among the European *émigrés* in the social sciences who came to reside in Britain in the course of the 1930s, for more radical social theorists, such as Franz Neumann (author of *Behemoth*, a study of Nazi Germany), took up residence in the United States.[40] It thus tended to reinforce the provincialism in British sociological thinking on race for it diverted attention away from the economic basis of racial segregationism in such areas of the Commonwealth as Southern Africa and linked racism almost exclusively with European, and to a lesser extent, American race theories. As a result of Hertz's book, John Robertson wrote, in the *Contemporary Review*: 'we may venture to believe that Europe has outlived the creed of Mr Houston Chamberlain, as it has outlived the more straightforward creed of Gumplowicz, who so grimly co-ordinated the feverish force-worship of Nietzsche . . . so long as nascent social service is mixed up with the creed of some inherent superiority of so-called 'Nordics', substituting that cheap order of generalisation for the dispassionate scrutiny of all the elements of national life, we are not visibly out of the wood of unscientific science'.[41] Further attacks on the unscientific nature of Central European racial thought continued throughout the 1930s, especially via the work of exiles from Nazi Germany. In 1938 another important study appeared entitled *Racism* (the first book so far traced to use the term 'racism' in its title), by Magnus Hirschfeld, who had died in exile from Germany in Nice in 1935. Here the earlier debunking of European racial theory was enhanced by its political use by German National Socialism and the manipulation of a 'blood myth' by such ideologues as Alfred Rosenberg.[42] In denouncing such racism, however, Hirschfeld, like Hertz earlier, did not develop an alternative category of analysis centred around notions of either 'culture' or 'class', and there was a lacuna in social thinking on this matter that sociologists did not tackle in any systematic manner before the Second World War. This became evident in 1935 when a joint committee was established by the Royal Anthropological Institute and the Institute of Sociology to investigate the meanings of the terms 'race' and 'culture'. The discussion was generally dominated by the anthropologists from the Royal Anthropological Institute and the only sociological contribution was from the secretary of the Institute of Sociology, Alexander Farquharson, who attended as an observer.[43] The independent sociological contribution to the discussion on race in the 1930s tended to be mostly derivative and second-hand, and the uninstitutionalised nature of the subject led to its failing to make a distinctive contribution before 1939. In December 1938 a 'racial relations group' was established under the auspices of the Institute of Sociology at Le Play House in Malvern, Worcestershire (following a visit to Britain by the director of the South African Institute of Race Relations, J.D. Rheinallt-Jones), as a means of reviving the work of the 1911 Universal Races Congress.[44] The work of the group did not start to take any significant form until the end of the Second World War and it eventually became absorbed into the work of the Racial Unity movement in the early 1950s.[45]

The sociological discussion of race in Britain thus tended to perpetuate throughout the 1930s rather second-hand ideas of both anthropometric classification into racial types and the classification of different blood groups as a means of discovering the patterns of settlement of different 'races'.[46] Its separation of 'race' from 'culture' tended to be rather confused and in 1938 Maximilien Beck, discussing the 'independence of culture from race', still argued that 'indirectly . . . man has the power to determine freely the development of his culture, that is, by the conscious application of racial eugenics',[47] though he also pointed out that 'culture, the true shaper of a Nation, is . . . by no means a natural product of race and heredity, but it is actively created, is a free achievement of individual creative personalities'.[48] The means by which such a 'culture' was created by 'individuals' eluded sociologists before the Second World War and it was developments in the anthropological theory of 'culture contact' which had a crucial role in eroding the idea that race had an independent causative role in social processes.

The anthropological contribution

Sociology in Britain, unlike its American counterpart, did not directly incorporate racial categories within its methodological assumptions since it was more of a clearing-house for the articulation of ideas derived from other disciplines, most notably eugenics and anthropology. The main battle with racial typologising and theories of race fitness in Britain tended, therefore, to be fought out within anthropology, which since the latter part of the nineteenth century had become increasingly linked with imperialism, as earlier ideas of Celtic ethnicity advanced by critics like Thomas Arnold gave way to theories of Anglo-Saxon and Nordic racial types.[49] As we saw in Chapter 1, many Victorian ideas on race derived from anthropological discussions on the physical measurement of races, an approach which had a wide-ranging influence on the emergent professional middle class in the nineteenth century. This concern with measurement became reinforced by the development of anthropometric ideas in measurement which, in Europe, became part of nationalist ideologies in France and Germany after the Franco-Prussian War of 1870–1.[50] Anthropometry had the advantage of appearing far more 'scientific' than previous methodologies for, unlike the earlier emphasis upon skull shape and size, it embraced measurements of the entire skeleton and tests of the brain's sense and motor functions.[51] In the wake of the decline of philology and language classification as a means of identifying races, anthropometry grew progressively popular among anthropologists in Britain in the last three decades of the nineteenth century. 'By the end of the nineteenth century', Andrew Lyons has written, 'the cephalic index had become not merely a practical tool but a pathological obsession.'[52]

In one sense, anthropometry as a 'science' of races allowed for the suspension of the earlier monogenesis–polygenesis debate, which had aided the growth of anthropology as a discipline in the years before the founding of the Anthropological Institute in 1871. It did not, either, conflict with the theme of cultural evolutionism that was expressed through the writings of Edward Tylor and Sir Henry Lubbock in Britain and Lewis Morgan in the United States.[53] While these exponents of scientific rationalism and its application to human classification had considerable appeal in a century gripped by the idea of materialism and social progress, the renewal of class conflict in the 1880s and 1890s, symbolised by the growing menace of Ireland, led to a progressive undermining of the faith in continuous social improvement. The anthropometrists' measurements could not be used to confirm conclusively the inherent separateness of different races and establish the linkage between both physical and mental ability and moral and social worth. The germ plasm theory of August Weismann also helped to undermine this anthropometric view for it stressed the continuity of the germ plasm through succeeding generations of different races and classes irrespective of the life history of parents, and could be used to throw doubts on the inherent racial superiority of the white Anglo-Saxon stock.[54]

This growth in the 'scientific' pretensions of anthropology in the 1880s and 1890s thus led it to forge a number of linkages with other disciplines which would later come to exert a critical impact on academic teaching and practice in the period after the First World War. In one sense, the doubts and uncertainty in the professional intelligentsia's own identity within the British class hierarchy led this to be a period of considerable fluidity, with a number of possible courses and directions open to it: a purely 'scientific' enterprise nourished by zoology and biology and centring on anthropological investigation of the measurement and classification of physical types; a more 'social' discipline, seeking nourishment from the infant subject of sociology and its pioneers centred around the Fabians and the summer schools of Patrick Geddes and the Outlook Tower in Edinburgh; an 'imperial' subject seeking, like many members of the professional middle class at this time, new pastures in colonial expansion and the study of 'subject races' in the British imperial sphere of influence. All these paths were at different times pursued by some members of the anthropological coterie in late Victorian Britain, with the latter option in the colonial sphere becoming increasingly popular in the period after the Anglo-Boer War of 1899–1902.

Anthropometry and physical anthropology

By the 1890s anthropometry had begun to achieve growing academic institutionalisation. In Scotland it was recognised as a branch of human anatomy in 1892 at the University of Edinburgh, while in Ireland an anthropological laboratory was opened at Trinity College, Dublin, in 1891, which led to the start of anthropological measurements of the student population there.[55] This anthropometrical research, under the control of Professor D. J. Cunningham, was seen as an important means to professionalise the hitherto amateur investigations of such gentlemen scholars as John Beddoe, whose study, *The Races of Britain*, appeared in 1885.[56] Such work also seemed to provide a more 'scientific' basis to the long Victorian debate over the nature of 'the Irish race' as well as searching into the nature and origins of isolated rural communities, such as the people of the island of Aran, whose independent identity was seen as increasingly threatened by the growth of modern communications and social mobility.[57] Furthermore, the measurement of populations was seen as complementing the biometrical work on inheritance initiated by Francis Galton. Indeed, the objectives of some physical anthropologists at this time were scarcely distinguishable from Galton's eugenical ideas on the need for race fitness in Britain's governing elite.[58]

The growing significance of anthropometry was reflected in 1892 when a committee was established by the British Association for the Advancement of Science to report on an ethnographical survey of the whole United Kingdom. Galton, Haddon and Cunningham were members, while representatives from the Folklore Society, the Royal Statistical Society and the Royal Irish Academy were also included.[59] Galton at this time undoubtedly exerted a considerable influence on the nature of anthropological work as it sought new directions.[60] The Anthropological Institute hoped to develop anthropometrical investigations at this time by mobilising a sufficiently wide degree of support from within the professional middle class in order to realise its hope for a nationwide survey. In the presidential address in 1896, E. W. Brabrook, the chairman of the Institute's

Ethnographical Survey Committee, urged the mobilisation of 'the educated classes' behind the idea, noting in particular 'the parochial and other clergy, the practioners of medicine, the board school masters and others of similar position, education and intelligence throughout the length and breadth of the land'.[61] The achievement of the committee by 1896, however, indicated the rather limited degree of support for a national survey: some measurements were made by individuals in villages, by the Buchan Field Club in east Aberdeenshire and by a naturalists' club at Nidderdale. The Cambridge Ethnographical Survey Committee also conducted measurements in the villages of Barrington and Foxton.[62] However, lack of funds prohibited further investigations and by 1899 the final report of the committee indicated that any more wide-reaching survey would depend upon a greater system of cooperation with local societies and the coordination of teams of volunteers by full-time survey organisers. The committee urged the establishment of a proper ethnological bureau under the auspices of the British Museum, a proposal taken up in greater earnest by the Institute after the Anglo-Boer War.[63]

The limited achievements of anthropometrical survey work thus belied the initial optimism of the early 1890s. In addition to a shortage of funds, it was clear that the scientific pretensions of anthropometry did not enjoy unchallenged sway in anthropological circles. Some historically minded traditionalists began to doubt the scientific worth of such work, and at the Ipswich meeting of the British Association in 1895, Professor Flinders Petrie defended an eclectic view of anthropology 'more as the study of man in relation to various and often independent subjects, rather than as an organic and self-contained science. Human nature is greater than all formulae; and we may as soon hope to compare its study to a logical structure, as to construct an algebraic equation for predicting its course of thought.'[64] While accepting some of the assumptions behind physical anthropology, Petrie questioned the methods by which permanent racial 'types' could be established given that the methods of measuring skulls were so unreliable:

> In skulls ... the main measurements are the length, which is compounded of half a dozen elements of growth, and the breadth and height, each the resultant of at least three elements. Two skulls may differ altogether in their proportions and forms, and yet yield identical measures in length, breadth and height. How can any but empirical results be evolved from such a system of measurement alone?[65]

Petrie's doubts were echoed by a growing scepticism amongst some physical anthropologists. By 1903, Cunningham privately confessed to

Haddon that he hated craniology as it was then taught for 'my whole soul revolts against it' though 'I suppose it is better to keep it going till it is replaced by something better'.[66] Cunningham still initiated, though, the following year, a scheme with the secretary of the Buchan Field Club, John Gray, for a nationwide anthropometric survey, which was submitted to a Privy Council Committee on Physical Deterioration. This involved measuring over ten years some 800,000 adults and 8 million children to add to existing knowledge of the 'distribution and origin of the races of our own country'. Furthermore, it was claimed that 'the connections that would be discovered between the different physical characters and between physical and mental characters would be new and valuable scientific discoveries'.[67]

The scheme reflected the growing influence on anthropology of eugenics and biometry led by Francis Galton and his follower, Karl Pearson. In 1902 Galton wrote that he hoped 'to induce anthropologists to regard human improvement as a subject that should be kept openly and squarely in view, not only on account of its transcendent importance, but also because it affords excellent but neglected fields for investigation'.[68] The following year, Karl Pearson, in his Huxley lecture at the Anthropological Institute, urged the correlation between 'home influence and moral qualities, and between education and mental power'.[69] He supported such claims by the analysis of the cephalic indices of 1,982 pairs of brothers in order to show the close physical resemblances. Using statistical correlations developed by Francis Galton, Pearson showed that the 'coefficient of resemblances' was .5 or 1 in 2, which was the 'measure of fraternal resemblance in brothers for cephalic index'.[70]

Such biometrical analysis of physical anthropological data indicated the closeness of eugenical work at this time to that of mainstream anthropology; the longer-term significance of this for a truly 'scientific' subject of anthropology was not lost on some of the members of the Anthropological Institute. In the presidential address at the Institute for 1903, Henry Balfour urged the importance of eugenics in the investigation of physical deficiencies within the British population and linked this to the proposal before the Anglo-Boer War for the establishment of a permanent bureau for the collection of large quantities of data.[71]

However, the mood for 'national efficiency' after the Anglo-Boer War led to growing differences between the anthropologists and eugenists, with the latter increasingly questioning the worth of anthropometric survey work.[72] In 1904, H. G. Wells complained of the 'degeneration theorists' who 'speak and write with ineffable profundity about the "criminal" ear, the "criminal" thumb, the "criminal" gland', and who 'gain access to gaols and pester unfortunate prisoners with callipers and cameras, and quite unforgiveable prying into personal and private matters, and they hold out great hopes that by their experiments they will evolve at last a scientific revival of the Kaffir's witch smelling'.[73] The founding of the Sociological Society the same year, strongly supported by Galton, and later the Eugenics Society itself in 1908, indicated that the earlier alliance between anthropology and eugenics was beginning to break up.

Anthropology did not remain theoretically static at this time: new developments occurred in the 1890s and early 1900s for links were forged by some anthropologists with sociology as interest grew in anthropological fieldwork amongst 'tribal' societies. The key figure in this respect was Alfred Court Haddon, who, whilst continuing anthropometric experiments in Ireland, also became acquainted with the ideas and work at Edinburgh of Patrick Geddes, who had moved from a career in biology to sociology and an amateur interest in eugenics. As early as 1891 Haddon taught at Geddes's Edinburgh summer school, to which a number of younger teachers and academics were drawn in the 1890s in pursuit of new avenues of inquiry that differed from the conventional modes of late Victorian thought. Geddes's chief significance for sociology in Britain was his introduction of much French social science thinking, especially that of Frédéric Le Play, whose environmental sociology of work, place and the family seemed to offer a third path of social reform as an alternative to both socialism and capitalism.[74] Methodologically this was to lead Geddes, after 1903, into the area of the regional survey and town planning, and a concomitant influence on the new infant subject of geography.[75] In the period of the 1890s, however, the main interest was still one of the classification of the various splintered sciences. From his study of Comte and Spencer, Geddes sought an ambitious synthesis in the work of the summer school so as to build up a team of lecturers for a 'university of the future' which would not subordinate 'technical education' under the heading of 'culture' since this seemed to him to have a number of class-bound connotations.[76] In seeking to harness Haddon to this project, Geddes hoped for a wider view of anthropology which would link it not so much to anatomy as to geography, 'with the concrete synthesis – the history of the world as we find it in all its aspects, rather than with the *autopsy of nature*'[77] (emphasis in original).

While Haddon later became somewhat sceptical of the ambitious nature of Geddes's project,[78] at this stage in his career he showed considerable enthusiasm. In 1897 he wrote to Geddes that the best way to organise a school of anthropology at Cambridge was to incorporate linguistic and psychological research, for he himself was interested in 'the psychology and sociology of savage peoples', which were 'of more importance and much wider interest'.[79] The Geddes school was also critical in Haddon's conceptualisation of the Torres Straits Expedition of 1898, which, in addition to including workers in anthropometry, was significant for including an analyst in psychology, W. H. R. Rivers.[80] From his understanding of Le Play, too, Haddon's notes reveal a considerable growth in interest in 'the externalist method' of 'direct observation' of social phenomena in order to determine the 'laws by which they are governed'.[81] Much of this can be seen as an important precursor of the development in fieldwork by Malinowski and Radcliffe-Brown within a functionalist paradigm during and after the First World War.[82] For Haddon, though, there was still as yet no complete break between physical and social anthropology and in a presidential address to the Anthropological Institute in 1903 both methods were seen as united within a single discipline. On the basis of a classification directly attributed to Geddes, Haddon put physical anthropology on 'the lowermost plane', which he termed 'Anthropography'. 'Ethnology' came on a plane higher and this he saw in terms of 'the anatomy of cultural man' or 'descriptive sociology'. Finally, on the highest plane, and probably reflecting the work of the Torres Straits Expedition, he put psychology, which, while it had 'roots in [man's] animal nature . . . flowers, so to speak, in a realm of its own'.[83]

This somewhat unstable definition of anthropology in some degree reflected the uninstitutionalised position of sociology in Britain at this time and the lack of clarity in its theoretical pretensions. There was thus some reason for Haddon, in seeking to further the academic institutionalisation of anthropology in the University of Cambridge, to seek only a limited and pragmatic alliance with sociology which could be defined essentially on anthropology's own terms. Sociology was still treated as one level within the anthropological enterprise, with considerable room being left for the more conventional pursuits of physical anthropology and craniometry. This 'lack of definiteness' for Haddon in anthropology was a positive advantage since it added 'charm to the subject' and was 'fertile in the production of new ideas'.[84] However, a lecture to a group of missionaries the same year by Haddon indicated that in the years after the Treaty of Vereeniging there were growing pressures on anthropology to adapt itself to become a more vocationally orientated subject suitable for training colonial administrators, teachers and missionaries.[85] In such a context the influence of sociological theory grew considerably.

The imperial factor

Despite the resurgence of popular enthusiasm in Britain in the 1890s for empire and imperial expansion, anthropology initially remained comparatively aloof in its devotion to the idea of unhampered scientific study. At best, anthropologists such as Flinders Petrie acted as forerunners of Mary Kingsley as they championed the notion of cultural relativism between races and impressed on public opinion as far as possible 'a clear idea of the great civilisations, ancient and modern, and their suitability to their conditions', for there would then be 'a readier toleration of what does not fit our ideas in the races we have now to deal with'.[86] These ideas, expressed privately and in small select circles, did not make much impact politically and in 1896, at the Liverpool meeting of the British Association for the Advancement of Science, a group of anthropologists from the British Museum, led by C. H. Read, initiated a scheme for establishing an Imperial Bureau of Ethnology. The plan was motivated in part by the desire to establish a British equivalent of the Bureau of American Ethnology, which accumulated data on the life and customs of American Indian peoples[87] and expressed an ethnographic ethos for accumulating data and material for unhampered 'scientific' research. Though arrangements were made for the establishment of the Bureau on the British Museum's premises before the start of the Anglo-Boer War in 1899,[88] the project did not gain an especially favourable reception in government circles since its main aim was the comparatively esoteric one of researching 'subject' races which would soon become too 'civilised' to have any great anthropological interest.[89]

In the wake of the Anglo-Boer War, the aim behind the Imperial Bureau scheme began to change as British anthropologists began to react to a new situation that was more favourable to 'applied anthropology' for use in colonial administration. The ideas of Mary Kingsley were of considerable importance for anthropologists of the late 1890s, since they were expressed in a public context freed from the more formal constraints of professional anthropological discussion.[90] This was especially important since some theorists of 'arrested development' amongst 'savages' had never considered cranial measurements as decisive to their arguments, preferring to view 'endless generations of savagery' as conferring predetermined characteristics in innate opposition to 'culture'. This view Mary Kingsley had been strongly able to refute.[91]

The opportunities thrown up by the South African war were important, too, for the establishment of British colonial government in the Transvaal under the governorship of Lord Milner appeared to offer the chance of linking anthropological research to the running of a modern system of imperial rule.[92] In 1905 the British Association significantly held its annual meeting in South Africa in the same year as an important report was published on the future of 'native policy' in South Africa and Rhodesia, and the times seemed to bode well for linking anthropology with the development of colonial policy in the region.[93] 'The day is past when the amassing of detailed information will satisfy the demands of science', declared

A.C. Haddon in an address to the anthropological section of the British Association in Johannesburg:

> The leaders, at all events, will view the subject as a whole, and so direct individual labour that the hewers of wood and drawers of water, as it were, shall not mechanically amass material of which no immediate use can be made, but they will be so directed that all their energies can be exercised in solving definite problems or in filling up gaps in our information, with knowledge which is of real importance.[94]

The assumption of 'leaders' being able to 'direct' such individual research implied some form of imperial relationship being established in British anthropological research, with the main body of theoretical systematisers being located in the imperial metropolis while the 'applied' body of researchers were located in the colonial periphery. This research relationship only became overturned, as Adam Kuper has pointed out, with the Malinowskian functionalist revolution of the periphery, which effectively unified both theory and practice within the notion of fieldwork.[95] However, the establishment of such an imperial set of relationships in anthropology led logically to some coordinating mechanism in the form of an Imperial Bureau and this idea was revived in the following years by the Anthropological Institute.

The chances of the Anthropological Institute finally gaining government support for the Imperial Bureau project were still hampered, though, by the general aim, as expressed in an Institute memorandum, of gathering data to test whether there was 'physical improvement or deterioration of all the races of the Empire'. It also urged that 'on political grounds' it was essential to gather knowledge on the 'mental attitudes and modes of life of the savage races within the Empire'. The general ethos thus still appeared to be one of gathering 'scientific' data, with a public policy application only a secondary consideration. Furthermore, the memorandum appeared as a continuation of the anthropological campaign before the Boer War for a nationwide survey of adults and children, though this time widened even further onto an imperial level.[96]

Though the Institute still hoped to secure a grant of £500 towards the Bureau's establishment, by 1910 the campaign was reported as a failure by its president, Professor William Ridgeway, despite claims that it had obtained support from members of parliament, shipowners, manufacturers and traders.[97] Anthropology was still clearly seen as too esoteric and specialised a subject to be of much use in the development of colonial administration, though it was hoped it would also be of use to missionaries.[98]

The retreat of physical anthropology

The onset of world war in 1914 led to a renewed upsurge in the efforts by anthropologists to get the government interested in a nationwide anthropometric survey. In March 1916 a number of scientific societies met under the aegis of the Royal Society to form a 'Conjoint Board' to advise government departments and this led to the appointment of an Anthropological Survey Committee which recommended a survey of the physical condition of the people dealt with by the new Ministry of National Service, the Board of Education and the Home Office.[99] This campaign was buttressed by the establishment of Medical Boards in 1917 by the Ministry of National Service, which commenced a survey of British men in November of that year according to a grading system from 1 to 4 for 'physical fitness' – which meant in effect the capacity for marching, carrying machines or their 'soundness in limb and wind'.[100] While this somewhat amateur approach represented a start, the anthropometrists hoped for a more 'scientific' survey. Arthur Keith argued for test areas of up to half a million people in both rural and urban areas and measurements that included teeth, mouth, nose, throat, ears, lungs, heart and feet and which were based upon an agreed set of anthropometrical measurements.[101]

The end of the war, though, prevented these hopes materialising and anthropometry only met the serious attention of the newly established Medical Research Council when it appointed, at the end of 1919, an Anthropometric Standards Committee.[102] Though Keith joined this committee, the leading influence on it was the Professor of Pathology at the University of Oxford, Professor Dreyer, whose methods of measurement, including the use of a contraption called a 'spirometer' to measure lung and chest capacity, met with ridicule from Karl Pearson. 'These methods are being used by all sorts of people', Pearson wrote to the Medical Research Council's chairman, Sir Walter Greenwood, 'who cannot possibly judge their value'.[103]

As a result the MRC's Anthropometric Methods Committee was dissolved early in 1924 and no further anthropometric work was undertaken by it, an application by Leonard Darwin of the Eugenics Education Society in 1925 being turned down on the grounds that there was no commonly agreed unambiguous standard of measurement which could make such a survey suitably scientific.[104]

In addition to this distrust by state and institutional bodies of anthropometry by the 1920s, the mainstream of anthropology increasingly veered in the direction of the social sciences. 'Anthropology', declared W. H. R. Rivers in his posthumous address to the Anthropological Institute in 1922, 'stands midway between the sciences that study nature on the one hand, and history and humanistic studies on the other.'[105] While this still left the door open for physical anthropology and anthropometry, physical measurements were pursued to some extent outside the formal confines of the discipline, especially within the emergent subject of geography. P.M. Roxby at Liverpool and H.J. Fleure both had an interest in linking geographical studies to the study of racial types and both, significantly, came from strong rural backgrounds with an attachment to long-established small communities as opposed to the more complex culture of large cities.[106] Fleure in particular conducted a fairly extensive set of anthropometric measurements in the village populations in Wales whilst teaching both geography and anthropology at Aberystwyth, where he became professor in 1918. For Fleure the linking of anthropology with geography was of crucial significance for, like Haddon, his early work had owed much to the thinking of Patrick Geddes. The synthetic classification of sciences begun by Geddes was especially important for Fleure in so far as it meant a suspension of the old Victorian nature–nurture debate. The implications of Darwinism were that the influences from both heredity and environment were inextricably interrelated such that a 'human geography' which incorporated both anthropological and geographical dimensions could move to a higher level of synthesis than the older anthropology inherited from the Victorian period.[107] To this extent the philosophical idealism running through Geddes's thinking that has been seen as a crucial feature of British sociology in the period before the Second World War may well be judged as having important ramifications beyond simply sociology itself.[108]

Within this new synthesis developed by Fleure a more traditional physical anthropology was still preserved which went back to the period prior to the development of biometry by Karl Pearson. On the basis of research into Welsh 'physical types', commenced in 1905 while still lecturing in zoology and botany,[109] Fleure became suspicious of attempts to deduce 'racial types' from statistical averages of physical forms. Equally, though, he was determined to preserve as far as possible the validity of the classification of racial types in the face of differing forms of criticism, especially that of Franz Boas, who had worked on immigrants and their children in the United States.[110]

Beginning in an important paper published in 1916 on the geographical distribution of 'anthropological types' in Wales, Fleure criticised the Boasian standpoint of rejecting racial typologies for serious anthropological purposes.[111] Suspicious of urban industrial societies, Fleure preferred to base his conclusions on work carried out in rural Wales, where anthropological research could pinpoint an identifiable 'race history' of the people. Carrying this even further in 1918 to a race history of Britain as a whole, Fleure applied the threefold category of European racial groups into 'Nordic', 'Caucasian' and 'Mediterranean' developed by the American, Ripley, early in the century. The 'Nordic type' was seen as an important component part of the landed aristocracy and country house life prior to industrialisation and was later a key component of overseas colonial expansionism. By contrast, the 'Mediterranean race type', which Fleure's research had identified as an important component part of the Welsh people, was the repository of life in the churches, medicine and the poetical imagination. It was, though, ill-adapted to life in towns, where it was likely to sink into slumdom – a version, in some respects, of a liberal paternalism that in the colonial context frequently expressed itself in the form of a benevolent segregation of colonised societies from life in the towns, which were seen as the abode of acquisitive, white coloniser races.[112]

Fleure's ideas on race were especially significant due to the strategic place he came to hold in the establishment of geography as a subject taught in both schools and universities. As early as 1911 he was keen to disseminate the methods of the 'new geography' that were being developed in Britain by H. L. Mackinder and H. J. Herbertson to a growing band of school teachers.[113] Furthermore, the influence of Geddes's ideas led Fleure strongly in the direction of regional geographical studies and this resulted in a questioning of a simple nation-state orientation behind anthropological studies. The spread of state systems over 'small regions' was for Fleure a matter of regret if this led to a failure to recognise 'varying modes of life and thought'.[114] These ideas Fleure propagated via the *Geographical Teacher* during the 1920s, after he became secretary of the Geographical Association in 1918. As the offices of the Association moved, too, to Aberystwyth, Wales became for a short period the locus of a burgeoning area of ethnic studies, though the inheritance of racial typology moved the work of some of Fleure's students, such as E. G. Bowen, in the direction of an early socio-biology in its emphasis on the interaction between environmental and inherited physical traits to explain the incidence of phthisis amongst South Wales coal miners.[115]

One of the more significant consequences, though, for race thinking in Britain of Fleure's work at Aberystwyth was the informal links established with eugenics. In 1919 Fleure responded positively to a scheme proposed by the Eugenics Education Society and the Royal Anthropological Institute for a study into the effects of mixed-race marriages and their 'half-caste' offspring, suggesting in particular that a female assistant of his, Rachel Fleming, could collate the existing material on the subject.[116] In the course of the 1920s, Rachel Fleming pursued research for the Medical Research Institute on the anthropometry of 'half-caste' children in dockland areas, including Liverpool, and it was as a consequence of this that the Liverpool

Association for the Welfare of Half Caste Children was formed in 1930 with close links to the University Settlement that was devoted to 'rescue work' in the poor dockland areas of depression-struck Merseyside.[117] Fleure himself left Aberystwyth for Manchester in 1930 and it was here that he increasingly turned to the question of genetics on the thinking about race.[118]

The impact of genetics

One of the reasons for the relatively slow response by anthropological circles in Britain to the political implications of race thinking was that the Mendelian revolution in genetics took a long time to seep through into anthropological analysis. This in part was a result of an educational climate dominated by an ethos of the gentleman amateur and an Oxbridge humanist tradition that was not strongly supportive of scientific research. Genetics thus remained seriously underfunded for many years in Britain compared to the United States,[119] while the division early in the century between the pioneer geneticists in Britain, led by Gregory Bateson, and the bio-metricians led by Raphael Weldon and Karl Pearson, also hampered the diffusion of genetical ideas.[120] It was only by the early 1930s, following the retirement of Pearson from his chair at University College, London, in 1933, that younger geneticists like Julian Huxley saw an opportunity for putting genetical research in Britain onto a really professional basis.[121]

Thus concepts of race derived from genetical research only began to make an impact on anthropological thought in the late 1920s. Until then the main intellectual context in which the genetical implications of inter-racial crossing had been discussed in Britain had been that of eugenics and few professional anthropologists addressed themselves to genetics before then.[122] In 1928 one British geneticist, R. Ruggles Gates, urged greater anthropological attention to inter-racial crossing since 'the purpose of the genetical method is to trace individual pedigrees, and so follow the inheritance of racial difference through succeeding generations. We shall never have an adequate knowledge of human racial inheritance until this has been done on a large scale with crosses between different races in various parts of the world.'[123] The general tone of Gates's conclusions, though, reinforced in many respects those of the eugenists. Deploring the creation of 'mongrels', especially when it occurred 'between an advanced and a more backward race', Gates argued that crosses between negroes and Eskimos were 'undesirable from any point of view'.[124]

Over the following years, the influences from genetics caused many anthropologists to realise that a rethinking was needed on racial typologies. A. C. Haddon, for example, reacted favourably in 1931 to a proposal for the establishment of an Institute of Research in Human Genetics,[125] while in 1933 he considered Charles Chamberlain Hurst's *The Mechanics of Creative Evolution* of 'profound importance' and considered it needed to be studied by both anthropologists and sociologists alike.[126] Discussions were also begun in the Royal Anthropological Institute, where a Human Biology Research Committee held its first meeting in January 1932. The anthropological diffusionist, Professor Grafton Elliot Smith, emphasised the importance of biological research into inheritance and blood groups and criticised the Institute for failing to pay enough attention to these, especially via its annual Huxley lectures.[127]

For the most part, the conservatism within the Royal Anthropological Institute prevented it from recognising the danger of the political use of racial typologies in Europe until well into the 1930s. The influx into Britain of refugees from Nazi Germany after 1933 certainly caused some rethinking in sociological circles and it was as a result of pressure from the Institute of Sociology at Le Play House that the joint meeting was arranged with the Royal Anthropological Institute in 1934 to determine the significance of racial factors on cultural development.[128] The main response, though, from the anthropologists in the Institute was to accept that there was a fundamental distinction between 'racial' and 'cultural' groups, with a third category of 'population' groups, and to seek if possible a common set of criteria by which to determine the anthropometrical study of race types.[129] This led to a general agreement, in the joint report of the Anthropological and Sociology Institutes in 1935, entitled *Race and Culture*, deploring the 'misuse' of anthropometrical research in the fostering of racial ideologies, though without there being any commonly accepted notion of 'race'.[130]

Thus throughout the 1930s physical anthropologists continued to defend research and investigation into 'physical types', which, as one leading RAI anthropologist, G. M. Morant, claimed, was of key importance 'to workers engaged in problems of racial hygiene'.[131] This research also continued to be buttressed by the old campaign for a nationwide survey, though the general enthusiasm for this was by no means so strong as it had been in the years before the First World War.[132] The main example to which the physical anthropologists looked was Scandinavia, where in 1922 the Swedish State Institute for Race Biology began a nationwide anthropometric survey. By the mid-1930s, following the collapse of the earlier work of the geography department at Aberystwyth, the main centre for this kind of survey work was Scotland, where the Scottish Anthropological Society pursued anthropometric research under its zealous president, G. R. Gair. In 1935 a Scottish anthropometric survey was begun to investigate the different 'race types' in Scotland,[133] and in 1937 the War Office agreed to supply the Society with data relating to recruits into the army from Scotland.[134] The work of the Society, though, came under increasing suspicion from many of the anthropologists connected to the RAI in England, especially after Gair fostered links with the Secretariat of the International Ethnological Association in Berlin, where he went as a delegate from the SAS in 1936.[135] This led to a charge from Professor C. G. Seligman that the Scottish Society was allowing itself to be used as a vehicle for Nazi propaganda.[136] Later in the same year Gair resigned his presidency of the Society, which moved increasingly in the direction thereafter of work on local folklore.[137]

Outside Scotland, physical anthropological research continued, though without the same degree of certainty as had been exhibited in earlier years. By the time of the outbreak of war, one study done of people in some Oxfordshire villages reflected the general loss of confidence in the methods of racial typology. Hinting at the possibility of links between the Oxfordshire villagers and the 'Mediterranean race type', the authors nevertheless concluded that they were 'sceptical of the validity of a procedure which appears to depend on subjective conceptions of racial stereotypes, and we prefer to take a group as we find it and try to associate it with similar groups'.[138]

This empiricism and absence of theory in physical anthropology undoubtedly reflected the growing impact of the more radical critique of racial typologies mounted by Julian Huxley and Alfred Court Haddon in 1935 in their seminal study entitled *We Europeans*.[139] Written in part as a result of a request by the publishers, Jonathan Cape, for an effective debunking of Nazi race propaganda,[140] the study rejected the whole idea that there were identifiable racial types in anthropology. It attacked the Nazi notion of a distinct 'Aryan race' by arguing for the discarding of the term 'race' in favour of 'ethnic group' and the classification of former 'race types' within major 'races' as 'ethnic types' or 'genetic types'.[141] The study was not especially original in the way it attacked racial typologies for it reflected the earlier doubts of Fleure, Lord Raglan and Grafton Elliot Smith, who in 1934 at an International Conference of Anthropology at University College London had denounced the 'Nordic legend' as 'witchcraft'.[142] However, as Nancy Stepan has argued, by focusing upon the Nazi use of the Aryan race myth, Huxley and Haddon used genetics to debunk the old race science without putting anything substantially new in its place. *We Europeans* thus marked the end of an era without ushering in a new theory paradigm,[143] and it is not clear how far their criticisms were understood by the public at large. Liberal attacks on race in the 1920s still looked to the anthropologists as a guide and H. J. Massingham in 1929 hoped that the diffusionists could provide a way out of the idea of racial superiority. Though diffusionism declined in the 1930s following the rise of structural functional anthropology, there still remained a considerable area of uncertainty and doubt even in liberal and missionary circles on the issue of race and race differences. For some 'experts' on the issue only a survey of world dimensions and based on a comparison of races segregated from each other could provide the data necessary to resolve the issue.[144]

Furthermore, Huxley and Haddon's employment of genetics produced no uniform agreement among anthropologists about the meaning of race in the 1930s. At a meeting of the British Association in 1936 at Blackpool, a number of questions were raised on the degree to which genetics could assist anthropological research. G. M. Morant defended the typological classifications of the physical anthropologists on the grounds that Mendelian genetics had failed to show that the theory of 'blended inheritance' was as incorrect for groups as it was for individuals. 'I am still prepared to defend the old-fashioned theory', he declared, 'that, as far as quantitative skeletal characters are concerned, the crossing of groups leads to blended inheritance, i.e. to the blending of the average values of the characters of the parent groups. A great deal of observational data may be brought forward to support this theory, and it seems to me that no valid objections to it of a theoretical nature have yet been advanced by geneticists.'[145]

This counterattack from physical anthropology was aided, too, by the fact that not all geneticists were themselves in agreement on the issues of races. R. Ruggles Gates argued for a polygenetic explanation of race differences, advancing in many respects a line of argument on race that stretched back, via Mary Kingsley, to Robert Knox in the middle of the previous century. He concluded:

> From a genetical point of view, if we apply the same criteria of species to man as are applied to the higher animals, it is necessary to recognise the existence of several species of living man. Recent critical studies of African monkeys show various genera containing a number of species, each with several sub-species or geographical races. 'Homo sapiens' is an anthropological convention, surviving from the time when intersterility was regarded as an essential criterion of species. Recent evidence indicates that the mongoloid, australoid, negroid and caucasoid types of man have been evolving independently since the beginning of the Pleistocene. This confirms the view that they should be regarded not merely as geographic sub-species of races but as species.[146]

Given this diversity of view, it was not altogether surprising that no uniform anthropological campaign could be organised against the advance of racist political ideology in the late 1930s in the period up to the Second

World War. The pace of political events in Central Europe in the 1930s was too swift in many ways to allow for the creation of any uniform consensus, though this was not despite attempts to evolve some form of establishment view.

Efforts at creating a consensus

For some British anthropologists, the absence of any uniform agreement in the 1930s on the nature of race represented both a challenge and an opportunity to influence informed official opinion in the direction of a common viewpoint. This was not an unprecedented intellectual climate for, as J. W. Burrow has pointed out, social evolutionary theory in Victorian times reflected efforts to reach a common basis for intellectual debate, 'a point of response at which the tension between the need for certainty and the need to accommodate more diverse social facts, and more subtle ways of interpreting them, than the traditional certainties allowed for, reached a kind of equilibrium'.[147] In some senses, by the 1930s there was a similar need perceived by some anthropologists to seek a new form of common intellectual ground.

The roots of this mood amongst some of the 'establishment' anthropologists went back to the break-up of the older Victorian consensus during the First World War. For the then president of the Royal Anthropological Institute, Sir Arthur Keith, the opportunity presented itself to develop a theory of race formation as a result of the historical catalyst of war within human societies.[148] As an anatomist who became curator of the Hunterian Museum of the Royal College of Surgeons, Keith was an influential figure in the 1920s and was able to impress his views on a wide section of the British establishment. As well as being a Fellow of the Royal Society, he was president of first the Royal Anthropological Institute and then the British Association and was elected to the Athenaeum Club.[149] He was also a fairly adept publicist who was keen to disseminate his ideas on the relationship of race to nation and patriotism to as popular a level as possible. 'The Caucasian stable alone had saddled a wealth of candidates and mounted them in national characters', he once wrote in the *Evening Standard*, 'I am putting my money on horses from the Caucasian stable – particularly the British breed.'[150]

Coming from a late Victorian background that was heavily influenced by Social Darwinism, Keith was typical of many of his generation in losing religious faith, and the belief in race became a surrogate religion. In the late 1920s he was strongly impressed by General Smuts's *Holism and Evolution* and this was a probable source of influence on his idea of linking race to human social evolution through the idea of 'ethnos'.[151] With a new map of Europe created by the Versailles Peace Treaty of 1919, this concept became for Keith a key means to explain both nationalism and the resurgence of race thinking. 'A nation always represents an attempt to become a race,' he argued in 1930, 'nation and race are but different degrees of the same evolutionary movement.'[152]

This evolutionary view of race found a limited degree of support among anthropologists in the 1930s in the search for a consensus on definitions of race. For George Pitt-Rivers, the concept of 'race formation' helped point the way to 'a new scientific synthesis, with a defined and surer method. Out of it there emerges the conception of race, population, and culture as tripartite aspects of Man in time, conditioning and being conditioned by his environment: the conception of race in evolution.'[153] The idea was even hinted at in Huxley and Haddon's *We Europeans* in 1935 when it was pointed out that ethnic groups were the product of 'partial geographical differentiations of the human species, of a kind rather different from anything found in animals . . . . Their latter intermixture produces wholly new combinations of characters which may be stabilized as new "ethnic types" – a process apparently without parallel in other organisms.'[154]

The concept of 'ethnos' or 'ethnogenics', however, became increasingly bound up with the debate over European racism as the 1930s progressed, and became compromised after Keith, in a debate in the correspondence columns of *The Times*, sought to defend German nationalism as an aid to the formation of a German 'race': 'Compounded out of diverse elements,' he argued, 'it is in the throes of fusion; psychologically it is being made one.'[155] Introducing a new psychological definition of race brought the retort from Julian Huxley that this merely added to the confusion in the thinking surrounding race and strengthened his own conviction that the term 'race' was inapplicable when applied to the human species.[156] In general, Keith's thinking was seen as failing to make the elementary distinction between race and national or cultural groups[157] and by the time of the Second World War his thought was linked to the older set of redundant theories on race which a more radical generation of anthropologists, such as the American, Ashley Montagu, were keen to see discarded in the postwar world.[158]

The outbreak of war in 1939 acted as a shock wave on many British anthropologists, who began to ask why no greater stand had been made in the 1930s against the use of anthropology in racist and Nazi ideologies.[159] 'The fact that anthropologists were not agreed regarding methods of *racial* analysis', wrote G. M. Morant in 1940, 'need not have prevented them from making an effective protest, and this would have been not merely negative, but also of positive value if it had led to some general appreciation of the elements of physical anthropology'[160] (emphasis added). Morant's continued belief, despite admitting the failure of anthropologists to move from their adopted position of ostensible scientific neutrality, that a 'racial' analysis could still be preserved, revealed some of the major methodological limitations endemic to much physical anthropology in Britain during this period. The survival of racial typology within British physical anthropology can be seen historically as an important part of European racial thought over the previous four to five decades[161] and is significant for failing, as George Stocking has pointed out in the case of American anthropology, to make ultimately any major significant distinction between a race 'type' and, in actual practice, a 'pure race'.[162] Racial typology thus survived throughout the period both of late nineteenth-century imperial expansionism and the onset of Fascism and racism after the First World War. Though this typology can be most easily located, after Hannah Arendt, as part of a pattern of 'race thinking' in European thought before the onset of an identifiable pattern of 'racism',[163] its ultimate contribution to the latter cannot be ignored. By 1945 a number of British anthropologists felt a degree of responsibility for the manipulation of anthropological ideas politically in the pre-war era; this, indeed, partly explained the greater degree of enthusiasm for reaching a common consensus within UNESCO in the late 1940s and 1950s on definitions of 'race' and 'racism'.[164] 'Let us beware of arguments about diversity of "race" that have sometimes crept into political discussions', declared H. J. Fleure in 1946 at the time of his retirement from the University of Manchester, '. . . let us beware of giving support to propaganda about so-called superior and inferior races, and let us try to see that this dangerous nonsense is effectively condemned by UNO and UNESCO in the most public manner possible'.[165] This delayed response from within anthropology in Britain reflected the new mood of the post-war era, anxious to forget the mistakes and inadequacies of the pre-war generation. With the establishment of the Colonial Social Science Research Council in 1940, research on race and the new, more commonly known area of 'race relations' increasingly shifted towards the field of social anthropology and sociology.[166] Here, as Chapter 8 shows, the American debate on the role of law to outlaw racial discrimination stimulated by Gunnar Myrdal's *An American Dilemma* (1944) had some impact. If the pre-war generation of physical anthropologists had been successful in either limiting or neutralising the ideas on race from such American scholars as Franz Boas, many of their post-war successors were now anxious not to repeat this mistake. Thus, by 1948, Friedrich Hertz was calling on his fellow sociologists in Britain to recognise that 'racialism' was 'a social factor' which needed extensive sociological and anthropological study. With the legacy of pre-war Fascism and Nazism, it was clear that racialism was a force incompatible with western democratic political systems, though

'racialism' was often 'admitted by the backdoor to the ideology of democratic nations'.[167] This meant that 'the only remedy' was for 'the different
sections of mankind, whether races or nations, to acquire a deeper
understanding of each other and to develop sufficient mutual sympathy'.[168]
Thus did social scientists try to mobilise their intellectual and educational
resources to meet a new political challenge in the post-war era, at a time
when 'race' was taking on a new set of meanings as the withdrawal from
empire began.

6

The 'half-caste' pathology

When Dorian Gray went down to London east and underworld in Oscar Wilde's novel, *The Picture of Dorian Gray* (1891), he came across a 'half-caste' dressed in a 'ragged turban and shabby ulster' who 'grinned a hideous greeting'.[1] This Victorian association of mixed-race people with both immorality and a slumland underclass standing outside the main social order of Britain grew in the early twentieth century to become a fairly common stereotype by the inter-war years, reflecting a growing consciousness of black–white race relations within the metropolitan society itself. In the nineteenth century, as has been seen, the issue of race and colour was perceived as mainly an imperial one, though from the 1880s onwards there grew up in a number of British towns and cities identifiable black communities of seamen, traders and students, together with a small group of entertainers and musicians. In the case of London, a black community had begun to emerge in the eighteenth century, though during the nineteenth century the numbers of blacks declined in the wake of the abolition of slavery and only started to rise again with the settlement of numbers of blacks and Asians in the 1880s and 1890s. Other black communities in Liverpool and Cardiff also grew up at this time.[2]

The presence of blacks in Britain raised the question of inter-racial sexual liaisons in a new and politically acute form. The black middle class, such as Henry Sylvester Williams and Harold Moody, were to some extent able to avoid extreme racial prejudice by marrying white women and attaining a degree of social respectability. The same, however, could not be said for black seamen settling in seaport towns such as Bristol, Liverpool, South Shields and London's dockland, where there were growing racial tensions with the indigenous white working-class population. These finally spilled over into anti-black riots in Liverpool and Cardiff in 1919.[3] During the First World War significant numbers of black seamen from colonial territories in West Africa, the Caribbean and the Middle East were engaged on British ships, and at the war's end found themselves out of work as the shipping

120

industry contracted and the Seamen's and Firemen's Union (later to form, with the Cooks' and Stewards' Union, the National Union of Seamen in the 1920s) campaigned to keep jobs on ships for white crewmen only.[4] Flung out into the slumland culture of the port towns, the black seamen focused upon themselves considerable racial hostility as they became linked in the public mind with growing crime rates and prostitution when they cohabited with white women and produced 'half-caste' children.

The issue came to a head during the months of April, May and June of 1919, when there were widespread inter-racial attacks in London, Cardiff, Liverpool and South Shields, resulting in several casualties and a few deaths. In Cable Street, Stepney, there was violent fighting and shots fired on 16 April, while in the latter half of May black seamen in Liverpool, of whom 500–600 were reported as unemployed and anxious to be repatriated, were subject to attacks from white gangs. On 8 June, mobs of between 2,000 and 10,000 roamed the streets of Liverpool attacking blacks at random and a house occupied by blacks was set on fire. With covert support from the local police, who perceived the blacks, in the words of one police officer, as 'only big children who when they get money like to make a show', the white crowds had all the trappings of lynch mobs and were often goaded on by demobbed servicemen. In Cardiff attacks on black houses in Bute Town, referred to by *The Times* as 'nigger town', were partly provoked by ex-soldiers without jobs and there were reports of 'colonial soldiers' at the head of the mobs. There was thus a probable element of orchestration behind the white racial attacks and the riots have been described as divisive in that they fomented a racial hostility which cut through an otherwise common working-class consciousness.[5] At a time when there was widespread industrial unrest, blacks in Britain emerged after the riots as a unique and distinct 'problem'.[6]

The longer-term significance of the 1919 riots, though, lay in the series of official responses over the following years as a result of pressure from the lower echelons of the civil service and local police forces. These latter elements, especially, pressed for a tightening-up of controls on black settlement and residence in Britain and for the deportation of seamen who could not prove they had British citizenship. The importance, therefore, of the 'coloured alien seamen' issue lay not so much in its magnitude – for the actual numbers of seamen involved was quite small, numbering a few hundred – but for the manner in which it exemplified that the ideas on race and empire generated at the heart of British imperial culture could penetrate down into the administrative petty bourgeoisie within the metropolis. At a time when the political will at the heart of British imperialism had begun to be eroded in the wake of the First World War, the establishment of the League of Nations and the doctrine of colonial 'trusteeship', this mobilisation of administrative resources within Britain for the purpose of excluding certain categories of black labour was of some significance. If imperialism represented, as A. P. Thornton has argued, the conferring of the privilege of will, room, time and money[7], then the ability by the British state within the empire to enforce these advantages for the British population by the 1920s became increasingly problematical. The 1919 riots in Liverpool for example, represented in many respects the extension of rising colonial nationalism into the heart of the British metropolis itself at a time when nationalist ferment was being expressed in many parts of the empire. The growing numbers of black colonials in British ship crews during the war itself provided an avenue of escape from the ability of the British imperial edifice to manipulate geographical space and labour time solely to its own advantage. The fact, too, that crewmen could jump ship in such ports as Liverpool and Cardiff indicated a willingness and ability to escape from total imperial control. This element of increasing mobility among the black colonial population together with growing political appeals to pan-Negro solidarity and the myth of back to Africa by the Universal Negro Improvement Association, led to a growing unease in imperial circles in the early 1920s.[8] The racial response from the police and some section of the Board of Trade during these years thus reflected a political imperative to tighten up governmental control within the metropolis as well as a wider economic and political response on the imperial plane during the inter-war years to dampen down the fires of colonial nationalism and deflect colonial political energies into channels which could be more easily controlled. The educational and political dimensions of this strategy are discussed in Chapter 7. The purpose of this chapter will be to examine this administrative response to internal racial tension within Britain in the 1920s and 1930s.

The 1925 Special Restriction (Coloured Alien Seamen) Order

The numbers of foreign seamen in British ships had been rising before the First World War, for between 1890 and 1903 it rose from 27,000 to 40,000 while the numbers of British seamen fell by 10,000. However, in 1911 a turning-point occurred in industrial relations in the industry when the first national seamen's strike occurred. The triumvirate of leaders involved in the strike – Captain Tupper of the Seamen's Union, J. H. Thomas of the Railwaymen and Ernest Bevin of the Transport Workers – were by no means extreme socialists and the importance of the strike lay in its combining an industrial militancy with an ethos of working-class patriotism that bordered on jingoism. During the course of the strike, there were attacks on Chinese laundries in Cardiff which were partly initiated by the Seamen's

Union and, by the time war started in 1914, the Union had evolved as a fervently nationalist and anti-pacifist organisation – in 1917 it refused to allow Ramsay Macdonald and fellow pacifists to sail to Stockholm to attend a peace conference.[9]

This combination of militancy and patriotism had a significant effect on the shipping industry, for by 1912 there was a reduction of 9,000 foreign crewmen in British ships, while British crewmen increased by 30,000.[10] The intervention of the war, however, was only a temporary respite in the campaign by white seamen to reduce the numbers of foreign crewmen and secure jobs for British men. By 1921, as a contraction occurred in British shipping, there were reports of numbers of black seamen left stranded in British ports unable to find ships on which to return home and some 250 West African seamen were apparently 'starving' in Cardiff, Liverpool, Glasgow and east London.[11] Some of these men sought whatever public assistance they could in order to get a passage on a ship out of Britain. Others, however, decided to stay in the dockland areas of the ports, a situation which gave rise to official concern for further measures of control. The Board of Trade took the view that 'Coloured seamen seem to imagine that the United Kingdom is a place where there are ample opportunities of obtaining remunerative seafaring employment' and, since it seemed 'impossible to disabuse their minds of this totally erroneous idea', sought 'all practical steps' to prevent their adding to the numbers of unemployed seamen. Immigration officers were instructed by the Home Office to refuse to allow 'coloured seamen' to land unless they could satisfy one of five different criteria:

(a) If he produces satisfactory evidence of British nationality.
(b) If he has signed on in the United Kingdom for the round voyage.
(c) If, though signed on abroad, he can prove that he is domiciled in this country, and has been in the habit of signing on at British ports.
(d) If he has signed on at any distant foreign port, so that his repatriation would be almost impracticable.
(e) If the owners or agents guarantee in writing his repatriation *as a passenger* and satisfy the Immigration Officer that a passage has been or is about to be booked for him. In such a case the seaman is given leave to land on condition that he leaves the United Kingdom within a specified time and (where possible) by a specified route.[12]

These were fairly broad criteria which gave a wide latitude of interpretation and, in practice, immigration officers sought to focus their attention on West African and West Indian seamen, together with Middle Eastern seamen from Egypt, Somalia, Aden and North Africa. Lascar and Chinese seamen were engaged upon Asiatic Articles such that shipowners could be required to return home any seamen who deserted ship while in Britain. In the case of 'negro' seamen, however, the issue revolved around the deserting crewmen claiming British nationality and thus escaping conviction by local magistrates who did not distinguish between 'British protected natives' and 'British subjects'. It was pointed out by the assistant chief constable of Cardiff that prosecutions could not be successfully pursued under the existing Aliens legislation against a person who claimed British nationality but had no documentary evidence of this.[13]

The issue revolved around redefining the existing Aliens Order in specifically racial terms to widen the net away from the more conventional 'alien', who could be identified as non-British on clear cultural grounds (i.e. East European and Jewish origins), to an identification based on racial grounds which could override any cultural affiliation that a colonial seaman might claim. This change in the law was urged in 1923 by a deputation to the Board of Trade of the Seafarers' Joint Council on the grounds that the difficulty in distinguishing between seamen with authentic British nationality documentation and those trying to slip through without them led to 'unfair methods' being used, especially by Arab seamen, in the competition for jobs on the labour market. The National Sailors' and Firemen's Union claimed that 'there are two standards of morality, the morality of the East and the morality of the West', and while 'men of the Western nations compete on the open market on equal terms without paying for the privilege of getting employment, men of the Eastern nations, especially the Arabs, are always paying to bribe the employer for purposes of getting their employment'.[14] Urged to take some form of action, the Board of Trade favoured a system of registration which would have the effect of identifying those 'coloured alien seamen' already here, though in general it favoured a more *ad hoc* policy of getting local immigration officials to impress on masters of ships the need not to sign on 'coloured seamen' unless they could show documentary proof that they were British subjects.[15] As far as the objections of the Seafarers' Union was concerned, it took the view that Arab seamen should be signed on under 'Lascar Articles' so that the owners or masters of the ships they were in were responsible for their deportation from England.[16] There was the nagging feeling held also that the 'dividing line' between Arab seamen who were British subjects and those who were aliens was 'narrow and not easy to trace'.[17]

The arguments of the Seafarers' Union, though, were by no means the deciding factor in the decision to proceed with a legislative measure to ensure the registration of 'coloured seamen'. An additional dimension was the strong campaign waged by the police in the dockland towns for further controlling powers to prevent a possible repetition of the 1919 'race riots' in Liverpool and Cardiff. The police were especially effective in making their opinions known through some of the allies of the white seamen's Union such as the various sailors' charities who carried out welfare activities in the docks. A retired sea captain, Henry T. A. Bosanquet, reported the police position after a visit to Cardiff in 1921. Here some 3,000 seamen, both black and white, were laid up, of whom some 1,110 were estimated to be 'coloured British seamen' and a further 300 were 'coloured aliens'. 'It is considered that these distressed coloured seamen constitute a very serious danger to the public peace', Bosanquet concluded, 'and the Chief Constable of Cardiff has warned the Lord Mayor that rioting must be expected at any time if steps are not promptly taken to do something to ameliorate the condition of these men. Added to which it is known to the authorities that a number of undesirables have recently been imported into Cardiff on purpose to stir up discontent and to foment disturbances.' The chief cause of this potential unrest lay in the inability of boarding house masters to continue keeping the men without payment as many had been doing for the provious five months or so. Some 639 seamen were likely to be turned adrift without any work or money and unable to claim benefit even from the Lord Mayor's Relief Fund, which only covered 'permanent residents' in Cardiff and not seamen domiciled there. With the only help coming from the Missions to Seamen Institute, which provided some 3,000 to 4,000 meals a week, the solution lay in the repatriation of these 'coloured seamen' in order to ward off the threatened unrest.[18]

Given the resistance to providing aid to the black seamen by local charities, the police effectively became the key local public spokesmen, warning of the consequences if the course of deportation was not taken. In 1923 similar warnings came from Cardiff police regarding the attempts of Arab seamen to get jobs. Echoing the claims of the Seafarers' Union, the Cardiff chief constable claimed that Arab stowaways crossed the Channel from French ports 'with the connivance of the firemen' and the ships' officers, who were bribed. The chief constable urged a thorough search of vessels arriving from French ports as a means of putting pressure on the Shipowners' Federation, who, when 'burdened with the repatriation of this class of stowaway . . . would very soon give drastic instructions to their masters to search the vessels immediately prior to leaving the French ports'.[19]

This role of the police in linking a variety of local interests behind the Coloured Alien Seamen Order was further reflected in their central role in the process of registration in the years after 1925. The measure provided for compulsory registration by 'coloured seamen' with the police after 6 April 1925 if documentary proof could not be produced to show that they were British subjects. The order, therefore, had a strong criminalising element to it, especially as police chiefs' views had some weight in the actual method of enforcement. The certificate of registration had the word 'seaman' stamped or written in red ink on the front cover and contained various particulars of the individual seaman's nationality, date of birth, profession or occupation, address of residence and date of arrival in the United Kingdom. It also contained some physical descriptions such as build, height and distinctive marks such as tattoo marks, together with a photograph with an especial emphasis upon a 'clear print'.[20] At a conference of representative staff of organisations dealing with the enforcement of the Order, one chief constable urged the use of photographs taken for prison record purposes as part of the identification procedure as it was 'the type that is recognised'.[21] The issue pinpointed in many ways the strength of racial stereotyping in the perceptions of this section of British society at this time. As a Home Office memorandum pointed out, explaining the provisions of the certificate of registration: 'the difficulties arise mainly from the fact that the racial resemblance between many coloured seamen is such that there is no satisfactory means of identifying individuals'.[22] On the general question of nationality the conference of chief constables decided that the best form of identification of the holder's 'race' would be such terms as 'Malay' or 'Arab' or 'West African', though where there was any doubt the section should be left blank or 'doubtful' inserted.[23]

The approach underlying the Order, therefore, did not manifest a cohesive racial ideology, and 'racial' distinctions were perceived in an *ad hoc* and piecemeal manner. With an uncertain approach to the clarification of the relationship between 'nationality' and 'race', the Order gave considerable leeway to the discretion of individual chief constables. In the case of Manchester, there was little support from the police for inclusion in the schedule of areas covered by the Order, given the relatively small number of men – about thirty in 1925 – to whom it applied.[24] In Glasgow, on the other hand, there were pressures from the police to have the city included in the list of scheduled areas under the Order in order to register the number of Lascar seamen who, it was claimed, had come there as deserters from ships in order to become pedlars.[25] Some 100 Lascar deserters were reported as living in Glasgow and Lanarkshire, having deserted from steamers trading with India, and a number had been living in Glasgow for several years and had formed a Glasgow Indian Union. The police urged a tighter control over the granting of pedlars' certificates to the seamen and linked their presence to pimping and liaisons with white women.[26] The Home Office Immigration Department took the same view, arguing that the granting of the pedlars' certificates encouraged desertion, while the issuing of passports would be an 'open sesame' into the UK.[27] The resulting tightening-up on registration and issuing of certificates for peddling brought protests from the Indian Union led by one G. S. Varma,

the president. The Lascars in question, the Indian Union pointed out, had
been living in Glasgow from 3 to 14 years and were mostly from the Punjab.
Many had been employed during the First World War as labourers, jobs
which some of them were still doing. Since all claimed British nationality,
the implementation of the Ordinance was condemned as 'harsh and
unwarranted' and an attack on their nationality status.[28]

The issue of peddling was not solely confined to Glasgow for in
Liverpool, too, there were similar cases of deserters gaining peddling licences,
though here there was a more overtly political tinge. The Lascar seaman,
Joffer Shah, was reported as having deserted from the SS *Maidan* in
Liverpool in May 1927 and gone to live in Glasgow. Moving to Liverpool in
1920, he applied for a pedlar's certificate, which the immigration office felt
it could not refuse, despite the operation of the Coloured Alien Seaman
Order. The 'problem' represented by Joffer Shah was increasingly being
pinpointed as the network of boarding houses for black seamen in the ports,
whose owners encouraged seamen to desert, it was claimed, in order to
pursue the comparatively 'lucrative employment' of peddling. The numbers
of Lascar deserters was reported as 'growing daily' while one immigration
officer commented on the links with political movements in India.[29] 'In all
the villages and suburbs in this part', he wrote in October 1930, 'one sees
these coloured pedlars going from door to door, and I was told by a CID
officer the other day that some of them were rampant propagandists on the
Indian question both by the remarks and innuendoes they make to the
people on whom they call with their wares and occasionally by taking part
in meetings, at which they are allowed to speak for India'.[30]

By the late 1920s the political limits on further governmental action at the
legislative level began to become clear. The Home Office Aliens Branch,
under its chief inspector, Sir Haldane Porter, considered in 1926 that issuing
emergency certificates at least had the effect of preventing further increases
in the number of incoming black seamen into Britain, while any further
action implied some form of restriction on the rights of British nationals to
enter Britain. On the latter point, given the pre-eminence of imperial notions
of equal British citizenship, the government felt unable to act.[31] This
opposition to an immigration control procedure that contained overt racial
features led some local police chiefs to adopt a segregationist and anti-
miscegenationist standpoint. The Cardiff chief constable, James A.
Wilson, argued before the local watch committee for legislation to prohibit
inter-racial sexual intercourse on lines similar to the recently passed
Immorality Act of 1927 in South Africa:

> In other parts of the Empire, including the British Isles, there is
> reason to believe that the knowledge, by the male members of the

white race, of social ostracism is a sufficient deterrent to them but, strangely, that feeling does not dominate a certain class of women in the British Isles. It may be that some of the inhabitants of the Motherland are more tolerant on this subject, but this tolerance has led to a state of affairs which demands the attention of serious thinking people.

The day may come when public opinion will awake to the fact that our race has become leavened with colour strain to such an extent that calls for action. Someone must have the courage to take the initiative, explain the position, and strike a warning note . . . . There appears to be no valid reason why steps should not be taken, on the grounds of good order and the welfare of the different races, so that Parliament may be urged to consider the desirability of bringing into existence in this country legislation similar to that which has been found necessary in the Union of South Africa.[32]

The appeal for anti-miscegenation legislation came as a logical accompaniment to the earlier campaign for social control in the docks through the Coloured Alien Seamen's Order. The same year, the chief constable complained that the black seamen in Cardiff came into contact with the white prostitutes 'with the result that children are born whose lineaments unmistakeably indicate the origin of the male parent. In other words their progeny are half-caste with the vicious hereditary taint of their parents.'[33] By pinpointing the issue in terms of 'half-castes', the Cardiff chief constable developed the previously *ad hoc* definitions of 'race' into a far more coherent ideology of racial decay that bore strong eugenic resemblances. The imperial model and the appeal to South African precedents were crucial in this racialising process, for 'welfare' in this context was assumed to accrue from implicit racial separation and the prohibition on inter-racial marriage and sexual contact.[34] This ideology of racial separationism was also functional in helping to crystallise public attitudes to more general aspects of the docklands issue where simple racial definitions in terms of colour did not easily apply. The arguments of the Cardiff chief constable to the watch committee were partly used, for instance, to sustain the case for further control over Maltese café owners who, it was argued, effectively connived at a system of pimping and prostitution which threatened the purity of the white race: 'They are debased and degenerate types. They practice, despite the vigilance of the police, those disreputable vices *ingrained in them from early environment*. They do not appreciate the British point of view with regard to prostitution. To them it is a commonplace of life and a matter of business'[35] (emphasis added).

The rationale behind these arguments was the increasing of police powers of control over the boarding houses in the ports in order to restrict the numbers of seamen in particular areas. These houses provided havens for those unemployed black seamen who had difficulty in appealing for help from the local welfare organisations and the Board of Guardians under the Poor Law, and were thus seen as the chief obstacle to a labour recruitment system on the ships that was free from bribery.[36] In 1930 the National Union of Seamen and the shipowners negotiated an agreement for a rota system to cover Arab and 'coloured' seamen to prevent the continuation of this bribery. All such seamen were obliged under the agreement to register at offices of the National Maritime Board Joint Supply, where they would receive registration cards. When a crew of Arabs or blacks was then required by a shipmaster the necessary men would be obtained through this joint supply system. The NUS saw the system as an effective method of control over the number of black seamen gaining jobs on British ships and, as its journal, *The Seaman*, argued, would 'give satisfaction to bona fide Arabs [*sic*] and will solve a very vexed question in addition to preventing any further racial disturbance'.[37]

The agreement, however, strengthened in some parts the arm of the police and immigration authorities against the unemployed black seamen and thus enhanced the case for deportation. In Barry Dock in South Wales, the number of boarding houses was reduced by the county authorities in 1930, after reports by the chief sanitary inspector, thus limiting the lodging facilities available for seamen seeking registration under the Joint Supply agreement. This drove a number of seamen back to living in Cardiff and, when a group of four Arab seamen sought to register in Barry in September 1930, they were refused by the police there and compelled to return to Cardiff. 'With a view to avoiding any possibility of having to provide relief for destitute coloured seamen', a sergeant of the Cardiff police complained, 'the authorities at other South Wales ports are taking every step to discourage these men to reside in those areas.'[38]

While the implementation of the rota system went ahead in Cardiff and South Wales without any significant opposition, things were somewhat different in South Shields and the North-East, where the left-wing Seamen's Minority Movement gained some following among Arab and Somali as well as some white seamen in the early 1930s. The Movement attacked in particular the strong degree of control given to the NUS by the rota system and the system of registration through the PC5 form, which, at a fee of £2, was essential for a seaman to get a ship.[39] At a time when 22,346 British seamen were unemployed, 2,051 of these in North and South Shields, the Minority Movement organised a protest meeting on 24 July 1930, and on 2 August there was a reported 'riot' at South Shields when the Arab crew of the ship *Linkmoor* refused to get a PC5 or register on the rota. When the NUS and the Shipping Federation sought to engage white firemen, a fight ensued and a number of seamen were arrested by the police and later charged, on 4 August, with a riot and riotous assembly. The sentences ranged from 3 to 16 months in prison, while the majority of the Arab seamen were deported.[40]

The Home Office took the view that it would 'go against the grain' for the police to grant registration under the 1925 Order to men who had 'probably taken an active part in disturbances against the system at S. Shields'.[41] Further deportations ensued the following year of Arab seamen who had been either convicted of offences in August or else dealt with by the local Public Assistance Committee, which sought deportation orders under the 1925 Aliens Order against men who were living on public assistance in local boarding houses, but could not claim British nationality.[42]

Overall, therefore, the 1925 Coloured Alien Seamen Order enhanced both the powers of the police, the National Union of Seamen and the Public Assistance Committees in the ports in establishing a system of control over the movements and job-seeking patterns of black seamen. It tended to enhance, too, the racial manner in which the presence of black seamen residing in British port towns was perceived by authorities and public alike, for the Order acted as a catalyst for a political debate about the general effects of 'mongrelisation' and 'miscegenation', which had been seen as a cause of the 1919 Riots.

This anti-miscegenation campaign was couched in strongly imperial terms throughout most of the inter-war period. In 1919 the *Daily Herald* reported a former missionary in South Africa, the Rev. Dr F. B. Meyer, arguing in Cardiff against 'a mixture of races' for 'mongrels were always despised and found it hard to hold their own'. Furthermore, 'the true policy of the Empire must be to govern so that each race should have the best chance of full development in its own country'.[43] In 1929, too, the proposal for a legal outlawing of miscegenation by the Cardiff chief constable, James Mitchener, was in terms of the South African model. In the early 1930s, however, the ideology behind which the campaign was conducted began to change as new interests, centred around the university settlement movement, particularly in Liverpool, began to focus on the issue. This led to a more eugenic and 'scientific' discussion of 'miscegenation', which was now seen more in national terms. By the mid-1930s the result was a more nationally focused campaign for the control of black immigration, organised from London.

'Half-caste' children and pressure for immigration control

While the main focus in the 1920s was on the presence of black seamen in the ports and their liaisons with white women, by the 1930s this had widened to the issue of mixed-race or 'half-caste' children who were the offspring of these sexual relationships. By 1929 the *Daily Herald* was already reporting that 'hundreds of half-caste children with vicious tendencies' were 'growing up in Cardiff as the result of black men mating with white women' while 'numerous dockland cafés run by coloured men of a debased and degenerate type are rendezvous for immoral purposes'.[44] The emergence of 'half-caste' children as a social problem resulted in social workers being brought into the debate and this led to a growing interest by the Liverpool University Settlement. This body had opened in 1908 in Nile Street, Liverpool, as part of the philanthropic concern of university social reformers in the tradition of Toynbee Hall in London's East End.[45] The Liverpool settlement served as an important centre for different interests in the city to come together to discuss current social issues. In December 1927, a meeting was organised by the University School of Social Science to discuss the question of the welfare of 'half-caste' children in the city and representatives of both the university, the settlement and the police were present.[46] Significantly, the main address came from the assistant to Professor H. J. Fleure at Aberystwyth, Miss R. M. Fleming, who had conducted research on 'half-castes' in Britain following pressure by the Eugenics Education Society on the Colonial Office for a survey of 'half-castes', in the early 1920s. Fleming had been schooled in an atmosphere where 'racial' and cultural traits tended to be confused and there was an implication within her research that separate races inherited certain cultural characteristics, though not necessarily within any rigid racial hierarchy.[47] At the meeting she spoke of the 'adverse factors' in 'half-caste' children's heredity 'which often involve not only disharmony of physical traits but disharmony of mental characteristics'. This resulted, she claimed, in 'great strain', for the children 'had no homes and were unable to obtain employment in any decent occupation'. Moreover, she concluded, a 'very high proportion of such children suffered from tuberculosis or similar diseases'.[48]

The meeting led to an executive committee being formed, chaired by Professor Roxby of the School of Geography in Liverpool, which launched an appeal for £2,000 to provide a fund both for alleviating the conditions of the children concerned and to pay the salary of a 'well-qualified social worker' to 'devote all her time to the finding of possible solutions to the problem'.[49] In the event, only £652 was collected by the following May in order to finance an investigation (despite a promise of $25,000 from the Rockefeller Memorial Fund).[50] Nevertheless, the executive committee, which was now the nucleus of the Liverpool Association for the Welfare of Half-Caste Children, decided to appoint a probation officer at Stoke-on-

Trent (and former student of the Liverpool University School of Social Science), Miss M. E. Fletcher, to conduct the survey from October of 1928.

The inadequate resources and amateur approach of the investigator led to a controversial report being produced in 1930 entitled *Report on an Investigation into the Colour Problem in Liverpool and Other Ports*. Though praised by Professor Roxby as 'the most thorough investigation of this particular problem that has so far been made',[51] the report reinforced the initial approach of R. M. Fleming in 1927 when it perceived the presence of 'half-caste' children in Liverpool and other ports as an intrinsic moral problem conducive to the perpetuation of prostitution and a slumland culture. It also strengthened the campaign by the police and the National Union of Seamen against the presence of black 'alien seamen' in British ports since the early 1920s. The claims of many seamen to British nationality could in many cases, the report concluded, 'hardly be substantiated', for many were in fact 'Liberians or at the most, British protected persons'. Furthermore, there were 'strong reasons' for believing that the passports which were issued were done so 'by native clerks on the West Coast of Africa to all coloured seamen who apply, without their claim being questioned'.[52] The report thus recommended the replacement of black firemen by white firemen on British ships, despite recognising the 'probable political reactions' which would result from this. It also urged that black seamen from West Africa should 'sign on' there so that they would have to make a 'round trip' since they would not be paid in Britain, while 'greater discrimination' should be exercised in the issuing of British passports'.[53] Not surprisingly, the report received strong support from the National Union of Seamen.[54]

Another important feature of the report was its portrayal of the social and economic conditions of mixed-race children within hereditarian and eugenical terms. M. E. Fletcher reported an estimated total of some 450 families in Liverpool with such children; with an average number of 3.3 per family she estimated a total of 1,350 coloured children.[55] The health and welfare of these children was judged within a framework heavily influenced by the research of R. M. Fleming, who in 1929 visited Cape Town with the British Association and wrote up her research on mixed-race children in British seaport towns under some influence from the South African model. In an article, 'Human Hybrids', in the *Eugenics Review* she noted the 'higher cultural level' of those Cape Coloureds 'with a larger admixture of white blood' and condoned the Coloured practice of 'passing for white'. In general, though, Fleming opposed any discrimination against mixed-race children:

They are British citizens, and as such need protection. Whatever action may be taken to prevent such intermixture in the future, if it can be proved to be undesirable, it certainly seems a bad policy of citizenship to penalize half-castes for a fault of birth for which they are in no way responsible.[56]

For the period, this was in some respects a 'liberal' perspective on the issue, despite the fact that it engrained both a middle-class paternalism and a view of 'miscegenation' as a 'fault of birth'. The same perspective lay behind the Fletcher Report, though the evidence collected from schools also indicated little support for a hereditarian pathology behind 'miscegenation':

> Opinions have been expressed from time to time that in the question of health the half caste children suffer in comparison with the white. In so far as school children are concerned, however, no evidence has been found to confirm these statements. Out of eighty teachers replying, sixty three stated that the half caste children were not more prone to infectious disease. In the matter of attendance at school, the half caste children appear to be quite up to standard and are quite as well clothed as the white children in the district, in some cases even better. With regard to intelligence and social aptitude, the majority of the replies received indicated that the half caste children were below average. Opinions had been stated that the Coloured children had marked ability in various branches of handwork, forty nine teachers replied, however, that the half caste children under their care exhibited no particular aptitude for handwork. In the matter of reliability, forty one teachers were of the opinion that the half caste children were up to the average of the white children, while thirty eight replied that they were below standard. Nothing startling emerges from this enquiry. The half caste children on the whole appear to be below the average, but only slightly so.[57]

The chief influence of the report, nevertheless, lay in its reinforcement of the view that the presence of 'half-castes' in British cities contributed to a process of moral decline. When reporting on the labour prospects of the children, the Fletcher Report indicated a marked unwillingness of employers to engage 'coloured' labour. Of 119 firms written to in Liverpool, only 56 replied and 45 of these gave a negative response.[58] Furthermore, the Committee of the Liverpool Association for the Welfare of Half-Caste Children itself initiated a training scheme for coloured girls, concentrating on five girls attending a class of one hour twice a week. The scheme was eventually abandoned after the girls exhibited little motivation to complete the course and Fletcher concluded that the girls 'easily tire and lack the power of application'.[59] The failure of the scheme was probably one reason behind her conclusion that the presence of coloured families in Britain 'presents a special problem both from a moral and an economic point of view' and that the employment of 'half-caste juveniles', especially girls, should be the subject of an official inquiry.[60]

The report's findings led to an angry response from some of the missions involved with the black population in Liverpool and the League of Coloured Peoples in London also took up the issue. Ernest Adkin of the African and West Indian Mission in Parliament Street, Liverpool, claimed that it would take 'months, or even years to repair the damage the publicity of the report has carried'. Miss Fletcher, he claimed, had 'posed as an interested worker with deep sympathy for these unfortunate people, and their half-caste children, and . . . they trusted her implicitly, many thinking more of her sympathy than of mine . . . . Some of them said that they could never trust a white person again; no matter what his pretensions. I have lost several whose help and sympathy I valued, and many more who came occasionally.'[61]

The furore shook both the University Settlement and the Association for the Welfare of Half-Caste Children, which failed in 1931 to secure any government interest in the issue.[62] M. E. Fletcher left Liverpool as a result of the report and the fact that no funds were available in the depression for her appointment as a permanent welfare officer for the Association.[63] The report represented a brief instrusion of eugenics into the 'half-caste' issue in Liverpool, and by the end of 1931 a different approach began with the publication of the first of the social surveys of Merseyside from the University of Liverpool by D. Caradog Jones, which perceived the issue within a much wider framework of immigration generally into the region, including Irish and Jewish immigration as well as that of black and Chinese immigrants. When seen in this wider context, the issue of black immigration into Merseyside was comparatively small, for the communities of Chinese and blacks was estimated at about 500 each. The Jewish population on Merseyside, on the other hand, was estimated at 9,000 while the total net immigration from Ireland between 1927 and 1929 was estimated at about 6,000 a year.[64] Taken as a whole, the immigration into Merseyside was estimated by Caradog Jones to have had strongly beneficial economic effects, for a higher percentage of the immigrant population was in regular work than the indigenous population while there was less overcrowding and poverty amongst them.[65] The survey noted, though, the general problem of 'Anglo-negroid' children in obtaining employment compared to the more successful Anglo-Chinese children.[66] This was not an issue that got taken up in any systematic way on Merseyside itself in the early 1930s after the Fletcher Report, though similar unpublished reports by F. S. Livie-Noble of the London Group on African Affairs on Cardiff and a survey of London and Cardiff in 1932 by Nancy Sharpe, using funds from the Methodist Church, emphasised both the environmental context in which such mixed-race children grew up and defended the right of black seamen to work on British ships and come to live in Britain if they had the necessary national documentation.[67]

The intervention of the Anti-Slavery Society

The Merseyside social survey led to some extent to a diverting of attention in Liverpool away from the 'half-caste' issue onto the more general question of immigration, especially from Ireland, in the early 1930s.[68] The black–white issue in Britain, however, began to attract the attention of groups in London.[69] In particular, John Harris of the Anti-Slavery Society became interested in the matter for he found the Fletcher Report an 'extraordinarily able document' containing 'the most impressive and authoritative detail'.[70] Over the next few years Harris tried to capitalise upon its arguments in order to mobilise a campaign to restrict black immigration into the ports. The 'growth of coloured and half-caste communities', he wrote, was a 'growing evil'. Estimating the total numbers involved as around 10,000 in such ports as Liverpool, Cardiff and London's dockland, Harris played upon the disease issue: only 10% of the tuberculosis and venereal disease cases in Liverpool hospitals were white, he claimed. The nature of 'this sordid evil' was thus so 'tragic' that 'no government' could 'continue to ignore it'. Bringing his colonial perspective to bear, Harris especially emphasised the social consequences of inter-racial sexual liaisons from the vantage point of colonial experience:

> It is true that many a white girl, no less than many Africans and West Indians are making a brave effort to lead lives in every respect worthy of British subjects, while several of them are regular and devoted members of Christian churches, but in the mass their conditions are so degrading that the ordinary decencies that exist even in an African village put to shame some of these areas in Cardiff, Liverpool and London.[71]

This linked mixed-race marriages and 'half-caste communities' with a slumland culture and a disease metaphor more strongly than the Fletcher Report. By the early 1930s, Harris's work for the Welfare of Africans in Europe Committee had led him to establish several contacts with seamen's societies, who had often referred to him cases of 'distressed black seamen' which they themselves did not wish to handle. The British Sailors' Society in 1930, for example, contributed a £5 donation to Harris's committee both in appreciation of its work and 'in view of the fact that the colour question has been, and is likely to be in the future, an acute problem'.[72] Thus, Harris's emphasis upon the racial aspects of the half-caste issue to some extent reflected a more general racialisation of thought in various charitable and welfare bodies within British dockland.

The importance, though, of Harris's taking up the issue lay in its growing national focus. While the Fletcher Report had highlighted the Merseyside issue, with some reference to a more general national context at the end, Harris sought to coordinate the various provincial organisations into a coherent national lobby, the first real lobby specifically opposing black immigration in British politics. At first, he moved cautiously, rejecting the idea from another member of the Welfare of Africans in Europe Committee, W. H. Grey, that an approach should be made immediately to the Colonial Office to get the shipping companies to sign on all their black crews in West Africa for a 'round trip', as the Fletcher Report had suggested.[73] Harris hoped to capitalise upon the existing momentum generated by the report and visited Liverpool in the autumn of 1930 to start a wider organisational coordination.[74]

The temporary demise of the Liverpool Association for the Welfare of Half-Caste Children at the end of 1930, however, dashed these initial hopes. Over the following four years further developments in the field of race relations activity occurred in London to put a damper on Harris's projected campaign. A number of church groups came together in 1931 under the leadership of the Quaker, John Fletcher, to establish The Joint Council to Promote Understanding between White and Coloured People in Great Britain, modelled to some extent on lines similar to the Joint Council developed in South Africa by white liberals after the First World War.[75] With relatively well-known personalities on the Council such as Winifred Holtby, the novelist, Vera Brittain, and the black doctor, Harold Arundel Moody, the limelight was stolen from Harris's campaign for immigration restriction. The Joint Council reflected a new mood in Britain in the early 1930s, epitomised by the success of such black actors as Paul Robeson and Norris Smith, of upper-middle-class liberalism on race. It was now fashionable to have well-known black personalities at parties and social functions, while there was also a growing interest in black music and singers such as John Payne and Leslie Hutchinson.[76] Thus, on the question of mixed marriages and 'half-castes', the Joint Council did not especially exhibit any particular enthusiasm, though at the end of 1932, following an interview between John Fletcher and Rachel Fleming, a group including Rachel Fleming, Professor Seligman, Lancelot Hogben, Harold Moody and Shoran S. Singha was set up to look into it.[77] The Joint Council, in fact, was far more concerned with the issue of 'the colour bar' as opposed to mixed marriages *per se*, for it had been a discussion on this in the Quaker journal, *The Friend*, in 1929 and a Conference on the Colour Bar in Great Britain which had led to the Joint Council being established in the first place.[78]

By 1932, the Joint Council began to run out of steam as the more politically significant League of Coloured Peoples was formed by Harold Moody. The LCP has been described as 'the first conscious and deliberate attempt to form a multi-racial organization led by blacks' in Britain, and its political significance lay in its bridging the gap between the mainstream white paternalistic bodies like the Anti-Slavery Society and the more locally based student bodies such as the West African Students' Union (WASU) led by Ladipo Solanke.[79] Certainly, it eclipsed the efforts of the white liberals led by John Fletcher and Winifred Holtby, who became increasingly disorganised during the 1930s, especially after Winifred Holtby's death in 1935.[80] Despite attacks from small groups of left-wing intellectuals organised in London through the Negro Welfare Association in the early 1930s and the international monthly magazine, *The Negro Worker*, which accused Moody of being an 'Uncle Tom' for supporting the establishment of a hostel in London for black students in Aggrey House,[81] the LCP was successful in filling an important middle position in English race relations. To some extent, Harris's committee was won over by Moody's search for support in missionary and Colonial Office circles during these years and Harris himself grudgingly gave his backing for the LCP's welfare and social work in such fields as hostel accommodation and employment finding.[82]

In 1935, however, renewed racial conflict in Cardiff, following pressure from the National Union of Seamen to reclassify jobs on British ships as white, provided a new opportunity for Harris to launch his campaign. Harris was surprised by the turn of events in the city,[83] though the causes of the renewed 'unrest' had been brewing for some years with demands from the NUS for a distinction to be made between 'foreign coloured seamen' and 'coloured seamen, natives of British possessions or protectorates, who are domiciled in this country' and who thus received the same standard of wages as British whites.[84] In April 1934, the Communist-dominated League Against Imperialism claimed that the 'Cardiff representative' of the NUS was urging captains and engineers in the city to sign on only white crews.[85] This agitation was exacerbated the following year when the British Shipping (Assistance) Act was passed in order to try and revive the industry by limiting the amount of British freight in order to meet overseas competition. While the shipowners were to scrap surplus tonnage, the government would reimburse them through a series of subsidy payments. The scheme was administered by a Tramp Shipping Administrative Committee (TSAC) which was empowered to grant the subsidies providing the shipowners gave first preference for employment on their surviving ships to seamen and firemen of British nationality. With unemployment in Cardiff Bute docks totalling some 5,236 at the end of 1935, the situation was explosive and a united movement of African, West Indian, Arab, Somali and Malay seamen called the Coloured Seamen's Union was formed to resist the discriminatory measure.[86]

A full-scale riot was narrowly averted in Cardiff in April 1935 only through pressure from the LCP on the chairman of the TASC to reinstate coloured seamen on the SS *Ethel Radcliffe*.[87] The LCP sent a team of investigators to Cardiff and tried to establish a branch in the city, Moody considering that the success of the League in its mediating efforts to be a full vindication of his previous work in building up the organisation.[88] The established missions and welfare bodies, such as the Salvation Army, the League of Goodwill and the Wesleyan Church Mission run by the Rev. Stanley Watson, were in some degree outmanoeuvred and John Harris wrote that Moody had been given an 'open cheque' to keep the chief constable of Cardiff informed of any new 'urgent cases'. 'The whole situation is so bad, so complicated socially and politically', he asserted, 'that we think it can only be met adequately by two or three of us going down and having a frank discussion with everybody concerned.'[89]

The intervention of the LCP in Cardiff, however, had really shown the increasing ineffectiveness of the old English welfare and missionary bodies, whose inability to influence matters at the local level partly explained the rechannelling of their energy the following year into pressure on the central government to tighten up on the recruitment procedure for black seamen. Considering the whole issue a 'festering sore',[90] Harris began planning a deputation to the Home Office at the end of 1935. The Liverpool Association for the Welfare of Half-Caste Children had been revived in the course of 1934, and in July 1935 it was stimulated to renew its work after the publication of a report by Captain F. A. Richardson on a survey conducted by the anti-venereal disease and strongly pro-imperial British Social Hygiene Council together with the British Council for the Welfare of the Mercantile Marine. Though focused on Cardiff, the Report reached conclusions substantially similar to the Fletcher Report, reproducing a classically Victorian teleological racism based on geographical differences:

> Morality and cleanliness are as much matters of geography as they
> are dependent on circumstances. The coloured men who have

come to dwell in our cities are being made to adopt a standard of civilisation they cannot be expected to understand. They are not imbued with moral codes similar to our own, and they have not assimilated our conventions of life .... . They come into intimate contact with white women, principally; those who unfortunately are of loose moral character, with the result that a half-caste population is brought into the world ...

The half-caste girl is characteristically disinclined to discipline and routine, and efforts made to encourage and train her have mostly met with failure. By nature and environment, and by the handicaps of colour and common prejudice, these girls have very little chance but to sink to an even lower level.[91]

This new input of survey research, combined with a eugenicist folk wisdom on race differences, helped define the approach of the Liverpool Association to Harris's efforts to widen the issue to British seaports generally.[92] Harold King, warden of the Liverpool University Settlement, and an active figure in the Association for Half-Caste Children, responded positively to Harris's overtures. The general impression of 'most people' in Liverpool, he claimed, was that the numbers of half-caste children was rising and this was confirmed by 'unofficial estimates' by headmasters. The problem was, however, complicated by the fact that the 'machinery for distinguishing half-caste negroid children is in a very elementary state'. The Association itself had established a 'special bureau' in cooperation with the local Juvenile Employment Committee for 'these unfortunate children', though for half-caste girls he concluded that 'there is apparently little alternative to prostitution'. Overall, the presence of black seamen had 'created a most disturbing moral and social condition which is tending to worsen steadily if slowly as time goes on'.[93]

The attitude of fatalism projected by the surveys of social conditions and employment opportunities of the 'half-caste' communities touched in some respects a traditional chord within the anti-slavery impulse. The image of hapless and passive hybrids created through the perceived immorality of black seamen cohabiting with white women in seaport towns (which the middle-class anti-slavers understood less then the more simple African villages) led them to see a new race of aboriginals emerging who were ill-equipped to survive in the inhospitable industrial society of Britain. 'The problem of these unfortunate people is, I fear, almost insoluble', John Harris despairingly wrote in early 1936, 'all we can do is to help them to the best of our respective ability.'[94] The tone here was considerably different from the image projected by the National Union of Seamen and the *Daily Herald* of the inherent 'viciousness' of the half-caste, though in this respect the Anti-Slavery Society was adopting its traditional Victorian posture of

translating political conflicts at the local level, which were strongly rooted
in economic competition and struggle for scarce jobs, into essentially moral
issues that could become acceptable to established political opinion in
Westminster and Whitehall.

Lobbying central government

The request for a formal deputation to the Home Office was made by Harris
in February 1936 after some discussion over the terms of his proposals with
the Liverpool Association for the Welfare of Half-Caste Children. Noting
that the black community in the seaports numbered some 10,000, Harris
emphasised the 'political danger' from their presence, especially as there
had been 'two serious race riots'. It was, however, the 'moral aspect' which
was most deplorable and in describing the situation of half-castes considerable documentation from the Fletcher Report was used. While the 'ideal
plan' would be 'to arrange for the progressive return of these men to their
respective countries', it was recognised that there were difficulties involved
in this and, in essence, the recommended measures strongly echoed the
demands of the NUS for the 'paying-off' of black seamen in their countries
of origin. Harris also sought the removal of grievances over registration
cards for seamen with British national status while 'an arrangement might
be made with the trade union to assist the men to obtain employment
without a precedent cash payment'. On the issue of half-caste children 'the
problem' was seen as 'almost insoluble', though it was urged that 'steps
might be found for raising the standard of these children nearer to that of the
white races, rather than to leave them to drift down to that of the black' – a
significantly colonial response that echoed similar calls from white liberals
in the Cape in South Africa to upgrade the Coloured population there in
order to act as some form of buffer between whites and Africans.[95]

The Home Office response to Harris's call for an enquiry was muted,
with the general climate of civil service opinion being to take a low keyed
response to the previous year's disturbances in Cardiff. E. H. Cooper
considered the idea a 'very questionable move, having regard to all the
racial prejudice and political issues which it would raise without being able
to suggest any proposals which could tend to appease an already difficult
situation'.[96] The Home Office did not consider itself especially well
equipped to deal with such unfamiliar race matters in the ports and its
interest in methods of 'appeasement' suggested that it was at least as
pleased by the mediating efforts of Moody's LCP in 1935 as it was with
Harris's contentious proposals. Furthermore, there was the all-important
question of whether tightening up even further the measures restricting
entry of black seamen should be extended to those seamen holding British

nationality documentation. In a memorandum it was pointed out that the Home Office, in consultation with the colonies and protectorates, had already made it difficult for black seamen to obtain passports to come to Britain, while the Tramp Shipping Administrative Committee favoured the allocation of jobs to white seamen. If, however, the purpose of the deputation was to suggest the amendment of the law to exclude or deport black British nationals, this 'would raise questions of far-reaching constitutional importance, which would be beyond the scope of any ordinary committee of enquiry set up to deal with a limited objective and any recommendation on the matter made by such a committee would only be a source of embarrassment to His Majesty's Government'.[97]

By the time of the actual deputation to the Home Office on 28 July 1936, therefore, the government response to the possible proposals was already fairly clear-cut, ruling out in particular any restrictions on the immigration of black British nationals. The case for this was put most forcibly by the representative on the deputation from the British Sailors' Society, the Rev. Geo. F. Dempster. Warning that there were unemployed black seamen 'at a loose end' in the provinces and villages of England, Dempster emphasised the political dimension. With the war in Abyssinia, 'the eyes of all Abyssinians and Africans are upon this country' for 'We have the mentality of the man of Southern Rhodesia.'[98] When pressed on the issue of legislative restriction, however, he urged the need for measures additional to simple repatriation.

The main thrust of the deputation's arguments was on the welfare dimensions involved in dealing with the presence of black communities in the ports. The Rev. J. H. S. Bates warned of the birth-rate of coloured children and of the possibility that schools would not be able to absorb them.[99] In a letter subsequent to the deputation, Harold King backed up his assertions on the increase in the coloured 'problem' in Liverpool by claiming that there was evidence of an 'organised influx of women' from other cities to Liverpool to meet the demands of the coloured men there.[100] For the most part, though, the Home Office sought to deflect the wilder claims of the deputation and the Under Secretary of State, Geoffrey Lloyd, concluded by emphasising the need for greater coordination of the work of the separate voluntary agencies involved in the welfare work in the ports – a theme that was to characterise much subsequent discussion on race relations in Britain in the late 1940s and 1950s.[101]

The deputation came away feeling that it had made some form of impact on government thinking and by November the one MP involved, Captain Arthur Evans, MP for Cardiff, reported that an inter-departmental committee had been established to review the issues discussed.[102] However, the response from the Home Office was not to set up a committee but to hold a conference, on 2 December 1936, which effectively decided to defuse the whole matter by instituting a series of local inquiries in four or five of the ports.[103] Home Office thinking was considerably influenced by pressure from both the Colonial Office and the India Office not to change the law on nationality and deport black British nationals,[104] while the Ministry of Labour reported that the claims regarding the poor employment position of half-caste juveniles were exaggerated. Labour exchanges reported a decrease in the number of such juveniles on their books since the Fletcher Report and there was a call for welfare work to be focused on a decentralised basis through the local Port Welfare Committees rather than be treated as a national issue on terms suggested by the deputation.[105]

The decision effectively stalled any further action by the Welfare Committee and the Liverpool Association at a national level, for much of their campaign had heavily depended upon evoking a positive governmental response. As organisations geared mainly towards lobbying established political opinion, they were not especially fitted towards launching a mass campaign. In December 1936 a conference was held in Liverpool to discuss whether further action could be taken to support the aims of the deputation the previous July to the Home Office. John Harris attended for the Anti-Slavery Society together with missionaries from Cardiff and Hull, while members of the local Liverpool Juvenile Employment Bureau also came. While the general mood of the conference favoured a widening of the issue to cover Arab and Lascar seamen, much of the future coordination of the various local work depended upon the intended government responses. When this became known the following January, Harris was to some extent left isolated, having lost face over his previous attempts to demonstrate his ability to influence central government.[106] The conference was noteworthy, though, for its raising the wider issue of black settlement in Britain as a whole, which was to occupy so much official thinking from the late 1940s onwards. 'The question of the dispersal of the coloured population owing to rehousing was discussed', the minutes noted, 'and it was suggested that Sir Kingsley Wood (the new Home Secretary) might be asked if there are any advantages in segregation.'[107]

After the December 1936 conference the issue was not taken up again in any systematic way before the Second World War. The coordination of local welfare work became difficult if the precise overall objectives remained vague, while the actual character of the different local organisations began to change. In Cardiff, the South Wales Association for the Welfare of Coloured People, led by a Wesleyan missionary from Trinidad, the Rev. Stanley Watson, conducted a campaign in 1937 in favour of easing the pressure on black seamen in Britain to produce documentary evidence of British nationality. It urged that the Coloured Alien Seamen Order be withdrawn as 'an insidious intrusion of the colour bar into the laws of this realm' and demanded a revision of the regulations against aliens who had been resident in Britain for several years. Such men, the Association argued, 'have no hope of obtaining employment in their own calling in their own countries . . . to retain unrevised regulations which force them to live in the direst poverty is unjust and a further disturbing factor in the present inter-racial situation'.[108] Such a stand against racial discrimination was also reflected by the increasing criticism being made by the League of Coloured Peoples, through its journal, *The Keys*, of racial discrimination against black seamen in the ports. The League held a conference in June 1937 in London which attacked the 'propaganda which is made in Parliament and elsewhere for the repatriation of the seamen or else for their segregation' and called for the LCP to 'take active steps' to 'remove any discrimination between British citizens on account of their colour or race'.[109]

In the period after 1937 up to Harris's death in 1940, the call for stepping-up repatriation of black seamen and dealing with half-caste children as a 'moral problem' came to be seen as increasingly outmoded. This growing racial toleration occurred, as F. Henriques has suggested, somewhat later than the period after the riots that immediately followed the First World War. The issue of 'half castes', as this chapter has shown, was still an important one in political debate in Britain until at least the late 1930s. But Harris and the Anti-Slavery Society were increasingly attacked for their paternalism in race relations, especially on the issue of control over Aggrey House, the centre for the West African Students' Union in London.[111] With little or no standing amongst the black political groups in London, Harris's credibility became further undermined by his association with the Liverpool Association for the Welfare of Half-Caste Children. Harold King's control over the Association had been marked by a refusal to establish any contacts with the LCP in its welfare work for 'half-castes', and Charles Collett, the general secretary of the LCP, accused the Association of contributing to 'anti-colour mongering' in Britain so that, while Harris urged the League to look to the work of King and the Association, it was clear that the previous record of the Liverpool organisation since the Fletcher Report prevented any real contacts being made.[112] Harold King left Liverpool in 1939 and in a sense an era had come to an end by then in British race relations. The Liverpool Association for the Welfare of Half-Caste Children was renamed the Liverpool Association for the Welfare of Coloured People and its thinking in the 1940s became heavily influenced by the Merseyside social surveys of D. Caradog Jones and the Liverpool University School of Social Science. Jones himself became Chairman of the Association's executive committee.[113]

The comparative success of the LCP in the latter part of the 1930s in establishing itself as an authentic voice of the small black middle-class elite in Britain indicated a new pattern of political collaboration after the start of the Second World War and the intrusion of the Colonial Office into race relations in Britain. The previous weaknesses of the Home Office in its dealings with the seaports in the 1920s and 1930s and the Victorian paternalism of the Anti-Slavery Society suggested that a new approach was needed.

To some extent, the issue became defused by the onset of war and a resurgence of employment. However, a sign of the new ideological climate was the publication of a new survey in 1940 by the Social Sciences Department of the University of Liverpool entitled *The Economic Status of Coloured Families in the Port of Liverpool*, which confirmed the conclusions of the previous social survey of 1931. Covering some 225 families, the 1940 survey found that unemployment of black seamen had been higher over the previous ten years than it had been for white seamen, though only 40% of the sample was currently in employment. Overall, though, it studiously avoided a pathological view of black living conditions in Liverpool for 'whilst visible evidence of healthier homes and better clad men, women and children exists today for English people', it concluded, 'there is similar evidence to show the increasing upgrading of similar conditions as affecting the coloured population'.[114] The survey broadly reflected the general mood favouring an enhancement of the welfare state in Britain as a means of alleviating poverty and deprivation and it was within this general social transformation that it was assumed the specific problems surrounding black employment and living conditions would disappear.[115] In a similar manner, thinking on colonial issues also moved towards one of development and welfare in the late 1930s and here, too, the presence of black students or immigrant workers in Britain in the 1940s was assumed to be linked to colonial development programmes overseas. Not until the early 1950s did it start to become apparent that this overlooked the specific question of racial discrimination affecting black people permanently resident in Britain, who were in effect 'black British'. Nevertheless, the British government now found that the 'colonial question' of race relations had moved into the heart of the imperial metropolis itself.

7

Colonial development, war and black immigration

The outbreak of the Second World War in 1939 ushered in the beginnings of a new era in British race relations which was to culminate in the relinquishing of the colonial empire in the 1950s and early 1960s. The long neglect of economic and social development in British colonies since the short-lived schemes of Joseph Chamberlain in the mid-1890s[1] now began to come to an end as British colonial administrators turned their attention to the question of formulating development programmes which would provide the infrastructure both for increased economic production as well as the creation of a trained class of colonial political leaders. British imperial history now took in many respects an ironical turn: after decades of indifference when the imperial presence was least challenged politically by colonial nationalism, the British establishment turned its mind towards colonial development at precisely the point when its rule began to be undermined. Perhaps in some respects, though, the ultimate logic of this process was the acceptance by British colonial planners of colonial nationalism as the continuation of imperialism by other means.[2]

Colonial development and the Hailey African Survey

Whatever the ultimate rationale, the impetus towards a change in British colonial policy was under way even before the actual declaration of war in 1939 and the passing of the Colonial Development and Welfare Act the following year. In 1929 a Colonial Development Act had been passed to establish a Colonial Development Fund of £1 million in order to promote both colonial economic development and trade with the UK. The main objective behind this measure tended to be the alleviation of unemployment levels in Britain, and the rigid administration of it from Whitehall prevented the growth of new development schemes in the colonies themselves.[3] By the time of the 1940 Act, thinking on colonial development had become some-

145

what transformed as a result of the political debate and academic analysis in various colonial territories during the course of the 1930s.

Pointing out that the colonial development programme would have occurred even if war had not been declared, Malcolm Macdonald, the Minister of Health, in introducing the Colonial Development and Welfare Bill in May 1940, defined the ethical content of the measure. The concept of 'development' in the Bill, he declared, had 'not a narrow materialistic interpretation', for though it covered the development of material economic resources of colonial territories it 'also covers everything which ministers to the physical, mental or moral development of the colonial peoples of whom we are the trustees'.[4]

This somewhat idealistic, if also paternalistic, conception of colonial development reflected the direction that colonial policy took during the course of the Second World War and the post-war Labour government of 1945–51. The colonial service had its heyday during the 1920s and 1930s when the conception of 'indirect rule' fostered by Lord Lugard underpinned an essentially aristocratic conception of the colonial civil servant.[5] However, things had begun to move towards a more dynamic and techno-cratic basis by the 1940s. Much of the idealism behind this new 'forward thinking' occurred from a reformulation of the British imperial mission in British imperial circles during the 1930s. Oxford and Rhodes House, opened as the centre of operations for the Rhodes Trust in 1929, were particularly important in this new thinking. General Smuts suggested a general survey of Africa in his 1929 lectures given at Rhodes House as part of a renewed 'colonising effort' by Britain to create a new white dominion in East and Central Africa.[6] A conference was thus held in November 1930 on the African colonies. Keenly aware of Britain's changed international position in the period after the 1919 Versailles Armistice, the Rhodes Trust circle of Lord Lothian (Philip Kerr), Lionel Curtis, L. S. Amery and Geoffrey Dawson sought to focus developmental thinking on the African parts of the empire and move attention away from the Far East and the Pacific, where it was recognised that American political and economic hegemony was increasingly holding sway. Whilst the more ambitious idea of renewing colonisation in Africa was not shared by all the Rhodes Trust circle, the climate of opinion was strongly in favour of a 'scientific' approach to African development. Smuts, contributing to the conference as a specially invited guest, argued for 'Africa's problems' being moved 'out of the political atmosphere and away from sentimentalists, and to let science speak'.[7] This marked an attack on the opponents of British policy towards the white settlers in Africa such as Norman Leys and Sydney Olivier, and received support from the main body of the Rhodes Trust lobby. Lionel Curtis argued that the 'existing relations of white and black populations rested less upon climate than upon tradition. The more rapidly the native's standard of living was raised the less effective would be his competition and the brighter the field of white immigration.'[8] The general objective was to transform societies economically through colonial social engineering so that they would present less of a political challenge to the white settler presence in Africa, and it was not surprising that liberal critics of British colonial policy, such as W. M. Macmillan, were passed over in the search for a coordinator of research on African colonial development.[9]

Within this ideological context work commenced on Lord Hailey's *African Survey* in 1933. Funds for the project came from the Carnegie Corporation in New York as well as the Rhodes Trustees and reflected the continuation of previous Anglo-American interest in African economic and social development since the early 1920s as expressed in the work of the Phelps-Stokes Fund on African education.[10] By the 1930s, there was a greater tendency towards seeing the African continent as a whole with common economic and social needs. The choice of Malcolm Hailey, a distinguished administrator from the Indian civil service, was by no means fortuitous. One of the central objectives behind the *Survey* was the promotion of a common pattern of Western control over the separate African territories, as had been produced in the Indian Raj. 'The problem before us in Africa', wrote Lionel Curtis, 'is to bring the most helpless family of the human race into right conditions with Europe, America and Asia.' The continent was 'exposed to the impact of Eastern civilisation' which would 'ruin the life of its child-like peoples unless it is controlled'. In order to control, though, it was necessary to study 'not only the ideas, institutions, customs and languages, but the effects which an economic revolution is having upon them in all its effects'.[11] The focus had thus shifted in some degree from the earlier Round Table interest in the South African segregationist model to that of the Indian Raj as a cohesive and unitary model of administration over an agrarian society. This was a legacy which was to have a significant impact on British thinking about race relations.[12]

There was in particular a concern for immediate administrative action, which was partly born of the experience of many of the Rhodes Trustees, such as Lothian, Curtis and Dawson, in the Milner Kindergarten.[13] It was by no means easy to gain the same positive response from the somewhat more cumbersome British colonial administrative machine as had been obtained in the autocratic conquest state of the Transvaal after the Anglo-Boer War.[14] The idea was as far as possible to avoid criticism of any particular government's colonial policy in Africa and rely on 'scientific' analysis pursued by what Gilbert Murray hoped would be a 'disinterested group of researchers'.[15] Nevertheless, via the influence of the Rhodes Trust circle and its links with Chatham House, a considerable mark was made on government thinking, not least on that of the Colonial Secretary, Malcolm Macdonald.[16]

When *An African Survey* finally appeared in 1938, a significant shift occurred in British colonial thinking in terms of seeing African development issues in terms of a common pattern of 'race relations'. 'Africa is not India', wrote Reginald Coupland, the Beit Professor of Imperial History at Oxford, in reviewing the work, 'but not only are the fundamental principles underlying the relationship of the white and coloured races everywhere the same, but the practical problems of government, however different the customs and conditions, are broadly the same kind of problem in an Indian province and an African colony.'[17] This conception of certain 'fundamental principles' lying at the heart of white–black relations was strongly reinforced by *An African Survey* and its concern to establish a centralised direction in research on African social and economic development which, it argued, had been frequently undertaken in response to an unrelated series of demands rather than as an outcome of comprehensive planning'.[18] In particular, it recommended the creation of a metropolitan research institution or 'Africa Bureau' which could 'maintain close contact with institutions and voluntary organisations in this and other countries interested in African development'.[19] This centralisation of the research effort in African colonial development in Britain (which bore fruit eventually in the establishment of the Colonial Social Science Research Council in 1940),[20] arose from the *Survey's* recognition of the need for guided social engineering in African colonies in order to confront the social tensions that were likely to arise within the existing indirect rule strategy that guided so much official thinking on colonial policy. In British colonies, the *Survey* argued, there was not 'the most important problem of a political nature' in the question of how far political representation for Africans in legislative councils should be increased.[21] Sooner or later, there was likely to be conflict with the existing policy of relying upon hereditary African bodies of chiefs or emirs, and the *Survey* sought greater coordination of representative government at the local level through the model of the Natives Representative Council of South Africa, introduced in 1936 as part of a political package that removed the African voters in the Cape from the common electoral role. 'Up to the present time', the *Survey* concluded, 'the fact that the system makes little provision for recognising educated opinion has not resulted in open opposition to it; in the future, however, it will inevitably have to meet pressure due to this cause.'[22]

The *Survey* was thus much in tune with the 'forward thinking' in British colonial circles that sought to meet future African political demands even before they were formulated. While nationalist pressure for political changes in African colonies was stimulated by the Italian invasion of Abyssinia in 1936,[23] the most significant upsurge of discontent with British colonial rule occurred in the Caribbean, where riots in 1936–8 shocked British colonial planners out of their earlier complacency and forced them to confront a new political situation where the old colour–class social order had to some extent become undermined by a new class-based political militancy which took the initiative away from the brown middle class which colonial analysts since Sydney Olivier had favoured as a stabilising factor.[24] From now on the black working class in a number of the Caribbean islands was a force to be reckoned with in the form of the 50,000 members of Bustamente's Maritime Workers' Union in Jamaica or the 8,000 members of the Oil Workers' Union in Trinidad. In 1942 Eric Williams, in an important pioneering study of Caribbean politics, argued that the brown middle class had to choose which political direction it wished to take: either with the black working class, or in collaboration with the colonial administration, for no middle way any longer existed.[25] This political volatility of the middle class also worried British propaganda experts in the Ministry of Information who were concerned with mobilising West Indian support for the Allied war effort, especially as now the emerging trade unions in the islands were seen to have some stabilising force in local communities but as yet little political weight.[26]

As a result of the changed set of political configurations both in the Caribbean and internationally due to the war, British governmental thinking in the early 1940s came increasingly to emphasise the colour-blind nature both of British colonial policy and public attitudes in Britain in general. The Ministry of Information urged that it was essential if the middle class in the Caribbean colonies was to stay loyal to British war aims that blacks had to be admitted into full participation in citizenship rights in Britain itself, especially in the armed forces, for otherwise numbers of them would return back to their countries of origin with unfavourable impressions.[27] This liberalisation of policy seemed especially essential in the wake of the disasters in the Far East in the war against Japan when Singapore fell on 15 February 1942 with some 85,000 British prisoners of war. These defeats represented, in Harold Macmillan's words, 'a staggering blow to British pride in Asia and Africa',[28] and there was a growing tendency to talk of colonial objectives less in terms of the more paternalistic 'trusteeship' and more in terms of 'partnership', which *The Times* considered 'a fact and not a phrase' for it was essential to avoid racial discrimination towards black students, seamen and other visitors, it being a 'duty as well as an interest that they return with an abiding impression of the tolerance, seemliness and good will of the English way of life'.[29] Such liberal pretensions were castigated by some black critics, like George Padmore, as hypocritical since they seemed to be mainly motivated by a desire to mobilise colonial support behind Britain's wartime struggle. Nevertheless, some £17 million was collected for planes from the colonies by November 1940 and racial barriers in the armed forces against blacks did start to come down, most notably in the exclusive Royal Air Force, where Harold Moody's son, Arundel, became a fighter pilot.[30]

The limits on the liberalisation of policy were perhaps best reflected in the working of the Colonial Office's Advisory Committee on the Welfare of Coloured People in the UK, which was established in September 1942 under the chairmanship of one of the Colonial Office civil servants who had been actively involved in the work for the Hailey *Survey* in the 1930s, J. L. Keith. A former employee of the British South Africa Company in Northern Rhodesia (Zambia) in the early 1920s, Keith was genuinely concerned to promote the Colonial Office's welfare role in Britain in the sensitive climate of the war years and after, whilst remaining anxious to steer clear of too direct a political involvement. Criticism was already being mounted from some quarters of the lack of coordination of government policy on race matters and in a memorandum sent to the Colonial Office in August 1942, Kenneth Little, then researching on Cardiff for his book *Negroes in Britain*, complained of the poor state of 'Anglo-Colonial relations' and called for 'a more imaginative and even a more constructive attitude towards the implications which arise simply out of the question of "colour"'.[31] Keith, however, doubted whether the Colonial Office could take up a propaganda mantle against the operation of colour bars in Britain in any systematic way, for this would mean usurping the government's public relations effort.[32] Furthermore, the work of the Advisory Committee would inevitably come up against the 'colour bar question', but in general it should be 'headed off from concerning itself with it beyond what is necessary for dealing with the particular point at issue', for this was 'a welfare, not a political committee'.[33]

Aiming, therefore, to control what Keith termed the 'enthusiasts' on the Advisory Committee such as Harold Moody, the Colonial Office did not carve out all that different a role in the welfare field than the previous *ad hoc* efforts by private organisations before the war such as the Anti-Slavery Society. The Anti-Slavery Society was represented on the Committee by Harris's successor, the lawyer and former sugar planter from Honduras, C. W. W. Greenidge, and the chief task of the Committee was to advise the government on policy. It thus tended to adopt a low-key approach and avoided as far as possible taking up the political dimensions of race relations in too direct a manner.

This objective, however, soon became complicated by the rapid increase in the latter half of 1942 of black American troops in a number of English towns and villages. The total number of American troops in Britain was some 170,000, and some 10% of these were black. In many respects, the presence of these black American troops marked the development for the first time of a significant race relations issue in Britain as a whole, for it had previously been largely restricted to the ports.[34] The issue pinpointed some of the strategic dilemmas confronting the British government at this particular phase of the war. The entry of the United States into the war and the presence of its forces in Britain reflected the widening of the war away from Europe onto a world-wide scale and the relative decline of the British military role in it. The signing of the Atlantic Charter in 1941 by Winston Churchill and President Roosevelt defined the Allied objectives in the war and respected 'the right of our peoples to choose the form of government under which they will live'. This was a strong fillip to American criticisms of British imperialism, including calls in the Senate Foreign Relations Committee for the use of American power to force a change in British policy towards its colonies.[35] Resistance to these American attacks occurred from a number of quarters in Britain, not least from the Colonial Office. The Colonial Secretary for nine months of 1942 (from 22 February to 23 November) was Viscount Cranborne, later 15th Marquis of Salisbury, who led a protracted resistance to any attempts to bend to American pressure. In particular, Cranborne was concerned to foster political alternatives to American proposals for international supervision of colonial territories through schemes for regional defence and economic cooperation, especially in the sensitive area of the Far East.[36] During Cranborne's stay at the Colonial Office, a close relationship developed between the Colonial Office and the Foreign Office on mobilising an effective propaganda campaign against American attacks on Britain.[37] It was in this context that the discussions on policy towards the presence of black American troops in Britain were conducted from August 1942 onwards.

British policy was concerned to prevent any unsettling of political relationships in those parts of the colonial empire, especially in Africa and the Caribbean, which had so far escaped direct involvement in the military action of the war. There was thus considerable doubt in some quarters of the British administration whether Britain should accept the formalised system of racial segregation which America exported to Britain with her army.[38] The main advocate within British governmental circles for the American segregationist model was the War Office, led by the Secretary of State for War, Sir James Grigg, who presented a memorandum to the Cabinet early in October 1942 that distinguished between the US army's 'combination of equal rights and segregation practised in the United States' with the British 'natural inclination to make no distinction between the treatment of white and coloured troops'. Attached to the memorandum was an appendix, written by a Major-General Dowler, who was in charge of administration in the Southern British Army Command. It was entitled 'Notes on Relations with Coloured Troops' and had been drawn up by Dowler for the War Office after consultation with US army officers. It noted that 'while there are many coloured men of high mentality and cultural distinction, the generality are of simple mental outlook' and went on to recommend conformity with 'the American attitude' and the avoidance of friendships with American black troops.[39] A key motive here was the concern that liaisons would develop between American blacks and British white women, and the Home Secretary, Herbert Morrison, noted on 10 October the traditional concern about such liaisons, harking back in some respects to the pre-war events in the seaports. 'I am fully conscious that a difficult sex problem might be created', he wrote, 'if there were a substantial number of cases of sex relations between white women and coloured troops and the procreation of half-caste children.' A general educational approach as suggested by the War Office in its guidelines for conduct would be unlikely, however, 'to have any influence on the class of women who are attracted by coloured men'.[40]

These negative reservations from the Home Office contrasted with the Colonial Office view which accrued from both a genuinely liberal concern to foster a more benign view of racial differences and a desire to promote a colonial policy that avoided charges of racial discrimination. The former influence stemmed in part from the employment by the Colonial Office of anthropological expertise in the early 1940s as part of the development and welfare programme. One of the letters in the Colonial Office file was to Audrey Richards, now working as a government anthropologist, from her former teacher and close friend and mentor, Gilbert Murray: 'As a matter of imperial policy', he wrote, 'we cannot encourage a colour bar to tolerate outrages on blacks and then make objections to keeping American and coloured people apart'.[41] The logical consistency of this view was underpinned in the following couple of months by what the Colonial Office saw as the potentially damaging intrusion into colonial policy by the War Office and its 'Notes on Relations with Coloured Troops'. On 12 September, J. L. Keith, reacting to the War Office guidelines and the resulting publicity in the *Sunday Pictorial*, minuted to Cranborne that 'if we believe in racial equality as an idea for the colonial empire' it would be impossible to accept two of the three options proposed by the War Office memorandum which proposed acceptance of the segregationist policy of the US army and the educational guidelines favouring the avoidance of liaisons with American blacks. 'It is the first step which counts in this sort of thing', Keith wrote, and, echoing the arguments of Gilbert Murray, he went on: 'how are we to persuade people to take one attitude towards the Coloured American and another towards our own [*sic*] coloured people . . . . We believe broadly in the brotherhood of man and any attempt to cut across this principle cannot fail to have the most serious reactions both at home and abroad.' It was important, therefore, to resist 'any nonsense about rape, VD, etc.' and to oppose 'the so-called Southern American attitude towards negroes'.[42]

This line of reasoning was one of the main buttresses behind Cranborne's opposition to the War Office proposals in the Cabinet meeting of 13 October. In a memorandum of 9 October, Cranborne argued that 'we cannot ask people to follow the American attitude on the colour question without asking them to set aside the British tradition'.[43] Policy on racial discrimination and the preservation of British colonial policy in the face of American attacks were thus, for Cranborne, crucially linked, and for the first time in British government policy there was exhibited a far-reaching understanding of the inter-relationship between race and wider public policy in both Britain and the colonial empire. After a somewhat stormy Cabinet meeting on 13 October in which Cadogan wrote that 'everyone spoke at once' while Churchill read the papers and Cranborne 'tried to impress Cabinet with his (Colonial) difficulties', the War Office guidelines were left to be revised by Grigg, Morrison and the Lord Privy Seal, Stafford Cripps, who had returned to Britain earlier in the year after an unsuccessful peace mission in India.[44] The new guidelines for the services emphasised the differences of American attitudes on race to those of Britain, whilst also emphasising the attempts by the Roosevelt administration to institute reform. In some respects, the description of American race relations bore some resemblance to a pluralistic analysis in that 'The Americans are making a great experiment in working out a democratic way of life in a mixed country, with races of very different characteristics and traditions. In doing so they have to take account of the legacy of the past and learn for the future.' It was furthermore 'a difficult task and it is not for us to embarrass them, even if we have different views of how relationships should be treated in our own country and in the empire'.[45]

The Cabinet document and the resulting publicity through the Army Bureau of Current Affairs (ABCA) journal, *Current Affairs*, represented an important decision by the British government at a critical stage in the war not to conflict openly with the American army's system of segregation. As one scholar, Graham Smith, has recently noted in a study of the black American troops in Britain, the British government sought 'on an important issue of racial tolerance' a 'shabby compromise and a blot on any kind of liberal ideals the war might have stood for'.[46] Though anxious not to antagonise black opinion in either the colonies or in Britain itself, the war-time government resisted pressure from Keith and the Colonial Office for a more assertive stand against the American army's system of segregation which had been announced by General Eisenhower on 14 July 1942 as implying separate facilities for whites and blacks, but equality of treatment, a principle that stemmed from the *Plessy* v *Ferguson* decision in the Supreme Court in 1896 and which was not to be overthrown until the 1954 decision in *Brown* v *Board of Education*. This led, though, to the extension of Jim Crow practices in Britain itself and by the middle of 1942 there was segregation in on-duty facilities in the American army in Britain, while by mid-1943 off-duty recreational areas had been demarcated between whites and blacks. Thus certain towns were designated off limits for one or other racial group and passes issued accordingly; in some cases this might mean a whole town would be excluded for American blacks, while in East Anglia, where Ipswich was a main centre, 10 pubs and dance halls out of 150 were for blacks only.[47]

The implementation of segregation did not prevent a number of racial disturbances occurring between white and black troops or of assaults against black British subjects. Harold Macmillan, the Parliamentary Under Secretary of the Colonies, proposed in September 1942 that the black British should wear Union Jacks in their buttonholes, though his suggestion seems to have met no positive response.[48] The American army itself did not respond to complaints over the US treatment of black Britons and a more definitive policy line from the Cabinet might well have had a more positive effect.[49] As it was, the Colonial Office found itself somewhat disarmed when it came to attacks on its policy by radical critics of British imperial policy, especially as there was evidence to show that the initially favourable reception of many British people of the black GIs in 1942 began to give way by mid-1943 to a more racially prejudiced view.[50]

The pressure on the Colonial Office under Cranborne, however, was such that the department felt a more immediate issue was the American hostility to the continuation of the British empire. By the second half of 1942, it was becoming apparent that a defence of the British empire would have to be mounted to meet the attacks of liberal critics in the United States. If this was, as W. T. Wells pointed out, now 'the American century' British imperial policy needed to stress the bond of common citizenship with the Empire–Commonwealth.[51] It was this climate of opinion which encouraged some Colonial Office officials such as the Under Secretary, Sir George Gater, to caution against suggestions that the American forces 'should be made fully aware of the British attitude toward coloured persons' since the Colonial Office would be likely to 'get into very deep water indeed'.[52]

The inconsistency of this policy does not escape radical critics of imperialism and Nancy Cunard and George Padmore, in a pamphlet, *The White Man's Duty*, in 1942, pointed out 'today (this has to be said) the coloured soldier of the USA over here in very large numbers records, that although he may be the same as a white American soldier in democracy, when democracy is a battlefield, he is not the same in daily relations with the people of Great Britain, because some of his chiefs have requested that this be not so'.[53] The authors also pointed out that the colour issue in Britain was part of a wider question of racial discrimination within the empire as a whole. 'I find it rather remarkable', Padmore claimed, 'that no responsible Colonial official has made any statement yet about the future of Colonial subjects. No promises have been made in this war as they were in the last.' Campaigning for the immediate application of Clause 3 of the Atlantic Charter, Padmore urged that 'the economies of all Colonial territories should be made for the benefit of the peoples there under their own direction and control'.[54]

This was a radical criticism of British colonial policy by a leading Pan-Africanist who had been an active organiser in London since 1935, especially at the militant International African Service Bureau.[55] However, the thrust of British policy in the wake of the 1940 Colonial Development and Welfare Act was the maintenance of imperial control in the colonial territories combined with an economic development programme that emphasised the educational advancement of political and economic elites in them as part of a process of progressive and evolutionary reform.[56] It made the Colonial Office all the more sensitive by the war years[57] to the attitudes and feelings amongst the colonial student population resident within Britain and here the question of the West African Students' Union was of especial significance.

WASU and black students in Britain

The Colonial Office had been successful in gaining the cooperation of the more moderate of the Pan-African groups in London, Harold Moody's League of Coloured Peoples, since the early 1930s. In 1934, Moody joined the committee of the hostel established by the Colonial Office for colonial students in London called Aggrey House.[58] A considerable part of the LCP's activities at this time were generally of an apolitical nature, centring around welfare work involving children's parties and outings and cases of racial discrimination against individuals, such as black nurses, on an *ad hoc* basis. By the late 1930s, however, in the aftermath of the Italian invasion of Abyssinia, the League's position began to change. In a memorandum to the Moyne Commission appointed to investigate conditions in the West Indies following the riots of 1937–8, the LCP urged 'with deference' that West Indian progress depended 'only to a limited extent on the Colonial Office'. 'If these colonies are to progress', it continued, 'it is their own people, led by their own leaders, who will play the major part.'[59] Thus, though the League still continued to work with the Colonial Office in its welfare activities after the outbreak of war in 1939, even the more moderate section of black political opinion in Britain was becoming critical of Colonial Office control and the policy of colonial development and welfare.[60]

In the early 1940s, the Colonial Office was confronted with an especially pressing need to accommodate black student feeling in the West African Students' Union. This organisation had been founded in London in 1925 by a Nigerian barrister, Ladipo Solanke, who was a Pan-Africanist with a vision of a 'United States of West Africa' and a strong proponent of educational regeneration through a 'West African Educational Fund' modelled on the lines of Tuskegee.[61] Over the following years, WASU grew from an original membership of some 25 students to approximately 252 by 1939, though it sank again to some 30 after the outbreak of war. Despite its tiny numerical size, the organisation was important for its numerous contacts with nationalist political leaders in British West African colonies and its establishment of branches there.[62] The Union had been stung into publishing a pamphlet in 1934 entitled *The Truth about Aggrey House*, attacking both the LCP and the Colonial Office for establishing the Aggrey House student hostel, which it saw as a segregationist measure to insulate African students from wider contacts in London.[63] The Union sought a hostel of its own and Solanke toured West Africa in 1929–30 to raise funds for one which was opened on 1 January 1933 at 62 Camden Road in London. Solanke himself became warden of this hostel, but the cost of running it soon proved beyond the resources of WASU, so that in 1936 Solanke approached John Harris of the Anti-Slavery Society for a loan of money in order to buy another property freehold.

Harris's Welfare of Africans in Europe War Fund Committee had been concerned since 1931 with establishing, together with the Colonial Office, an African student hostel in London.[64] Some £1,500 was collected from donations from both West Africa and Liverpool and Manchester firms with West African interests and the funds were paid into an account managed by John Harris's daughter, a Mrs Anderson, from which Harris alone was able to withdraw. The key figure who was instrumental in getting this financial support was Major Hans Vischer, a Colonial Office official and anthropologist, who was a leading member of the International Institute of African Languages and Cultures. As a result, no loan was necessary from Harris's Welfare of Africans in Europe War Fund Committee and in 1938 new premises at 1 South Villas, Camden Square, were purchased, which WASU thought were freehold. However, Harris persuaded Solanke to accept that his Welfare Committee should act as trustees for the hostel due to possible hostility from the surrounding residents, though this resulted in WASU not being freeholders, as they had imagined, but the tenants at will of the trustees, who were Harris and General Grey of the Anti-Slavery Society. A sum of £200 was also to be paid to Mrs Anderson as commission for the money she had collected as a result of the appeal.[65]

Harris's actions served to dash the hopes of Vischer and the Colonial Office, who were attempting to bridge the differences between WASU and Aggrey House.[66] WASU refused to accept the tenancy agreement and defaulted on the rent, leading Harris to threaten to take legal action to remove the Union from the hostel premises. Vischer, though, remained an ally of WASU, arguing that they ran the hostel efficiently. In 1939 he suggested a Joint Board could run both WASU's Africa House along with the Colonial Office's Aggrey House, since he believed it important to develop a 'better understanding' between whites and Africans in both Britain and the colonial territories generally.[67] The aged Harris remained a stalwart opponent of this for the last year of his life, considering that the original 'spirit' behind the scheme had been destroyed.[68] After the outbreak of war in 1939, however, and Harris's death the following year, a new policy started to prevail as the Colonial Office got drawn further into the issue. The chairman of the Welfare of Africans in Europe War Fund Committee, General Grey, hoped to drum up support for the Anti-Slavery Society's case by alleging in July 1940 that some of the black Africans living in London were 'agitators and known to be disloyal'.[69] Vischer, however, saw 'the problem' of the black students as 'an extremely important one',[70] and urged Harris's successor as secretary of the Anti-Slavery Society, C.W.W. Greenidge, to take a more conciliatory line on the whole issue. 'One thing that has always helped me in my dealings with Solanke', he wrote to Greenidge in July 1941, 'has been the realisation that in his way he is fighting for exactly what we want him to have, if only we spoke the same way of reasoning.'[71] This more conciliatory view increasingly prevailed in the wartime atmosphere and in August the Deputy Prime Minister, Clement Attlee, visited the WASU hostel. For Solanke, the whole question of the hostel property represented 'the first test case to prove and confirm that the old conception that Africans are an inferior race and should be treated as such has passed away'.[72]

The Colonial Office by 1941 had already realised that there was a need to appease Solanke and WASU and in April of that year J. L. Keith indicated a willingness of the Colonial Office to increase its financial assistance which, since 1937, had been some £250 a year.[73] This was aided by the growth in political support for WASU's case from sections of the British left, most notably the Labour MP, Reginald Sorensen, who became one of the Union's trustees. The Union hoped it would become an important participant in a dialogue between the British government and nationalist opinion in the colonies and it was this possibility which attracted some of the left-wing critics of British imperial policy to assist WASU's cause. 'For the past 16 years', Solanke wrote to Sorensen, 'we have been trying to establish and build up WASU as the *People's Institution to Serve* as one of the machineries through which the government may, by sympathetic cooperation, understand the mind and wishes of the native people of West Africa with a view to training and leading them to self-government on democratic lines.'[74] There was some element of truth in these claims, for the occupants of the hostel were by no means solely students and a number of African political leaders, including Dr M. A. S. Margai and Rev. John Dube, had stayed at the hostel. However, the Colonial Office still tended to give most of its support to Aggrey House, to which it contributed some £2,000 per annum, on the grounds, as Keith minuted, that it was 'of interest throughout the whole of the Colonial Empire'.[75] While WASU received some £378 for 1942–3 and £274 for 1943–4, the Colonial Office was wary of too close an involvement with the body. As the war progressed, it became clear that the Anti-Slavery Society was unlikely to proceed with legal proceedings to recover the property at 1 South Villas and Keith considered it important that the Colonial Office should 'steer clear' of the dispute. Solanke he considered a 'very difficult and contentious person' and likely to draw the Colonial Office into opposition to the Anti-Slavery Society.[76] However, later the same year, it was proposed that the Colonial Office pay off the mortgage and convey the property to the trustees on behalf of WASU and keep an informal control over the Union's activities via Reginald Sorensen, who in addition to being a WASU trustee was also a member of the Colonial Office's own Advisory Committee for the Welfare of Colonial People in the United Kingdom.[77] This went ahead in October and November of 1942, with the mortgage of some £1,350 being redeemed by the Colonial Office, and the new trustees, who included Lord Listowel and Reginald Sorensen, tended to represent more of an establishment-orientated Anglican interest in race relations compared to the previous Nonconformist Anti-Slavery lobby. The Colonial Office hoped that this reorganisation would lead to an increase in private fund-raising for the Union, and WASU and the Anglo-African Committee and the Dean of Westminster held a series of meetings to raise funds for a second hostel. This was eventually opened after the war at 13 Chelsea Embankment in 1949.[78]

By the time the war ended, WASU had begun to become a respectable institution and at the 1945 Pan-African Congress in Manchester there were complaints that the black students' body in Britain 'had cut itself aloof' from the main body of the black British community.[79] In the early 1950s the Union was receiving some £2,000 per annum from the Colonial Office for the running of its hostels.[80] The role of the hostel had developed from one of providing accommodation for African students to acting also as a refuge for many black immigrants to post-war Britain who, while nominally 'students', were often unemployed for long periods. 'The numbers of our boys who idly roam the streets of London', wrote the WASU honorary secretary, D. A. Okusaga, in 1949, 'is daily getting bigger and bigger. Some of them, when thrown out of their digs for default in payment of rent, now steal under cover of night into the WASU hostel and during the past month or so groups of them have been found in several corners of the hostel trying to catch a bit of sleep there.' 'It is not in every country of the world', he added, 'that Negro students find it hard to get jobs or acquire technical skills in factories and technical schools as is the case in Britain'.[81] The two hostels had become increasingly bound up with the emerging issue of race relations in Britain by the early 1950s and one complainant from the St Pancras Moral Welfare Association echoed pre-war sentiments by claiming that numbers of white girls with 'half-caste' babies were claiming the WASU hostel as their address.[82] The continuing support, though, from white sympathisers such as Reginald Sorensen in the early 1950s ensured that the Union continued to receive Colonial Office backing after the return of the Conservative government in 1951, despite an allegation by Lord Milverton in the House of Lords that the Union was 'a common medium for the contact of Communists with West Africans when they come to this country'.[83] By this time, Solanke had himself become vehemently anti-Communist in orientation and WASU became effectively a strong ally of Colonial Office policy.

In these new circumstances, there was far less concern expressed in official circles by the mid-1950s on the whole student issue. In the war years, the question of providing adequate social facilities for black students in Britain, who were alleged to have 'a very serious colour inferiority complex', was seen by some to be of greater importance than the question of 'entertaining' the black American GIs.[84] The Colonial Office welfare role had thus been expanded in 1941 and some financial aid was made available from the Colonial Students Loan Fund, which had been modelled on an earlier Indian Student Loan Fund established in 1910. The money from this fund was used to alleviate any distress and hardship amongst black students in England and also to reduce as far as possible any bitterness that might result from this. This was an issue that concerned a number of the Colonial Office welfare officials,[85] though the Colonial Office's role in this was eventually taken over by the British Council at the start of 1950.[86] Nevertheless, there was still a feeling of some 'anxiety' when a Political and Economic Planning survey of the conditions of 'colonial students' in Britain was commenced in 1951. By the time the report, entitled *Colonial Students in Britain*, appeared in 1955, however, there was a more optimistic note, as the British Council actively sought to desegregate the student hostels under its control.[87] The report outlined the by now familiar set of 'problems' that surrounded black students in Britain – alienation, loneliness, racial discrimination – but rejected the assertion that the students were being systematically met and indoctrinated by the Communist Party and argued that the students did not represent a homogeneous group for they came from a variety of countries, ethnic backgrounds and political and religious affiliations.[88] The report buttressed the work of the British Council and urged the widening of its work from existing colonies to territories that were to receive independence.[89] In general, by the mid-1950s, the welfare and reception service for students had been considerably extended by the universities themselves and the adviser to overseas students at the University of London claimed that efforts were being made to bring African students, especially, 'into our midst, bringing them wholly into our lives, giving them real friendship'.[90]

Although the reality for many black students in Britain in the 1950s was still much racial discrimination from a society in the process of withdrawing from empire,[91] the period was one marked by an absence of black political militancy in the wake of the decline of Pan-Africanism. The late 1940s was quite an important period for African political leaders and intellectuals in Britain, coming as it did after the 1945 Pan-African Congress at Manchester.[92] However, in the 1950s a number of leaders such as Kwame Nkrumah, Jomo Kenyatta, George Padmore and Julius Nyerere (later followed by Hastings Banda) had returned to Africa and the Pan-Africanist solidarity in the British diaspora began to go into decline. The revival of black political activity was to pick up again in the 1960s as a new wave of political exiles from South Africa and Rhodesia ushered in a new wave of political militancy, though without the same degree of Pan-Africanist consciousness.

While the issue of black students and the racial discrimination they experienced never entirely went away, for in some respects it acted as a kind of barometer of racial attitudes generally within British society, by the 1950s the main area of interest increasingly centred around the question of the immigration of black workers from the colonial empire into British industry. This had widened the pre-war race relations situations in the seaports to a national issue by the middle 1950s, and Britain now found herself with a general issue of race that had hitherto been seen mostly in colonial and external terms.

The growth of black immigrant labour

The immigration of black workers into British industry started slowly during the Second World War to help alleviate the labour shortage in a number of crucial sectors of the economy. A group of West Indians were imported to work as 'Bevin boys' on air-bases or munitions factories at Kirkby outside Liverpool. A group of Hondurans were also brought over to work on the forestry plantations in Scotland. They found themselves on several occasions discriminated against in pubs and dance halls, frequently on the pretext that their presence would cause hostility from white American servicemen. Learie Constantine, for example, who was appointed in 1940 as welfare officer in the Ministry of Labour for the north-west region of England, reported the 'bitterness' being created amongst the 180 West Indian technicians at Kirkby through attacks on them by white Americans. Furthermore, he wrote that 'I have been informed that when the police have intervened they complain of being baffled by the situation. It seems by inference that the individual is left to take the law into his own hands.'[93] Constantine himself became a victim of racial discrimination in 1943 when he was refused accommodation by the Imperial Hotel in Russell Square at a time when over two hundred American officers were staying there, though he successfully sued and was awarded £5 damages.[94]

The response from the Colonial Office was to apply its policy of 'welfare colonialism' to Britain itself in the form of a voluntary segregationism aimed at defusing racial hostility. To some extent, this policy arose from the previous pattern of inter-racial conflict in the inter-war period and the traditional Colonial Office policy of seeking to rest colonial rule on stable and identifiable community structures, as far as possible outside main urban areas.[95] Thus, the small black community at Barry in South Wales of some four to five hundred families, mostly of African origin, was held up as a model of the kind of race relations policy which could be pursued within Britain. In a report on the community in August 1942, the Sierra Leonean welfare officer of the Colonial Office, Ivor Cummings, emphasised its high degree of homogeneity and freedom from 'Colonial factions' that were 'trying to run shows of their own' and also its isolation from the main black community in Cardiff itself. The leaders of the community were a couple from Barbados, Mr and Mrs Abel, who ran a licensed boarding house in which Ministry of Labour transferred workers stayed. As the organisers of the Barry Coloured Society, the Abels sought Colonial Office financial backing for a clubhouse which could contribute to the community's identity. 'I think these people in Barry pride themselves upon being a little united group', wrote Cummings, 'and I must say that I am in sympathy with them as regards their attitude towards Cardiff and in some ways I think it is a good thing that they keep themselves to themselves.'[96] As a general policy, though, Cummings, who had formerly been warden of Aggrey House in the 1930s, emphasised the need for Colonial Office tact in the way it liaised with the community leaders: 'We shall have to be very careful indeed not to make the members feel that we are trying to impose a new organisation upon them, because they are very jealous of their independence and rights'.[97] One of the chief arguments by the end of 1942, however, was that if such a clubhouse were established it would also be a social centre for black American GIs as well as the members of the Barry community.[98]

In comparison with this relatively orthodox colonial approach, the Colonial Office found itself in a far more difficult and unfamiliar situaton in the case of black workers in more industrial situations. The ethos of the Colonial Office administrators was very much one of colonial economic development, born out of the thinking of the Hailey *Survey*, the Moyne Commission and the work of such academic researchers as W. M. Macmillan from his book *Warning from the West Indies*.[99] It was not very readily geared to understanding a specifically British race relations situation and the pioneering work on this, drawing extensively on the American example and the sociological school of Robert Ezra Park at the University of Chicago, was not to appear until after the war. The emphasis within Colonial Office policy at this stage was on training black workers in the UK for expanded wartime production who could later return to their colonies of origin as part of the post-war development programmes. These men were thus subordinated to a longer-term colonial policy of establishing a class of skilled and semi-skilled workers who were in some degree shielded from the full impact of living in an urbanised and industrialised society.[100] Ivor Cummings, for example, in his various reports on the situation of imported black workers in Britain during the war, emphasised the post-war theme. 'The African territories, both East and West', he wrote, were 'in urgent need of an industrial revolution which must take place before these territories will be able to take their rightful place in the world'. Furthermore, this was linked to the consideration that 'the great coloured social problem' in Liverpool and other port towns would be 'greatly eased by the resettlement of African peoples in West Africa where they could obtain proper and adequate employment'.[101]

There was much in this view which coincided with the growing developmental thinking in the Colonial Office in the early war years. J. M. Lee has pointed out that during this period the Colonial Office effectively 'ceased to be an organisation which was principally designed to supervise specific territories and became one which had to balance "subject" and "geographical" considerations in the formulation of development policy'. There was also a strong carry-over of some of the pre-war commitment to colonial development as numbers of the Colonial Office planners and administrators reacted with some sensitivity to the charge that the development planning was merely a wartime device to maintain the loyalty of colonial peoples.[102] Thus the thinking on the position of the various groups of 'colonial' blacks in

British ports and cities tended to be increasingly centred around a wider geographical development policy, with West Africans linked to plans for West Africa and West Indians linked to planning in the Caribbean and so on. With this concern to foster and develop links between black students and seamen and overseas colonial territories, the Colonial Office was reluctant to get too deeply drawn into a welfare role in Britain itself. In the case of children born as a result of liaisons between English women and black GIs, the LCP tried to take on a welfare role, especially in the city of Liverpool.[103]

This line of thinking continued to prevail after the end of the war as immigration from the West Indies began in earnest with the arrival of some 800 workers between December 1947 and October 1948 in such ships as the *Empire Windrush* and SS *Orbita*. For the Colonial Office this initially represented a continuation of the earlier questions they had had to tackle of finding accommodation for the men and trying to divert them to areas where there were adequate employment opportunities, for there was a general fear that if the new wave of black immigrants went to existing areas of black settlement in the seaport towns this would only revive the racial hostilities of the pre-war years in Cardiff and Liverpool. 'There can be no doubt', stated a Colonial Office memorandum submitted to the inter-departmental Working Party on the Employment in the United Kingdom of Surplus Colonial Labour, 'that the most undesirable thing which can happen is that large numbers of new coloured workers should be forced or encouraged to go into these areas. It is true to say, however, that if they are to be in these seaport towns their chances of obtaining accommodation outside of these "ghetto" districts are negligible'.[104]

The Colonial Office itself had ceased to run industrial hostels at the end of the war and its main role was one of trying to find accommodation for the immigrant men, two hundred of whom from the *Empire Windrush* had to be temporarily placed in air-raid shelters on Clapham Common. Fears began to be expressed in some circles in the Home Office that continued immigration would lead to 'undesirable elements' coming, which would 'present a formidable problem to the departments concerned'.[105]

The Colonial Office was especially worried that conditions in Liverpool would exacerbate racial tensions, especially with the continued influx of black stowaway seamen, whom it considered to be unemployable. The department's structure only allowed for the giving of information on job opportunities for the new arrivals for there were no legal powers for job allocation and there were complaints from some liberal quarters that labour exchanges were unsympathetic to the job requirements of black immigrants. Ivor Cummings, though, wrote that it was impossible to plan ahead for the immigrants' immediate employment and the details of their respective skills could only be taken by the local Ministry of Labour department. Further, it was necessary in these circumstances to 'impress upon the men the need for patience on their part if things are difficult for them on arrival here and that it is only by good behaviour that they can expect to obtain help of employment'.[106] But even this limited government role met with opposition for it was seen as leading to a possible segregationist policy which could have damaging political implications for colonial policy generally. J. L. Keith, for example, questioned whether the Colonial Office was the proper authority to be engaged in the reception, accommodation, employment and 'general welfare' of the black immigrants who were not temporary visitors but British citizens. 'The establishment of the latter as a permanent segregated minority population under the protection of the Colonial Office', he continued, 'would be most undesirable. It would go against the idea, which is highly important to establish, that the Colonial people are in no sense aliens and are entitled to regard this country as their home and to be regarded and treated as fellow citizens.'[107] This view was shared by some of the ministers of the post-war Labour government who were aware of the wider political implications of black migration to Britain from colonial territories. The Under Secretary of State at the Colonial Office, Lord Listowel (already familiar with the issue of black students and WASU), pointed out in 1948, on the question of the *Empire Windrush* immigrants, the 'political importance of seeing that everything possible is done to assist them. They are British subjects (some, at any rate, ex-servicemen) and we can neither prevent their landing nor compel their deportation. We must see that the smoothest possible arrangements are made to minimise the risk of any undesirable incidents or complaints that the Mother country does not bother to look after colonial British subjects.'[108]

This benign paternalism was not shared by all sections of the civil service, however, when the question arose of where the black immigrants were to be allocated jobs and what pattern of settlement they were to establish. In October 1948 the Working Party on the Employment in the United Kingdom of Surplus Colonial Labour met to discuss the possible employment openings available and strongly reflected a resistance from organised labour to the absorption of black immigrant workers into such industries as mining, agriculture, textiles and iron and steel. The Ministry of Labour, in particular, argued that West Indians were 'not . . . of the type required in the UK',[109] and the general consensus was that, since the immigration was likely to be permanent, it was necessary to oppose any scheme of 'mass immigration'.[110] A further meeting led to renewed opposition from the Ministry of Labour to immigration of workers who, they argued, could not be absorbed into British industry, and the openings that were seen as feasible centred around the employment of female immigrants as hospital domestics, which Cummings of the Colonial Office considered 'attractive from the administrative angle since the women involved would be living a regulated life and subject to supervision'.[111] This did not, though, tackle the more fundamental question of the employment of male immigrants (though the following year an experimental scheme was begun to train Barbadian women as hospital domestics) and in January 1949 a Ministry of Labour conference with its regional representatives led to a modification of its stance, when it emerged that some West Indians were beginning to settle into employment in iron foundries and engineering firms like Lucas and BSA in the West Midlands. While 'racial prejudice' among the white workforce was noted, the general opinion regarding the 'Jamaicans' was that 'they were usually of good type, inclined to be childish, and with inflated ideas of their ability, but intelligent in their work and easily managed'.[112] Thus, at an inter-departmental committee meeting the following month, the Ministry of Labour representatives urged that 'coloured people were well adapted to iron and steel manufacturing and engineering work'. While the question of the accommodation of the men was still considered a major problem, their employment in these areas was seen as a major means of tackling the 'larger aggregations' in such places as London and Liverpool, thus reducing the resulting 'difficulty' to the government departments concerned as well as the police. The resurgence of racial hostility in Liverpool the previous autumn undoubtedly fuelled this concern for a dispersal policy which had the advantage of avoiding any immediate government policy on either positively promoting or opposing the employment of black immigrants in specific sectors.[113] As one Ministry of Labour representative stated: 'if special steps were taken to provide employment for the coloured people a fairly large number of white unemployed would feel strongly. On the other hand, if nothing were done at all, the coloured population would feel that they were being victimised at the cost of other British subjects.' This meant that 'anything done by Government agencies would have to be done discreetly'.[114]

While the Ministry of Labour publicly backed this *laissez-faire* approach to job dispersal to areas of employment opportunities, privately it had considerable reservations about the continued influx of black immigrants. The Colonial Office at this stage continued to resist all proposals for immigration control through fear of the wider political implications on colonial opinion,[115] and some Ministry of Labour officials feared this would lead to an increase in the number of immigrants, which they felt could not be absorbed into industry. Far indeed from wanting a pool of unemployed labour, the Ministry of Labour considered a scheme of 'rehabilitation' and industrial retraining essential for those immigrants already entering employment. 'The idea of converting coloured men into acceptable units in the British industrial machine in a short period is ambitious and would seem to call for a special educational and training course', wrote one Ministry of Labour official, A. W. Davies. Such a scheme should be argued against the Colonial Office claim that it was unable to provide either accommodation or training for the immigrants, whilst it could also be used against the Colonial Office's opposition to any segregation. Davies continued: 'Too much stress seems to have been laid in discussion on the segregation point. This is quite secondary, and we would not be embarrassed if the Colonial Office run coloured hostels for their own people. Neither would a special training course for such persons provided by this Department necessarily lay us open to the charge of inconsistency, as the trainees would naturally live together.' Davies's views, though, were not shared by the department as a whole, which agreed with the Colonial Office in avoiding segregation.[116]

There were, nevertheless, differences between the Ministry of Labour and the Colonial Office on employment policy, which emerged in July 1949 at a meeting of the Inter-Departmental Committee on Colonial People in the United Kingdom. When a suggestion was mooted to recruit black officials to the Ministry of Labour to help in the allocation of black immigrants to jobs, the Ministry of Labour officials objected that this would not help control the placement of the immigrants, for employment exchanges throughout the country were 'doing all they could to disperse colonial labour'.[117] While Cummings of the Colonial Office defended the Office's welfare scheme, citing the example of the Honduran foresters brought over during the war, the Ministry of Labour replied that this was a special scheme and did not apply to the more recent immigration.[118] One of the Colonial Office representatives, L. S. Smith, also conceded that many of the immigrants had lived in Britain for years and should be treated as part of the resident population for 'it would prove most difficult to single out those of genuine origin'.[119] In effect, by the middle of 1949 it was becoming recognised in administrative circles that existing methods of control over black immigrant labour derived from the wartime schemes were breaking down and that the new phase of immigration was too complex for departments to cope with on a piecemeal basis. It was felt by the chairman of the committee, J. B. Williams, that a 'thorough social survey' was needed 'in the main centres of colonial population',[120] and there was rising pressure for more coordinated government action. This view reflected a wider feeling by 1949-50 that a more general social survey would in some manner lead to the kind of solution to the emerging race relations situation in Britain. Kenneth Robinson, from the Institute of Colonial Studies at the University of Oxford, suggested such a survey conducted in a 'disinterested' manner by that body in July 1950 and it became a basic demand of the Racial Unity movement in the early 1950s.[121]

The pressure for a survey accrued to some extent from the inability of the government to pursue any more coordinated action.[122] On 19 June 1950, the Cabinet agreed to a review of existing methods of immigration control and this led to the appointment of an *ad hoc* committee of ministers to consider legislation on the matter which met on 24 July 1950 and 10 January 1951.[123] A memorandum submitted to this committee by the Home Office, Ministry of Labour, Colonial Office and Ministry of Transport in July 1950 rejected outright any colour bar or policy of racial discrimination and urged that any law controlling immigration would have to be 'of general application irrespective of race or colour'.[124] The committee estimated a black population approaching some 30,000, with the main groups domiciled in Merseyside (10,000), London (5,000), Cardiff (5,000) and Tyneside (2,000). For the most part it considered the 'problems' resulting from the immigration of black people as 'not very great' and accepted that the Shipping Federation had done all it could be expected to do in the area of returning stowaways to their countries of origin. 'Until there is some evidence that the situation is becoming markedly worse', the memorandum concluded, 'it is unnecessary to proceed with legislation'.[125] This argument was accepted by the Cabinet committee on 24 July 1950 and subsequent discussions tended only to reinforce this view. Though it was hoped that the British government might try and get the colonial governments to agree to restrictions on emigration to Britain, the Colonial Office strongly backed the position of the colonial territories, especially Jamaica, which argued that this was a British government responsibility.[126] The government thus resorted to administrative methods of control, especially in the case of stowaways, and the Colonial Office sent notes to colonial governors in January 1950 suggesting such methods as the controlling of dock areas, the registration of dock workers, the policing of harbours, the licensing of small craft and gangway checks. Travel certificates were also to be issued to those leaving from West Africa before they could gain entry into the UK.[127]

This informational approach, based on what the Home Secretary, James Chuter Ede, termed 'palliative measures', left the government with no coordinated strategy *vis-à-vis* the black communities already established, or becoming established in Britain. It was recognised by 1949 that increased reliance would have to be placed on the work of voluntary and welfare bodies at the local level in order to cope with the specific questions of finding employment and accommodation for blacks. On 6 July 1949 Lord Listowel, in an address to the London Council of Social Service, appealed to the fund of moral concern over the problems facing immigrant communities in such towns as Liverpool, Cardiff and Manchester, for 'it would be a reproach to our national reputation if anything in the nature of a modern ghetto were to become an established feature of certain large cities of the twentieth century and we must do everything we can to prevent the occurrence of such a shameful state of affairs'. In the case of London, this question was largely confined to the East End and 'a great deal could be done by individuals and voluntary organisations to bring about improvement'.[128]

This *laissez-faire* policy of relying on the work of the voluntary bodies quickly gained widespread favour in government circles as it meant a reduction in direct government control of the situation and less expenditure and manpower involved. For the Colonial Office, furthermore, it represented the internal application of indirect rule methods within Britain itself. Officials such as Keith had come round to the idea of some form of immigration control by September 1950,[129] though the direction of government policy indicated that this was not politically feasible, at least in the short term. 'We can expect no support', minuted Sir Charles Jeffries, 'until we have done a good deal more to discourage the flow at its source'.[130] Thus, the best strategy was one that confined Colonial Office activities substantially to the national level, centred around the general surveying of the issue, while more detailed work was done informally by the welfare bodies at the local level. This resort to voluntary effort received the backing of Creech Jones, the Colonial Secretary up to 1950, who argued that Colonial Office should give 'advice and moral support' for local ventures such as at Stepney in east London, while the main initiative should come from voluntary effort.[131] On 10 July 1950 a conference of 'non-official organisations', such as the British Council of Churches, the National Council for Social Service, the Association of British Chambers of Commerce and the Rotary Institute, was held at Church House, Westminster, which led to the establishment of a small consultative committee to liaise with the Colonial Office's welfare department, a wider national committee being deferred at this stage because the department resisted a strong committee that could interfere with its field of action.[132] Nevertheless, the era of a modern 'race relations' question in Britain had clearly begun and by September 1951 the chairman of the Inter-Departmental Committee on Colonial People in the United Kingdom, J. B. Williams, spoke of the need to mobilise such voluntary and non-official effort for the 'integration' of the 'colonial coloured people' into British society. This question, he concluded, was a matter 'entirely outside the scope of official action'.[133]

8

End of empire and the rise of 'race relations'

The growing interest by various voluntary bodies and welfare associations in Britain with black immigrants signalled the emergence of a new field of political debate in the post-war years, that of 'race relations'. Arriving comparatively late, for the area had already been developed in the United States and in some colonial areas such as East and Southern Africa, 'race relations' soon took on a new significance in British society as it came to be associated both with the question of promoting harmonious political relationships in colonies about to gain independence and of 'absorbing', 'assimilating' or 'integrating' black New Commonwealth immigrants into British towns and cities. 'Race relations', as a subject area both for social science analysis as well as political debate, represented a new need for political concepts and analytical tools at a time of quite rapid political and social change in the immediate post-war years. It thus marked what A. Sivanandan has seen as a need for a 'totalising approach' to social analysis,[1] in comparison to the more microcosmic and invidious concept of the 'colour bar' in the 1930s and early 1940s, defined by Kenneth Little in 1945 as a 'vicious circle of inter-racial misunderstanding' which needed to be more widely appreciated by 'thoughtful and progressive citizens'.[2] 'Race relations' as a commonly acknowledged anchoring-point for the thinking on race in Britain began to entrench itself in British political debate in the late 1940s following the independence of India, growing racial polarisation in Southern Africa following the 1948 election defeat of Smuts's United Party by the National Party of D. F. Malan, and rising opposition to segregation in the American South, leading to the 1954 Supreme Court decision in *Brown* v *Board of Education* outlawing the notion that 'separate' facilities in education could be 'equal'.

The decline of white racial segregation

This changing ideological climate in the post-war years thus led to political attacks on white segregationism which, as we have seen, had been able during the inter-war years to adapt to changing international circumstances, including those of the British 'Commonwealth of Nations'. The wartime changes in the United States, however, led to a renewed impetus behind the campaign for full black American citizenship,[3] and this was reflected in the report of Gunnar Myrdal in 1944, *An American Dilemma*, counterposing Southern segregationism with the dominant 'American creed' of enlightenment humanism and the liberal notion of the rights of man. Foreseeing the eventual destruction of the minority segregationism in the South by the dominant values of American society, Myrdal reflected a new optimism in the American debate on race which was in marked contrast to the pessimism of earlier years. He particularly challenged the idea of William Graham Sumner in his book, *Folkways* (1906), that Southern values were rooted in a set of traditional 'folkways' or 'mores' which could only gradually change through time and that little in the way of practical legislative action could be done to alter this.[4] While folkways might be of some use in the analysis of primitive or folk cultures, Myrdal argued, the theory was 'crude and misleading when applied to a modern society in process of rapid industrialisation', characterised by a 'virtually universal expectation of change and a firm belief in progress'. In essence, Sumner's theory concealed more than it exposed by failing to acknowledge how rapid social and intellectual change could be induced in modern industrial societies. The theory was thus attacked by Myrdal for containing too conservative a vision of social change in the context of rising black political demands by the Second World War.[5]

Myrdal's critique of an earlier and more conservative sociological tradition in America had a wide-ranging impact on post-war relations thinking both in America and internationally, though radical critics attacked his approach for overemphasising the role of cultural as opposed to economic and social determinants.[6] 'Race relations' as a subject area had grown up in the 1920s centred around the sociology department at the University of Chicago and was dominated by such figures as Robert Ezra Park, Louis Wirth, Franklin Frazier, E. B. Reuter and St Clair Drake. The main body of empirical studies published by this school of race relations researchers was between 1928 and 1948 and the central stress was on the 'moral assimilation' of the values of black American society to those of the dominant white one as well as the 'economic integration' of the blacks migrating to the urban areas, a strategy aimed at reducing the competition with white labour.[7] Much of this work was dictated by analogies with the natural sciences and Park, in particular, stressed a regular race relations cycle of contact, competition, adaptation and eventual assimilation as a means by which the trajectory of evolving race relations patterns could be understood.[8] This natural science and positivist methodology tended, however, to lead the race relations researchers into de-emphasising both the role of political competition and the normative element of law and public policy in transforming race relations. In this respect, Myrdal's *An American Dilemma* crystallised some of the reservations felt by some more radical race relations researchers before the war, such as W. E. B. Du Bois,[9] and acted as a watershed in the development of a more politically engaged social theory in the 1940s. Louis Wirth, for example (who had taught from the late 1930s at Chicago, while also helping to organise the American Council on Race Relations), in 1950 published an article in the new *British Journal of Sociology*. He considered that Myrdal's work had been 'a major influence' in producing a new sensitivity in the United States towards the role of action agencies, for while it was recognised that 'formal control through law cannot by itself bring about a fundamental change in attitudes', nevertheless it could be 'a powerful deterrent to discrimination and other overt acts which undermine the peace and order of society'.[10]

The response in Britain

This growing enthusiasm for public engagement by American race relations experts was not initially shared by the more conservative scholarly establishment in Britain. At the end of the war this was still strongly organised around anthropology, especially via the work on colonial development and welfare organised, after 1944, through the Colonial Social Science Research Council. The key intellectual forum in which this anthropological debate was conducted was the International African Institute, where the dominating figure was Lord Hailey, the *éminence grise* in political thinking on colonial development and welfare, along with Andrew Cohen at the Colonial Office. In reply to a circular from the International African Institute in April 1945, Hailey expressed his 'disappointment' with *An American Dilemma*. 'It is not indeed', he wrote, 'so much a scientific study of the negro problem as a direct attack on the opponents of negro rights':

> The anthropologist, like any other scientist, must of course start with certain general assumptions which will guide him in assessing the value to be placed on many of his lines of enquiry or his deductions from them. In some way the scientist examining nutrition problems must start with certain assumptions regarding the value of a well-balanced diet and the like. But that is something different from starting with prepossessions in favour of a particular line of policy or directing research in such a manner as to demonstrate its merits.[11]

Hailey also likened Myrdal's apparent attack on social science 'neutrality' with the posthumously published work of Bronislaw Malinowski, *The Dynamics of Culture Change* (1945), which was based on material drawn from seminars at the London School of Economics between 1936 and 1938. Here Malinowski began to revise some of his earlier and rather static functionalist ideas of anthropological research in terms of a more dynamic study of 'culture contact' between 'three distinct orders of cultural reality', that of the 'African', the 'western' and of 'transition' which might well involve disorganisation and even social breakdown:

> Between the two boundaries of color bar on the one side and the dead weight of tribal conservatism on the other there lies the no-man's-land of change. This is not a narrow strip but really embraces what is going on in Africa. As yet it is but partly accomplished; adaptation is imperfect and piecemeal; conflict is open or concealed; and at times there is fruitful cooperation or else disorganisation and decay.[12]

Malinowski went on to attack an important article of Audrey Richards in 1935 on tribal authorities among the Bemba in Northern Rhodesia (Zambia), which had proved a strong justification for the colonial policy of indirect rule in that she had showed that these tribal authorities were not moribund as a result of the new culture contact and that the chief or *Citimukulu* had been able to retain a considerable element of his mythological and religious legitimacy.[13] Malinowski, however, stressed that this continuing importance of tribal authority did not imply that the older pre-colonial tribal values were being retained completely intact, for the impact of labour migration and land alienation in the colony showed the growing influence of external forces, which meant that the colonial administration could not act as a completely free agent to the exclusion of 'European vested interests'.[14] There was, he considered, an onus on the anthropological investigator to take into account the role of the administration in the assessment of the 'total culture contact situation'. The ethnographer needed 'to formulate his conclusions in a manner in which they can seriously be considered by those who frame policies and those who carry them out' whilst also having 'the duty to speak as the Natives' advocate', though Malinowski did not consider any further role.[15] This rethinking of 'applied anthropology' led to conclusions in the colonial context substantially similar to those of Myrdal in the American case and challenged the dominant idea of the anthropologist as an 'objective observer'. Hailey remained, though, a strong advocate of employing anthropologists in the formulation of colonial administration, considering that their brief lay outside the realm of policy formulation, for 'where he deals with policies his aim should be a factual examination of the results that have followed from the implementation of different policies, not an attempt to advocate policy'.[16] This stress on a 'neutral' role was supported by many anthropologists themselves, such as A. R. Radcliffe Brown and Audrey Richards, who wrote 'we should limit ourselves to Sociological judgments rather than Political ones'.[17]

This debate reflected in part the emergence of a distinctive profession of social anthropology that distanced itself from the more engaged and politically orientated subject area of race relations. In the colonial context, anthropology in the early 1940s took for a period a more politically orientated turn after the foundation of the Rhodes-Livingstone Institute in Central Africa in 1937. The work of Godfrey Wilson in particular sought at this time a kind of theoretical merger between Malinowski's ideas and those of Marx.[18] By 1945, however, both Malinowski and Wilson were dead, and social anthropology itself was increasingly coming under the aegis of academic departments in the British metropolis. In 1946 the Association of Social Anthropologists of the (British) Commonwealth was formed, which continued to support the Royal Anthropological Institute but with a distinctly more academic emphasis.[19] In the following year Max Gluckman moved to the University of Manchester and integrated the work of the RAI more firmly with this academic tradition, leading it to become, in Richard Brown's words, less an 'institute of colonial apologists' and more 'a surprisingly independent centre of learning and . . . a means of outdoor academic relief for a tightly knit group of sociologically motivated men'.[20] This 'academic' school of anthropology did not enjoy an unquestioned supremacy in the late 1940s for there was still a strong rival from an 'administrative' school at Oxford,[21] but the two were to some considerable degree integrated in their research efforts via the Colonial Social Science Research Council, which was then coming under the strong intellectual guidance of Andrew Cohen as part of the post-war colonial development and welfare programme.

The Colonial Office was anxious to appease the Oxford school as much as possible, despite the heavy predominance from academic anthropology on the CSSRC, in pursuit of its strategy of a 'middle course'.[22] Andrew Cohen, especially, placed considerable faith in Kenneth Robinson at the Institute of Colonial Studies at Oxford, as well as Evans-Pritchard, despite the evident hostility of the latter to the Colonial Office role in anthropological research in the wake of his own experiences in the Sudan.[23] To some extent this strategy bore fruit over the coming decade of progressive withdrawal from colonial rule in the 1950s, for a critical reassessment of social anthropology's theoretical base and its continuing preoccupation with order as opposed to change only began to emerge in the early 1960s.[24] At the same time, the work of the CSSRC began to attract wider publicity in the late 1940s as social science research was seen as a crucial means for the understanding and resolution of colonial 'development' problems. Audrey Richards wrote of the 'machinery of cooperation between Government departments and the social scientists' in the colonial development and welfare programme,[25] while Lord Hailey linked the work of anthropology with that of scientists engaged in agricultural or geological research as part of 'an attack by the allied forces of science on the multiple problems involved'.[26] Here was an approach resembling the 'holistic' social engineering in the colonial context which the Popperian paradigm of 'piecemeal' social engineering condemned within the British metropolis itself.[27]

The growing adoption by the colonial service in the 1940s of a scientistic vocabulary disguised, though, an ideological lacuna when it came to the question of inter-racial 'relations'. The Accra riots in the Gold Coast (Ghana) in 1948 were the first major post-war sign of nationalist hostility to British colonial policy in Africa,[28] while the election the same year of D. F. Malan in South Africa frightened sections of the British establishment and increased pressures for the establishment of a Central African Federation which could neutralise Afrikaner nationalist influences stemming from the South.[29] At the 1949 Commonwealth Relations Conference held at Bigwin Inn, Ontario, there was more discussion on 'racial problems' than on 'colonial policies' while the United Kingdom delegate condemned as 'reactionary' the policies of the South African government.[30] By the following year the Seretse Khama affair began to blow up as the British government came under South African pressure to prevent Khama from returning to his country of Bechuanaland (Botswana) with his English wife, Ruth, as this directly conflicted with its own segregationist policy of outlawing marriages between black and white. The same year the Malan government passed the Immorality Act, which made marriages between different racial groups illegal and Arthur Creech Jones, who lost his seat in the general election in March 1950, wrote the following month that Britain's 'traditional colonial policy' was being 'influenced by illiberal policies elsewhere . . . because of her moral responsibilities as well as her own long-term interests Britain cannot afford to graft on to her own traditional policy the compromises of "segregation" or "parallel development", or weaken her authority and leadership by promising something less worthy than the position and active principles which she has hitherto proclaimed as basic in her administration of overseas territories'.[31] Clearly, a crisis was becoming apparent in British colonial policy as far as the racial dimension was concerned and this was being admitted by those on the right, too. The Tory peer, Lord Milverton, wrote that 'race relations in Africa' were 'deteriorating', though his solution lay on the 'psychological plane' of inspiring confidence among visiting black students to Britain rather than on the economic or social level.[32] This general political consensus about the saliency of 'race relations' in colonial policy stimulated a more professional discussion on the issue in the early 1950s which was to have long-lasting ramifications on British political thought.

The Institute of Sociology and Racial Unity

The immediate post-war period was marked by a gradual increase in the awareness of race and its relationship to Britain's declining position as a world power. As the last chapter showed, the arrival of black American troops and small numbers of West Indian technicians in the war years had signified the arrival of a nationwide race relations situation, which became slowly embedded in the public consciousness. There was still, though, widespread public ignorance of basic political facts, which in some measure reflected an insular society that had only become periodically enthusiastic about external imperial involvements. A 1951 survey of British attitudes to colonies by the Central Office of Information, revealed that many people in Britain were unaware that white settlers lived in British colonies.[33] Much of the ignorance was a reflection, too, of a society still unused to the presence of black people in its midst, certainly outside London and the major cities. Learie Constantine recollected that when he went to Lancashire to play League cricket he went to a house where there were two small boys aged four and six. After he had shaken hands with them one turned to his brother and whispered: 'None's come off on me – look!'[34] This public ignorance on race was to persist through the 1950s, and the first generation of black immigrants came to experience considerable racial hostility due to a lingering public doubt that they all came from primitive jungle societies or had tails or were cannibals, a set of stereotypes that was often aided by cartoonists in the popular press, the continuing popularity throughout the 1950s of adventure films such as *Tarzan* and pulp fiction such as that of Ian Fleming's James Bond. 'I believe that most black races have more fears than the whites', Fleming wrote in the *Spectator* in 1952. 'They are timid experimenters and inept or unwilling rationalisers of their fears of superstitions.'[35] Fleming's James Bond novel, *Live and Let Die* (1954), linked this stereotype of a superstitious and credulous black population to an international conspiracy fomented by the Soviet Smersh in the black American underworld of Harlem, via the use of voodoo and the supernatural. Older colonial racial stereotypes were thus being updated to fit a new world order based on the Cold War.[36]

This idea of linking black political assertion internationally in the post-war years with the Cold War superpower rivalry became quite an important theme in the conceptualisation of race relations in Britain. It began in earnest in 1948 at the time of the *Empire Windrush* and continued through the early 1950s and was undoubtedly strengthened by the emergence in the United Nations in the late 1940s of increasingly vocal criticism of white settler colonialism in Africa. For liberals in Britain this became an object of profound moral concern as South African segregationism became further entrenched under *apartheid* and the society began a long trek into international isolation.[37] Until 1948 the white liberals in the South African Institute of Race Relations enjoyed a quite respectable status internationally, and considerable contacts had been maintained with fellow liberals in Britain and America. The Welshman and Director of the SAIRR, J. D. Rheinallt-Jones, was especially adept at forging links with Anti-Slavery circles in Britain and had helped establish the Racial Relations Group of the Institute of Sociology in 1938.[38] This body ceased activities during the wartime years as its members became dispersed and only started up again on a limited basis in 1945. In 1948, Rheinallt-Jones (now an adviser on black labour with the Anglo-American Corporation) sought to renew contacts with the Group, for the South African Institute of Race Relations was becoming increasingly isolated from African political leadership. The British Racial Relations Group initially welcomed this South African interest and announced an expansion of its activities into a body on the lines of an 'institute' or 'council' of race relations.[39] 'It is not nearly sufficiently realised here how dangerous racial tension may become', one of the group's members, H. S. L. Polak (the former chairman of the Joint Council to Promote Understanding between White and Coloured People in the early 1930s), wrote to Rheinallt-Jones, 'especially when related to colour problems and prejudice . . . the coloured folk of the world are getting more self-conscious and embittered, especially as a result of experiences gained in the war. It is upon this emotional material that the Communists are bound to play successfully, until the white peoples awaken to the inherent dangers of the situation.'[40]

The Institute of Sociology, however, declined that year to continue its annual subsidy to the Group to pay off its debt,[41] and the secretary thus invited six other societies – the East and West Friendship Council, the League of Coloured Peoples, the Council of Christians and Jews, the Anti-Slavery Society, the Fabian Colonial Bureau and the Friends International Centre – to a meeting to consider establishing an Institute of Race Relations.[42] This resulted in broad agreement, though the fact that the initiative came from a white liberal group can be partly ascribed to the general vacuum in black political activity in Britain following the demise of Harold Moody's campaign in the League of Coloured Peoples for a Caribbean centre in London with his death the previous year. Though a committee was appointed by the meeting of the seven bodies, no substantial progress was made until the Autumn of 1949, when it was announced by C. W. W. Greenidge that there were funds in the hands of the Charity Commissioners for the establishment of an institute for the encouragement of research on race relations, 'the promotion of friendship between people of different races', a bureau of advice and assistance and the (non-political) discussion of legislative or administrative measures affecting race relations. No agreement was reached on the aspect of promoting 'friendship' between races, though the committee, which divided itself into two sections, became supportive of a more academic research body.[43] By early 1951, however, the move by the Racial Relations Group for establishing an institute was to some extent upstaged by the decision of the rival British Sociological Association, centred on the London School of Economics, to establish a separate race department of its own. Though there was a call the same year for a committee of social science experts to examine the purposes and ethics of social research, especially in the field of race relations, no initiative was taken at this stage by the BSA. Most social science interest in the area remained centred in the United States and the Racial Relations Group began seeking amalgamation with a larger liberal body concerned with race relations which was launched early in 1952, Racial Unity. This eventually occurred in 1953, while in 1955 the Institute of Sociology was itself dissolved.[44]

Unlike the Racial Relations Group, Racial Unity started with a more Christian and evengelical basis. Indeed, it was primarily as a result of a suggestion by John Fletcher of the Society of Friends that it was conceived of as a 'movement'.[45] The impetus for it came in the wake of a letter sent by six societies (including the Racial Relations Group, The British Commonwealth League, The Society of Friends and the Anti-Slavery Society) to the Colonial Secretary, James Griffiths, in September 1951, urging the establishment of a committee of inquiry into the position of coloured people in Britain. Expressing concern about evidence of discrimination in employment and housing, the letter pointed out 'the increase in the number of coloured students and workers in this country in recent years has also brought about closer contacts between white and coloured people' such that it had 'now become more than ever desirable to relieve any racial tension and also to obviate colour prejudice'. The letter welcomed the government's existing support to voluntary work in the field of inter-racial contacts which, as we saw in the last chapter, developed in the late 1940s. But this situation was not regarded as 'wholly satisfactory' for there were cases of black people feeling isolated in Britain whilst also having difficulty in gaining employment or accommodation. Picking up a theme already common in the field of social welfare for black students, the letter also argued that it would be 'regrettable if coloured people returned to their homelands with any feeling of hostility to this country, its people, social order and administrative machinery'.[46] Overall, the signatories of the letter felt that they had a role to play in the welfare dimension with respect to black immigration to Britain, a view reinforced by both a global analysis of changing race relations and a fear, exacerbated by the Cold War climate of opinion, that welfare facilities were necessary to prevent black students and intellectuals in Britain going overseas with a racial bitterness or political radicalism induced by their living in a racially hostile society.

This welfare approach was given added impetus in the following months by the work of a former white female missionary in South Africa, Mary Attlee, who on retirement returned to Britain and was appalled by the apparent public apathy and ignorance regarding racial discrimination. As a result, an inaugural meeting was held at the Central Hall, Westminster, in February 1952, attended by over 2,000 people, to establish Racial Unity.[47] The organisation was founded with ambitious aims, for it stood by the United Nations Declaration of Human Rights and called for 'the support of all who wish to see that justice and goodwill prevail among the races of the world'.[48] In one sense, the movement was a direct successor of the original Universal Races Congress of Gustav Spiller in 1911, which the Racial Relations Group had sought somewhat half-heartedly to maintain after 1938. Part of the renewed liberal impetus behind it undoubtedly grew out of a rising Christian concern with international issues relating to race in the early 1950s, especially in Southern Africa. This was in part a result of the strong Quaker influence on the organisation, for the one organisation with a ready list of potential members (up to 40) was the Society of Friends; the only other organisations present at the start of Racial Unity were the African Relations Council, which was new and poorly organised, and the isolated and split Racial Relations Group.[49]

Beyond the more general objectives of promoting 'justice and goodwill' between races, Racial Unity had no obvious and easy function to fulfil in its initial stages. It started with a chronic financial debt of £380, compounded by its expensive launching, and £20 a week running costs, and there was no ready or automatic path forward. The task it set itself, however, soon rested on the sphere of education and promoting a moral concern about race through the wider knowledge of different societies and races. Its first secretary, Colin Turnbull, spelt out these tasks in terms of it being 'a broad-minded, wide organisation covering all creeds and shades of opinion'. It thus set out to 'convert' those who were 'wavering but are liberal-minded', particularly to the dominant ideological creed of the 1950s, in the wake of the foundation of the Central African Federation in 1953, of 'partnership between the races'. The function of the Racial Unity movement was that it was to act as a 'grand coalition' of all the various local bodies concerned with these issues.[50] The objectives certainly stretched beyond the more restricted research focus of the Racial Relations Group and implied the uniting of the study of race relations with a more engaged moral concern for changing attitudes, albeit on a 'non-political basis'. One of the most coherent intellectual sources of this proselytising view of race relations was the former president of the Racial Relations Group, Frank Norman, who had been a secretary at the original 1911 Universal Races Congress and later a UK representative at the ILO. After 1939 he was at the Ministry of Labour and, until 1944, acted as a labour adviser to the Jamaican government and to the West Indies Development and Welfare Commission under Sir Frank Stockdale. He thus had considerable knowledge of British colonial policy in the Caribbean and an understanding of the Caribbean model of race relations. His ideas were similar in some respects to those of Sydney Olivier in that he championed the rights of peasants to their land as a means of resisting proletarianisation:

> It is the most crying injustice in the world to enact that a people shall not be free in their own land, shall not have inseparable rights to move in it, and shall suffer the most evil wickedness of not being allowed to train and develop their own abilities. We have destroyed their own compact, closeknit strongly ruled community life – even if it was almost of stone age period, forced them into a different complex circumstances and not allowing [*sic*] them to develop their own powers in accordance, as Scott-Elliott says, with a tendency for a 'growth in mental ability to keep pace with complex environment'.[51]

Norman urged the study of the subject 'comprehensively if not too technically',[52] and sought through Racial Unity to keep the study and discussion of race relations from the total domination of professional sociology.

> It may prove that some of the methods and conclusions of some modern sociology are still too mechanical and its exponents too assured that the laboratory and test tube type of investigation can solve all questions of human behaviour. *Perhaps it cannot catalogue and pin down the living spirit like a butterfly in a show case*. Nevertheless the sociological approach is a practical one, and if this particular approach is used with sincerity and not wrested to suit a particular form of action desired by any arbitrary powers, should prove of inestimable value in the training of administrators and such officials.[53] (emphasis added)

This distrust of a more academic and behaviourist sociology was thus geared substantially to an administrative view of race relations. It was not clear how far Norman wished to see Racial Unity move in a wider task of political mobilisation to attack racial discrimination. Certainly he represented that more radical breed of Colonial Office civil servants who were anxious to break down notions of white supremacy. He was 'revolted' by the 'insulting and impolite behaviour to black people' by certain whites in the West Indies and later criticised the Racial Unity executive for referring to its white members as 'Mr' and to its black members by their Christian names.[54] In essence, though, the task Racial Unity set itself in the early 1950s was a mediating one between various small organisations, which in varying degrees reflected the demands of black people at the local level, and the machinery of government. Norman, as chairman of Racial Unity after 1954, and E. J. Turner, the treasurer, had connections with government as former civil servants and in October 1954 they took the initiative in presenting a second letter to the Colonial Secretary, who was now Alan Lennox-Boyd, urging a comprehensive survey of the black population in Britain. The letter was certainly representative of a more broadly based section of opinion than its predecessor in 1951. On the basis of consultation with a number of organisations via a coordinating committee that included the Stepney Coloured Peoples' Organisation, the Nigeria Union, Afro West Indian Services and the West African Arts Club, the letter urged legislation, on the lines of a Bill introduced in the Ontario legislature, to outlaw racial discrimination in public places, to introduce Fair Employment Practices legislation on the lines of the United States, and to remodel education in schools to inculcate 'racial tolerance and harmony'. It also urged that the teaching of history and geography in schools were apt to present a 'one-sided, inadequate and distorted picture' such that 'young people form a false mental picture and have a fallacious belief that the white races are inherently superior to all others and are permanently higher in the scale of humanity',[55] a theme originally stated at the 1911 Universal Races Congress.

These demands, though, were eclipsed the following year by the publication of *A Report on Jamaican Migration to Great Britain*, by Clarence Senior and Douglas Manley, which gained a fairly extensive press coverage and was also noteworthy for publicising the conclusions of the academic survey by Anthony Richmond in 1954, in a book entitled *The Colour Problem*, that one-third of the British population was 'tolerant' of coloured people in their midst, one-third was 'mildly prejudiced' and the remaining third was 'extremely prejudiced'.[56] The report concluded that there was a general British tendency to exaggerate the cultural 'backwardness' of 'coloured' people and urged a model of racial 'integration' that was strongly shaped by the West Indian pattern. It noted the 'absence of deep-seated hostility between natives and foreigners' and optimistically recommended schemes to promote 'Community Relations' via sports clubs, churches, civic groups and 'outstanding individuals of goodwill'.[57] Norman, as chairman of Racial Unity, saw the report as marking a strong ideological reinforcement to the movement's objectives for it supported the view that race relations in Britain were 'fluid in character and susceptible to education and modification'.[58]

This widespread liberal optimism in the 1950s was based on the fact that racial attitudes in Britain then were far less fixed than they were to become in the 1960s and 1970s. Michael Banton, on the basis of a 1951 government social survey and one he conducted from the University of Edinburgh in 1956, has questioned whether Richmond's description of race attitudes in the early 1950s did not *underestimate* the degree of tolerance of black immigration, especially in the context of low unemployment.[59] Politically, however, the rise in West Indian immigration from some 2,000 in 1952 to 10,000 in 1953–4 and 24,473 in 1955 and 26,441 in 1956, soon led to a rise in racial hostility. As early as 1951, an article in the *New Statesman* by Mervyn Jones began raising fears that the presence of some 15,000 black people in London would lead in time to the creation of a black ghetto situation on the lines of Harlem in New York. This process, in particular, seemed likely to erode the existing urban structure in which a liberal intelligentsia traditionally placed great faith for, as Jones pointed out, the presence of 'distinctly Negro quarters, on the American model' were replacing 'the old cosmopolitan neighbourhoods normal before the war'.[60] Such conclusions were in harmony with other warnings from Anthony Richmond in Liverpool that careful selection procedures would be necessary to ensure that only those West Indians with sufficient skills should be allowed to immigrate into the UK. Faced with a pattern of race relations in a city with a far higher level of unemployment (over 6% compared with the national average of 1.5%), Richmond's conclusions reflected the experiences of an area with far higher racial tensions than those generally confronted at this time by the Racial Unity groups in the south of England, or the inter-racial bodies that so impressed Manley and Senior. 'One or two severely maladjusted workers', wrote Richmond to the Ministry of Labour, 'can, as a result of their irresponsible behaviour, do untold damage to the good name of all coloured people . . . . In the interests of coloured peoples themselves, it is important that colonial workers should be recruited under a properly organised scheme rather than be allowed to drift here in ones and twos in hope of finding employment. Only in this way can the colonies be sure that they are sending their best men who will make a real contribution to production in this country, benefit themselves from the experience, and act as ambassadors for their country.'[61] This view placed the onus for the establishment of 'good race relations' to a considerable degree on the type and recruitment of the black immigrants themselves and the argument fairly quickly developed that it was thus the *number* and *quality* of the immigrants that mattered rather than any transformation in underlying racial sterotypes or values within British society itself.

Thus, despite the educational efforts by groups like Racial Unity in the mid-1950s, there was by no means a clear and united stand even within the British liberal intelligentsia on the matter and this progressively undermined the small efforts that were made. The work of Racial Unity was on a limited scale and, apart from a branch at Oxford, the organisation had developed no branch network outside London by the mid-1950s. The membership in 1955 was some 300 and a series of lectures and public talks on race was organised, including John Hatch, the Commonwealth adviser to the Labour Party, and the writer Cedric Dover, on China and 'The Colour Problem in Britain'.[62] The smallness of the organisation, though, meant that its more radical liberal ideals tended to get blurred as the field became increasingly dominated by more professional welfare organisations from the mid-1950s onwards. In 1956, the London Council of Social Service held a conference on the migration of West Indian workers to Britain, which four representatives from Racial Unity attended. A new phase of race relations welfare work began to take off which progressively eclipsed the more educational objectives of Racial Unity. Though the movement continued into the early 1960s, it lost the limited popularity it had enjoyed from 1952 and 1955 among certain sections of informed public opinion. A more professional social welfare approach began to lead to an ideological reformulation away from the liberal ideal of unity between 'races' towards one of fostering harmonious relationships between separate 'communities', a term which increasingly entered public vocabulary in this period.[63]

Fostering 'communities': the social welfare approach

The interest of voluntary welfare bodies and social workers in black immigration to Britain was by no means completely new in the 1950s. In the case of Liverpool the involvement went back to the early 1930s with the Liverpool Association for the Welfare of Half-Caste Children. In the late 1940s, too, the Labour Under-Secretary of State for the Colonies, Lord Listowel, appealed to the London Council of Social Service to get involved with the welfare of immigrants at the local level. By the mid-1950s the welfare interest had thus progressively increased in the wake of rising immigration figures.[64]

The voluntary bodies brought to the field a different set of interests and expertise to those of former civil servants like Norman and Turner in Racial Unity. For the most part they did not have colonial backgrounds and came from an indigenous philanthropic tradition of 'social service' that had first become embodied in the British Institute of Social Service in 1904 and later the National Council of Social Service, which was established in 1919. The central concept in this approach was that of fostering new forms of 'community service' to take account of changing patterns of urbanisation and suburbanisation in inter-war Britain. The movement was strongly localised in its efforts both to promote neighbourhood community centres on the new housing estates that were springing up in this period and to foster clubs for the unemployed and rural community councils in the villages, where traditional patterns of social life were seen as under threat in an increasingly urbanised society. Over the years the voluntary service movement developed quite a comprehensive pattern of local involvement, especially as it was successful in getting funds from the Carnegie United Kingdom Trust. It was thus able to develop a position, in G. D. H. Cole's words, of 'collaboration between state and voluntary agencies in the field of social services as against the old attitudes of antagonism or at most mutual delimitation of spheres'.[65] For politicians and opinion formers in the 1950s who were anxious, no matter what political party they belonged to, for a complete break with the memories of the 1930s and high unemployment, the movement epitomised the operation of political 'consensus' and the harnessing of local voluntary involvement with limited state involvement in a mixed economy.

Thus, by the mid-1950s the voluntary services carried some political influence, though there were worries that they attracted mainly elderly people.[66] An additional element of local public concern was that of the churches, and in 1949 the social responsibility department of the British Council of Churches held a conference on black students and workers in Britain, and in December of that year its international department established a Race Relations Committee to monitor the stand of the churches on race issues in both Britain and internationally. As the chairman of the committee, the Rev. R. K. Orchard, noted: 'the conscience of the churches as a whole' was 'not sufficiently alive either to the size or the importance' of the question of 'Africans in Britain'.[67] In March that year the Archdeacon of Birmingham established a Birmingham Coordinating Committee for Coloured People involving representatives of local bodies such as the University, the Colonial Office, the Birmingham Council of Social Service and the British Council; there were, however, no immigrant representatives until 1958 despite the existence of an Afro-Caribbean Association in the city.[68] This rather paternalistic approach was repeated in other cities, such as Bristol, where the local Committee for the Welfare of

Colonial Workers was formed in 1952 under the chairmanship of the Bishop of Bristol's adviser on industrial and social questions. In Nottingham a Consultative Committee for the Welfare of Coloured People was established in 1955 by the Council of Churches, the Council of Social Service and some local black immigrants and was rather exceptional in gaining a three-year grant from the Pilgrim Trust. The local Council of Social Service went on to establish a Nottingham Coloured People's Housing Society which provided an economic basis to the idea of local community relations. In 1955 a similar housing society was established in Leeds, known as Aggrey Housing Limited after the black liberal missionary J.E.K. Aggrey. In just over a year the society bought 16 houses and converted them for 40 families: 15 West Indian, 14 African, 1 Indian and 10 Europeans. The movement was centred on local voluntary effort and seemed by the mid-1950s to act as a possible 'solution' to race relations and probably encouraged the idea that active state intervention at this stage was not really necessary. 'This movement is still in its early stages', commented *The Times*, 'it needs ideas, enterprise, and voluntary service perhaps even more than funds. If it prospers it will help substantially to put a stop to talk of "politically explosive" problems.'[69]

The Nottingham example illuminated the general reluctance of the voluntary bodies to realise that existing methods of social policy were by no means entirely adequate when confronting a situation of black migration into inner-city areas, which were themselves in a process of economic decline towards 'twilight zones' hit by changes in the local urban economy and suburban migration.[70] This was especially exemplified in London by the Family Welfare Association, which opened in 1954 a special Citizens Advice Bureau in Lambeth to take up the issues of the West Indian migrants settling in the area. Though a West Indian family caseworker was employed in the Association's area offices and a West Indian social worker, Albert Hyndman, was on its central staff as a liaison officer, a report of the Association on West Indian family settlement that was begun in 1954 and published in 1959 manifested a strongly social welfare-orientated view of West Indian family values. The object of the report was to study the 'problems of assimilation of West Indians' and the issue was seen substantially in terms of 'racial' differences and consequentially the different pattern of cultural inheritance due to the legacy of slavery:

> The example of the masters was enough to impress on the mind of the slave that work was the badge of slavery. In freedom the ex-slave cared little for the type of work which was formerly his lot. This tendency is still manifested in current attitudes. Many pay little regard in the West Indies to the force of economic

circumstances and there is a tendency to look down on certain jobs even if well paid because they carry with them lower social status.[71]

This emphasis on the cultural legacy of slavery overlooked the processes of urbanisation and proletarianisation involved in the migration to Britain, but led to the view that West Indian family values were likely to inhibit the chances of eventual full 'assimilation' into British society. 'The savings efforts which are made even when the income is below average', the report continued, 'are sometimes amazing, and one is forced to the conclusion that the aim is to accumulate as much as possible, either because they plan in a few years to return home much better off financially than when they came or first own a house or two, and then if things go well a car, for they too, *and to a much greater extent than other racial groups*, pay a great deal of regard to the material aspect of status'[72] (emphasis added).

This conclusion contradicted a popular stereotype of West Indian cultural rootlessness prevalent in the 1950s and made famous through such novels as Samuel Selvon's *The Lonely Londoners* (1956) and Colin MacInnes's *City of Spades* (1957). This image derived substantially from the first group of single male West Indian immigrants in Britain, who were forced into a relatively marginal life-style based on low-cost digs, flats or boarding houses and who came to be seen as typifying the West Indian life-style generally. The report's emphasis upon both the family and the accumulation of savings was partly derived from the Victorian values of the middle class in the West Indies and took little account of the transformation that occurred in the process of immigration to Britain. Nevertheless, at one level it looked beyond the conventional view of a slick gangland culture of drugs, prostitution and criminal activity, and indicated a less pathological image of West Indian culture in Britain. While some sociological research has been subject to the accusation that it still perpetuates certain pathological images of ethnic minorities in British society,[73] later work went some way beyond the social welfare conception of immigration of the 1950s that tended to reinforce a largely Fabian view of administrative control and regulation of immigrant settlement. John Rex and Robert Moore's *Race, Community and Conflict* (1967), especially, began a sociological re-evaluation of immigrant settlement in Britain that emphasised the degree to which black minorities fell outside the dominant structures of the welfare state as well as their marginalisation in the 1950s and early 1960s in cheap, privately let boarding-house accommodation.[74] To this extent, the debate within the emergent field of race relations in Britain exposed many of the political and ideological limitations of the Fabian political tradition which, with its rather narrow cultural parochialism that went back to the Webbs, could only poorly adjust to a new situation of cultural diversity and social pluralism in British society.[75]

Indeed, contrary to the view that the 1950s was a period of *laissez-faire* and absence of state intervention, the period saw some evolution of social policy on immigration. The Colonial Office only reluctantly accepted this role in Britain and by the early 1950s was progressively trying to withdraw itself from the area. Until 1955 J. L. Keith continued in his post as Welfare Officer and Director of Colonial Students at the Colonial Office, where he maintained informative contacts with Racial Unity.[76] The same year, though, the Senior and Manley report recommended a separate West Indian welfare office in Britain and this led to the establishment from June 1956 of a British Caribbean Welfare Service under the control of a welfare liaison officer, Ivo de Souza, who was a civil servant seconded from the government of Jamaica. The service was divided into six different sections: welfare, industrial relations, public relations, reception and travel, community relations and administration. The welfare section was described as 'not attempting in any way to duplicate the multifarious activities in the general field which are now available in Great Britain' and was generally intended as a consultative section dealing with matters arising from 'problems' between the immigrants and the existing agencies.[77] Similarly, in the area of 'community relations', the objective lay 'in the organisation of the migrants to help themselves' for 'self-help activities would in turn aid tremendously in arousing the interest of the broader community'. In the administrative section the objective reflected the classic conception of American race relations of 'promoting the social and industrial integration of West Indian migrants and *attempting the difficult adjustment inherent in any group of workers migrating from a predominantly agricultural economy into a highly developed industrial one*'[78] (emphasis added).

In practice, the establishment of the Caribbean Welfare Service enabled the government to take quite a strong lead in the development of thinking about the question of 'integrating' the black immigrants into British society. At the end of June 1956 the first speaker at the London Council of Social Service conference on West Indians in London was Ivo de Souza, along with Miss M. E. Nicholson of the Lambeth Citizens Advice Bureau, Miss M. V. Raynes of the Southwark Diocesan Association for Moral Welfare, Albert Hyndman of the Family Welfare Association and Miss M. L. Harford of the London Council of Social Service.[79] Some of the conference discussion revealed the continuing grip of traditional ideas of social welfare in the area of black immigration: one speaker suggested the role of university settlements,[80] while Hyndman, of the Family Welfare Association, stressed the role of individual case work. Some of the more radical ideas came from de Souza, who urged the importance of immigrants joining trade unions and the provision of information to them on this. He also welcomed the idea of the Caribbean Welfare Service establishing a consultative committee to encourage the formation of housing associations and 'their special needs'.[81]

In general, the 1956 conference indicated the generally low level of understanding by the welfare bodies both of immigration processes and the dynamics of race relations. For the most part the comparative lessons drawn from other societies, especially the United States, were not at this stage understood by the voluntary bodies, reflecting in some measure their insulation from wider social influences and ideas. The 1958 'riots' at Notting Dale and Nottingham acted as a minor shock wave on both voluntary bodies and 'concerned' public opinion generally.[82] Though there was some attempt to blame the whole issue upon the particular 1950s social phenomenon of the 'teddy boy', then entering its last phase, the actual experience of racial conflict in British cities drew attention towards wider structural and sociological causes behind racial or social 'tensions'.[83] 'Attacks upon coloured people', wrote Kenneth Little in the *New Statesman*, 'should not be seen as racial hostility alone, but as the symptom of much deeper social tensions'. These tensions existed 'because of rapid change and unevenness in our society's development', especially due to the rise to 'affluence' of former working-class youth as expressed in the teddy boy phenomenon. Thus 'the whole programme of coloured integration may require reconsideration' and there was a need for 'the general life of the community' to be 'invigorated'.[84] Thus argument shifted attention in the direction of 'inter-racial bodies', or 'friendship' or 'international' councils on a local basis. Typical of such associations was the progressive Willesden International Friendship Council, which started off on the unfortunate premises of a children's kindergarten where its black members had to sit in kiddies' chairs, thus personifying, in some degree, a continuing Victorian stereotype of the 'childlike races'.[85]

These developments, however, led to a growing coordination in the work of the voluntary bodies. Even before the 1958 'riots' a National Council of Social Service Group on the Welfare of Coloured Workers was established by eight councils of social service in 1957, while in London, Nadine Peppard was appointed assistant secretary for coordinating fieldwork for the London Council of Social Service. By the early 1960s, the voluntary bodies were turning increasingly to professional and academic opinion and research as the vocabulary of race relations shifted from the notion of 'assimilation' to one of 'integration' as it became evident that black immigrants consisted not simply of 'colonial' West Indians anxious to be in some manner accepted as 'black English', but also Asians with a strongly cohesive family-based culture that resisted complete 'assimilation' to British culture and mores. At a London Council of Social Service conference at Oxford in September 1961 on 'Racial Integration', Dr Marie Jahoda and Judith Henderson spoke on 'The Roots of Discrimination', Alderman J. E. MacColl on 'Housing and Health' and Sheila Patterson of the Institute of Race Relations on 'Social and Economic Aspects of Housing'. The titles also indicated a development of interest away from the 'problems' in 'adjustment' by the immigrant 'newcomers' in the mid-1950s towards a more sociologically penetrating analysis of the immigrants' patterns of settlement and the question of housing and health care. The analysis of Dr Jahoda reflected the growing awareness of the psychological dimension of racial hostility, which had been a significant preoccupation in social psychology in the immediate post-war years, especially in the United States, and was now beginning to seep through into the British political debate on race.[86] The ingrained nature of racial stereotyping, however, and the interrelationship between anti-semitic hostility and hatred of blacks led Jahoda to warn that the creation of a climate of opinion where colour differences were accepted as a matter of course 'would take a very long time'. This belied the earlier liberal optimism of Racial Unity that simple education and publicity would alleviate racial hostility, and it was becoming evident that racial hostility was not only an in-bred attitudinal question but also strongly linked to structural issues relating to housing and employment. As Mrs Henderson pointed out: 'tolerance and aversion were so evenly balanced that any sudden change in the social situation, such as a shortage of jobs, or even the number of individual cases of friction, might well tip the balance towards intolerance'.[87]

In this changing political climate in the early 1960s, the government felt increasingly compelled to intervene in the area of race relations, especially with the increase in black immigration, which from 1957 onwards was including growing numbers of Asians as well as West Indians.[88] A Bill to restrict immigration had been originally suggested in Winston Churchill's Cabinet in 1955 and it has been argued that legislation at this relatively early stage in black immigration would have posed the issue in terms of control of migration rather than as an issue of domestic race relations.[89] By the late 1950s and early 1960s the rise in racial consciousness in Britain had destroyed this rather thin possibility. By the end of 1959 the West Indian population was estimated at 126,000 and the overall black population residing in Britain was estimated at 336,600 compared to some 74,500 in 1951. Black persons per 1,000 of the population had increased from 1.70 to 7.30 over the same period. There were growing signs of unease from some commentators. Even before the 1958 disturbances Clarence Senior wrote of a 'British Dilemma', though he placed great faith in those institutions 'working towards a structuring of the situation *against* prejudice and discrimination'.[90] By September 1958, in the wake of the summer disturbances, Norman Manley was urging the mobilisation of 'the solid traditional and powerful British opinion which set its face against colour prejudice and all forms of intolerance'.[91] But who was to initiate such a mobilisation? What indeed became apparent during this period is the bewilderment and confusion of many sections of the liberal intelligentsia in grappling with the immigration issue at the same time as they had difficulties in understanding the new elements of the youth culture brought on by the emergence of what was in popular parlance being termed an 'affluent society'. Pathological terminology describing black immigration became increasingly prevalent in the press by the late 1950s and there was a growing use of biological and geographical metaphors as a means of understanding this process. The *Spectator*, for example, in warning of a ghetto-style situation emerging in the cities, pointed out that the black immigrants '*flood* into a few slum and near slum areas, creating antagonisms among the poor whites already installed there, and providing the kind of community where crime and gangsterism can easily *breed*'[92] (emphases added). This fear that immigration would undermine the social order and threaten moral values was taken up in earnest by analysts and commentators on the right. 'The rising generation of British youth is already being handicapped in the evolutionary struggle by the moral degradation which was involved in, and has resulted from the last war combined with the wholly unspiritual atmosphere of thought engendered by Scientific materialism', wrote one commentator in the *Contemporary Review*. The consequence was that 'the young people of Britain are not sufficiently ethical to instruct their [black] companions how to rise. It is far easier to sink than to rise. We have an object lesson of this in modern America which has badly suffered from close propinquity with its less evolved immigrants.'[93] Victorian Social Darwinism was still alive in the late 1950s and, in so far as it shaped the vocabulary of 'maintaining social standards' used by the supporters of immigration control like Cyril Osborne, it contributed to a climate of opinion favouring immigration control.[94]

By 1961, R. A. Butler, the Conservative Home Secretary responsible for introducing the Bill, began to consider it questionable, so he later recalled, whether 'we' (i.e. the British people) could 'absorb' what he saw as 'largely unskilled immigrant labour in such large and uncontrolled numbers'.[95] The essence of the measure was in fact 'control, for the government at this stage was beginning to worry whether the immigration might not lead to a situation potentially threatening to the other structures of the post-war economic and political consensus, which had been based around the incor-poration of capital and labour into a stage-managed "liberal corporatism"'.[96] Butler, who had been one of the architects of the post-war Conservative Party's accommodation towards the welfare state and the mixed economy, was Home Secretary at the time of the 1958 disturbances. He strongly supported Mr Justice Salmon in his harsh sentencing of the white rioters convicted at Notting Dale.[97] He was also aware that the existing informal methods of social welfare organised through the voluntary bodies, valuable though they might be, would prove inadequate in the event of more significant immigration in the future. The voluntary sector, he told the House of Commons, 'can deal with limited numbers only, and, if the numbers of new entrants are excessive, their assimilation into our society presents the gravest difficulty, as many Hon. Members on both sides have informed me in the course of private conversation'.[98] Indeed, it was probably because most Labour opponents of the Bill recognised that increased immigration would strain the welfare bodies that they pitched most of their criticism in terms of more general political principles, especially those of Commonwealth multi-racialism. Only James Macfie, the member for Widnes, and a chairman of a committee of the LCSS, opposed the Bill in terms of the argument that the million pounds to be spent on enforcing immigration control could be better spent aiding the voluntary bodies and local authorities.[99]

The passing of the Bill into law strengthened government coordination of welfare through the establishment of a Commonwealth Immigrants Advisory Council under the chairmanship of Lady Reading. One of its functions was to examine the arrangements made by local authorities 'to assist immigrants to adapt themselves to British habits and customs, and to report on the adequacy of the efforts made'.[100] A more interventionist strategy was now under way, boosting the informal efforts already initiated by local inter-racial councils at the local level, which were broadly focused on the five areas of conciliation, fostering, social contacts, individual welfare work, political activity and educational work.[101] This led in 1964 to the establishment of the National Committee for Commonwealth Immigrants under the chairmanship of Philip Mason, the director of the Institute of Race Relations, which received an annual £11,000 grant from the government. A more professional approach was in the offing as the government saw the need for the greater institutionalisation of what was coming to be known as the 'race industry'. In essence, what was occurring at the most visible level was the active restructuring of an etiquette of race relations to fulfil the dominant moral norms of the British social order. As 'newcomers' to Britain, black immigrants did not readily fall into the customs and traditions of mainstream British social relations, and the systematisation of etiquette through inter-racial contact could be formalised as part of the process of social control.[102] The Institute, from the early 1960s onwards, thus began to play an increasingly active role in both the research and discussion of British race relations, though only in the wake of social research developed in the Department of Social Anthropology at the University of Edinburgh.

The 'Edinburgh School' of anthropological research

Despite the reluctance of the main body of anthropologists in Britain to get involved in formal research in the area of race relations in Britain, an important centre of research was established at the University of Edinburgh in the early 1950s under the auspices of Dr Kenneth Little. Having spent a sabbatical year at Fisk University in 1949–50, Little was keen to see race relations research in Britain geared to an educational programme that would widen public knowledge of race relations in Britain as well as introduce some concepts developed in the American context. He hoped also that the Labour Party could be made more aware of the race issue and in 1953, in response to a request from the party's National Executive Committee, submitted a memorandum that drew attention to colour discrimination on the basis of racial prejudice and recommended legislation modelled on the Fair Employment Practices Committee in the US that would outlaw the 'colour bar' as well as 'stirring the national conscience and ... creating a new standard of *public* behaviour in relation to coloured people'.[103] The Commonwealth Sub-committee of the Labour Party's NEC, however, was persuaded against legislation 'for a purely propaganda value',[104] and thereafter Little's formal links to actual policy-making on race relations declined, though he continued to remind the Labour leadership of the growing need for education on the matter. Mere 'book knowledge', he wrote to Hugh Gaitskell in the wake of the 1958 riots, was not enough for it was necessary to know 'the sociology of one's audience itself to meet their questions and explain them in terms that make sense'.[105]

The short-lived involvement in race relations at Edinburgh in the early 1950s did nevertheless lay important foundations for later research. The work of the Edinburgh School undermined the 'culture contact' model so favoured by anthropologists studying isolated 'tribal' societies in the colonial context. Working in such a highly urbanised metropolitan society as Britain, the Edinburgh researchers sought to develop new concepts linking race relations processes to the dominance of social structures defined around class loyalties. One student, Violaine Junod, who commenced a study of the coloured 'social elite' in Britain, began to rethink the issue in terms of the 'coloured middle class' since a focus on the attitudes of an 'elite' would render the study 'more psychological and individualistic'.[106] Similarly, Michael Banton, in a study of the 'coloured quarter' in Stepney considered that 'the integration of coloured immigrant groups will occur along class lines', with immigrants increasingly thinking of themselves as 'belonging to a certain class'.[107]

Despite the message of moral engagement bequeathed by the Myrdal study, the overall impact of American race relations thought on the Edinburgh researchers remained generally limited, for there seemed to be no precise definition of the end states of 'accommodation' and 'assimilation'. There was, furthermore, observable social and cultural resistance to this process not only from the dominant white society in Britain but even from some of the immigrant communities themselves. Sydney Collins, especially, emphasised the cohesive Muslim community of male immigrants on Tyneside drawn from Aden, Yemen, Somaliland and Pakistan, who maintained a separate social identity through the cafés and boarding houses of the seaport. Though there was a gradual process of assimilation, he nevertheless concluded that 'what seems to be observed in Britain in general is a process of accommodation between the racial groups, interrupted by occasional incidents of social conflict'.[108] Banton elaborated on this by distinguishing between those immigrant groups that sought to 'accommodate' themselves to British society and those who tried to 'adapt' to it, though the main variables seemed to be both the size and pattern of distribution of the black communities, its social and cultural bonds and the degree of 'social mobility' out of it via marriages with whites.[109] In general the School tended to take a cautiously optimistic view of the pattern of race relations in Britain and were not really prepared for the political mobilisation of nativist resistance in the wake of the 1958 riots. As a small group of social researchers who were working before the boom in academic sociology in Britain in the 1960s, they tended to follow the liberal educational goals of more involved white groups such as Racial Unity and the voluntary bodies, at the same time seeking to inject a greater degree of sociological sophistication into what was seen as a generally uninformed public. This educational emphasis was in part produced by the failure of the Labour Party before 1958 to take any strong lead on the issue – indeed, the party locally often bowed to white pressure to resist any favouritism to the black immigrants, as in 1955 when the London Labour Party, reporting on *Problems of Coloured People in London*, concluded that it was 'unthinkable' that immigrants 'no matter what their country of origin' should be allowed to 'jump the queue' for local authority houses.[110] It was also produced by the absence of any single black political body with which the white researchers could work – like the NAACP in the United States in the campaign for civil rights – and the general picture of the recent black settlers as only an emergent 'political minority'.[111] By and large the small black bodies that were formed in the 1950s tended to look to the Labour Party for a political lead as when the secretary of the West Indian Workers and Students Association, James Cummings, wrote to the secretary of the Labour Party in 1958 asking for 'positive action on all sides' which could 'serve to reduce the number of such outbursts in the future, if not prevent them altogether'.[112]

By the time the Labour Party did begin to apply a greater sociological sophistication to British race relations in the wake of the 1958 riots, the Edinburgh School had effectively dispersed and the main axis of academic interest shifted southwards to London as the newly formed Institute of Race Relations began to approach the issue. If the School had been given a stronger lead in the late 1950s, this centralisation of research expertise could possibly have been avoided and the later attack and transformation of the Institute by black militants in the early 1970s perhaps pre-empted.[113] Kenneth Little, however, eschewed involvement with the funding behind the emergent 'race industry', preferring to maintain a more detached academic role, and it was into this general lacuna of engaged university interest that the Institute under its director, Philip Mason, stepped in to coordinate a new programme of research far more closely geared to immediate political needs.

The emergence of the Institute of Race Relations

The establishment of the Institute in 1958 came a decade after initial efforts by the Institute of Sociology and the Anti-Slavery Society in the late 1940s. These had failed for a variety of reasons, including lack of adequate funds, worries that such a body might infringe the charitable status of the welfare societies, and the poor connections that the members involved, such as C. W. W. Greenidge and E. J. Turner, had with members of the Westminster–Whitehall establishment, a factor of no mean importance when it came to the question of establishing the status and credibility of race relations research and political activity. Furthermore, the small body of interested academic opinion, like Kenneth Little, strongly favoured the proposed Institute leaning mainly towards a research and propaganda role rather than a social welfare function, in which bodies like the Anti-Slavery Society had expertise.[114] The humanitarian and philanthropic lobby hoped the main purpose of the Institute would be to influence white racial attitudes rather than black ones, especially via the role of information, which, so the rational mind assumed, would lead to a more just and humane set of views, eventually emerging to promote a harmonious pattern of race relations. As one correspondent wrote to Greenidge: 'it is our own people who are the objects rather than the others whom we refer to as coloured. The main idea I

think is to hit on something which will appeal, but which is not mere sentiment, something academic, but not above the man in the street.'[115]

This intermediary role of race relations bodies, filling a role between
formalised academic research in the university context and wider political
opinion, had become fairly well known by the late 1940s with the precedent
of the South African Institute of Race Relations and the American Council
of Race Relations. But not all the activists in the welfare camp shared these
aims, for 'race relations' was not seen as an appropriate term in the early
1950s when only small numbers of blacks lived in Britain. Philip Eastman,
of the Commission of Churches on International Affairs, even pressed for
the inclusion of 'ethnic' relations in the light of the recent UNESCO documents refuting racism.[116]

The proposal for a British institute was raised more seriously in 1950 in a
more establishment-orientated context when H. V. Hodson, the deputy
editor of *The Sunday Times*, made an important address on the subject of
'Race Relations in the Commonwealth' at the Royal Institute of International Affairs. Hodson's intrusion in the field of race relations was by no
means coincidental. As a former editor of the *Round Table* and a director of
the Empire Division of the Ministry of Information between 1939 and
1941, where he had been concerned with dealing 'tactfully and
sympathetically' with Indian nationalist opinion,[117] he was in an important
position to see the changing nature of British political power and status
internationally. In one sense he represented the emergence of a new generation which had been educated, unlike Lionel Curtis and the original Round
Table group, in the less jingoistic years after the First World War. While
Curtis had to some extent declined in intellectual status by 1945 (though his
presence would still be a dominating one in Chatham House circles),
Hodson was very much on the rise. In contrast to Curtis's idealistic vision of
linking the British Commonwealth in organic union with America in *World
Order: its Cause and Cure* (1945), Hodson wrote of the idea of an evolving
'fourth empire' in his book, *Twentieth Century Empire* (1948), in which he
saw pre-war British imperialism as irretrievably moribund. Though
considerably indebted to Curtis's organic notion of the British Commonwealth, Hodson emphasised that it would live or die by its relationship to
the rest of the society of nations. The fourth British empire would indeed
only survive through 'an attitude of mind which makes the commonwealth
system work: the attitude of tolerance'. It was only on this basis that
everlasting world peace could be secured.[118]

Hodson, indeed, saw race relations as deteriorating in the Commonwealth and as being the single biggest threat to its ideals. His work as a
newspaper man and in the Ministry of Information had undoubtedly given
him a strong sense of the importance of communications and media in the

post-war international order and the interconnected nature of racial relations, which could not be isolated onto national terrains: 'a minor administrative act like the British Government's decision over Seretse Khama, or a social incident like a rebuff to a West Indian cricketer in a London hotel, many engage the sympathies and emotions of hundreds of millions of people who feel some sense of colour solidarity'.[119] The Commonwealth was an intinsically 'multi-racial' organisation and Hodson saw that it was ultimately incompatible with white supremacy in South Africa for 'sooner or later the one must overcome or be overcome by the other'. Hodson was thus concerned that the Commonwealth should progressively evolve on a basis that would erode white supremacy, which in Myrdalian terms acted as a minority segregationist opposition to a dominant liberal creed which was then seen to form the basis of the political values behind the Commonwealth. For Hodson, the Commonwealth was 'a unique laboratory for life-size political experiment while imperial authority still enables that experiment to be controlled'. The proposed Institute of Race Relations should thus be on a Commonwealth basis for 'the scientific and objective study of matters relating to race and colour'.[120]

Hodson's proposal led to a provisional council of an Institute of Race Relations in Britain being established at Chatham House in April 1951 with a strong orientation to research on Commonwealth race relations.[121] The Chatham House tradition of objective neutrality was still to be maintained in research and Lord Hailey became the first chairman of the Institute's council. The strong commitment, however, against white supremacy in Southern Africa in favour of ideals of multi-racialism generally ensured that the terrain of race relations research would confront political values far more directly than had been the case with the anthropology of the Colonial Social Science Research Council.

Support from Chatham House was vital at this early stage for it was clear that there would be no organised government support for such a scheme. While there had been suggestions for the establishment of an independent Social Science Research Council free from Colonial Office control and able to develop the social sciences as a whole, the Chatham Committee on the Provision of Social and Economic Research had opposed this in 1946 on the grounds that it was liable to lead to a 'premature crystallisation of spurious orthodoxies'.[122] Thus, Chatham House, with its prestigious tradition of contemporary history formed through study groups built up by Arnold Toynbee in the inter-war years, was left virtually unchallenged in the field in the 1950s as academic interest grew in the question of multi-ethnic 'plural societies' in the emerging post-colonial world and in the problems of inter-racial 'partnership' in such areas as the Central African Federation and South Africa.[123]

The Institute was initially organised, in 1952, as a body inside the RIIA under the directorship of a former Indian civil servant, Philip Mason. It initially started on a budget of only £5,000 a year, following an inaugural dinner at Brooks's Club arranged by Dougall Malcolm, chairman of the British South Africa Company. The growing availability of funds for research on race relations at this time ensured that the Institute would quickly grow, especially after a £93,000 grant came from the Nuffield Foundation for a survey of British race relations between 1962 and 1968 and a Ford Foundation grant between 1962 and 1967 of $250,000 for a comparative race studies project.[124] The increasingly academic commitments, though, of Chatham House ensured that a break with the Institute would be more or less inevitable at some stage. The Institute went off to form a separate body in April 1958 at the same time as an interest began in internal British race relations. While social science in British universities still remained heavily conservative in the 1950s and under the control of anthropology, there were the beginnings of academic interest in the subject and in 1956 a Rhodes Professorship of race relations at Oxford was created, leading to the appointment to the post of a white South African liberal, Kenneth Kirkwood. In 1957 Mason began to circularise the universities to find out their level of interest and to try to cement a partnership with Edinburgh, under Kenneth Little, and the London School of Economics, where Maurice Freedman lectured on race relations.[125] Even at this early stage, a grand survey as a 'Myrdal for Britain' was being mooted in the Institute, though the initial published works were a pamphlet by James Wickenden in response to the 1958 disturbances entitled *Colour in Britain* and a lengthier volume in 1960 edited by J. A. G. Griffiths called *Coloured Immigrants in Britain*.

The Institute was controlled by a fairly elite body through its governing council, 80% of whom had entries in *Who's Who* and had been to public school (14% to Eton).[126] The domination of the board by big business such as Barclays DCO and the British South Africa Company, indicated the links with capitalist interests in Southern Africa, and Harry Oppenheimer of the Anglo-American Corporation was a nominal board member, though he never attended meetings. The Institute thus represented a set of interests which were rooted in an earlier phase of British imperial expansion, especially in Africa, but which were now concerned to adapt to the rapidly changing post-colonial world order in which race and racism were seen as a potentially destabilising dimension.[127] In the case of internal British race relations, the Institute successfully adapted the notions of pluralism, adaptation and integration from the post-colonial arena into the metropolitan context and this had important implications for the reformulation of 'middle opinion' on race relations matters. Until the 1950s, political discourse in Britain had been relatively lax on race, reflecting the generally loose definitions of British citizenship and the cultural standards that were generally seen as accompanying it.[128] In Southern Africa, Cecil Rhodes's dictum of 'Equal Rights for All Civilised Men South of the Zambesi' had formed a rallying cry for a defensive liberal tradition in the Cape which opposed the mounting white settler segregationism following Union in South Africa in 1910 with the notion of the eventual 'assimilation' of an educated African elite into a common Westernised society.[129] As has been seen in earlier chapters, this had vaguely lain behind liberal views on race and colour in Britain before the Second World War in such bodies as the Joint Council and the League of Coloured Peoples in the 1930s and the opposition to the 'colour bar'. However, large-scale immigration of black labour had tended to scare even middle opinion and in 1947 Political and Economic Planning, in a report on immigration policy, had welcomed only the interchange of 'top level' manpower between Commonwealth countries, warning that 'the large-scale import of non-European workers' would 'meet with great difficulties for social and climatic reasons'.[130]

The Institute was careful not to identify itself with a policy of unchecked black immigration to Britain, but rather with how a controlled flow of black immigrants could be accommodated in British society without any upset in basic British social values. In this objective it sought to educate and catalyse middle-class opinion and that of the voluntary organisations in order to widen and deepen the structures of containment that the government sought to coordinate after 1962 through the Commonwealth Immigrants Advisory Council. The objective by the middle 1960s thus became one of 'integration' of the different immigrant groups into British society, an objective which was defined by the Home Secretary, Roy Jenkins, in 1966 as 'Equal opportunity accompanied by cultural diversity in an atmosphere of mutual tolerance'. The point was that an informal process of educational and informative contact should take place to promote harmonious inter-group relations between the black and white communities in Britain. It was hoped a mutual process of inter-racial accord could thus be fostered between black and white communities, for, as Philip Mason wrote in clarification of the 'integration' concept, there 'should be a steady increase in the two processes of adaptation and acceptance until such a stage is reached in mutual accommodation which may be called inclusion. This would be integration but not assimilation.'[131]

The work of the Institute was thus a more sophisticated version of the work of the voluntary bodies and their concern with the etiquette of race relations. It was not at this stage innovative in new patterns of race relations thinking, though this was in general a broader reflection of the poor state of academic thinking on the subject as a whole in Britain at this time. The Institute's journal, *Race*, founded in 1959, reflected a static and ahistorical view of race relations, which Anthony Richmond saw as an 'applied social science' and Michael Banton as rooted in the study of 'social distance'.[132] Despite the historically minded Round Table and Chatham House tradition which had led to the original conception of the Institute, the researchers it proceeded to ally itself to, came from a domestic tradition of British social science which by the 1950s had abandoned much of the former historical interest of the Institute of Sociology in favour of empirical analysis in the tradition of structural functional anthropology.[133] This led to a failure to link black immigration and the formation of black communities in Britain to a wider historical pattern of colonisation and its liquidation in the post-war world, and there was a tendency to engage in a static comparative analysis and compare West Indian 'assimilation' by the yardstick of the more successful Chinese pattern of 'adaptation'.[134]

There was a strong tendency in many of the early sociological studies of the black communities in Britain to analyse them in an isolated manner typical of the tradition of anthropological fieldwork. The class location of the emergent black communities thus tended to be frequently overlooked in favour of certain inherent traits which were seen as isolating black immigrants, especially the fissiparous West Indians, from the rest of British society. The 1950s were a bleak period for West Indian political leadership in Britain following the death of Harold Moody, the decline of the League of Coloured Peoples and the growing involvement by the radical Pan-Africanists such as George Padmore with African politics. British liberal opinion generally took the view at this time that West Indians had no culture of their own. Furthermore, they were seen as continually prone to factionalism. As Anthony Richmond wrote in 1956:

> It appears that any organisation which attempts to weld together the diverse interests of the various national groups within the coloured population is likely to disintegrate unless the sense of external threat is great enough to overcome the lack of common sentiments among people from as far afield as the West Indies, Africa and Asia. In the case of specifically West Indian organisations, status competition between individuals is often so acute as to prevent effective leadership from emerging.[135]

This view was born out of the general absence of black political organisation in the early 1950s, though local black bodies existed in the areas of longer-term residence such as Cardiff, where there was a Cardiff Coloured Defence Association. Many post-war immigrants were unable to appeal to any coherent political groups to take up any grievances and thus had sometimes to resort to the method of the petition in order to bring a particular issue to public attention, such as a group of former black workers in the army and RAF in Manchester who petitioned the Colonial Secretary, James Griffiths, in 1951, complaining that they were unable to obtain employment in local factories.[136] Though West Indian opinion began to obtain some coherence with the emergence of the *West Indian Gazette*, edited by the Trinidadian, Claudia Jones, in the late 1950s, the West Indian Standing Conference was a rather volatile organisation that was unsuccessful in organising nationally.[137] In its early phases it kept up contacts with both the Institute of Race Relations and the various inter-racial bodies such as the Clapham Inter-Racial Club, the Paddington Overseas Club and the Willesden International Social Club.[138] The initial liberalism of the WISC became replaced by a growing hostility to the Migrant Services Division of the West Indies Federal High Commission, which itself collapsed in 1961 with the break-up of the West Indies Federation. The publication the same year of the Commonwealth Immigrants Bill led to a growing opposition to alliances with whites, especially with the revival of Harold Moody's old ideal of a West Indian social centre.[139] No overall black organisation existed politically at this stage to mount a strong opposition to the 1962 Commonwealth Immigrants Bill and black political thinking was still governed more by the idea of asserting rights as citizens of the Commonwealth than as permanent members of British society. Claudia Jones thus condemned the Bill on the grounds that it 'knocked down the very foundations of the Commonwealth' and appealed to 'the British working class, with its rich tradition of human brotherhood and unity of working people', which she was sure would be 'appalled by this dangerous government policy'.[140] The main white support for this opposition came from libertarian and religious groups such as the National Council for Civil Liberties, the Society of Friends and the Movement for Colonial Freedom, who had originally backed Fenner Brockway's bills in Parliament in the 1950s to outlaw racial discrimination. The WISC was to a considerable degree dependent on these allies in order to make its protest heard.[141]

The direction of white middle opinion in the wake of the 1962 Act, though, was increasingly in the direction of further measures of control combined with policies to promote either the 'assimilation' or 'integration' of those black immigrants already living in Britain. The interventionist approach was well reflected in Sheila Patterson's study of West Indians in Brixton, *Dark Strangers*, which was published in 1963. The work was the result of research between 1955 and 1958 while Dr Patterson taught in the Department of Social Anthropology at the University of Edinburgh, and in some respects reflected support for increased government involvement in the sphere of anti-discriminatory legislation, a campaign for changes in the educational programme to reduce racial prejudice, and 'integrative social action' to promote greater migrant involvement in the life of the communities in which they settled.[142] Significantly, though, in the aftermath of this research Sheila Patterson moved on to further research on the integration of migrant groups in industry under the auspices of the Institute of Race Relations, reflecting the changing focus of academic initiatives in race relations from Edinburgh to London. This change in liberal initiatives in the sphere of race thus formed the basis of the Institute of Race Relation's 'domestic liberal approach' which Philip Mason impressed on the new Labour government from the autumn of 1964 onwards and which helped shape the climate of thinking which led to the 1965 White Paper, and the appointment of a junior minister in the Home Office, Maurice Foley, to coordinate integration policy.[143] While this was condemned by the Campaign Against Racial Discrimination, formed the previous year after a visit to Britain by Martin Luther King, as a 'spur to racialism',[144] there had already occurred a reorientation of British official thinking as the Labour government entered into a political consensus with the Conservative opposition on the basic thrust of race relations policy.

The Institute of Race Relations sought both to guide and mould public opinion towards meeting the transformation of British society from a relatively culturally and ethnically homogeneous one into a pluralistic and multi-racial one, though its entry into this arena was relatively late and its influence beyond government circles limited. For the most part, the initial interest in establishing the Institute had been to assist a number of multi-national companies to adjust to the new realities of political independence in former colonial territories. Its understanding of 'race relations' was mainly a developmental one, and studies were promoted on the 'modernisation' of ex-colonial territories.[145] By the mid-1960s, however, this conventional wisdom started to change, especially in the light of the influential volume edited by Guy Hunter, *Industrialisation and Race Relations*, which argued that industrialisation generally tends to adapt to the social order that exists in a society before its advent. This reformulation in social-scientific language of what has been termed in historiography as the frontier thesis generally absolved industrialists of moral and political responsibility for racial conflict and relegated 'race relations' issues to the sphere of the enlightened liberal conscience.[146]

The IRR did seek in the period of the late 1950s and 1960s to assist in the transformation of the older imperial perception of colonies as the abodes of 'backward races' to one informed by a more social-scientific analysis of 'backward' or 'underdeveloped' societies, in which 'race' as a biological phenomenon had no relevance. There was a strong sociological dimension to this reorientation of knowledge, though Philip Mason was concerned that this should not be pursued to the exclusion of a wider historical understanding of the manner in which 'patterns of dominance' had been maintained on the international plane.[147] Some critics such as V.G. Kiernan have pointed out that this intellectual project of liberal scholarship in the 1960s still maintained the essential idea of the *separateness* of European societies, making the distinction now one not of civilisation versus barbarism but of affluence versus poverty.[148] Furthermore, for some radical critics such as Hugh Tinker, who succeeded Mason in the Institute, there was a certain Toynbee-esque aloofness to this research enterprise, which failed to grapple with the immediate policy issues that could transform race relations.[149] These divisions were to become clearer as the crisis in the Institute blew up in the early 1970s.

The Crisis in the Institute

The developmental mode of thinking on race in the Institute in the 1960s began to come under attack by the end of that politically turbulent decade for failing to see that the hoped-for 'liberal hour' was unlikely to come. The liberally inclined managers of the Institute under Philip Mason became easy targets of a younger group of radical sociologists who began to surface in academic research in the wake of the university expansion after the Robbins Report. This sociological radicalism was a reflection of a breakup of cultural consensus in Britain and a growing attack on most of the visible symbols of authority through a new source of authority, social science research.[150] The cleavage became especially profound in the case of the Institute, which was not an institution with the same degree of prestige as a formal university, while its sources of funding were clearly drawn from private business. The general ideology underpinning the Institute's activities was also uncertain by the late 1960s, reflecting the somewhat dazed attitude of a generation which had not expected the relinquishment of imperial control to occur with the speed it had, or such a rapid growth in colonial nationalism challenging western values.

The crisis in the Institute in 1971–2 was symptomatic of a wider pattern of political and cultural cleavages in Britain by the late 1960s and early 1970s which were to have a considerable impact on the way race became defined in the media and public discussion over the following years. The immediate precipitating factor in the dispute was the publication of the Institute's survey, *Colour and Citizenship*, edited by Jim Rose, in 1969. This had been the long awaited 'Myrdal for Britain' which, with the support of a £70,000 grant from the Nuffield Foundation, attempted to portray in a scholarly and relatively neutral manner the state of race relations in Britain on the basis of extensive documentation. The study was generally pessimistic over the future state of race relations in Britain, since it appeared that the hoped-for 'liberal hour' in which there would be a broad movement in social policy on the issue had passed. It rejected, though, the view that British society was burdened by its imperial past, for it considered the direct influence of imperialism on political attitudes 'remarkably transitory'.[151] There was, however, no equivalent in Britain of an 'American creed' to which political and ideological goals in race policy would be orientated, and the study preferred to fall back on the more traditional concept of citizenship as the yardstick through which to evaluate policy. The report recommended a new citizenship law for the United Kingdom and the ending of the combined citizenship of the United Kingdom and Colonies under the 1948 British Nationality Act.[152]

The report appeared optimistic over the state of public attitudes towards race, on the basis of a survey conducted by the Institute in 1966 in which 30-40% of those surveyed revealed 'tolerant' scores, 34-42% 'tolerant inclined scores', 12-20% 'prejudice-inclined' scores and only 6-14% 'prejudiced' scores.[153] The response was not uniform over the whole country, and Britain could not be considered a monolithic society. In general, the report accorded with the view in the middle to late 1960s of a multi-cultural approach to race policy which accepted that immigrant communities would not simply disperse and abandon their cultural identities, but believed that measures should be taken to 'compensate' minorities for any disadvantages they might experience. It considered that the next ten years would be decisive for race relations in Britain, and that it was essential to take action to prevent the emergence of black ghettoes like those of the United States, though policies for repatriation as advocated by Enoch Powell were simply an evasion of the problems at hand.[154]

Colour and Citizenship appeared at the same time as Mason's own retirement as director, and he was succeeded by the then director of the Institute's International Race Studies Programme (IRSP), Hugh Tinker. The new regime that Tinker introduced at the Institute sought to break with much of the old Chatham House legacy which had been perpetuated under Mason, despite the difficulties that Mason had had in trying to gain official Chatham House recognition for the subject area of race relations in the 1950s. A newer generation of sociologists began to be recruited who were far less sensitive to the pressures for candour and caution in order not to jeopardise the sources of overseas funding from bodies such as the Ford Foundation.

For some of the younger generation of researchers at the Institute in the late 1960s, *Colour and Citizenship* appeared to fail in its efforts to promote a new climate of thinking on race. In a particularly outspoken paper, one of the Institute's younger researchers, Robin Jenkins, attacked the report for producing recommendations that were mainly geared to central government and failing to promote knowledge for the 'sub-proletariat' of the immigrant communities in the inner cities. The notion of 'citizenship', he charged, was without any firm theoretical foundation, while the survey reported in *Colour and Citizenship* failed to grapple with the class locations of those reported as 'tolerant' or 'prejudiced'. In general, the 'knowledge' produced by the IRR was serving the interests of social surveillance, for the Institute was acting as 'watchdog for the ruling elite', making sure that it received 'ample information on the subproletariat and ample warning of impending revolts'.[155]

These charges provided further ammunition for a group of radical researchers who had come together within the IRSP and were deeply suspicious of the policy-oriented research of the Joint Unit for Minority Policy Research (JUMPR) programme under Nicholas Deakin at the University of Sussex. The resulting demands by Jim Rose for Jenkins's resignation brought the white and black radicals, who were now being led by the Institute's Sri Lankan librarian, A. Sivanandan, into a political alliance under the figurehead of Hugh Tinker, who saw academic freedom at stake.[156] To Tinker, the advent of the government of Edward Heath in 1970 appeared to confirm that the previous Fabian strategy of permeation of officialdom by the Institute was effectively dead as a political strategy and that what was now needed was an alliance of moderates and radicals against the longer-term threat from the right represented by the Powellites.[157] Tinker refused to defend the Institute's Council over the Jenkins paper and merely suggested that Jenkins apologise for any 'personal distress' he may have caused. On 29 March, however, Tinker was forced to suspend Jenkins and the row within the Institute grew in its intensity.

A new campaigning style had entered into the work of the Institute after 1970, symbolised by the more engaged tone of the Institute's magazine *Race Today*, edited by Alexander Kirby. For the Council members this appeared to infringe the Institute's charitable status, while there was the threat that money from overseas foundations would be jeopardised if the Institute's activities became too overtly political. To Tinker, though, the older style of Philip Mason had smacked too much of Chatham House elitism, and all the staff members, including telephonists, typists and research assistants, were invited to staff meetings. This was the era of 'participation' and it seemed in the months of 1970–1 that a new era was being born in the Institute.

In practice, the Institute in its old format came to a rather dreary demise at a critical Extraordinary General Meeting of 18 April 1972 which had been called as a result of the Council's decision to sack Tinker and close down *Race Today*. For the traditionalists the objectives of the Institute should be studiously impartial, while for the radicals the Institute should re-orientate its work towards the black minorities in Britain and also champion third-world revolutionary movements, especially in southern Africa. A strong newspaper battle was fought by both sides, while there was a considerable degree of organised packing of the Institute's membership by sympathisers of the radical position. In addition, the radicals' cause was championed by a number of prominent left-wing sociologists such as John Rex at the University of Warwick and Robert Moore at the University of Aberdeen, which appeared further to undermine the academic credentials of the Institute's Council. With a train strike preventing some members from attending the final meeting, the Council's cause was lost by some 87 votes to 48 and over the following few days all the old Council members resigned. A new regime was ushered in that saw the Institute's journal *Race* become retitled *Race and Class* and a committed stance initiated which some observers have seen as having a significant long-term effect on the way that race issues have been perceived and debated in British politics.

The divisions within the Institute certainly appear at one level to have presaged a much more bitter pattern of polarisation over the following decade which eventually blew up in the riots in Bristol, Toxteth and Brixton in the early 1980s. From 1971–2 the former advocates of liberal reform at the level of the political centre in Britain around Westminster and Whitehall went on to the defensive, while the intellectual initiative in the area passed to those championing various forms of marxist analyses of race and class. At another level, though, it can be argued that from an historical angle the Institute's crisis marked the playing out of one pattern of responses to race and colour in British politics and their replacement by only a confused paradigm based on the model of third-world liberation. In the longer term, the demise of the older Institute may well be seen as exemplifying the continuing marginalisation of blacks in Britain from political decision-making and their failure to engage directly with the vital undercurrents that were to dictate the course of politics in the 1970s. These related in fact to the re-emergence of free market ideology in the Conservative Party allied to a strong upsurge in nationalism, and were to surface after 1979 in the phenomenon of 'Thatcherism'. In the absence of any strong levers on the centre of power and political decision-making, the black communities in Britain failed to be able to shape or influence these developments on the right.

The longer-term effect of the Institute's crisis of 1970–2 was thus to confirm the peripheralisation of black British communities from the apparatus of political power. The language of third-world liberation struggle which Chris Mullard, in particular, has identified as one of the features of the radicals' discourse in the Institute has no especial engagement with British politics and diverts intellectual effort away from formulating a domestic agenda.[158] To this extent, the challenge remains of developing a political programme of black economic and political advancement which can command credibility within British electoral politics.

Conclusion

The British imperial experience from the heyday of Victorian expansionism to the withdrawal from the colonial arena in the 1950s and 1960s left an indelible mark on British attitudes towards race and colour. While much of the Victorian thinking on race was shaped by the debate on liberal manhood, it is a limited view of the nature of imperialism and the governance of black 'subject races' to suggest, as has George Watson, that this was not linked in any causal way with Victorian doctrines of race.[1] The lurch into popular imperialism and jingoism in the late nineteenth century acted as a crucial vehicle for the reinforcement and bolstering-up of racial notions which had already taken hold of a considerable section of middle-class and informed opinion by the middle years of the century. The fundamental basis of British nationalism from the time of its emergence as a secular body of ideas in the seventeenth century had always been closely associated with Puritan ideas of liberty, though this was always expressed in a quiet and covert manner.[2] As imperial ideology developed in the late nineteenth and early twentieth centuries to reflect the emergence of the 'third British empire', these liberal ideas became incorporated into imperialism and ultimately acted to shape the emergence of the Commonwealth concept before and after the First World War. But in this respect, it also acted to reinforce a strong sense of liberal paternalism towards colonised and black races and shaped the early emergence of ideas within the liberal intelligentsia on inter-racial relations that were best expressed in their early phase by the 1911 Universal Races Congress.

A broad consensus of 'middle opinion' on a benevolent civilising mission towards black societies thus typified the climate of opinion on race in the first half of the twentieth century, maintaining strong links back with the Victorian consensus that emerged in the wake of the Indian Mutiny and the Governor Eyre controversy in the 1860s. With its benign faith in the inherent superiority of British institutions, overt racism became progressively suppressed in most respectable establishments and middle-

205

class circles in the years up to the Second World War. Much of what continued to be tacitly felt, though, can be gleaned from the more private thoughts of civil servants and politicians in memoranda and diaries as well as such popular literature as the ethos and thinking of clubland.[3] Within English society itself, however, there had emerged by the inter-war years a fairly tolerant climate of opinion on matters of race and it was partly for this reason that some black nationalist leaders such as George Padmore, C. L. R. James and Jomo Kenyatta chose to reside in the British imperial metropolis and develop and systematise their thinking on black nationalism. While there were issues surrounding the 'colour bar' and open discrimination against the relatively small number of blacks living in Britain then, the application of the imperial model of consultation with the established authorities by respectable black petty bourgeois bodies had brought certain results in terms of a growing sensitivity in some areas of government, especially the Home Office and the Colonial Office, to racial discrimination by the late 1930s and 1940s. It especially led to the growth of consultation on matters relating to the welfare of black students and workers in British towns and cities. The West African Students' Union and the League of Coloured Peoples of Dr Harold Arundel Moody (which has been described as 'the most successful attempt (in Britain) to create a unified organization based on the common factor of colour')[4] thus acted as an important black buttress for the liberal paternalist view of guided evolutionary reform towards growing political and social citizenship in an inherently liberal Commonwealth structure that tolerated limited and 'responsible' political opposition and criticism.

Though this liberal imperial model helped in guiding mainstream British opinion away from the more systematised pattern of European racist thought rooted in a rejuvenated nationalism, it nevertheless contained important racist dimensions. British colonial policy eschewed from a relatively early date the model of formalised racial segregation in the settler societies of Central and Southern Africa and verged towards the conception of Kingsleyite cultural relativism in West Africa, leading to indirect rule after the First World War, and the colour–class model of rule in the West Indies. However, when the colonial and paternalist trappings of these models of imperial control were removed and the model transposed in a neat form back to the imperial metropolis, then its more nakedly racist aspects could be observed at close hand. This colonial racism reinforced current anthropological ideas based on a polygenist view of race differences that emphasised the territorial and geographical distribution of racial groups. It also implied the need for strong controls on the emigration of black races out of their 'natural' environment. This was the essence of E. D. Morel's campaign against black French troops in the Rhineland and John

Harris's campaigns for the welfare of black troops in Europe during the First World War and for restricting the immigration of black seamen to the ports to prevent the emergence of 'half-caste' children. It shaped, too, the early movement to establish greater control and welfare provision for black students in Britain by both Harris's Africans in Europe War Fund Committee and the Colonial Office, and it was only with the advent of the Second World War and the need to mobilise colonial resources for the war effort that a more liberal attitude began to develop. If British imperial ideology can be seen as still a fairly self-confident force in the inter-war years,[5] it was the shock of military defeat in the early phases of the Second World War, especially by the Japanese in the Far East, that began a radical re-evaluation of both British colonial policy and policies on race. This played a crucial factor in the debate in governing circles on the response to black American troops in Britain in 1942–3 and the political compromise arrived at by the British government on the issue of their segregation.

In this internal debate and reshaping of attitudes within the governing class, the pressure of white left-wing opinion ultimately played a remarkably small part. While opinion in the Labour Party remained substantially indifferent to colonial issues before the First World War, the achievement in the inter-war years of some socialist critics of empire, such as Norman Leys, W. M. Macmillan and Sydney Olivier, was the shifting of thinking towards the idea of colonial development and welfare policies, which eventually became the accepted wisdom by the time of the 1940 Colonial Development and Welfare Act, passed partly in response to the 1936–8 West Indian riots. British left-wing opinion on race and empire remained ultimately restricted both by its predominant concern with the fostering of black agrarian societies free from penetration or exploitation by white settler capitalism and the championing of the cultural values and folkways of peasant, as opposed to proletarian, social groupings. To this extent the mainstream liberal and left-wing thinking on race relations before the Second World War echoed the dominant concern of the establishment-orientated and pro-imperial bodies, such as the Round Table and the Rhodes Trust, to avoid the path of American race relations and perceive it as the process of interaction between urban, metropolitan and capitalist societies with peasant, agrarian and folk ones. With the exception of some more acute observers, such as Leonard Barnes, of industrialisation in some parts of the Commonwealth, especially in South Africa with its burgeoning black working class, British radical opinion remained unreceptive to the notion of permanently urbanised black working-class communities as an inevitable concomitant of British imperial expansion and colonial development. The nineteenth-century mythology of black races as essentially rural and pastoral peoples governed by norms and values inherently antithetic to those of the urbanised and advanced metropolitan races of Western Europe and North America thus continued to shape and guide much of mainstream thinking in Britain on race up to the Second World War and left the society unprepared to cope with the advent of black immigrants into urban working-class communities in the post-war years. While some lobbying was done by white radicals such as Reginald Sorensen and Fenner Brockway on behalf of black students and workers complaining of racial discrimination, little attention was paid by a liberal British sociological body that had little academic standing and was poorly funded to the more sophisticated aspects of early race relations research in the United States.

'The contact of races in the States', declared W. E. B. Du Bois at the 1911 Universal Races Congress, 'with the peculiar problems it involved, was but a foreshadowing of what was going to happen in the world generally.'[6] This problem of racial contact had, however, a vital *urban* dimension, involving the formation of a black industrial working class and the establishment of permanent black residential patterns in the urban metropolitan network. From at least the time of the Chicago Commission on Race Relations of 1919–22 there had been a growing urban sociology of black residence and status in the northern cities of the United States.[7] In the case of the black suburb of Harlem in New York, James Weldon Johnson wrote in 1930 that by 1917 it had 'rid itself entirely of the sense of apology for its existence. It was beginning to take pride in itself as Harlem, a Negro community.'[8] Such images did not readily filter into British political thinking very easily and as late as 1954 Ian Fleming's novel, *Live and Let Die*, still portrayed the community as superstitious and liable to control through voodoo. Harlem and the American parallel indeed came to serve as a negative image in British race thinking and was used eventually by the anti-immigrant lobby in the 1950s and 1960s.[9]

The experience, furthermore, of even limited black settlement in the seaport towns of Cardiff, Liverpool, South Shields and elsewhere in the years before and after the First World War, brought a strong nativist reaction which reinforced a Victorian attitude towards race that stressed the climatic unsuitability of British cities for blacks from tropical societies and the probable eugenic unfitness of their 'half-caste' progeny. The external imperial mission thus helped buttress racial attitudes amongst the police and civil service and interacted with a tradition of indigenous and nativist hostility to alien immigration which went back to the campaign against Jewish immigration from Eastern Europe at the turn of the century.[10] Imperialism, therefore, even in its late and relatively benign phase, perpetuated a climate of opinion in Britain well into the twentieth century that buttressed a set of social models based upon a hierarchy of races, with the white Anglo-Saxon at the top, and upon the inherent antipathy of races to 'miscegenation' and inter-racial liaisons, for these produced a 'mongrelisation' of the white race. These attitudes appeared again in the 1950s as part of an immediate public response to the presence of black immigrants in white British industrial communities, and were also buttressed by a eugenic argument that it ran 'counter to a great developing pattern of human evolution' based on an 'array of variants', and the argument that black immigrants had 'measurable, and largely inheritable, physical attributes below the average for the United Kingdom'.[11]

The signal achievement of the liberal intelligentsia, however, was the progressive refutation of biological notions of inherently inferior or superior characteristics between races. This came substantially within the emergent discipline of anthropology, which managed to achieve professional and academic status substantially earlier than sociology. The rise of genetics and the retreat of physical anthropology contributed to a substantial loss of confidence in the subject areas of craniology and anthropometry by the time of the Second World War. This development within the intellectual conceptualisation of anthropology did not occur in isolation for it was part of a world-wide move amongst anthropologists and biologists to denounce the political manipulation of race for political purposes, especially with the advent of fascism and Nazism in the late 1920s and 1930s.[12] However, it had important British features as well and was noteworthy for refuting by the 1930s early notions of ethnobiology formulated by a conservative anthropological rearguard led by Sir Arthur Keith.[13] Even if the earlier British use of 'race' had been mainly in terms of the idea of a British 'nation' or 'culture', which until at least 1914 was 'still underpinned by a strong Christian ethic and leavened by the values of Victorian liberalism',[14] this became increasingly subject to the charge of 'racialism', which was an ideology substantially born of the twentieth century and virtually unknown to the Victorians.[15] The importance of 'race', though, in British establishment discourse was that it acted substantially as an anchoring-point for a more familiar class ideology. It particularly served to heighten middle-class fears of a widening of class divisions and the prospect of an eventual 'war' between classes. One writer, for example, warned of the threat of 'social disintegration', in 1867 at the time of the Reform Bill agitation, 'in which the moral unity of the nation is broken – in which the rich and the poor begin to form two separate castes, losing mutual comprehension, mutual sympathy, mutual regard, and becoming to each other as distinct races with separate organisations, ideas and interests'.[16] This lining of class and race formed a powerful ingredient to the Victorian imagination and H. G. Wells, in his novel *The Time Machine* (1895), linked it to Darwinian evolution when the two separate classes of owners and workers in Victorian England evolve into the two separate 'races' of Eloi and Morlochs who live above and below ground respectively.

The Victorian social order was governed by a dominant ideal of 'culture' or 'civilisation' which many Victorian opinion formers likened to the classical civilisations of Greece or Rome. The fixity of this order and its sense of permanence, which so impressed liberal observers of race like James Bryce, gave way in the course of the twentieth century to a less humanistic and more ahistorical 'science of man'. The classical analogy was applied fleetingly to the Commonwealth concept but lacked the holding power of the authentic vision of empire, and A. P. Thornton is probably right in concluding that the British ruling class never invested much emotional capital in the Commonwealth concept anyway.[17] What did emerge under the aegis of a Commonwealth-orientated mission of colonial development and welfare by the late 1930s and 1940s was the engagement of professional anthropological research in the processes of social and economic change and 'development' in colonial societies. Out of such a social science came the first professional discourse on the nature of 'race relations' in the British cultural arena. As the Commonwealth, however, verged more towards a 'multi-racial' ideal in the late 1940s and 1950s at the time of the last phase of colonial withdrawal, its meaning and significance, for the Conservative right at least, lay in its possibly providing a political model for a return to a system of 'informal imperialism', with all the rights and less of the responsibilities that characterised British imperial policy in the mid-nineteenth century before the scramble for colonies in the 1880s and 1890s.[18] The decline of the British economy, however, and its subordination to American power led to an erosion of faith in the Commonwealth by most sections of political opinion by the mid-1960s. Though the Commonwealth credo had been a major reason for Labour's opposition to the 1962 Commonwealth Immigrants Bill,[19] its hold even in Labour circles started to decline despite the hopes of some enthusiasts that a 'multi-racial Commonwealth' could even eclipse the empire itself as 'Britain's greatest contribution to the development of the world'.[20]

The post-war years represented a profound transformation in Britain's power status which meant that the former pattern of development, which had survived up to the Second World War, became interrupted and 'superseded by a pattern of development determined to a real extent by the interests of other powers'.[21] Opinion on both the right and left in Britain took some time coming to terms with this new status. Some Conservative critics of the Commonwealth reacted vengefully against it, equating it with a multi-racialism that was breaking down in the colonial context, such as the Central African Federation and its policy of 'partnership'.[22] By the 1960s this had led, in some cases, to a revival in a new form of the liberal racialist case against imperial federation. Just as E. A. Freeman had feared the domination of the British empire by coloured races, especially from India, so Lord Elton, in 1965, concluded that 'the Commonwealth is almost as far as it could possibly be from multi-racialism in the sense in which Britain is becoming multi-racial' for the Commonwealth consisted 'overwhelmingly of coloured citizens'. Furthermore, there could be no worthwhile classical analogy in an age of imperial demise and Elton saw the immigration of black people to Britain as emulating more the Roman empire in decline, when 'in its decadence' it 'imported subject races to discharge its menial tasks'.[23]

This growing pessimism in the 'ersatz assurance' of the Commonwealth by the early 1960s, especially in Conservative political circles, formed the climate of opinion which led to the development of the phenomenon of 'Powellism'.[24] It indicated that the Commonwealth acted as only a very uneasy and ill-understood ideological mechanism on the right to ensure the transition from imperial to national status. Hannah Arendt has argued that it is usually racism which serves this ideological bridging role for only 'in theory' is there 'an abyss between nationalism and imperialism' since 'in practice it can be and has been bridged by tribal nationalism and outright racism'.[25] It was this racist dimension of a more inward-looking and 'tribal' nationalism which Powell employed in his populist quest against the Commonwealth and for a new English national identity in the 1960s. History, for Powell, was always a series of myths and the point was to choose the most appropriate ones for the hour of national need.[26] The imperial legacy and its development into the Commonwealth he saw as an illusion, for the notion of imperial grandeur and a *Pax Britannica* only took hold of public consciousness at a relatively late date when the imperial star was already starting to decline.[27] It was thus essential to debunk all remaining illusions about the Commonwealth and 'the legal fiction' of Commonwealth citizenship.[28] Having achieved a somewhat painful transition from an earlier enthusiasm for empire (indeed Powell had originally hoped the Churchill government in the early 1950s would retake India), his little-England vision of nationalism saw no place for a multi-racial society. As a classical scholar, Powell, too, used images from ancient Rome, but this time it was of the River Tiber foaming with much blood, and the growth of black communities in Britain signalled for Powell the prospect both of civil unrest on a massive scale and a warning that race rioting on the pattern of the United States could also occur in Britain.

The importance of Powell's ideas lay not simply in their fitting into a longer pattern of anti-immigrant hostility employed for partisan political purposes, but for their cognisance of the growing crisis in establishment ideology in the late 1960s and 1970s.[29] Powell was in many ways an archetypal representative of 'middle opinion' – a 'one nation' Conservative of the 1950s along with such politicians as Iain MacLeod, Edward Heath and Angus Maude – he had a concern both for a regeneration of a capitalist market economy and for a measure of social welfare to protect the most poorly off members of British society. By the 1960s, however, this 'middle opinion' was itself being increasingly squeezed as the liberal corporatist consensus that had been established during the inter-war years began to come under increasing pressure, though it was not until 1979 with the election of Margaret Thatcher's Conservative government that a public disavowal took place of the very idea of political consensus. Powell warned that there was no illusory 'Commonwealth preference' to protect the internal British market from foreign competition and that a regeneration of British capitalism depended to a considerable degree upon a restructuring of domestic British society. The advent of black communities in British cities, which he depicted in terms of the riots and chaos of American urban experience, seemed to threaten and jeopardise this.

The long-term legacy of Powellism was the heightening of racial consciousness in British society. The establishment declined to take up the recommendation for a large-scale programme of 'voluntary repatriation' of black immigrants, though this idea continues to be mooted in some sections of the Conservative establishment.[30] Nevertheless, immigration restrictions have continued to be tightened, and in the 1971 Immigration Act there was a redefinition of British nationality on the basis of 'patriality' and the place of territorial abode – a concept that would have been well understood by the Victorians, engraining as it does the polygenist notion that separate races are mainly delimited to certain geographical spheres. But it did legally entrench the nationality rights of the black population already residing in Britain. The 1981 British Nationality Act went much further, however, by undermining the right of *ius soli* and the right of citizenship for anyone born in the United Kingdom and moved it more towards *ius sanguinis* and the right to citizenship through right or 'blood'. Anglo-Saxon racism may thus be in the process of resurfacing in British political discourse under the guise of a more nationalist conception of British identity articulated by the populist Thatcher government.[31]

The final withdrawal from empire took longer than most observers had imagined in the early 1960s for it was not until 1980 that the last colonial problem was removed with the attainment of Zimbabwe (formerly Rhodesia) to majority rule under Prime Minister Mugabe after the brief restoration of direct British rule under the governorship of Lord Soames. The outbreak of rioting in Bristol in the summer of the same year and in other cities the year following led to the appointment of the Scarman Commission and the formal shift in official nomenclature from 'race relations' to 'community relations'. As a judge with no former imperial connections, Lord Scarman gave a view that more closely resembled that of the mid-Victorian era before the advent of the last phase of imperial expansion. Scarman was especially concerned with the 'plight' of the ethnic minority communities in the inner cities and their relationship with the rest of the national 'community'. It was essential, he concluded, that 'people are encouraged to secure a stake in, feel a pride in, and have a sense of responsibility for their own area'.[32] While it was important to have community involvement in policing, Scarman pointed out that the main area of concern lay in 'community redevelopment and planning'[33] and even a policy of 'direct coordinated attack on racial disadvantage', which was 'a price worth paying if it accelerates the elimination of the unsettling factor of racial disadvantage from the social fabric of the United Kingdom'.[34] This represented a considerable advance on previous inner-city policy, based upon what John Rex has termed 'the crude environmentalist ideology' of the 1977 white paper, *Policy for the Inner Cities*,[35] and indicated that for the first time a major rethinking of ethnic policy was occurring in the context of an awareness of permanent black urban communities at the heart of British society.

Thus the colonial legacy may possibly have begun to decline in official discourse in the wake of significant and widespread social disruption. However, at the heart even of the notion of local community 'pride' is a Victorian idea of a pleasant and ordered society that is still ultimately rooted in a pastoral myth of rural gentility.[36] The century of imperial experience from the 1880s onwards had helped to freeze this notion in public consciousness, aided by a strong Kiplingesque injection of respect for the 'law' as an ordered part of nature. While black challenges to this seemingly natural order were subsumed to some extent by the wider biological notion propounded by Scarman of 'the natural aggression of youth',[37] the inference was that black communities still lay considerably outside the cultural bondage that holds 'British' communities together. In this sense the imperial legacy may still be said to have left its mark on the conceptualisation of ethnic minority communities as Britain completed the transition from imperial status to that of a more parochial and inward-looking nationalism in the course of the 1980s.

Notes

Introduction

1 James Walvin, *Passage to Britain* (Harmondsworth, Penguin, 1984), p. 119. See also Centre for Contemporary Cultural Studies, *The Empire Strikes Back* (London, Hutchinson, 1982).

2 John Rex and Sally Tomlinson, *Colonial Immigrants in a British City* (London, Routledge and Kegan Paul, 1979), esp. pp. 36–69. See also Frank Reeves, *British Racial Discourse* (Cambridge, CUP, 1983), pp. 112–27.

3 Stefan Collini, Donald Winch and John Burrow, *That Noble Science of Politics* (Cambridge, CUP, 1983), esp. pp. 3–21.

4 George Stocking, 'The limits of "presentism" and "historicism" in the historiography of the behavioural sciences' in *Race, Culture and Evolution* (New York, Free Press, 1968), pp. 1–12. See also Michael Biddiss, 'Myths of the blood', *Patterns of Prejudice*, 5, 5 (September–October 1975), pp. 11–19; Michael Banton, 'The idiom of race: a critique of presentism', *Research in Race and Ethnic Relations*, 2 (1980), pp. 21–42; Paul Rich, 'The long Victorian sunset: anthropology, eugenics and race in Britain, c. 1900–1948', *Patterns of Prejudice*, 18, 3 (1984), pp. 3–17.

5 George Mosse, *Toward the Final Solution: a History of European Racism* (New York, Howard Fertig, 1978). See also the review by Keith L. Nelson in the *Journal of Modern History*, 52, 2 (June 1980), pp. 284–5.

6 Pierre van den Berghe, *Race and Racism* (New York, John Wiley, 1978), p. 11.

7 Ruth Benedict, *Race and Racism* 1st edn, 1942 (London, Routledge and Kegan Paul, 1983). For a critique of the view of racism in terms of social attitudes, see John Rex, 'Racism' in *Race Relations in Sociological Theory* (London, Routledge and Kegan Paul, 1970), p. 137.

8 Marc Bloch, *The Historian's Craft* (Manchester, Manchester University Press, 1954), p. 151.

9 *Ibid.*, p. 144.

10 Cited in Howard Zinn, *The Politics of History* (Boston, Beacon Press, 1971), p. 17.

11 See, for example, Dante Puzzo, 'Racism and the Western tradition', *Journal of the History of Ideas*, 25, 4 (October–December 1964), pp. 579–86; Cedric Robinson, *Black Marxism* (London, Zed Press, 1983).

12 Christine Bolt, *Victorian Attitudes to Race* (London, Routledge and Kegan

214

Paul, 1971), pp. 17, 207. For a critique of this view, see Michael Biddiss, 'Racial ideas and the politics of prejudice, 1850–1914', *Historical Journal*, 15, 3 (1972), pp. 570–82.

13 Magnus Hirschfeld, *Racism* (London, Victor Gollancz, 1938).

14 Rex, *op. cit.*, p. 136. This problem is examined more fully in Paul Rich, 'The politics of "race relations" in Britain and the West', in Peter Jackson, ed., *Race and Racism* (London, Allen and Unwin, 1986), pp. 94–118.

15 Peter Fryer, *Staying Power: the History of Black People in Britain* (London, Pluto Press, 1984), p. 134.

16 Anthony Barker, *The African Link: British Attitudes to the Negro in the Era of the Atlantic Slave Trade, 1550–1807* (London, Frank Cass, 1978), pp. 23–4.

17 *Ibid.*, p. 48.

18 Fryer, *op. cit.*, pp. 134–5; W. Ross Johnston, *Great Britain, Great Empire* (St Lucia, London, New York, University of Queensland, 1981), p. 21.

19 Barker, *op. cit.*, pp. 53–8.

20 Arthur Marwick, 'Middle opinion in the thirties: planning progress and political "agreement"', *English Historical Review*, 79 (April 1964), pp. 285–98.

21 Noel Annan, *The Curious Strength of Positivism in English Thought*, L. T. Hobhouse Trust Lecture, No. 28 (London, 1959).

22 Hugh Tinker, 'Race and neo-Victorianism', *Encounter* (April 1972), pp. 47–55. Walvin, *op. cit.*, p. 42.

23 Felix Gilbert, 'Intellectual history: its aims and methods', *Daedalus*, 2 (Spring 1971), pp. 80–97.

24 Leonard Krieger, 'The autonomy of intellectual history', *Journal of the History of Ideas*, 34, 4 (October–December 1973), p. 500.

25 *Ibid.*, p. 507.

26 Quentin Skinner, 'Meaning and understanding in the history of ideas', *History and Theory*, 8, 1 (1969), p. 53.

27 Ronald Robinson, *The Decline, Revival and Fall of the British Empire* (Cambridge, CUP, 1982); J. M. Lee and Martin Petter, *The Colonial Office, War and Development Policy* (London, Maurice Temple Smith, 1982), pp. 249–54.

1. Empire and Anglo-Saxonism

1 Philip Curtin, ' "Scientific" racism and the British theory of empire', *Journal of the Historical Society of Nigeria*, 11 (1969), p. 44.

2 Thomas Carlyle, 'Occasional discourse on the nigger question', in *Critical and Miscellaneous Essays*, Vol. 4 (London, Chapman and Hall, 1849). See also Iva G. Jones, 'Trollope, Carlyle and Mill on the negro: an episode in the history of ideas', *Journal of Negro History*, 52, 3 (July 1967), pp. 185–99; Ian Campbell, 'Carlyle and the negro question again', *Criticism*, 13, 3 (Summer 1971), pp. 279–89.

3 See, for example, 'The West Indies, as they were and are', *Edinburgh Review*, 109, 222 (April 1859), pp. 421–60.

4 For the Governor Eyre case, see Bernard Semmel, *The Governor Eyre Controversy* (London, Macgibbon and Kee, 1962), pp. 173–7; Arvill B. Erickson, 'Empire or anarchy: the Jamaica rebellion of 1865', *Journal of Negro History*, 44, 2 (April 1959) pp. 99–122.

5 Michael Biddiss, 'The politics of anatomy: Dr Robert Knox and Victorian racism', *Proc. Roy. Soc. Med.*, 69 (April 1976), pp. 245–50; John Burrow,

'Evolution and anthropology in the 1860s: the Anthropological Society of London, 1864–1871', *Victorian Studies*, 7 (1963), pp. 137–54; George Stocking, 'What's in a name? The origins of the Royal Anthropological Institute, 1837–1871', *Man*, 6 (1971), pp. 369–90; Ronald Rainger, 'Race, politics and science: the Anthropological Society of London in the 1860s', *Victorian Studies*, 22 (1978), pp. 51–70; Douglas Lorimer, *Colour, Class and the Victorians* (New York, Holmes and Meier, 1978), pp. 130–61. Curtin, *op. cit.*, pp. 43–4.

6 David Owen Williams, 'Racial ideas in early Victorian England', *Ethnic and Racial Studies*, 5, 2 (April 1982), pp. 196–212; Nancy Stepan, *The Idea of Race in Science: Great Britain, 1800–1960* (London and Basingstoke, Macmillan Press, 1982), esp. pp. 20–46.

7 Hugh MacDougall, *Racial Myth in English History* (Montreal and Hanover, Harvest House and University of New England Press, 1982). See also Asa Briggs, *Saxons, Normans and Victorians*, 1066 Commemoration Series, Pamphlet No. 5 (Bexhill on Sea, Hastings and Bexhill Branch of the Historical Association, 1966); Donald A. White, 'Changing views of the Adventus Saxonum in nineteenth- and twentieth-century English scholarship', *Journal of the History of Ideas*, 32 (1971), pp. 585–94; Reginald Horsman, 'Origins of racial Anglo-Saxonism in Great Britain before 1850', *Journal of the History of Ideas*, 37, 3 (July–September 1976), pp. 387–410; L. P. Curtis, *Anglo-Saxons and Celts: a Study of Anti-Irish Prejudice in Victorian England* (Cambridge, University of Bridgeport, 1968); L. P. Curtis, *Apes and Angels: the Irishman in Victorian Caricature* (Newton Abbot, Davis and Chambers, 1971); Reginald Horsman, *Race and Manifest Destiny* (Cambridge, Mass., Harvard University Press, 1981), pp. 62–77.

8 A. V. Dicey, 'A common citizenship for the English race', *Contemporary Review*, 71 (April 1897), p. 467; 'The third empire', *Nineteenth Century*, 54 (December 1903). Not all Victorians shared this view, though, for Walter Bagehot scorned the idea of reducing the world to the 'dead level of "Anglo-Saxon" common-placeness' ('An Anglo-Saxon alliance', *The Economist*, 29 (1877), repr. in Norman St John Stevas (ed.), *The Collected Works of Walter Bagehot*, Vol. 8 (London, The Economist, 1974), p. 358).

9 Horsman, *Race and Manifest Destiny*; Anderson, *Race and Rapprochement: Anglo-Saxonism and Anglo-American Relations, 1895–1904* (London and Toronto, Associated University Press, 1981).

10 Philip Reynolds, 'Race, Nationality and Empire: Aspects of Mid-Victorian Thought, 1852–1872', Ph.D. thesis, Queens University, Ontario, 1978, p. 100.

11 Matthew Arnold, *The Study of Celtic Literature* (London, Smith, Elder and Co., 1905), p. 104.

12 *Ibid.*, pp. 147–8.

13 James Anthony Froude, *Oceana or England and her Colonies* (London, Longmans, 1886), pp. 8–9. See also J. W. Burrow, *A Liberal Descent* (Cambridge, Cambridge University Press, 1981), pp. 279–85.

14 Sir Charles Wentworth Dilke, *Greater Britain* (London, Macmillan, 1890).

15 Froude, *op. cit.*, pp. 10–11.

16 Dilke, *op. cit.*, p. 34.

17 'The Irish abroad', *Edinburgh Review*, 127, 260 (1868), pp. 509, 523.

18 Sir Henry Sumner Maine, *Village Communities in East and West*, 3rd edn (London, John Murray, 1896), pp. 9–14. See also J.W. Burrow, '"The village

community" and the uses of history in late nineteenth-century England', in Neil McKendrick (ed.), *Historical Perspectives: Studies in English Theory and Society* (London, Europe Institute, 1974), pp. 256–301; Stefan Collini, Donald Finch and John Burrow, *That Noble Science of Politics* (Cambridge, CUP, 1983), pp. 210–12.

19 Maine, *op. cit.*

20 H. M. Hyndman, *The Bankruptcy of India* (London, Swan Sonnenschein, 1886), pp. 9–10.

21 Arnold, *op. cit.*, p. 60. For the application of philological theories to race differences in India, see Joan Leopold, 'British applications of the Aryan theory of race to India, 1850–1870', *English Historical Review*, 89 (July 1974), pp. 578–603.

22 Edward Freeman, 'Imperial federation', *Macmillans Magazine* (March 1885), p. 444; C.J.W. Parker, 'The failure of liberal racialism: the racial ideas of E. A. Freeman', *Historical Journal*, 24, 4 (1981), pp. 825–46.

23 Edward Freeman, 'Race and language', *Contemporary Review*, 29 (1877), p. 724, repr. in Michael Biddiss (ed.), *Images of Race* (Leicester, Leicester University Press, 1979), p. 218.

24 Edward Freeman, *Comparative Politics*, 2nd edn (London, Macmillan, 1896), pp. 4–9. See also Margaret Hodgen, *The Doctrine of Survivals* (London, Allison and Co., 1936); C. J. W. Parker, *op. cit.*

25 Carlton Hayes, *A Generation of Materialism, 1871–1900* (New York, Harper and Row, 1941).

26 Freeman, *Comparative Politics*, p. 29.

27 Douglas Lorimer, 'Racist theory in British anthropology, 1870–1900', paper presented to the Conference on the History of Anglo-Saxon Racial Ideas, *c.* 1870–1970, Selly Oak Colleges, Birmingham, September 1982, p. 23.

28 Hayes, *op. cit.*, p. 255.

29 H. N. Hutchinson, J. W. Gregory, R. Hydeken, *The Living Races of Mankind* (London, Hutchinson, 1900), p. ii.

30 Lorimer, *op. cit.*, p. 161.

31 Hutchinson, Gregory and Hydeken, *op. cit.*, p. 216.

32 H. H. Johnston, *The Negro in the New World*, 1st edn, 1910 (New York and London, Johnson Reprint Corp. 1969), esp. pp. 2–6.

33 Charles Pearson, *National Life and Character*, 1st edn, 1893 (London, Macmillan, 1894), p. 68.

34 Benjamin Kidd, *The Control of the Tropics* (New York, Macmillan, 1898), pp. 50–1. For the genesis of the idea of the climatic unsuitability of the tropics for the white race, see Philip Curtin, ' "The white man's grave": image and reality, 1780–1850', *Journal of British Studies*, 1 (1961), pp. 94–110; and for a discussion of the ideas of the racist, Dr Robert Knox, see Curtin, *The Image of Africa* (Madison, University of Wisconsin Press, 1964), pp. 379–80.

35 *Mr Gladstone and the Nationalities of the United Kingdom: a Series of Letters to the 'Times' by Sir John Lubbock with Rejoinders by Mr J. Bryce, MP* (London, Bernard Quaritch, 1887), pp. 7–13 (letter of 18 March 1887).

36 *Ibid.*, p. 13 (letter of 21 March 1887).

37 *Ibid.*, p. 15.

38 James Bryce, *The American Commonwealth* (London, Macmillan, 1889), p. 308.

39 James Bryce, *Impressions of South Africa* (London, Macmillan, 1899), pp.

319–42. By 1912 Bryce had begun to acknowledge that the impact of migrant labour was eroding Basuto social structures. As a result of reading W. C. Scully's *The Ridge of the White Waters* he considered 'it would be the greatest pity to interfere with Basutoland' (*W. C. Scully Papers*, A2, J. Bryce to W. C. Scully, 28 October 1912).

40 John Stone, 'James Bryce and the comparative sociology of race relations', *Race*, 13, 3 (1973), p. 326. For Max Weber's ideas on race, see Ernst Moritz Manasse, 'Max Weber on race', *Social Research*, 14, 1 (June 1947), pp. 191–221.

41 James Bryce, *The Relations of the Advanced and the Backward Races of Mankind* (Oxford, Clarendon Press, 1902), p. 9.

42 Greta Jones, *Social Darwinism and English Thought* (Sussex, Harvester Press, 1980), pp. 158–9.

43 Bryce, *Relations*, p. 10.

44 Stone, *op. cit.*, p. 323.

45 Bryce, *Relations*, p. 13.

46 *Ibid.*, p. 15.

47 *Ibid.*, p. 19.

48 *Gilbert Murray Papers*, MS 148, N. Leys to G. Murray, 10 October 1902.

49 Raymond Betts, 'The allusion to Rome in British imperialist thought of the late nineteenth and early twentieth centuries', *Victorian Studies*, 15, 2 (December 1971), p. 156.

50 James Bryce, 'The Roman empire and the British empire in India', in *Studies in History and Jurisprudence*, Vol. 1 (Oxford, Clarendon Press, 1901), p. 33.

51 *Ibid.*, pp. 63–6.

52 Betts, *op. cit.*, p. 158. See also M. E. Chamberlain, *Lord Cromer's 'Ancient and Modern Imperialism': a Proconsular view of Empire* (London, Beverley Hills, Sage Publications, 1974), pp. 113–28.

53 Bryce, 'The Roman empire and the British empire', p. 33.

54 *Ibid.*, p. 83.

55 *J. L. Hammond Papers*, f. 15, J. Bryce to J. L. Hammond, 26 February 1900.

56 Viscount Bryce, *Race Sentiment as a Factor in History* (London, University Press, 1915), p. 25. This was a lecture given to the University of London on 22 February 1915.

57 *Ibid.*, p. 27.

58 *Ibid.*, p. 35.

59 *Ibid.*, p. 36.

60 Edward Carr, *Nationalism and After* (London, Macmillan, 1945), p. 21.

61 *Bryce Papers*, MS 3, A. V. Dicey to J. Bryce, 19 December 1918.

62 George Boxall, *The Anglo-Saxon: a Study in Evolution* (London, Grant Richards, 1902), p. 36.

63 *Ibid.*, p. 37. A similar view critical of the Roman modes of the Raj was expressed by B. L. Putnam Weale, who wrote in 1910 that 'the idea that any kind of loyalty can be fostered under a system resembling the Roman system is only held by those who in the practical business of life have much to learn. It is fear – and largely traditional fear – which in Asia is the white man's chief safeguard; and on such an emotion no permanent edifice can be reared' (*The Conflict of Colour* (London, Macmillan, 1910), p. 105).

64 Peter Jacobson, 'Rosebery and liberal imperialism, 1899–1903', *Journal of British Studies*, 13 (November 1973), pp. 83–107; G. R. Searle, *The Quest for National Efficiency* (Oxford, Blackwell), 1971, p. 126.
65 Anderson, *op. cit.*, p. 176.
66 Paul Rich, 'The long Victorian sunset: anthropology, eugenics and race in Britain, *c*. 1900–48', *Patterns of Prejudice*, 18, 3 (1984), esp. pp. 5–10.
67 Major Stewart Murray, *The Peace of the Anglo-Saxon: to the Working Man and their Representatives* (London, Watts and Co., 1905), p. 10. For the role of the National Service League, see Paul Kennedy, *The Rise of Anglo-German Antagonism, 1860–1914* (London, Allen and Unwin, 1980), pp. 361–85.
68 Murray, *op. cit.*, p. 94.
69 *Ibid.*, p. 103.
70 *Ibid.*, p. 104.

2. Mary Kingsley and the emergence of cultural relativism

1 *Graham Wallas Collection*, 1/12, Herzel Cary to G. Wallas, 12 November 1892. For a view of Indians as a 'hopeless' people and as 'indolent, improvidently lying, thieving scoundrels, everyone of them', see *Alfred Zimmern Papers*, II, Arthur Herbert Ley (from Motiliari, Bengal) to A. Zimmern, 6 September 1904.
2 Hugh Tinker, *Separate and Unequal: India and the Indians in the British Commonwealth, 1920–1950* (London, C. Hurst and Co., 1978), p. 23.
3 F. H. Barrow, 'Disturbances in Bengal', *Westminster Review*, 171 (March 1909), pp. 270–1.
4 J. Keir Hardie, *India: Impressions and Suggestions* (London, ILP, 1909), p. 102.
5 D. F. Pocock, 'Notes on the interaction of English and Indian thought in the nineteenth century', *Journal of World History*, 4, 4 (1958), pp. 846–7.
6 Josiah Oldfield, 'The failure of Christian missions in India', *Hibbert Journal*, 1 (April 1903), pp. 487–97; Christine Bolt, *Victorian Attitudes to Race* (London, Routledge and Kegan Paul, 1971), pp. 161–2.
7 E. A. Wodehouse, 'Racial feeling in India', *Nineteenth Century* (April 1910), p. 628.
8 Andrew Lyons, 'The Question of Race in Anthropology from the Time of Johann Friedrich Blumenbach to that of Franz Boas, with Particular Reference to the Period 1830–1890', D.Phil. thesis, Oxford University, p. 543.
9 Joseph Maxwell, *Advantages and Disadvantages of European Intercourse with the West Coast of Africa* (London, Smart and Allen, 1881), p. 19.
10 Joseph Maxwell, *The Negro Question: Or Hints for the Physical Improvement of the Negro Race* (London, T. Fisher Unwin, 1892), p. 10.
11 *Ibid.*, pp. 39–40.
12 *Ibid.*, p. 103.
13 *Ibid.*, pp. 136–7.
14 A. B. C. Merriman-Labor, *Britons through Negro Spectacles* (London, The Imperial and Foreign Company, 1909), pp. 134, 177.
15 Bernard Porter, *Critics of Empire* (London, Macmillan, 1968), p. 150.
16 Mary Kingsley, *West African Studies*, 1st edn 1899 (London, Frank Cass, 1964), p. 313.

17 *Ibid.*, p. 236.
18 J.E. Flint, 'Mary Kingsley – a reassessment', *Journal of African History,* 4, 1 (1963), pp. 95–104.
19 William Hynes, *The Economics of Empire* (London, Longman, 1979), p. 140.
20 Kingsley, *op. cit.*, p. 318.
21 *Ibid.*, p. 323.
22 Hollis Lynch, *Edward Wilmott Blyden: Pan-Negro Patriot 1832–1912* (London Oxford University Press, 1966), p. 206.
23 Porter, *op. cit.*, p. 155.
24 Owen Mathurin, *Henry Sylvester Williams and the Origins of the Pan-African Movement, 1868–1911* (Westport, Greenwood Press, 1976), pp. 60–82.
25 'The revolt against the Paleface', *Review of Reviews* (August 1900), p. 121; Mathurin, *op. cit.*, pp. 73–4.
26 Rudyard Kipling, 'Mary Kingsley', in *To the Companions* (New York, Doubleday, 1933), pp. 3–4.
27 J. A. Hobson, *Imperialism*, 1st edn 1902 (London, Allen and Unwin, 1961), p. 132. For the influence of Mary Kingsley on Hobson's attack on the colonial administrative ineptitudes, see p. 121, footnote 1, citing *West African Studies*. The fear over the fitness of the recruits for the army in South Africa was partly caused by the fact that the trade boom induced by the war led to numbers of able men, formerly unemployed, being able to find other jobs and thus not needing to go into the army. See Gareth Stedman Jones, *Outcast London* (Harmondsworth, Penguin, 1971), p. 78. For Hobson's ideas on eugenics, see J. A. Hobson, 'Eugenics as an art of social progress', *South Place Magazine*, 14 (1909), pp. 168–170.
28 Hobson, *Imperialism*, p. 136.
29 *Ibid.*, p. 138.
30 Hobson first worked out his theory of imperialist expansionism as a product of an underconsumptionist drive for external markets in 'Capitalism and imperialism in South Africa', *Contemporary Review*, 76 (January 1900). There was, though, a strong linkage between the economic and political determinants in his theory, for, as he pointed out, 'The causa causans of the present trouble in South Africa is the growing need of these economic rulers [the mine magnates] to become political rulers' (p. 5). The economic determinants behind imperialism in turn created the political attitude of jingoism to foment war, 'that race-lust of dominance, that false or inverted patriotism . . . whose essential immorality is summed up in the doctrine that British paramountcy is a "right" ' (p. 16). Hobson pursued his analysis of jingoism further in an early study of mass psychology in *The Psychology of Jingoism* (London, Grant Richards, 1901).
31 L. T. Hobhouse, *Democracy and Reaction* (London, T. Fisher Unwin, 1904), p. 28.
32 *Gilbert Murray Papers*, 8, J. A. Hobson to Gilbert Murray, 7 August 1902.
33 *E. D. Morel Papers*, f. 65, H. R. Fox-Bourne to E. D. Morel, 24 July 1901.
34 Catherine Cline, *E. D. Morel, 1873–1924: The Strategies of Power* (Belfast, Blackstone Press, 1980), p. 6.
35 *Ibid.*, p. 16.

36 *Ibid.*, p. 27. See also Alice Stopford Green, 'Mary Kingsley', *Journal of the Africa Society*, 1 (October 1901), For Harry Johnston's work and ideas, see Roland Oliver, *Sir Harry Johnston and the Scramble for Africa* (London, Chatto and Windus, 1964), and James Casada, 'Sir Harry H. Johnston as a geographer', *Geographical Journal*, 143, 3 (November 1977), pp. 393–406.

37 Johnston persuaded Dilke to support the CRA (Oliver, *op. cit.*, p. 348). It was Roger Casement who originally funded the CRA with a £100 cheque in 1903 after visiting the Congo and writing a scathing report on the forced labour system there. But from then on he tended to act as little more than an adviser to it, (William Louis, 'Roger Casement and the Congo', *Journal of African History*, 5, 1 (1964), p. 117).

38 *E. D. Morel Papers*, H. Johnston to E. D. Morel, 23 April 1904 and n.d. See also H. H. Johnston, 'The white man's place in Africa', *The Nineteenth Century* (June 1904).

39 H. Johnston, 'Introduction', in E. D. Morel, *Red Rubber*, 2nd edn (London, T. Fisher Unwin, 1908), p. xvi. Johnston's arguments reflected the current political agitation in both Britain and South Africa over the 'Black Peril' of independent African church movements. The scare had gained especial importance as a consequence of the Bambata Rebellion in Natal of 1906–7. 'I venture to warn those who are interested in African politics', he wrote, 'that a movement is already begun and is spreading fast, which will unite the negroes against the white race.' See also Shula Marks, *Reluctant Rebellion* (Oxford, Clarendon Press, 1970).

40 *Ibid.*, p. 209.

41 *Ibid.*, p. 208.

42 *E. D. Morel Papers*, E. D. Morel to Walter Langley (from Paris) 26 February 1909. See Catherine Cline, 'E. D. Morel and the crusade against the Foreign Office', *Journal of Modern History* (June 1967), who points out that Morel's crusade came at a time when British policy on the Congo had brought considerable reform in the labour system (p. 128).

43 *E. D. Morel Papers*, E. D. Morel to Edward Grey, 28 December 1906.

44 *E. D. Morel Papers*, E. D. Morel to Walter Langley, 27 February 1909.

45 John Harris, *Dawn in Darkest Africa* (London, Smith, Elder and Co., 1914), p. 126.

46 Susan Kaplan, 'The mudfish and the crocodile: underdevelopment of a West African bourgeoisie', *Science and Society*, 41 (1977–8), pp. 328–30. For racial hostility in Britain, see Merriman-Labor, *op. cit.*

47 Harris, *op. cit.*, p. 114.

48 John Harris, *Africa: Slave or Free* (London, SCM, 1919), p. 112. See also Brian Willan, 'The Anti-Slavery and Aborigines Protection Society and the South African Natives Land Act of 1913, *Journal of African History*, 20 (1979), pp. 83–102. Harris also visited Rhodesia in 1914 to collect evidence against the British South Africa Company and he was eventually deported. See Robin Palmer, *Land and Racial Domination in Rhodesia* (London, Heinemann, 1979), p. 112.

49 Harris, *Africa: Slave or Free*, pp. v–xiv.

50 Willan, *op. cit.*

51 Harris, *Africa: Slave or Free*, pp. 54–5; 'South Africa – the golden opportunity', *Contemporary Review*, 115 (June 1919), p. 642.

52 Harris, *Africa: Slave or Free*, p. 41. For the Webbs' attitude to race, see J. M. Winter, 'The Webbs and the non-white world: a case of socialist racism', *Journal of Contemporary History*, 9 (1974), pp. 181–92. For Harris's views on shaping Labour Party thinking, see *Gilbert Murray Papers*, 378, J. Harris to G. Murray, 17 November 1922.

53 Brian Willan, 'The South African Native Labour Contingent, 1916–18', *Journal of African History*, 19, 1 (1978), p. 71.

54 Sir H. C. Sloley, 'The African Native Labour Contingent and the Welfare Committee', *Journal of the African Society*, 17 (1918), p. 208.

55 MSS Brit. Emp. S22 G427, minutes of the committee meeting of the Edinburgh Council of the Committee for the Welfare of Africans in Europe, 14 December 1916.

56 *Ibid.*, John Cowley to John Harris, July 1917, enclosing Glasgow committee's appeal. The committee had collected £750 already.

57 John Harris, 'Colonial dependencies: "possession" or "trusteeship"?', *Contemporary Review*, 113 (February 1918), pp. 207–12. See also William Louis, 'Sir John Harris and "colonial trusteeship" ', *Bulletin des sciences d'outre mer*, 3 (1968), pp. 832–56.

58 John Harris, 'Peace terms and colonial reconstruction', *Fortnightly Review*, 105 (March 1919), pp. 424–33. See also Noel Buxton, 'The international factor in African settlement', *Contemporary Review*, 635 (November 1918), pp. 513–20.

59 E. D. Morel, *Africa and the Peace of Europe* (London, National Labour Press, 1917), pp. 80–1. See also E. D. Morel, *The Black Man's Burden* (Manchester and London, National Labour Press 1920). Morel had linked his ideas to those of the cooperative movement by the end of the war and saw the two forces of 'womanhood' and 'economic cooperation' being the factors crucial for a new world order (E. D. Morel, *The Cooperative Movement and World Problems* (London, Union of Democratic Control, 1921). For Morel's views on Kenya and 'paramountcy', see 'Two African policies', *Contemporary Review*, 124 (September 1923), pp. 310–20.

60 Robert Reinders, 'Racialism on the left: E. D. Morel and the "Black Horror on the Rhine" ', *International Review of Social History*, 1 (1968), pp. 1–28; Keith L. Nelson, 'The "Black Horror on the Rhine": race as a factor in post World War One diplomacy', *Journal of Modern History*, 42(1970), pp. 606–27; Sally Marks, 'Black watch on the Rhine: a study in propaganda, prejudice and prurience', *European Studies Review*, 13, 3 (July 1984), pp. 297–333. For Morel's role in the Union of Democratic Control, see A.J.P. Taylor, *The Trouble Makers* (London, Hamish Hamilton, 1957), pp. 132–66. See also Peter Fryer, *Staying Power* (London, Pluto Press, 1984), pp. 316–21.

61 E. D. Morel, 'The black scourge in Europe', *Daily Herald*, 10 April 1920, repr. as a pamphlet by the Union of Democratic Control (London, 1920), p. 6.

62 E. D. Morel, 'The black scourge in Europe', p. 6; *The Horror on the Rhine* (London, Union of Democratic Control, 1920).

63 H. W. Massingham, 'A glance at the French occupation', *Nation and Athenaeum*, 22 October 1921, p. 139; 'The question of responsibility', *ibid.*, 29 October 1921. See also Norman Angell, 'France and the black power', *Contemporary Review*, 121 (1922), pp. 226–9; Josiah Wedgwood, 'Big business and the black races', *New Leader*, 7 September 1922. See also Cline, *E.*

D. Morel, pp. 126–8 noting support from the *Daily Herald* and the *Labour Leader*.

64 See Chapter 6.

65 Porter, *op. cit.*, p. 155.

66 Michael Freeden, *The New Liberalism* (London, Clarendon Press, 1978).

67 Noel Annan, *The Curious Strength of Positivism in English Thought*, L. T. Hobhouse Memorial Trust Lecture, No. 28 (London, Athlone Press, 1962). Kipling's notion of 'the law' did not go totally unchallenged, though, for H. G. Wells's novel, *The Island of Dr Moreau* (1896), to some extent undermined the idea of 'the law' by linking it to the eugenic monstrosities of Moreau's half-men/half-beasts. Unlike Kipling, Wells did not hold that scientific progress was necessarily beneficent.

68 Perry Anderson, 'Components of the national culture', *New Left Review*, 50 (1968), pp. 3–57. Stefan Collini has argued that the philosophical idealism of L. T. Hobhouse did provide the basis for such a coherent social theory in England ('Sociology and idealism in Britain, 1830–1920', *Archives européenes de sociologie*, 19 (1978), pp. 3–50).

69 Philip Abrams, *The Origins of British Sociology, 1834–1914* (Chicago and London, University of Chicago Press, 1968).

70 *Gilbert Murray Papers*, MS 8, J. A. Hobson to G. Murray, 7 August 1902.

71 J. W. Burrow, *Evolution and Society* (Cambridge, CUP, 1966), p. 263. See also George Stocking, 'The persistence of polygenist thought in post-Darwinian anthropology', in *Race, Culture and Evolution* (New York, Free Press, 1968), pp. 42–68.

72 D. S. Margoliouth, 'The First Universal Races Congress', *Sociological Review*, 4 (1911), pp. 216–31; H. H. Johnston, 'Racial problems and the Congress of Races', *Contemporary Review*, 100 (August 1911), pp. 149–68; Michael Biddiss, 'The Universal Races Congress of 1911', *Race*, 13, 1 (1971), p. 37; Paul Rich, 'The baptism of a new era: the 1911 Universal Races Congress and the liberal ideology of race', *Ethnic and Racial Studies*, 7, 4 (October 1984), 534–50.

73 Spiller was the organiser of this congress. See Agnes Grove, 'The Meaning of the International Moral Education Congress', *Fortnightly Review* (July 1908), pp. 69–73.

74 MSS Brit. Emp. S22 C441, G. Spiller, circular, 30 March 1909, encl. memorandum, n.d.

75 *Ibid.*, R. Felkin to Travers Buxton, 7 December 1909; L. G. Harrington (Congo Reform Assoc.) to Travers Buxton, 10 December 1909; notes on a gathering of the Universal Races Congress, 13 December 1909, at Westminster Palace Hotel presided over by Professor L. T. Hobhouse. The discussion was described as 'most desultory, the object of the Congress being barely referred to' (22 December 1909).

76 G. Spiller, quoted in report, *Review of Reviews* (25 October 1910).

77 R. J. Halliday, 'The sociological movement, the Sociological Society and the genesis of academic sociology in Britain', *Sociological Review*, 16, 3 (1968), pp. 377–98.

78 Johnston, 'Racial problems and the Congress of Races', p. 149.

79 *Ibid.*, p. 160.

80 Reported in *Review of Reviews* (April 1911).

81 Jean Finot, 'The races myth', *Review of Reviews* (April 1911), pp. 363–4. See

also Jean Finot, 'Long heads and broad heads', *Contemporary Review*, 99 (April 1911), pp. 479–85.
82 Jean Finot, *Race Prejudice* (London, Archibald Constable and Co., 1906), p. 319.
83 *Ibid.*, p. 320.
84 Johnston, 'Racial problems and the Congress of Races', pp. 165–8.
85 G. Spiller, 'The problem of race equality', *Papers on Inter-Racial Problems communicated to the First Universal Races Congress held at the University of London, 26–29 July, 1911, edited for the Congress Executive by G. Spiller, Hon. Organiser of the Congress* (London, P. S. King and Boston, The World's Peace Foundation, 1911), p. 35.
86 *Ibid.*, pp. 38–9.
87 Edwin Mead, 'International organisation for inter-racial goodwill', in *ibid.*, pp. 443–53.
88 Biddiss, *op. cit.*, p. 45.
89 *The Times*, 28 July 1911.
90 Sydney Olivier, letter in *The Times*, 6 August 1911.
91 Biddiss, *op. cit.*, p. 45.
92 *Ibid.*, p. 45.
93 *A. C. Haddon Papers*, 5406, Duse Mohammed Ali to A. C. Haddon, 30 April 1912; *Review of Reviews*, 276 (December 1912), p. 669.
94 Duse Mohammed, *In the Land of the Pharaohs* (London, Stanley Paul and Co., 1911), pp. 3–4. See also Ian Duffield, 'The dilemma of Pan-Africanism for blacks in Britain, 1760–1950', paper given at the International Conference on the History of Blacks in Britain, Institute of Education, London, September 1982.
95 Stanton Coite, 'The ethical movement and the non-European', *African Times and Oriental Review* (June 1913).
96 Marcus Garvey, 'The British West Indies in the mirror of civilisation', *African Times and Oriental Review* (October 1913).
97 F. E. M. Hercules, 'The African and nationalism', *African Telegraph* (December 1918). See also W. F. Elkins, 'Hercules and the Society of Peoples of African Origin', *Caribbean Studies* (January 1972), pp. 47–9 and Fryer, *op. cit.*, pp. 313–16.
98 George Shepperson, 'Pan-Africanism and "Pan-Africanism": some historical notes', *Phylon*, 23 (1962), p. 354.
99 R. J. Vincent, 'Race in international relations', *International Affairs*, 58, 4 (1982), pp. 658–70.

3. The Commonwealth ideal and the problem of racial segregation

1 John Cell, *The Highest Stage of White Supremacy: the Origins of Segregation in South Africa and the American South* (Cambridge, CUP), p. 18.
2 C. Van Woodward, *The Strange Career of Jim Crow*, 3rd edn (New York, Oxford University Press, 1974), p. 69. Segregation did start to be implemented in some cities in the South before the Civil War. See Roger Fischer, 'Racial segregation in ante bellum New Orleans', *American Historical Review*, 74, 3 (February 1969), pp. 926–37.
3 Van Woodward, *op. cit.*, pp. 72–4; I. A. Newby, *Jim Crow's Defense* (Baton

Rouge, Louisiana State University Press, 1973), pp. 19–51; Stuart Anderson, *Race and Rapprochement: Anglo-Saxonism and Anglo-American Relations* (London and Toronto, Associated University Press, 1981).

4 Newby, *op. cit.*, p. 15; Van Woodward, *op. cit.*; John Higham, *Strangers in the Lane: Patterns of American Nativism, 1860–1925* (New York, Atheneum, 1978).

5 Theophilus Scholes, *The British Empire and Alliances: or Britain's Duty to the Colonies and Subject Races* (London, Elliot Stock, 1899), p. 378.

6 *Ibid.*, p. 379.

7 Anthony Trollope, *The West Indies and the Spanish Main*, 1st edn 1859 (London, Frank Cass, 1968), p. 64.

8 Grant Allen, *In All Shades* (London, Chatto and Windus, 1886); Sydney Olivier, *White Capital and Coloured Labour* (London, ILP, 1906), p.35.

9 *Edinburgh Review*, 217, 342 (April 1888), p. 322. Another reviewer saw the book as indicating the complete unfitness of the West Indian colonies for representative government, *Quarterly Review*, 166, 332 (April 1888), p. 498.

10 William Archer, *Through Afro-America: an English Reading of the Race Problem* (London, Chapman and Hall, 1910), p. xiii.

11 *Ibid.*, p. 73.

12 *Ibid.*

13 William Archer, 'Black and white in the southern states of America', *The State*, 3, 1 (January 1910), p. 72.

14 Archer, *The State*, 3, 2 (February 1910), p. 281. See also *The State*, 3, 3 (March 1910), pp. 426–31.

15 J. A. Hobson, *The Crisis of Liberalism*, 1st edn 1910 (Sussex, Harvester Press, 1972), p. 244.

16 D. M. Schreuder, *The Scramble for Southern Africa, 1877–1895: the Politics of Partition Reappraised* (Cambridge, CUP, 1980).

17 For an analysis of the decline in the hope that the Cape liberal values would spread northwards, see Paul Rich, 'Industrialisation, Fabianism and race: Sydney Olivier and the liberal critique of South African segregation' (London, ICS seminar paper, 1984).

18 C. C. Eldridge, *Victorian Imperialism* (London, Hodder and Stoughton, 1978), p. 216.

19 Henry Wilson, 'Some notes on imperialism', *Saint George*, 6, 21 (January 1903), p. 88.

20 C. Enoch, 'Democracy and empire', *Nineteenth Century* (November 1910).

21 A. P. Thornton, *The Imperial Idea and its Enemies* (London, Macmillan, 1866), p. 81.

22 Deborah Lavin, 'Lionel Curtis and the idea of Commonwealth', in Frederick Madden and D. K. Fieldhouse (eds.), *Oxford and the Idea of Commonwealth* (London and Canberra, Croom Helm, 1982), p. 97; 'History, morals and the politics of empire: Lionel Curtis and the Round Table', in John Bossy and Peter Jupp (eds.), *Essays presented to Michael Roberts* (Belfast, Blackstone Press, 1976), pp. 117–32.

23 Harold Wolpe, 'Capitalism and cheap labour power: from segregation to apartheid', *Economy and Society*, 14 (November 1972), pp. 425–56.

24 Shula Marks, *Reluctant Rebellion* (Oxford, Clarendon Press, 1970).

25 Paul Rich, 'Milnerism and a ripping yarn: Transvaal land settlement and John

Buchan's novel *Prester John*, 1901–1910', in Belinda Bozzoli (ed.), *Town and Countryside in the Transvaal* (Johannesburg, Ravan Press, 1983), pp. 412–33.

26 Parlt. Deb. H. of C., 152, 28 February 1906, cols. 1241–3. C 537/513, Report of Maj. R. H. Massie, 29 February 1904, warning of the political changes in Independent Church activity among Africans in South Africa. See also Roderick Jones, 'The black peril in South Africa', *Nineteenth Century* (May 1904), pp. 712–27. For a critical view of the 'black peril' idea, see H. H. Johnston, 'The white man's place in Africa', *Nineteenth Century* (June 1904), pp. 937–46.

27 R. W. Rose-Innes, *The Glen Grey Act and the Native Question* (Lovedale, Lovedale Press, 1903).

28 See for example, Archer, *op. cit.*, p. 192; H. H. Johnston, *The Negro in the New World*, 1st edn 1910 (New York and London, Johnston Reprint Corp., 1969), pp. 405–20. The ideals of Tuskegee received 'institutionalised recognition' at the first World Missionary Conference in Edinburgh in 1910 (Kenneth King, *Pan-Africanism and Education* (Oxford, Clarendon Press, 1971), p. 50).

29 Gilbert Murray, 'The exploitation of inferior races in ancient and modern times' in *Liberalism and the Empire* (London, G. Briarly Johnson, 1900), p. 144.

30 Leo Amery to Sir Valentine Chirol, 7 July 1900, in John Barnes and David Nicholls (eds.), *The Leo Amery Diaries, Vol. 1, 1896–1929* (London, Hutchinson, 1981), p. 36.

31 Ken Jordaan, 'Iberian and Anglo-Saxon racism: a study of Portuguese Angola and South Africa', *Race and Class*, 20, 4 (1979), pp. 391–412; A Sivanandan, 'Race, class and caste in South Africa', in *A Different Hunger: Writings on Black Resistance* (London, Pluto Press, 1982), pp. 161–71. The caste view of South African stratification has been recently restated by No Sizwe, *One Azania, One Nation* (London, Zed Press, 1981).

32 Lionel Curtis, 'The place of subject peoples in the empire', *Fortnightly Club Papers* (Church of the Province Archives, University of the Witwatersrand, n.d. (1906?)), p. 4.

33 *Ibid.*, p. 5.

34 Lionel Curtis, *With Milner in South Africa* (Oxford, Basil Blackwell, 1951), diary entry for 24 November 1900.

35 Lionel Curtis, 'The place of subject peoples in the empire'.

36 Lavin, *op. cit.*; S. R. Mehrota, 'Imperial federation and India, 1868–1917', *Journal of Commonwealth Political Studies*, 2, 1 (November 1961), pp. 29–40; John Kendle, *The Round Table Movement and Imperial Union* (Toronto, University of Toronto Press, 1975); Richard Symonds, *Oxford and the Empire* (London, Macmillan, 1986), pp. 62–79.

37 Kendle, *op. cit.*, p. 18.

38 Mehrota, *op. cit.*

39 *Round Table Papers* MS Eng. Hist. C864, Lord Hailey, 'LC – Lionel Curtis' (mimeo), 1958, p. 1.

40 Philip Kerr, *What the British empire stands for: an Address to the Toronto Round Table 31 July 1912* (Toronto, Toronto Round Table, 1912), pp. 15–16.

41 'India and the empire', *Round Table*, 2 (1911–12), p. 591. 'It is almost cer-

tain', wrote one correspondent, 'that what we have lately seen will continue and that the Indian people will more dislike our rule the more prosperous and educated they become. The ruin of the Empire through the utter alienation of all the races in our Eastern dependencies may be a real possibility' ('Viator', 'Asia contra mundum', *Fortnightly Review* (1 February 1908), p. 192). See also 'Vidvan', 'India in England', *English Review* (November 1909), pp. 707–15.

42 'India and the empire', p. 620; W. S. Urquhart, 'The alleged waste of higher education in India', *Westminster Review*, 192 (July 1909).

43 Gilbert Murray 'Empire and subject races', in *Nationalities and Subject Races: Report of the Conference held in Caxton Hall, Westminster, 18–30 June 1910* (London, P. S. King and Son, 1910), p. 9.

44 Lieut. Gen. Sir J. Bevan Edwards, 'The necessity for an imperial parliament', *United Empire*, 2, 1 (January 1911), p. 20; Arthur Page, 'Imperialism in the future', *Blackwoods Magazine* (October 1912), p. 445 – 'the very existence of Great Britain as a Sovereign Power is contingent upon the scheme of Imperial Federation'; 'Pelops', 'Greater Britain in 1911: a retrospect', *United Empire*, 3, 1 (January 1912).

45 Robert Huttenbach, *Racism and Empire: White Settlers and Colonial Immigration in British Self-Governing Colonies, 1830–1910* (Ithaca and London, Cornell University Press, 1976), p. 279. See also Hugh Tinker, *A New System of Slavery: the Export of Indian Labour Overseas, 1830–1920* (London, Oxford University Press, 1974).

46 'Labour Migration', *United Empire*, 12, 3 (March 1921), p. 135. Not all observers agreed with this view. 'The Asiatic demands not merely to be recognised as an equal', wrote one observer, 'he demands a share in the new lands of the world . . . In South or Middle Africa, in Australia, or in South America, in some or all of these regions, room must be found for the crowded myriads of Asia' (Fleetwood Chidill, 'Imperial migration and the clash of races', *Quarterly Review*, 233, 463 (April 1920), p. 367).

47 Tinker, *op. cit.*, pp. 346, 403, n. 11. See also the same author's 'Colour and colonization: a study in rival Commonwealth ideals of human settlement', *Round Table*, 240 (November 1970), pp. 405–16.

48 Bernard Semmel, *Imperialism and Social Reform* (London, Allen and Unwin, 1960), p. 27.

49 George Louis Beer, 'Lord Milner and British imperialism', *Political Science Quarterly*, 30, 2 (June 1915), p. 303.

50 *Round Table Papers*, MS Eng. Hist. C817, L. Curtis to A. E. Zimmern, 14 February 1914.

51 Alfred Zimmern, *The Greek Commonwealth* (Oxford, Clarendon Press, 1911).

52 Alfred Zimmern, 'German culture and the British Commonwealth', in R. W. Seton-Watson et al., *The War and Democracy* (London, Macmillan, 1915), pp. 348–84.

53 *Ibid.*, p. 364.

54 MSS Brit. Emp. S403 1/2(10), Reginald Coupland, notes on the colour problem for the Ralegh Club.

55 Lionel Curtis, *The Commonwealth of Nations*, Part 1 (London, Macmillan 1916), p. 15.

56 *Ibid.*, p. 24.

57 See pp. 13–15.

58 Lionel Curtis, *The Commonwealth of Nations*, Part 1, p. 180.
59 *Ibid.*, p. 210.
60 *Ibid.*, p. 220. See also Lionel Curtis, 'A criteria of values in international affairs', *Journal of the British Institute of International Affairs* (1 and 2 November 1922), pp. 165–80.
61 *Ibid.*, p. 697.
62 J. A. Hobson, *Manchester Guardian*, 11 September 1916.
63 *Round Table Papers*, MS Eng. Hist. C817, A. Zimmern to J. A. Hobson, 13 September 1916.
64 *Ibid.*, John Hobson to A. Zimmern, 16 September 1916. See also J. A. Hobson, *Towards International Government* (London, Allen and Unwin, 1915), in which British imperialism was attacked for maintaining 'large areas rife with the spirit of unsatisfied nationality' (p. 122).
65 *Ibid.*, A. Zimmern to J. Hobson, 29 September 1916.
66 *G. Wallas Collection* 1/82, A. Zimmern to G. Wallas, n.d. (1916?).
67 *Daily Herald*, 27 October 1919.
68 M. S. Donnelly, 'J. L. Dafoe and Lionel Curtis – two concepts of the Commonwealth', *Political Studies*, 8, 2 (1960), p. 178.
69 Alfred Zimmern, 'The British empire in 1924', *Nation*, 26 June, 9 August and 30 August 1924; *The Third British Empire*, 3rd edn (London, Oxford University Press, 1934); Lavin, 'Lionel Curtis', p. 101.
70 Corelli Barnett, *The Collapse of British Power* (London, Eyre Methuen, 1972), pp. 426–8.
71 George Foster, 'Imperial unity', *Nineteenth Century*, 627 (March 1925), p. 345. See also Frank Fox, 'A way out of our troubles – empire resettlement', *National Review*, 199, 472 (June 1922), pp. 562–7.
72 G. Dawson, *The Times*, 27 October 1925.
73 Vladimar Halperin, *Lord Milner and the Empire* (London, Odhams Press, 1952), p. 201, quoting a letter from Lady Milner of 2 May 1946 to the author stating that Milner 'greatly regretted' the fact that Curtis, Lothian and Brand became internationalists.
74 Stanley Baldwin, 'Democracy and the empire', in *On England* (London, Hurst and Spottiswoode, 1926), p. 236.
75 'If there are those who want to fight the class war', he wrote, 'we will beat them by the hardness of our heads and the largeness of our hearts.' Cited in Keith Middlemas and John Barnes, *Baldwin* (London, Weidenfeld and Nicolson, 1969), p. 209. See also Paul Rich, 'British imperial decline and the forging of English patriotic memory, *c*. 1918–1968' *History of European Ideas*, 9, 6 (1988), pp. 659–80.
76 Virgina Woolf, 'Thunder at Wembley', *Nation*, 23 June 1924; E.M. Forster, *Abinger Harvest*, 1st edn 1936 (Harmondsworth, Penguin, 1976), pp. 55–62.
77 David Cannadine, 'The context, performance and meaning of ritual: the British monarchy and the "invention of tradition", *c*. 1820–1977', in Eric Hobsbawm and Terence Ranger (eds.), *The Invention of Tradition* (Cambridge, CUP, 1983), pp. 149–60.
78 C 875/19/17, Viscount Bledisloe, Empire Day message, 24 May 1943.
79 *Britain and the Colonies* (London, HMSO, 1946), p. 3.
80 Cannadine, *op. cit.*, p. 157. The coronation itself was still, however, essentially an imperial occasion and Empire Day was celebrated well into the 1950s. See report entitled 'Empire Day luncheon at the Mansion House',

United Empire, 46 (July–August 1955), p. 126.
81 William Archer, *India and the Future* (London, Hutchinson, 1917), p. 23.
82 *Ibid.*, p. 24.
83 *Ibid.*, p. 25.
84 *Ibid.*, p. 26.
85 Beatrice Webb to Catherine Courtney, 18 September 1911; to Clifford Sharp, 15 January 1912; to Mildred Buckley, 24 January 1912; to Clifford Sharp, 7 April 1912, in Norman Mackenzie (ed.), *The Letters of Sidney and Beatrice Webb: Volume 2, Partnership 1892–1912* (Cambridge, CUP, 1978), pp. 372–90. The Webbs' ethnocentric views have been rather falsely interpreted as 'socialist racialism' and as the propagation of 'a number of crude assumptions about racial character which were widely shared in late-Victorian society' (J. M. Winter, 'The Webbs and the non-white world: a case of socialist racialism', *Journal of Contemporary History*, 9 (1974), p. 181).
86 Basil Matthews, *The Clash of Colour: a Study in the Problem of Race* (London, Church Missionary Society, 1926), p. 109. Some opinion on the left, though, was already championing Indian independence by the end of the First World War. See George Lansbury, 'India for the Indians', *Daily Herald*, 23 August 1919.
87 King, *op. cit.*, p. 28.
88 Paul Rich, *White Power and the Liberal Conscience* (Manchester, Manchester University Press, 1984), pp. 18–20; King, *op. cit.*, p. 85.
89 CBMS H/PB/4/140, broadcast by Dr Thomas Jesse Jones on the BBC, 19 July 1931.
90 Rich, *op. cit.*, pp. 28–30.
91 James Bryce, *International Relations* (London, Macmillan, 1922), p. 128. Bryce's book was based on eight lectures given in the USA in 1921.
92 Cited in J. W. Gregory, *The Menace of Colour* (London, Seele and Co., 1925), p. 232.
93 *Ibid.*, and *Race as a Political Factor* (London, Watts and Co., 1931), with an introduction by Sir Arthur Keith.
94 Gregory, *The Menace of Colour*, p. 235.
95 *South Place Ethical Society*, Minutes of special meeting of the general committee, 15 July 1931; Minutes of the general committee of 29 July, 7 October and 4 November 1931 and 6 January 1932. The Conway Memorial Committee declined to relinquish its powers to the general committee and this was accepted by the general committee. The total membership of the Society in 1931 was 424, with 166 associated members.
96 General J. C. Smuts, *Africa and some World Problems* (Oxford, Clarendon Press, 1930), p. 63.
97 J. H. Oldham, *White and Black in Africa: a Critical Examination of the Rhodes Lectures of General Smuts* (London, Longman Green and Co., 1930), p. 44.
98 See pp. 145–150.

4. The widening critique of empire

1 MSS Brit. Emp. S22 G432, N. Angell to J. Harris, 6 May 1922.
2 Leonard Barnes, unpublished autobiography (London, School of Oriental and

African Studies, n.d.), p. 27.

3 James Bryce, *The American Commonwealth* (London, Macmillan, 1889), p. 308.

4 J. A. Hobson, 'The negro problem in the United States', *Nineteenth Century* (October 1903), p. 593. See also anon., 'The colour question in the United States', *Edinburgh Review*, 411 (January 1905), pp. 55–76. For the triumph of Southern segregation, see C. Van Woodward, *The Strange Career of Jim Crow*, 3rd edn (New York, Oxford University Press, 1974) and Howard Rabinowitz, 'From exclusion to segregation: Southern race relations, 1865–1890', *Journal of American History*, 63, 2 (1977), pp. 325–50.

5 W. P. Livingstone, *Black Jamaica: a Study in Evolution* (London, Sampson, Low and Co., 1899), p. 84. See also Owen Mathurin, *Henry Sylvester Williams and the Origins of the Pan-African Movement, 1869–1911* (Westport, Conn., Greenwood Press, 1976), pp. 87–8. For the failure of Creole nationalism, see G. K. Lewis, *Slavery, Imperialism and Freedom* (New York and London, Monthly Review Press, 1978), p. 48.

6 Livingstone, *op. cit.*, pp. 165–6, 183–4.

7 H. H. Johnston, 'The native problem', *Nineteenth Century* (August 1909), p. 236.

8 Sydney Olivier, *White Capital and Coloured Labour* (London, ILP, 1906), p. 14.

9 *Ibid.*, p. 5.

10 *Ibid.*, p. 17.

11 *Ibid.*, p. 18.

12 *Ibid.*, pp. 38–9.

13 *Ibid.*, p. 56.

14 *Ibid.*, p. 86.

15 *Ibid.*, p. 137.

16 *Ibid.*, p. 160.

17 *Gilbert Murray Papers*, MS 148, N. Leys to G. Murray, 13 January 1900.

18 *Ibid.*, N. Leys to G. Murray, 7 February 1902 and 29 August 1910.

19 *Ibid.*, N. Leys to G. Murray, 25 February 1918.

20 Barnes, unpublished autobiography, p. 102.

21 Diana Wylie, 'Confrontation over Kenya: the Colonial Office and its critics, 1918–1940', *Journal of African History*, 18, 3 (1977), pp. 427–47; 'Norman Leys and McGregor Ross: a case study in the conscience of African empire, 1900–39', *Journal of Imperial and Commonwealth History*, 5, 3 (May 1977), pp. 294–309.

22 Norman Leys, *Kenya*, 1st edn 1924 (London, The Hogarth Press, 1926), pp. 207–8; 'New style imperialism in Kenya', *New Leader*, 25 May 1923.

23 Leys, *Kenya*, p. 381 and *passim*; Wylie, 'Confrontation over Kenya', p. 430.

24 Leys, *Kenya*, p. 254.

25 Wylie, 'Confrontation over Kenya', p. 445.

26 Sydney Olivier, *The Anatomy of African Misery* (London, The Hogarth Press, 1927), p. 62; *White Capital and Coloured Labour* (London, The Hogarth Press, 1929). See also Paul Rich, 'Industrialisation, Fabianism and race: Sydney Olivier and the liberal critique of segregation', mimeo (London, ICS 1984).

27 Olivier, *Anatomy of African Misery*, p. 64.

28 *Ibid.*, p. 78.
29 *Ibid.*, p. 75.
30 *Ibid.*, pp. 66–7.
31 Godfrey Lagden, 'The issue in South Africa', *United Empire*, 13, 3 (March 1921), p. 143.
32 Martin Channock, *Unconsummated Union: Britain, Rhodesia and South Africa, 1900–1945* (Manchester, Manchester University Press, 1977), p. 194.
33 Colonel P. A. Silburn, 'The racial problem in South Africa – territorial segregation', *United Empire*, 19, 1 (January 1928), p. 15.
34 Olivier, *Anatomy of African Misery*, p. 64.
35 Commander D. C. Lamb, 'Our heritage – the empire', *United Empire*, 17, 8 (August 1921), p. 449; W. R. Inge, 'The white man and his rivals', *Quarterly Review*, 235 (April 1921), p. 251; L. E. Neame, 'The white race in South Africa', *Contemporary Review*, 127 (June 1925, p. 765; A. M. Chirgwin, 'Is South Africa a white man's land?', *Nation*, 14 January 1928, p. 561.
36 *W. M. Macmillan Papers*, N. Leys to W. M. Macmillan, n.d. (1929/30).
37 Quoted by David Goldsworthy, *Colonial Issues in British Politics, 1945–1961* (Oxford, Clarendon Press, 1971), pp. 117–18.
38 Leonard Woolf, *Empire and Commerce in Africa: a Study in Economic Imperialism* (London, Labour Research Dept. and Allen and Unwin, 1919), p. 364.
39 *Ibid.*, pp. 357–8.
40 *Ibid.*, p. 362.
41 *Ibid.*, p. 365.
42 *Ibid.*
43 Neal Malmsten, 'The British Labour Party and the West Indies, 1918–39', *Journal of Imperial and Commonwealth History*, 5, 2 (January 1977), p. 175.
44 *The Empire in Africa: Labour's Policy* (London, The Labour Party, 1926), pp. 7–9; Goldsworthy, *op. cit.*, pp. 118–19.
45 Malmsten, *op. cit.*, p. 178.
46 Labour Party, *The Colonies*, report adopted at the Annual Conference at Hastings, October 1933 (London, Transport House, November 1933), pp. 5–6.
47 *Ibid.*, pp. 8–9.
48 *Ibid.*, p. 5.
49 Stephen Howe, 'Anti-colonialism in British politics: the left and the end of empire, 1939–1964', Ph.D. thesis, University of Oxford, 1984.
49 *Nation*, 23 April 1927, review of *The Anatomy of African Misery*.
50 *Winifred Holtby Papers* G 15, S. Olivier to W. Holtby, 18 October 1930.
51 *Report of the West Indian Sugar Commission, 1929*, Cmnd 3517 (London, HMSO, 1930).
52 W.M. Macmillan, *My South African Years* (Cape Town, David Philip, 1975), pp. 193–203. See also Paul Rich, 'W. M. Macmillan, South African segregation and Commonwealth race relations', paper presented to the conference on W. M. Macmillan, London, Institute of Commonwealth Studies, 2–4 October 1985.
53 W. M. Macmillan, *Warning from the West Indies*, 1st edn 1936 (Harmondsworth, Penguin, 1938), pp. 159–60.
54 *Ibid.*, p. 168.

55 Mona Macmillan, 'The making of *Warning from the West Indies*: extract from a projected memoir of W. M. Macmillan', *Journal of Commonwealth and Comparative Politics*, 18, 2 (July 1980), p. 218.
56 *W. M. Macmillan Papers*, unpublished MS, 'A student of British Africa looks at America', 1935, p. 10.
57 *Ibid.*, p. 9.
58 *Ibid.*, p. 7.
59 Diana Wylie, 'Confrontation over Kenya', p. 431.
60 W. M. Macmillan, *Democratise the Empire!: a Policy for Colonial Change* (London, Kegan Paul, 1941), p. 50.
61 See, for example, F. Furedi, 'The social composition of the Mau Mau movement in the White Highlands', *Journal of Peasant Studies*, 1 (1973–4), pp. 486–505; M. Tamarkin, 'Mau Mau in Nakuru', *Journal of African History*, 18, 1 (1976), pp. 119–34.
62 A. W. Stadler, 'Birds in the cornfield: squatter movements in Johannesburg, 1944–1947', *Journal of Southern African Studies*, 6, 1 (October 1979), pp. 93–123; 'The politics of subsistence: community struggles in war-time Johannesburg', inaugural lecture, University of the Witwatersrand, Johannesburg, 1981.
63 Anthony McAdam, 'Leonard Barnes and South Africa', *Social Dynamics*, 3, 2 (1977), p. 43.
64 Barnes, unpublished autobiography, p. 10.
65 Leonard Barnes, *Caliban in Africa* (London, Victor Gollancz, 1930), p. 43.
66 Leonard Barnes, *The New Boer War* (London, The Hogarth Press, 1932), p. 39.
67 *Ibid.*, p. 40.
68 *Ibid.*, p. 42.
69 *Ibid.*, p. 40. For Ballinger's arrival in South Africa in 1928 and work there, see P. L. Wickens, *The Industrial and Commercial Workers Union of South Africa* (Cape Town, Oxford University Press, 1978), esp. pp. 167–86.
70 Paul Rich, *White Power and the Liberal Conscience: Racial Segregation and South African Liberalism, 1921–1960* (Manchester, Manchester University Press, 1984), pp. 45–6.
71 Leonard Barnes, *The Duty of Empire* (London, Victor Gollancz, 1935), p. 21.
72 *Ibid.*, p. 117.
73 *Ibid.*, p. 95.
74 *Ibid.*, p. 102.
75 *W. M. Macmillan Papers*, N. Leys to W. M. Macmillan, 23 April 1936.
76 Betty Reid, 'The Left Book Club in the thirties', in Jon Clark *et al.* (eds.), *Culture and Crisis in Britain in the 30s* (London, Lawrence and Wishart, 1979), p. 195.
77 Leonard Barnes, *Empire or Democracy* (London, Victor Gollancz, 1939), p. 195.
78 *Ibid.*, p. 197.
79 *Ibid.*, pp. 215–22. See also Wolfe Schmokes, 'The hard death of imperialism: British and German colonial attitudes, 1919–1939', in Prosser Gifford and William Louis (eds.) *Britain and Germany in Africa* (New Haven and London, Yale University Press, 1967), pp. 301–35.
80 See, for example, V. G. Kiernan, *European Empires from Conquest to*

Collapse, 1815–1960 (London, Fontana, 1982, pp. 194–205.

82 A. G. Russell, *Colour, Race and Empire* (London, Victor Gollancz, 1944), pp. 21–2. For the change in Left Book Club policy, see Stuart Samuels, 'The Left Book Club', *Journal of Contemporary History*, 1, 2 (1966), p. 81.

83 Martin Kilson and Robert Rotberg (eds.), *The African Diaspora: Interpretive Essays* (Cambridge, Mass., Harvard University Press, 1976), esp. the introduction by George Shepperson, pp. 1–10.

84 George Padmore, 'The British empire is the worst racket yet invented by man', *New Leader*, 15 December 1939. For the Pan-Africanist experience in Britain, see Cedric Robinson, 'Black intellectuals in the British core, 1920s–1930s', paper presented at the International Conference on the History of Blacks in Britain, Institute of Education, London, 1982.

85 James Hooker, *Black Revolutionary: George Padmore's Path from Communism to Pan-Africanism* (London, Pall Mall Press, 1967), pp. 6–17.

86 George Padmore, *The Life and Struggles of Negro Toilers* (London, RIIU for ITUC-NW, 1931), p. 8.

87 *Ibid.*, pp. 60–78.

88 Hooker, *op. cit.*, p. 49.

89 See, for example, Padmore's article 'Race prejudice in England', *Negro Worker* (March 1932), repr. in Nancy Cunard, *Negro: An Anthology* (London, Lawrence and Wishart, 1934), pp. 551–4. See also Ann Chisholm, *Nancy Cunard* (Harmondsworth, Penguin, 1979), pp. 297–9.

90 F. M. Leventhal, 'H. N. Brailsford and the New Leader', *Journal of Contemporary History*, 9, 1 (January 1974), pp. 91–113.

91 Fenner Brockway, *Inside the Left* (London, Allen and Unwin, 1942), p. 237. See Alan Mackenzie 'British Marxists and the Empire: Anti-Imperialist Theory and Practice, 1920–1945', Ph.D. thesis, Birkbeck College, London, 1978, pp. 233–4.

92 Sir Stafford Cripps, 'Foreword' to George Padmore, *Africa and World Peace* (London, Secker and Warburg, 1937), p. x; *International African Opinion* (September 1938), p. 3.

93 C. L. R. James, 'George Jackson', in *The Future in the Present* (London, Allison and Busby, 1977), p. 268.

94 *New Statesman*, 17 February 1945. For the proceedings, see George Padmore (ed.) *The Voice of Coloured Labour* (Manchester, Panaf Services, 1945).

95 George Padmore, *History of the Pan-African Congress* (London, Hammersmith Bookshop, 1947); Immanuel Geiss, *The Pan-African Movement* (London, Methuen, 1974), pp. 385–400; Adekunle Ajala, *Pan-Africanism: Evolution, Progress and Prospects* (London, Andre Deutsch, 1973), p. 11.

96 George Padmore to W. E. B. Du Bois, 17 August 1945, in Herbert Aptheker (ed.), *The Correspondence of W. E. B. Du Bois*, Vol. 3 (Cambridge, University of Massachusetts Press, 1978), p. 77.

97 *NCCL Archives*, University of Hull, DCL 92/1 G. D. Ekarte to R. Kidd, 11 February 1941.

98 Leonard Barnes, *Soviet Light on the Colonies* (Harmondsworth, Penguin, 1944); Hooker, *op. cit.*, p. 73.

99 George Padmore, *How Russia Transformed her Empire* (London, Dennis Dobson, 1946), p. 164.

100 Leonard Barnes, 'A policy for colonial peoples', in Lord Latham *et al., What*

Labour Could Do (London, World Book Services, 1945), p. 64.
101 Basil Davidson, 'Prisoners of prejudice', *New Statesman*, 28 July 1951; 'The hope for white and black', *ibid.*, 4 August 1951; *Report on Southern Africa* (London, Jonathan Cape, 1952), pp. 138–43. 'The contemporary revolution in South Africa', Davidson wrote, 'transforming the economy from a primarily imperialist pattern, to one of expanding industrialism, overturns the old assumptions about the white man and the black man, but that is a lesson that is scarcely perceived, far less learnt' (*Report*. p. 142). See also Paul Rich, 'The impact of South African segregation and apartheid ideology on British racial thought', *New Community*, 13, 1 (Spring–Summer 1986) pp. 1–17.
102 T.O. Ranger, 'From humanism to the science of man: colonialism in Africa and the understanding of alien societies', *Trans. of Roy. Hist. Soc.*, 5, 26 (1976), pp. 115–41.

5. Sociology, anthropology and race

1 The problem was perceived by liberal critics at the time. See, for example, John Robertson, 'The inertia of the English universities' in *Essays in Sociology*, Vol. 2 (London, A. and H. B. Bourne, 1904), pp. 72–100.
2 Perry Anderson, 'Components of the national culture', *New Left Review*, 50 (1968), pp. 3–57. See also E. P. Thompson, 'The peculiarities of the English', *Socialist Register* (1967), pp. 310–62, for a different view of English thought.
3 Anderson, *op. cit.*, and 'Origins of the present crisis', *New Left Review*, 23 (January–February 1967), pp. 26–48.
4 Philip Abrams, *The Origins of British Sociology*, 1834–1914 (Chicago and London, University of Chicago Press, 1968), pp. 5–6.
5 Stefan Collini, 'Sociology and idealism in Britain, 1880–1920', *European Journal of Sociology*, 19 (1978), pp. 3–50; ' "Cambridge idealism": utilitarian revisionists in late nineteenth-century Cambridge', *Historical Journal*, 17, 1 (1974), pp. 63–78.
6 Stefan Collini, 'Hobhouse, Bosanquet and the state: philosophical idealism and political argument in England, 1880–1915', *Past and Present*, 72 (1976), pp. 86–111.
7 J. Rumney, 'British sociology', in George Gurvitch and William Moser (eds.), *Twentieth-Century Society* (New York, Free Press, 1945), p. 571.
8 *Institute of Sociology Collection*, AF 170, Victor Branford to Francis Galton, 14 April 1904.
9 Rt. Hon. James Bryce, 'The use and purpose of a sociological society', in Francis Galton, E. Westermarck *et al., Sociological Papers, 1904* (London, 1905), p. 3, address delivered at the London School of Economics, 18 April 1904.
10 Michael Freeden, 'Eugenics and progressive thought: a study in ideological affinity', *Historical Journal*, 22, 3 (1979), pp. 645–71.
11 See the essay by George Watson, 'Race and the socialists', in *Politics and Literature in Modern Britain* (London, Macmillan, 1979), pp. 120–34; Freeden, *op. cit.*, p. 654.
12 Michael Freeden, *The New Liberalism: an Ideology of Social Reform* (Oxford, Clarendon Press, 1978), pp. 85–93; Stefan Collini, *Liberalism and Sociology: L. T. Hobhouse and the Political Argument in England, 1880–1914* (Cambridge, CUP, 1979). See also Peter Weiler, 'The new liberalism of

L. T. Hobhouse', *Victorian Studies* (December 1972), pp. 142–61.
13 L. T. Hobhouse in Galton and Westermarck, *op. cit.*, p. 63.
14 D. Kidd in Galton and Westermarck, *op. cit.*, p. 63.
15 *Institute of Sociology Collection*, AF 170, F. Galton to V. Branford, 20 December 1904.
16 *Ibid.*, V. Branford to F. Galton, 16 May 1904.
17 R. J. Halliday, 'The sociological movement, the Sociological Society and the genesis of academic sociology in Britain', *Sociological Review*, 16, 3 (1968), pp. 377–98.
18 L. T. Hobhouse, editorial in the *Sociological Review*, 1 (January 1908), p. 8.
19 The 1911 Universal Races Congress was described in D. S. Margoliouth, 'The first Universal Races Congress', *Sociological Review*, 4 (1911), pp. 216–31.
20 John Robertson, 'The tutelage of races', *Sociological Review*, 1 (1908), p. 172.
21 *Ibid.*, p. 174.
22 See pp. 36–43.
23 John Robertson, 'The sociology of race', *Sociological Review*, 4 (1911), p. 125.
24 *Ibid.*, p. 130.
25 *Ibid.*, p. 126.
26 'Gustav Spiller' *Sociological Review*, 32 (1940), pp. 108–10; Nina Spiller (ed.) *Autobiography of Gustav Spiller* (Chelmsford, Essex, 1940).
27 G. Spiller, 'Science and race prejudice', *Sociological Review*, 5 (1912), p. 340; 'Darwinism and society', *ibid.*, 7 (1914), pp. 232–53.
28 Spiller, 'Science and race prejudice', p. 347.
29 L. T. Hobhouse, G. C. Wheeler and M. Ginsburg, *The Material Culture and Social Institutions of the Simpler Peoples – an Essay in Correlation* (London, Chapman and Hall, 1915), p. 1.
30 *Ibid.*, p. 3
31 *Ibid.*, p. 7.
32 *Ibid.*, p. 28.
33 Sydney Olivier, 'Colour prejudice', *Contemporary Review*, 12 (1923), p. 456.
34 Friedrich Hertz, *Race and Civilisation* (London, Routledge and Kegan Paul, 1928), p. 3.
35 Cited in *ibid.*, p. 14.
36 *Ibid.*, p. 36.
37 *Ibid.*, p. 172.
38 *Ibid.*, p. 251. For Arthur Keith's ideas, see pp. 116–17.
39 *Ibid.*, p. 8.
40 Anderson, 'Components of the national culture', pp. 18–20. For Neumann, see H. Stuart Hughes, 'Franz Neumann: between Marxism and liberal democracy', in Donald Fleming and Bernard Bailyon (eds.), *The Intellectual Migration: Europe and America, 1930–1960* (Cambridge, Mass., Harvard University Press, 1969), pp. 446–62.
41 John Robertson, 'The illusion of race', *Contemporary Review*, 134 (July 1928), p. 33.
42 Magnus Hirschfeld, *Racism* (London, Victor Gollancz, 1938), pp. 138–48.

See also Michael Biddiss, 'Myths of the blood: European racist ideology, 1850–1945', *Patterns of Prejudice*, 9, 5 (September–October 1975), pp. 11–19.

43 Royal Anthropological Institute and the Institute of Sociology, *Race and Culture* (Le Play House Press and RAI, Malvern and London, 1935), p. 2.

44 *The Racial Relations Group*, leaflet printed by the Institute of Sociology (Le Play House Press, Malvern, 1938); *J. D. Rheinallt-Jones Papers*, C26/3, Mrs John Jones to J.D. Rheinallt-Jones, 24 April 1948.

45 See p. 177.

46 Allison Davis, 'The distribution of the blood groups and its bearing on the concept of race', *Sociological Review*, 47 (1935), pp. 19–29, 183–200. Davis, though, pointed out that there were few homogeneous 'races' and the term could only be used to denote 'aggregates of physical characteristics when such types inhabit the same locality and inter-breed' (p. 196).

47 Maximilien Beck, 'The independence of culture from race', *Sociological Review*, 30 (1938), p. 49.

48 *Ibid.*, p. 56.

49 Philip Reynolds, 'Race, Nationality and Empire: Aspects of Mid-Victorian Thought', Ph.D. thesis, Queen's University, Ontario, 1972, pp. 104–26; Richard K. Barksdale, 'Thomas Arnold's attitude toward race', *Phylon*, 18 (1957), pp. 174–80.

50 Daphne Herzstein, 'Anthropology and racism in nineteenth-century Europe', *Duquesne Review*, 14, 2 (Fall 1969), p. 123; Nancy Stepan, *The Idea of Race in Science: Great Britain, 1800–1960* (London and Basingstoke, The Macmillan Press, 1982), p. 83.

51 Douglas Lorimer, 'Racist theory in British anthropology, 1870–1900', paper presented at the Conference on Anglo-Saxon Racial Attitudes, *c.* 1870–1970, Selly Oak, Birmingham, September 1982.

52 Andrew Lyons, 'The Question of Race in Anthropology from the Time of Johann Friedrich Blumenbach to that of Franz Boas with Particular Reference to the Period 1830–1890', D.Phil. thesis, University of Oxford, pp. 108–9.

53 Idus Murphree, 'The evolutionary anthropologists: the progress of mankind', *Proceedings of the American Philosophical Society*, 105, 3 (June 1961), pp. 265–300; Irving Goldman, 'Evolution and anthropology', *Victorian Studies*, 3, 1 (September 1959), pp. 55–75; J. W. Burrow, *Evolution and Society: a Study in Victorian Social Theory* (Cambridge, CUP, 1966). As late as 1920 it was argued that 'the battle between monogenists and polygenists cannot be decided until more facts are at our disposal, and much will doubtless be said on both sides for some time to come' (A. H. Keane, *Man, Past and Present* (Cambridge, CUP, 1920), p. 3).

54 Freeden, *The New Liberalism*, pp. 88–9.

55 Sir W. H. Flower, *Address to the Anthropological Section of the British Association* (Oxford, The British Association 1894), p. 6.

56 John Beddoe, *The Races of Britain*, 1st edn, 1885 (London, Hutchinson, 1971). See also Sir Arthur Keith, 'Anthropology: old and new' (The Beddoe Memorial Lecture, Bristol, 5 September 1930), *JRAI*, 47, 178 (1930), pp. 287–306.

57 For the influence of Victorian ethnology on middle-class conceptions of 'the Irish race', see L. P. Curtis, *Anglo-Saxons and Celts: a Study of Anti-Irish*

Prejudice in Victorian England (Cambridge, University of Bridgeport, 1968), esp. pp. 66–73; *Apes and Angels: the Irishman in Victorian Caricature* (Newton Abbot, Davis and Chambers, 1971). For a criticism of Curtis's earlier book showing how the middle-class conception did not necessarily shape popular views, see Sheridan Gilley, 'English attitudes to the Irish in England, 1780–1900', in Colin Holmes (ed.), *Immigrants and Minorities in British Society* (London, George Allen and Unwin, 1978), pp. 81–110.

58 D. J. Cunningham and A. C. Haddon, 'The anthropometric laboratory of Ireland' *JAI*, 21 (1892), pp. 35–7. The 'ethnical islands' of Aran were seen as important for identifying 'the persistence or otherwise of various characters' (p. 36). See also Charles Myers, 'The future of anthropometry', *JAI*, 33 (1903), pp. 36–40. Myers hoped for a 'one united science', in the future, of biometry and anthropometry, 'concerned in the quantitative investigation of the phenomenon of life' (p. 40).

59 See for example, *Ethnographical Survey of the United Kingdom – Fourth Report of the Committee*, in British Association, *Proceedings*, Section H, Liverpool, 1896, pp. 1–50.

60 Galton asked John Beddoe to become president of the RAI in 1891 (*A. C. Haddon Papers*, J. Beddoe to A. C. Haddon, 24 January 1911).

61 E. W. Brabrook, 'Presidential address', *JAI*, 25 (1895–6), p. 406.

62 *Ethnographical Survey*, pp. 1–3.

63 Anthropological Institute, Annual Report, *JAI*, 28–9 (1898–9), pp. 215–16.

64 W. M. Flinders Petrie, *Address to the Anthropological Section of the British Association* (Ipswich, British Association for the Advancement of Science, 1895), p. 2. See also *Discussion: 'On the Contact of European and Native Civilizations', held at the Meeting of the British Association* (Ipswich, 1895).

65 Flinders Petrie, *Address*, p. 3. Flinders Petrie became an ardent exponent of Galton's view of hereditary intelligence, which he saw as rooted in those Puritan and Quaker families that practised self-denial and hard work. These he thought were increasingly being threatened by the *nouveaux riches*, 'who have sprung forward on some lucky speculation or trade enterprise' but who 'usually go to pieces in the next generation' (*Janus in Modern Life* (London, Archibald, Constable and Co., 1907), p. 5).

66 *A.C. Haddon Papers*, D.J. Cunningham to A.C. Haddon, 14 March 1903.

67 John Gray, *An Anthropometric Survey: its Utility to Science and the State* (Cambridge, The British Association, 1904). See also *Physical Degeneration: a Survey of the Discussion at the Anthropological Section of the British Association Meeting in Cambridge by Vratsch*, (Newry, Joseph Wright, 1904).

68 Francis Galton, 'The possible improvement of the human breed under the existing conditions of law and sentiment', *Popular Science Monthly*, 60 (January 1902), p. 218.

69 Karl Pearson, 'On the inheritance of the mental and moral characters in man, and its comparison with the inheritance of the physical characters' (Huxley lecture for 1903), *JAI*, 33 (1903), p. 179.

70 *Ibid.*, p. 185. For the development and formulation of Francis Galton's concept of biostatistics, which Pearson employed in the service of the 'science' of

biometry, see Ruth Cowan, 'Francis Galton's statistical ideas: the influence of eugenics', *Isis*, 63, 219 (December 1972), pp. 509–28.
71 Henry Balfour, 'Presidential address', *JAI*, 35 (1905), p. 17.
72 G. R. Searle, *Eugenics and Politics in Britain, 1900–1914* (Leyden, Noordhoff International Publishing, 1976), pp. 9–10. Donald Mackenzie has argued that the resurgence of class politics in Britain after the First World War explained the demise of the eugenics movement during the 1920s ('Eugenics in Britain', *Social Studies of Science*, 6 (1976), pp. 499–532).
73 H. G. Wells, *Mankind in the Making* (London, Chapman and Hall, 1904), p. 53.
74 For Geddes's use of Le Play's ideas, see Philip Abrams, *The Origins of British Sociology, 1834–1914* (Chicago and London, University of Chicago Press, 1968), pp. 113–20; Michael Brooke, *Le Play: Engineer and Social Scientist* (London, Longman, 1970), pp. 134–6.
75 Abrams assessed Geddes's influence as a failure for his premature diversion from urban sociology into propaganda for town planning (Abrams, *op. cit.*, p. 120). See also H. J. Fleure, 'Patrick Geddes (1854–1932)', *Sociological Review*, 1, 2 (1953), pp. 5–13.
76 *A. C. Haddon Papers*, P. Geddes to A. C. Haddon, 1891.
77 *Ibid.*, P. Geddes to A. C. Haddon, 6 April 1891. Geddes wrote from Paris.
78 *Ibid.*, A. C. Haddon, 'Environment and culture progress among primitive peoples', unpublished lecture delivered in London, 26 October 1927, p. 1.
79 *A. C. Haddon Papers*, A. C. Haddon to P. Geddes, 4 January 1897.
80 For Rivers's influence on British anthropological thought, see Richard Slobochin, *W. H. R. Rivers* (Columbia University Press, New York, 1978).
81 *A. C. Haddon Papers*, A. C. Haddon, 'Notes on Le Play', n.d.
82 Adam Kuper, *Anthropologists and Anthropology: the British School, 1922–72* (Harmondsworth, Penguin, 1975), esp. Chapters 1–2.
83 A. C. Haddon, 'Presidential address: anthropology, its position and needs', *JAI*, 33 (1903), pp. 11–13.
84 *Ibid.*, p. 11.
85 *Manchester Guardian*, 15 January 1903.
86 *A. C. Haddon Papers*, Flinders Petrie to A. C. Haddon, 24 April 1898; Petrie, 'Presidential address', *op. cit.*
87 The bureau was formed in the Smithsonian Institution in 1879 under the leadership of John Wesley Powell. See Robert Berkhofer, Jr., *The White Man's Indian: Images of the American Indian from Columbus to the Present* (New York, Vintage Books, 1978), p. 54 and *passim* for the bureau's relationship to nineteenth-century American ethnology.
88 *British Museum Central Archives*, Original papers 3611, Memorandum on Bureau of Ethnology, 1897.
89 Bernard Porter, *Critics of Empire* (London, Macmillan, 1968), p. 147.
90 *Ibid.*; Mary Kingsley, *West African Studies*, 1st edn, 1899 (London, Frank Cass, 1964), esp. pp. 327–34.
91 See, for instance, Frederick Boyle, 'The capacity of savages', *Macmillans Magazine* (November 1898), pp. 36–43.
92 C. H. Read, 'Presidential address', *JAI*, 30–1 (1900–1); report in *Nature*, 13 March 1902.

93 A. C. Haddon, *Address to the Anthropological Section, British Association for the Advancement of Science* (Johannesburg, The British Association, 1905), pp. 1–2. The South African venue of the British Association's 1905 conference has been described as combining 'the political thrust of the British Association's imperial ambitions with the wider political purpose of improving British South African relations in the wake of the Boer War' (Michael Worboys, 'The British Association and empire: science and social imperialism, 1880–1940', in Roy Macleod and Peter Collins (eds.), *The Parliament of Science* (London, Science Reviews Ltd., 1981), p. 175).

94 Haddon, *Address to the Anthropological Section*, p. 1.

95 Adam Kuper, 'The man in the study and the man in the field: ethnography, theory and comparison in social anthropology', *European Journal of Sociology*, 21, 1 (1980), pp. 15–16.

96 *RAI Archives*, Memorandum on the establishment of an Imperial Bureau of Anthropology presented to the imperial government by the Royal Anthropological Institute, n.d.; draft memorandum on the establishment of an Imperial Bureau of Anthropology.

97 William Ridgeway, 'The application of zoological laws to man', *Nature* (24 September 1908), p. 531; 'The influence of environment on man', *JRAI*, 40 (1910), pp. 1–13. Porter (*op. cit.*, pp. 154–5) notes the failure of the Anthropological Institute to impress Chamberlain at the Colonial Office, though undoubtedly the seeds had begun to be sown for greater Colonial Office interest after the First World War as indirect rule was developed. Anthropology also failed to make any significant headway in South Africa before the end of the First World War. See the article by H. H. Johnston, 'The empire and anthropology', *Nineteenth Century* (July 1908), pp. 133–46, arguing for the teaching of anthropology in British schools. 'The time may come', he hoped, 'when the mass of the people will flock to the discussions at the Royal Anthropological Institute or the Entomological Society as they now flock to the music halls' (p. 139).

98 *A. C. Haddon Papers*, A. C. Haddon to Canon Weinbrecht, December 1911: 'I am convinced that a good general knowledge of ethnology . . . is more essential as a preparation for missionary work than anything else'.

99 Arthur Keith, 'Anthropometry and national health', *Journal of State Medicine* (February 1919), p. 3; Sir Arthur Keith, *An Autobiography* (London, Watts. and Co., 1950), pp. 404–5.

100 Keith, 'Anthropometry and national health', p. 4.

101 *Ibid.*, p. 8.

102 MRC, f. 2025, Anthropometric Standards Committee 1, Sir Walter Fletcher to Professor Arthur Keith, 23 December 1919.

103 *Ibid.*, Karl Pearson to Sir Walter Fletcher, 26 October 1922 (marked 'confidential'); 'Notes for observers', n.d.

104 Sir Walter Fletcher to Arthur Keith, 7 May 1924; MRC/f. 1278, Leonard Darwin to the secretary of the Medical Research Council, 18 May 1925; Major Greenwood to Sir Walter Fletcher, 28 May 1925; Sir Walter Fletcher to Major Darwin, 23 June 1925.

105 W. H. R. Rivers, 'The unity of anthropology', *JRAI*, 111 (1922), p. 14.

106 For Fleure and Rosby's importance in the development of British academic geography, see H. C. Darby, 'Academic geography in Britain, 1918–1946', *Trans. Inst. Br. Geogr.*, NS 8 (1983), pp. 14–26. I am grateful to Mark

Johnson for bringing this article to my attention.

107 Alice Garnett, 'Herbert John Fleure, 1879–1969', *Biographical Memoirs of Fellows of the Royal Society*, 16 (1970), p. 259.

108 For the idealist influences on the growth of sociology in Britain, see Stefan Collini, 'Sociology and idealism in Britain, 1880–1920', *European Journal of Sociology*, 19 (1978), pp. 3–50.

109 Garnett, *op. cit.*

110 For criticisms of the anthropometrical method, see W. M. Flinders Petrie, 'Migrations', *JAI*, 36 (1906), pp. 189–220; Ridgeway, 'The application of zoological laws to man'; and Franz Boas, 'Changes in bodily form of descendants of immigrants' (1912), repr. in Franz Boas, *Race, Language and Culture* (New York, The Free Press, 1948).

111 H. J. Fleure and T. C. James, 'Geographical distribution of anthropological types in Wales', *JRAI*, 46 (1916), p. 37. Fleure considered the Boasian standpoint on the 'impermanence of race types' as 'extreme', considering that it could be 'discarded in serious anthropology'. 'Descent with modification is obviously a slow process', he wrote on the basis of the Welsh survey research, 'for in every parish of our country markedly contrasted types live side by side, and yet, in spite of intermarriage as well as of substantial similarity of conditions, they remain distinct' (*The Races of England and Wales: a Survey of Recent Research* (London, Benn Bros., 1923), pp. 84–5). Fleure's research made quite a considerable impact on anthropological thought in Britain before and after the First World War. See, for example, A. H. Keane, *Man, Past and Present* (Cambridge, CUP, 1920), pp. 522–4; A. C. Haddon, *The Races of Man and their Distribution* (Cambridge, CUP, 1924), p. 57; Sir Arthur Keith, 'How did Britain's racial divisions arise?', *Discovery* (January 1929). The general theory was that around 2500 BC a cross between Anatolians and Mediterraneans gave rise to restless mariners named 'The Prospectors', who played a key role in the dissemination of early culture and whose descendants can still be traced in parts of the Mediterranean and Wales, where they form the basis for an identifiably distinct 'race type'.

112 H. J. Fleure, 'The racial history of the British people', *Geographical Review*, 5 (January–June 1918), pp. 230–1.

113 E. G. Bowen, *et al., Geography at Aberystwyth* (Aberystwyth, University of Wales Press, 1968), p. xxi.

114 H. J. Fleure, 'Regions in human geography', *Geographical Teacher*, 14 (1917–18), p. 44. See also Fleure, 'Patrick Geddes', pp. 8–9 for the influence of Geddes on regional geography.

115 E. G. Bowen, 'The incidence of Phthisis in relation to race types and social environment in South and West Wales', *JRAI*, 58 (1928), pp. 363–98; 'A clinical study of miners' phthisis in relation to the geographical and racial features of the Cardiganshire lead-mining area', in *Studies in Regional Consciousness and Environment: Essays presented to H. J. Fleure* (Oxford, Oxford University Press, 1930), pp. 189–202.

116 MRC/f. 1278, President of the Eugenics Education Society and the president of the RAI to Viscount Milner, 24 January 1919, encl. letter from H. J. Fleure.

117 This work was published as R. M. Fleming, 'A study of growth and development: observations in successive years on the same children', *Med. Res. Ser. No. 190* (London, HMSO 1933). See also R.M. Fleming, 'Human hybrids: racial crosses in various parts of the world', *Eugenics Review*, 21, 4 (1930), pp. 257–63; R.M. Fleming, 'Physical heredity in human hybrids', *Annals of*

Eugenics, 9, 1 (1939), pp. 55–81.

118 H. J. Fleure, 'The nordic myth', *Eugenics Review*, 22 (1930) pp. 117–21.

119 Daniel Keyles, 'Genetics in the United States and Great Britain, 1890–1930: a review with speculations', in Charles Webster (ed.), *Biology, Medicine and Society, 1840–1940* (Cambridge, CUP, 1981), pp. 193–215. In some cases, the initial impact of Mendel's thought was to reinforce ideas of racial 'purity'. 'Owing to the discoveries of Mendel', wrote one observer in 1911, 'and his disciples, we may well believe that the primary races of mankind, like certain substances of chemistry, may possess the power of shedding off alien elements, and reverting to a state of purity' (Arthur S. Herbert, 'De Gobineau's ethnological theory', *The Nineteenth Century*, July 1911, p.134).

120 Lyndsay Farrall, 'Controversy and conflict in sciences: a case study – the English biometric school and Mendel's laws', *Social Studies of Science*, 5 (1975), pp. 269–301. The dispute mainly centred around how the question of human variation fitted into the general evolutionary biology bequeathed by the Darwinians. Weldon and his disciple, Karl Pearson, sought to understand evolutionary processes in biology as a population question that could be operationalised through statistical theory. Bateson considered that the best method was through concentrating on animal species that had clearly distinguishable varieties, for it was by observation and breeding experiments that biologists could understand what happened to different species when they were bred together. This difference in method also led to differences over the nature of evolutionary change, which for Weldon occurred through a series of small variations and for Bateson happened as a result of a sudden and large mutation. Keyles has noted that the dispute did not arise with the same acerbity in the USA as in Britain (Keyles, *op. cit.*, p. 201).

121 See the letters of Julian Huxley to Hunt on the proposal to establish an independent Institute of Human Genetics in Britain in the early 1930s which could neutralise the influence of Pearson's biometry at UCL and also link up with the work of the anthropologists (Add 7955/18/212, *Human Genetics Scheme 1931*, University of Cambridge Library).

122 See the attack by Ruggles Gates on anthropologists' neglect of the issue in Britain (R. Ruggles Gates, 'Mendelian heredity and racial differences', *JRAI*, 55 (1925), p. 468).

123 R. Ruggles Gates, 'A pedigree study of Amerindian crosses in Canada', *JRAI*, 58 (1928), p. 511. See also *Heredity and Eugenics* (London, Constable, 1923); *Heredity in Man* (London, Constable, 1930). Gates's views on the biological dangers attached to such inter-racial 'crossing' were fairly widely shared by biologists and anatomists during this period. For a similar view, see J. W. Gregory, *Human Migration and the Future* (London, Seeley Service and Co., 1928), pp. 37–8.

124 Gates, 'A pedigree study', p. 529. See also Leonard Darwin, *The Need for Eugenic Reform* (London, John Murray, 1926), pp. 494–7.

125 Add 7955/18/167, A. C. Haddon to Major Hurst, 21 June 1931.

126 C. C. Hurst, *The Mechanics of Creative Evolution* (Cambridge, CUP, 1932); Add 7955/20/42, A. C. Haddon to Major Hurst, 21 May 1933.

127 *RAI Archives*, A3 Minute Book, Human Biology Research Committee, 4 March 1932.

128 *Ibid.*, 24 April 1934. See also Royal Anthropological Institute and the Institute of Sociology, *Race and Culture* (Malvern and London, RAI, Le Play House Press, 1935), p. 2.

129 Human Biology Research Committee, 27 May 1932; In the report entitled

Standardization of the Techniques of Physical Anthropology, G. M. Morant, M. L. Tildesley and L. H. Dudley Buxton concluded that 'one of the main purposes with which the physical anthropologist is concerned is the documentation and comparison of different races from the anatomical standpoint'.

130 *Race and Culture*, pp. 3–4; Stepan, *op. cit.*, p. 168.
131 G. M. Morant, 'Physical anthropology and ignorance in Great Britain', *Sociological Review*, 26 (1934), p. 176.
132 *Ibid.*, p. 180.
133 *SAS Archives*, Minutes of Council, 7 April 1935; *Glasgow Weekly Herald*, 25 May 1935. For attacks on the Society, see *The Times*, 13 March, 22 May 1935.
134 *SAS Archives*, Minutes of Council, 1 June 1937.
135 *Ibid.*, 14 April 1936; *The Scotsman*, 5 May 1936.
136 *SAS Archives*, 14 July, 19 August 1936.
137 *Ibid.*, 15 December 1936.
138 L. H. Dudley Buxton, J. C. Trevor and Beatrice Blackwood, 'Measurements of Oxfordshire villagers', *JRAI*, 69 (1939), pp. 1–10.
139 Julian Huxley and A. C. Haddon, *We Europeans: a Survey of 'Racial' Problems* (London, Jonathan Cape, 1935).
140 Julian Huxley, *Memories* (Harmondsworth, Penguin, 1972), p. 207.
141 Huxley and Haddon, *op. cit.*, p. 269. For the British conception of this Aryanism, see the two articles by Joan Leopold, 'British applications of the Aryan theory of race to India, 1850–1870', *English Historical Review*, 89 (1974), pp. 578–603; 'The Aryan theory of race', *Indian Social and Economic History Review*, 7 (1970), pp. 271–97. See also G. L. Hersey, 'Aryanism in Victorian England', *Yale Review*, 66, 1 (1976), pp. 104–13; and Stepan, *op. cit.*, pp. 99–100.
142 *The Times*, 4 August 1934.
143 Stepan, *op. cit.*, p. 168. This absence of a new paradigm was reflected in Haddon's last lectures at Cambridge in the late 1930s. 'In the endeavour to classify mankind', he wrote, 'it is essential to keep the consideration of physical characters, culture and language quite apart from one another, or much confusion will arise. The problems of racial affinity are purely zoological, thus in considering race only external and internal physical characters, or occasionally to some extent, physiological characters can be taken into account. Unfortunately, there is still a lack of uniformity in the use of the word "race" ' (*A. C. Haddon Papers*, 4034, lecture, 'The races of Man', Cambridge, 1938, p. 1).
144 H. J. Massingham, 'The new anthropology', in *The Heritage of Man* (London, Jonathan Cape, 1929), p. 137. See also G. Cons, *Racial Superiority* (London, Friends Council for International Service, 1927), pp. 10–11.
145 *Report of the British Association for the Advancement of Science* (Blackpool, 1936), p. 462. See also Morant's remarks in *Race and Culture*, pp. 19–24.
146 *Ibid.*, pp. 462–3.
147 Burrow, *Evolution and Society*, p. 263.
148 See, for example, Arthur Keith, 'War as a factor in racial evolution', *St Thomas's Hospital Gazette* (December 1915), pp. 1–9. 'On certain factors concerned in the evolution of human races', *JRAI*, 46 (1916), pp. 1–25; *Nationality and Race* (London, Oxford University Press, 1919).
149 For Keith's career, see *Dictionary of National Biography, 1951–1960*, pp. 565–6; and Sir Arthur Keith, *An Autobiography, passim.*

150 *Evening Standard*, 14 October 1927. For the resurrection of Max Müller's
     Aryan theory and the Asiatic origin of the 'Caucasian race', see A. H. Keane,
     Man, Past and Present, pp. 502–4 and also G. R. Gair, 'The cradle of man-
     kind', paper read to the Ethnic Research Society, 1931–2 session, *Evangelical
     Quarterly* (January 1933).
151 See, for example, Sir Arthur Keith, 'Science and religion', *The Sunday Times*,
     3 October 1926, for the influence of Smuts's *Holism and Evolution*
     (1926).
152 Sir Arthur Keith, *Ethnos – or the Problem of Race* (London, Kegan Paul,
     Trench, Trubner and Co., 1931), p. 28.
153 George Pitt-Rivers, 'An anthropological approach to ethnogenics: a new
     perspective', in E. E. Evans-Pritchard *et al.*, (eds.), *Essays presented to C. G.
     Seligman* (London, Kegan Paul, Trench, Trubner and Co., 1934), p. 247. See
     also Pitt-Rivers's remarks in *Race and Culture*, pp. 15–18 and his contri-
     bution to the debate in *The Times* in a letter of 17 August 1934.
154 Huxley and Haddon, *We Europeans*, p. 269.
155 *The Times*, 18 July 1936.
156 *The Times*, 20 July 1936.
157 *The Times*, 22 July 1936, letter from W. E. Le Gros Clark.
158 Ashley Montagu, *Man's most Dangerous Myth: the Fallacy of Race* (New
     York, Columbia University Press, 1942), pp. 155–66. See also Montagu's
     articles, 'A cursory examination of the relations between physical and social
     anthropology', *American Journal of Physical Anthropology*, 26 (1940), pp.
     41–61; 'The genetical theory of race and anthropological method', *American
     Anthropologist*, 94 (1942), esp. pp. 369–72; and Henry Wallace, 'Racial
     theories and the genetical basis for democracy', *Science*, 89, 2303 (February
     1939), pp. 140–3.
159 For the employment of eugenics and pseudo-anthropological material in a
     'positive' affirmation of Nordic race theory, see Geoffrey Field, 'Nordic
     racism', *Journal of the History of Ideas*, 38, 3 (1977), pp. 523–40.
160 G. M. Morant, 'Racial theories and international relations', *JRAI*, 69, (1939–
     40), p. 161.
161 For an important survey of this wider European tradition of racial thinking, see
     George Mosse, *Toward the Final Solution: a History of European Racism*
     (London, Dent, and New York, Fertig, 1979); and the review article by
     Michael Biddiss, 'Towards a history of European racism', *Ethnic and Racial
     Studies*, 2, 4 (1979), pp. 508–13.
162 George Stocking, 'American Social Scientists and Race Theory, 1890–1915',
     Ph.D thesis, University of Pennsylvania, 1960. 'The type concept implies
     some sort of quantitative treatment of the data of physical characteristics . . .
     Once derived, it is easily abstracted from the variability upon which it is based
     and then used as a substitute for the older concept of "pure race" ' (p.
     218).
163 Hannah Arendt, *The Origins of Totalitarianism* (London, George Allen and
     Unwin, 1951), Chapter 6. See also Earl Count, 'The evolution of the race idea
     in modern Western culture during the period of the pre-Darwinian nineteenth
     century', *Transactions of the New York Academy of Sciences* (28 January
     1946), p. 141, for a similar distinction between *racism* and *raciology* as a
     'bona fide science'.
164 The history of this debate in UNESCO and the political context in which it
     was conducted remains to be written. See, though, the early review article for

the output of the early 1950s by Maurice Freedman, 'Some recent work on race relations: a critique', *British Journal of Sociology*, 5 (1954), pp. 342–54. The standard work is Ashley Montagu, *Man's most Dangerous Myth: the Fallacy of Race* (New York, Columbia University Press, 1942). See also Stepan, *op. cit.*, pp. 170–89; and Ashley Montagu, *Statement on Race* (London, Oxford and New York, Oxford University Press, 1972). The general objective in UNESCO was the mobilisation of expert opinion as part of an 'educational offensive' against public misconceptions on race and to ensure a wider acceptance of the conclusions of social science. See Otto Klineberg, '32 social scientists testify against segregation', *Unesco Courier*, 6 (1954), p. 24.

165 H. J. Fleure, 'The Institute and its development', *JRAI*, 76 (1946), p. 2.

166 In 1956 T. H. Marshall noted the shift of focus towards the treatment of race in anthropology. 'At one time the concept [of race] was treated more as a thing to be identified than as a tool to be used', he argued. 'Today the emphasis shifts to a study of processes, genetic and social, producing stabilizing distributions of traits within groups socially delimited or geographically located' ('Anthropology', *British Journal of Sociology*, 7 (1956), p. 61).

167 Friedrich Hertz, 'Racialism as a social factor', *Sociological Review*, 4 (1948), p. 8.

168 *Ibid.*, p. 10.

6. The 'half-caste' pathology

1 Oscar Wilde, *The Picture of Dorian Gray*, 1st edn 1891 (Harmondsworth, Penguin, 1949), p. 208.

2 James Walvin, *Black and White: the Negro and English Society, 1555–1945* (London, Allen Lane, 1973), pp. 46–73; Peter Fryer, *Staying Power* (London and Sydney, Pluto Press, 1984), pp. 66–88, 191–5, 227–36.

3 In the case of the riots at Cardiff and Barry in 1919, see the *Daily Herald*, 13, 14, 16 and 17 June 1919.

4 For a short discussion on the emergence of the NUS as an effective 'company union' of the British Shipping Federation, see David Byrne, 'The 1930 "Arab riot": a race riot that never was', *Race and Class*, 18, 3 (1977), pp. 263–6 and *passim*.

5 Fryer, *op. cit.*, pp. 298–313, on which much of the above is based.

6 James Walvin, *Passage to Britain* (Harmondsworth, Penguin, 1984), p. 80.

7 A. P. Thornton, *Imperialism in the Twentieth Century* (London and Basingstoke, The Macmillan Press, 1980), p. 32; 'Imperialism in the twentieth century', *Journal of Imperial and Commonwealth History*, 2, 1 (October 1973), pp. 38–55.

8 R. May and R. Cohen, 'The interaction between race and colonialism: a case study of the Liverpool race riots of 1919', *Race and Class*, 16, 2 (1975, pp. 111–26; W. F. Elkins, 'Marcus Garvey, the negro world and the British West Indies, 1919–1920', *Science and Society*, 36 (1972), pp. 63–77. See also G. Dimmock, 'Racial Hostility in Britain with Particular Reference to the Disturbances in Cardiff and Liverpool in 1919', M.A. dissertation, University of Sheffield, 1975; Jacqueline Jenkinson, 'The Glasgow race disturbances of 1911', in Kenneth Lunn (ed.), *Race and Labour in Twentieth-Century Britain* (London, F. Cass, 1985), pp. 43–67.

9 Campbell Balfour, 'Captain Tupper and the 1911 seamen's strike in Cardiff',

Morgannwg, 14 (1970), pp. 75–6, 79; 'Jack ashore: seamen in Cardiff before 1914', *Welsh History Review*, 9 (1978–9), pp. 176–203; E. Tupper, *Seamen's Torch: Life Story of Captain Tupper* (London, Hutchinson and the National Book Association, 1938).

10 Little, *Negroes in Britain*, 1st edn 1948 (London, Routledge and Kegan Paul, 1972), p. 58.

11 *West Africa*, 6 August 1921.

12 HO 45/11897, G. E. Baker (Board of Trade), letter dated 13 May 1921.

13 *Ibid.*, Report by E. N. Cooper, Immigration Office, Liverpool, 17 February 1921.

14 *Ibid.*, Deputation to the Board of Trade (Viscount Woolmer) from the Seafarers' Joint Council regarding the employment of Arabs to the detriment of British seafarers, Monday, 15 January 1923, evidence given by Mr Hewson.

15 *Ibid.*, Minute CR 18/1/15.

16 *Ibid.*, Minute 26/1/23.

17 *Ibid.*, Minute 19/1/23.

18 HO 45/11897/027246, Henry T. A. Bosanquet to Capt. Sir A. W. Clarke, Deputy Chairman, King George's Fund for Sailors, 10 June 1921; Little, *op. cit.*, p. 79. For a more detailed account of the Cardiff situation, see Neil Evans, 'Regulating the reserve army: Arabs, blacks and the local state in Cardiff, 1919–45' in Lunn (ed.), *Race and Labour*, pp. 68–115.

19 HO 45/11897, Chief Constable, Cardiff, to the Under Secretary of State, Home Office, 24 September 1923.

20 *Ibid.*, Memorandum, 'Instructions as to the registration of coloured alien (other than Chinese and Japanese) under the Special Restriction (Coloured Alien Seamen) Order, 1925, paras. 3 and 4.

21 HO 45/12314, Memorandum of a conference of chief constables, superintendents, merchant marine officers and immigration staff.

22 *Ibid.*, John Peddar, Circular to chief constables entitled 'Registration of coloured alien seamen (other than Chinese and Japanese)', 23 March 1925.

23 *Ibid.*, Minutes of conference of chief constables.

24 *Ibid.*, Chief Constable, Manchester, to Under Secretary of State, Home Office, 14 April 1925 encl. report of detective officer on coloured alien seamen, 14 April 1925.

25 *Ibid.*, Chief Constable, Glasgow, to Under Secretary of State, Home Office, 11 September 1925 encl. report by Aliens Registration Department, 10 September 1925.

26 *Ibid.*

27 *Ibid.*, Minute by E. N. Cooper, 24 September 1925.

28 *Ibid.*, G. S. Varma *et al.*, President, Glasgow Indian Union, to Secretary of State for India, 17 February 1926; Little, *op. cit.*, p. 87.

29 *Ibid.*, Immigration Office report re Joffer Shah, 27 October 1930.

30 *Ibid.*, Minute, 28 October 1930.

31 HO 45/11392, Coloured Seamen, Minutes of a conference held at the Home Office, 13 December 1926, evidence given by Sir Haldane Porter. In 1928 Porter complained that because it was difficult to explain 'even to the educated person' the difference between a 'British Subject' and a 'British protected person', the Home Office was 'being gradually driven to the position of treating British protected persons almost on the same footing as British Subjects as regards the grant of leave for discharge and registration under the Coloured

Seamen Order' (*Ibid.*, Coloured Seamen: Notes of a conference held at the Home Office on 5 November 1928).

32 MSS Brit. Emp. x23 HI/22, James A. Wilson, Chief Constable, Cardiff, to chairman and members of the watch committee, 10 April 1929, p. 4.

33 *Ibid.*, James A. Wilson, Chief Constable, Cardiff, to chairman and members of the watch committee, 8 January 1929.

34 See Paul Rich, *White Power and the Liberal Conscience: Racial Segregation and South African Liberalism* (Manchester, Manchester University Press, 1984).

35 HO 45/14299, James A. Wilson to Under Secretary of State, Home Office, 14 October 1930.

36 *Ibid.*, Minute by J.P., 3 October 1930, pointing out that the rota system was 'brought off by the collaboration of the NUS and the employers in certain ports'. 'No Government department could have managed it with existing powers', he noted, 'but it looks like being a success.' For the operation of the boarding house system, see Little, *op. cit.*, pp. 60–3.

37 *Seaman*, 2 July 1930. The allegation of corrupt practices was denied by the Arabs in South Shields (Byrne, *op. cit.*, p. 270).

38 HO 45/14299, Report by Sergeant T. Holdsworth, Cardiff, 27 October 1930. However, as the chief constable of Cardiff wrote: 'Unless the coloured population at Barry Dock, Cardiff and elsewhere, are kept under complete control, there is a possibility that they may endeavour to remove from one port to another, causing endless trouble to the Police, and, incidentally, they may devise some scheme whereby they may obtain relief from the Public Assistance Officers at both ports' (*ibid.*, Lionel Lindsay, Chief Constable, Cardiff, to James A. Wilson, Head Constable, 23 October 1930).

39 Byrne, *op. cit.*, p. 266.

40 *Ibid.*, p. 273.

41 HO 45/14299, Minute by J. H. J., 25 September 1930.

42 Byrne, *op. cit.*, p. 274. See also the *Daily Herald*, 1 October 1930.

43 *Daily Herald*, 13 June 1919; May and Cohen, *op. cit.*, pp. 111–26.

44 *Daily Herald*, 11 January 1929.

45 For a study of charitable effort in Liverpool in which the University Settlement developed, see Margaret Simey, *Charitable Effort in Liverpool in the Nineteenth Century* (Liverpool, Liverpool University Press, 1951); and Lord Woolton, *Memoirs* (London, Cassell, 1952), pp. 17–37.

46 Constance and Harold King, '*The Two Nations': the Life and Work of Liverpool University Settlement and its Associated Institutions, 1906–1937* (London, Hodder and Stoughton with the University of Liverpool Press, 1938), pp. 127–8.

47 See pp. 110–12.

48 King and King, *op. cit.*, p. 128.

49 *Ibid.*, p. 129. Roxby still had a strong belief in different racial 'types' at this time. See Percy Roxby, 'Geography and nationalism', *New Era* (July 1931), pp. 224–6.

50 King and King, p. 129; Minutes of the Council of the University Settlement, 22 October 1928.

51 Percy Roxby, 'Foreword' to M. E. Fletcher, *Report on an Investigation into the Colour Problem in Liverpool and Other Ports* (Liverpool, Association for the Welfare of Half-Caste Children 1930), p. 6.

52 Fletcher, *Report*, p. 9.
53 *Ibid.*, p. 39.
54 *Seaman*, 2 July 1930.
55 Fletcher, *Report*, pp. 10–11.
56 M. Fleming, 'Human hybrids', *Eugenics Review*, 21, 4 (1930), p. 260. See also R. M. Fleming, 'Physical heredity in human hybrids', *Annals of Eugenics*, 9, 1 (1939), pp. 55–81. Cedric Dover considered by 1937 that the view of 'biological disharmony' being produced by 'inter breeding' had become somewhat undermined, though he noted the lingering belief in 'Hybrid infertility' (*Half-Caste* (London, Secker and Warburg, 1937), pp. 30–1).
57 Fletcher, *Report*, p. 28. See also M. E. Fletcher, 'The colour problem in Liverpool', *Liverpool Review*, (October 1930), pp. 421–4.
58 *Ibid.*, p. 33.
59 *Ibid.*, p. 37.
60 *Ibid.*, p. 39.
61 MSS Brit. Emp. S23 H1/15, Ernest Adkin to J. Harris, 7 August 1930.
62 King and King, *op. cit.*, p. 130; St Clair Drake, 'Value Systems, Social Structure and Race Relations in the British Isles', Ph.D. thesis, University of Chicago, 1954, pp. 80–1.
63 Interview with Lady M. Simey; King and King, *op. cit.*, p. 130.
64 *University of Liverpool Social Survey of Merseyside, No. 2: A Study of Migration to Merseyside, with Special Reference to Irish Immigration* (Liverpool, University of Liverpool Press, 1931), p. 2.
65 *Ibid.*, p. 7.
66 *Ibid.*, pp. 5–6.
67 MSS Brit. Emp. S1427 4/3, F. S. Livie-Noble, Memorandum on 'Distressed coloured seamen at Cardiff and elsewhere'. Livie-Noble asserted that repatriation was not acceptable to the black seamen, whose unemployment should be seen as part of the wide issue of unemployment within Britain generally (p. 2). For the Nancy Sharpe report, see St Clair Drake, *op. cit.*, p. 83.
68 See 'Merseyside social survey', *Liverpool Review*, 3, 1 (January 1932) for an attack on Irish immigration. See also G. R. Gair, 'The Irish immigration question', *Liverpool Review*, 9, 1 (January 1934), pp. 11–14; 9, 2 (February 1934), pp. 47–50; 9, (March 1934), pp. 86–8.
69 See St Clair Drake, 'The "colour problem" in Britain', *Sociological Review*, 3 (1955), pp. 201–2, for the London interest in race relations.
70 MSS Brit. Emp. S23 HI/18, J. Harris to Ernest Adkin, 22 December 1931.
71 *Ibid.*, John Harris, 'An open sore', n.d.
72 *Ibid.*, Rev. Geo. F. Dempster, British Sailors' Society, to J. Harris, 6 August 1939.
73 *Ibid.*, W. H. Grey (from Africa House, Kings Way), to J. Harris, 8 August 1930.
74 *Ibid.*, J. Harris to W. H. Grey, 19 August 1930.
75 *Winifred Holtby Papers*, John Fletcher, Circular, 6 January 1931. The Joint Council was formed 'to overcome colour prejudices in this country'.
76 Edward Scobie, *Black Britannia: a History of Blacks in Britain* (Chicago, Johnson Pub. Co., 1972), pp. 174–9. For Paul Robeson's impact on Britain in the late 1920s and early 1930s, see Phil Foner (ed.) *Paul Robeson Speaks* (London, Quartet Books, 1978), pp. 76–94.

77 Joint Council, Minute No. 86, 8 December 1932; St Clair Drake, 'Value Systems', p. 83.
78 *The Friend*, 6 December 1929 and 10 January 1930; C. F. Andrews, 'Toward the solution of the race problem', *The Friend*, 3 October 1930.
79 Roderick Macdonald, 'Dr Harold Arundel Moody and the League of Coloured Peoples, 1931–1947: a retrospective view', *Race*, 14, 3 (1973), p. 291.
80 Mona Macmillan, *Champion of Africa: the Later Life of William Milner Macmillan*, unpublished MS in author's possession, argued that Winifred Holtby had an important intermediary role amongst a number of liberal welfare organisations in London in the early 1930s and was important in getting them to cooperate as a kind of lobby. This was not a role that was taken on after her death by other liberal notables such as Leonard Barnes, Norman Leys or Macmillan himself. Holtby's success was undoubtedly stimulated by her reputation as a novelist; her novel, *Mandoa Mandoa* (1934), was an attack on some aspects of British colonial rule.
81 St Clair Drake, 'Value Systems', p. 202.
82 MSS Brit. Emp. S23 HI/18, H. A. Moody to J. Harris, 28 January 1932; HI/19, J. Harris to H. A. Moody, 22 May 1932.
83 MSS Brit. Emp. S23 HI/20, F. de Courcy Hamilton to J. Harris, 14 October 1933; J. Harris to F. Hamilton, 12 December 1933; J. Harris to Alistair Smith, 20 July 1934; A. Smith to J. Harris, 5 January 1935.
84 *Daily Herald*, 8 December 1933.
85 *Colonial News*, April 1934.
86 Little, *op. cit.*, pp. 94–7; Byrne, *op. cit.*
87 Little, op. cit., p. 96, n. 2; *Western Mail and South Wales Daily News*, 17 April 1935.
88 St Clair Drake, 'Value Systems', p. 105.
89 MSS Brit. Emp. S23 H/22, J. Harris to Charles Roden Buxton, 21 June 1935.
90 *Ibid.*, J. Harris to Hans Vischer, 27 December 1935. The deputation was organised, Harris boasted, because of his 'rather well-known personal relationship with Sir John Simon' (J. Harris to H. King, 20 December 1935).
91 Cited in Little, *op. cit.*, p. 104. The British Social Hygiene Council was established in 1914 to carry out the recommendations of the Royal Commission on Venereal Disease. It worked with various government departments under its secretary general Mrs Neville Rolfe; T. Drummond Shiels was its medical secretary.
92 MSS Brit. Emp. S23 HI/22, J. Harris to Harold King, 11 December 1935.
93 *Ibid.*, Harold King to J. Harris, 19 December 1945; Minutes of the Council of the University Settlement, Liverpool, 3 June and 8 October 1935. Contacts were established between the Liverpool Association for Half-Caste Children and the Juvenile Employment Committee. The Association also considered the Richardson Report with the education committee of the Settlement (Minutes of Fin. and Gen. Purposes Committee, 19 July 1935).
94 MSS Brit. Emp. S23 HI/22, J. Harris to H. King, 14 January 1936.
95 *Ibid.*, J. Harris to The Secretary of State for Home Affairs, 20 February 1936; Harold King to J. Harris, 14 January 1936, influenced Harris's letter in a more

specifically racial direction by getting him to concentrate specifically on 'half-caste children', since it was 'very important to differentiate in this problem between half-caste and pure negroid types'.

96 HO 213/349, E. H. Cooper, Minute, 11 April 1936.
97 *Ibid.*, Minute, n.d.
98 HO 213/350, Deputation from the Welfare Committee on Africans in Europe and various other societies in the ports of Great Britain to the Parliamentary Under Secretary of State, Home Office, 28 July 1936, p. 8.
99 *Ibid.*, pp. 20–1.
100 *Ibid.*, H. King to E. H. Cooper, 31 July 1936.
101 *Ibid.*, Deputation, p. 27.
102 MSS Brit. Emp. S23 HI/22, A. Evans, MP to J. Harris, 23 January 1937.
103 *Ibid.*, G. Lloyd to J. Harris, 20 January 1937.
104 HO 213/352, Minutes of a conference held at the Home Office on 2 December 1936, to consider matters relating to the welfare of coloured persons in the United Kingdom, evidence given by Messrs. Bigg (Colonial Office) and Morley (India Office), p. 2.
105 *Ibid.*, evidence given by Mr Stewart, Ministry of Labour, pp. 4–5.
106 MSS Brit. Emp. S23 HI/23, Summary of a conference in Liverpool by the Association for the Welfare of Half-Caste Children on 8 December 1936, p. 4.
108 DCL 92/1, Stanley Watson, and George Young, Secretary, The South Wales Association for the Welfare of Coloured People, to Rt. Hon. Sir Samuel J. G. Hoare, 21 June 1937, encl. report of a deputation to the chief constable; MSS Brit. Emp. S23 HI/20, S. Watson to J. Harris, 14 September, 1 October 1937.
109 *The Keys*, 5, 1 (July–September 1937).
110 Fernando Henriques, *Children of Caliban: Miscegenation* (London, Secker and Warburg, 1934), p. 143.
111 Immanuel Geiss, *The Pan-African Movement* (London, Methuen, 1974), pp. 297–304.
112 MSS Brit. Emp. S23 HI/22, Charles Collett, LCP, to J. Harris, October 1937.
113 MSS Brit. Emp. S23 HI/28, S.J.K. Baker to J. Harris, 8 February 1940.
114 University of Liverpool Social Science Department, Statistics Division, *The Economic Status of Coloured Families in the Port of Liverpool* (Liverpool, Liverpool University Press, 1940), pp. 8–10.
115 Colin Holmes, *John Bull's Island* (London, Macmillan, 1988), p. 156. For the climate of the time, see Paul Addison, *The Road to 1945* (London, Quartet Books, 1977).

7. Colonial development, war and black immigration

1 See William Hynes, *The Economics of Empire* (London, Longman, 1979), for an analysis of the growth of commercial imperialism in the 1880s and 1890s, which were years of economic panic. After 1895 when confidence returned, interest in the tropical economies of West Africa waned and it was not until the 1930s that interest in their economic development started to pick up again.

250   *Notes*

2 An idea suggested by Ronald Robinson in 'Andrew Cohen and the transfer of power in tropical Africa, 1940–1951', in W. H. Morris-Jones (ed.), *Decolonisation and After: the British and French Experience* (London, Frank Cass, 1980), p. 50.

3 George Abbott, 'A re-examination of the 1929 Colonial Development Act', *Economic History Review*, 24, 1 (1971), pp. 68–81; Sir Charles Jeffries, *The Colonial Office* (London, George Allen and Unwin, 1956), p. 151; David Meredith, 'The British government and colonial economic policy, 1919–39', *Economic History Review*, 28, 4 (1975), pp. 484–99.

4 *Parlt. Deb.*, House of Commons, 5 Ser., 361, 21 May 1940, p. 47, col. 1.

5 Bernard Porter, *The Lion's Share: a Short History of British Imperialism, 1851–1970* (London and New York, Longman, 1975), p. 294; Robert Heussler, 'The legacy of British colonialism', *South Atlantic Quarterly*, 61 (1961), pp. 301–10.

6 General J. C. Smuts, *Africa and some World Problems* (Oxford, Clarendon Press, 1930), p. 64 and *passim*.

7 *Lothian Papers*, GD 40/17/120, Conference on Africa, minutes of the first meeting, Rhodes House, Saturday, 9 November 1930.

8 *Ibid*. Curtis thought it might take 'three or four centuries under the white man before the black had real civilisation' and after observing the 'quickness and intelligence of the so-called young Arabs with perhaps not more than one sixteenth part of Arab blood', he wondered whether 'in the last resort the best could be got from the African without mixing his blood with other stocks' (*ibid.*).

9 W. M. Macmillan, *My South African Years* (Cape Town, David Philips, 1975), pp. 243–4.

10 Kenneth King, *Panafricanism and Education* (London, Oxford University Press, 1971).

11 *Lothian Papers*, GD 40/17/120, L. Curtis to X. Keppel, 20 July 1931.

12 It especially shaped the thinking of Philip Mason, later the first director in the Institute of Race Relations, who saw India as 'the last of the old pre-industrial empires in the world'; Philip Mason *A Shaft of Sunlight* (London, Andre Deutsch, 1978), p. 93.

13 See Shula Marks and Stanley Trapido, 'Lord Milner and the South African state', *History Workshop*, 8 (Autumn 1979), pp. 50–80.

14 *Lothian Papers*, GD 40/17/120 Minutes of the second meeting, 10 November 1930.

15 *Ibid*.

16 Malcolm Macdonald was one of the members of the initial committee established to consider the African Research Project at the end of 1932 (*ibid.*, Ivison Macadam to Lothian, 20 December 1932). Though Lothian complained of the Colonial Office putting 'obstacles' in the way of the project (*ibid.*, Lothian to Macadam 29 March 1933), undoubtedly the project was able to use continual channels with the government, of whom Macdonald was one of the most prominent, being the son of the prime minister. See, for example, *ibid.*, Lothian to M. Macdonald, 27 June 1933.

17 R. Coupland, 'The Hailey Survey', *Africa* 12, 1 (January, 1939), p. 4.

18 Lord Hailey, *An African Survey* (London, Oxford University Press, 1938), p. 1624.

19 *Ibid.*, p. 1631.

20 *Ibid.*, p. 1640.
21 *Ibid.*, p. 1646.
22 *Ibid.*, p. 1656.
23 S. K. B. Asante, *Pan-African Protest: West Africa and the Italo-Ethiopian Crisis, 1934–41* (London, Longman, 1977).
24 Partha Sarathi Gupta has argued that the chief credit for the 1940 Act goes to Malcolm Macdonald and the West India desk of the Colonial Office. See *Imperialism and the British Labour Movement, 1914–1964* (London, The Macmillan Press, 1975), p. 248.
25 Eric Williams, *The Negro in the Caribbean*, 1st edn 1942 (New York, Negro Universities Press, 1969), p. 85.
26 Inf. 1/560, Overseas Policy Committee, Plan of Programme for West Indies, Paper No. 241, *Plan of Programme for Jamaica*, p. 7.
27 *Ibid.*, Paper No. 250, *Plan of Operations*, 21 September 1942.
28 Harold Macmillan, *The Blast of War, 1939–1945* (London, Macmillan, 1967), p. 163. 'We are nothing but failure and inefficiency everywhere', wrote Sir Alexander Cadogan on the collapse of Singapore, 'and the Japs are murdering our men and raping our women in Hong Kong'. See *The Diaries of Sir Alexander Cadogan, 1938–1945* (London, Cassell, 1971), entry for Thursday, 12 February 1942, p. 433.
29 *The Times*, 24 September 1942; Macmillan, *op. cit.*, p. 117. H. Duncan Hall noted in 1943 that 'the principle of partnership for the dependent Empire' and 'the extension to it of the Commonwealth principle of self-government and partnership in the common family of the British Commonwealth of Nations' was an 'essential condition' of the American guarantee of 'the territorial integrity of the British empire' into peacetime (*William Hailey Papers*, H. Duncan Hall to Lord Hailey, 18 January 1944, encl. memo entitled 'British Commonwealth – American post-war policy', 9 August 1943, p. 1).
30 George Padmore, 'Why the RAF has dropped the colour bar', *New Leader*, 25 January 1941. At the start of the war, though, an unofficial colour bar was operated in the armed forces and Arundel Moody was rejected from the Tank Corps on the grounds that he was not of pure white descent (Marika Sherwood, *Many Struggles: West Indian Workers and Service Personnel in Britain (1939–45)* (London, Karia Press, 1984), pp. 4–5).
31 CO 875/19/14 K. Little to J. L. Keith, 20 August 1942. It was also noted that 'the matter of colour prejudice receives constant consideration in this office' (*ibid.*, Minute by W. Keating, 7 November 1942).
32 *Ibid.*, J. L. Keith, Minute, 9 October 1942.
33 CO 876/16, J. L. Keith, Minute, 30 September 1942.
34 It was estimated that there were some 11,200 black American troops in Britain in August 1942 (CO 876/14, Bolero Combined Committees, Minutes of 12 August 1942, 'Problem of American coloured troops').
35 Christopher Thorne, 'Britain and the black GIs: racial issues and Anglo-American relations in 1942', *New Community*, 3, 3 (Summer 1974), p. 268. See also W. T. Wells, 'The British empire in the American century', *Fortnightly Review* (October 1942), pp. 248–54; and J. T. Harris, 'Britain and her colonies', *New Republic*, 4 October 1943, pp. 444–6.
36 William Lewis, *Imperialism at Bay: the United States and the Decolonisation of the British Empire, 1941–1945* (New York, Oxford University Press, 1978), p. 187; J. M. Lee and Martin Petter, *The Colonial Office, War and*

Development Policy (London, Maurice Temple Smith, 1982), p. 135.

37 *Ibid.*, p. 188. See also Christopher Thorne, *Allies of a Kind* (London, Oxford
University Press, 1978), pp. 222–3.

38 For a contrasting view, see Thomas Hachey, 'Jim Crow with a British accent: attitudes of London government officials towards American negro soldiers in England during World War II', *Journal of Negro History*, 59, 1 (January 1974), pp. 65–71, and a critique of this by Neil Wynn, *The Afro-American and the Second World War* (London, Paul Elek, 1976), pp. 33–4. See also Graham Smith, 'Jim Crow on the home front (1942–1945)', *New Community*, 8, 3 (Winter 1980), p. 320.

39 CO 876/14, Appendix to Grigg memorandum, September 1942; Thorne, 'Britain and the black GIs', pp. 264–5.

40 CO 876/14, Home Secretary, Memorandum, 10 October 1942. Wynn (*op. cit.*) places Morrison in the liberal camp with Stafford Cripps and Brendan Bracken on the issue (p. 34).

41 *Ibid.*, G. Murray to A. Richards, 24 June 1942. Murray attached great importance to anthropological work in the formulation of colonial policy. See *The Anti-Slavery Reporter and Aborigines Friend*, Ser. V, 31, 3 (October 1941), pp. 72–3.

42 CO 876/14, J. L. Keith, Minute, 12 September 1942; *Sunday Pictorial*, 6 September 1942; *New Statesman*, 22 August 1942.

43 CO 876/14, Cranborne memorandum, 9 October 1942.

44 Cadogan, *op. cit.*, entry for 13 October 1942, p. 483. Cranborne also mentioned the case of a black official in the Colonial Office who had always lunched at a certain restaurant and now had to stay away as it was patronised by American officers. 'That's all right', said Churchill, 'if he takes a banjo with him they'll think he's one of the band.' Cadogan thought the solution arrived at regarding the rewriting of the notes 'quite sensible'. For the Cripps mission to India, see Paul Addison, *The Road to 1945* (London, Quartet Books, 1982), pp. 201–5.

45 CO 876/14, Lord Privy Seal memorandum, 17 October 1942. Thorne, 'Britain and the black GIs', p. 267, has argued that 'some traces of the original Southern Command notes were still present in the new " Instructions as to the advice which should be given to British Service Personnel" '.

46 Graham Smith, 'Black American Soldiers in Britain, 1942–1945', Ph.D. thesis, University of Keele, 1982, p. 120.

47 *Ibid.*, pp. 150–63.

48 CO 876/14, Memo by H. Macmillan, 14 September 1942.

49 Smith, 'Jim Crow on the home front', p. 321.

50 Smith, 'Black American Soldiers', p. 205. Nevertheless, Roi Ottley reported in the US press in 1944 the lack of formality in British racial distinctions and the fact that there was no significant racial prejudice exhibited to the black GIs. 'The negro soldier', he concluded, 'has appealed to the British heart' (Roi Ottley, 'Dixie invades Britain', *Negro Digest*, 3, 1 (November 1944), p. 7). See also Roi Ottley, *Black Odyssey* (London, John Murray, 1949), pp. 311–12.

51 CO 876/14 G. Gater, Minute, 27 October 1942.

52 PREM 4/26/9 P.G. Grigg to Churchill, 2 December 1943.

53 Nancy Cunard and George Padmore, *The White Man's Duty* (London, W. H. Allen and Co., 1942), p. 4. See also Randolph Dunbar, 'Colonial rights', *Time and Tide*, 24 (July 1943).

54 *Ibid.*, p. 19.

55 Immanuel Geiss, *The Pan-African Movement* (London, Methuen, 1974), pp. 352–6; 'Pan-Africanism', *Journal of Contemporary History*, 4, 1 (January 1969), pp. 187–200.
56 This question, though, went back to before the war when a number of key critics and analysts of colonial policy asked what the role of trained African teachers would be back in their own societies. See, for example, Lord Lugard, 'Colonial administration', *Economica* (August 1933), pp. 250–1.
57 MSS Brit. Emp. S23 HI/25, G. C. F. Tomlinson to J. Harris, 18 March 1938, mentioning that a Colonial Office committee had been formed to assist colonial students in the UK.
58 Geiss, *The Pan-African Movement*, p. 349.
59 League of Coloured Peoples, *Memorandum on the Recommendations of the West India Royal Commission*, 1 (May 1940), p. 16.
60 Roderick J. Macdonald, 'Dr Harold Arundel Moody and the League of Coloured Peoples, 1931–1947: a retrospective view', *Race*, 3 (1973), pp. 299–300; Sam Morris, 'Moody – the forgotten visionary', *New Community*, 1, 3 (1972), pp. 193–4.
61 Ladipo Solanke, *United West Africa (or Africa) at the Bar of the Family of Nations*, 1st edn 1927 (London, African Publication Society, 1969), pp. 58–64. For Solanke, WASU served as 'the training ground for practical unity and effective cooperation between all West African students' (p. 64).
62 Geiss, *The Pan-African Movement*, p. 300; Philip Garigue, 'The West African Students' Union – a study in culture contact', *Africa*, 23 (1943), pp. 58–9; Paul Rich, 'The Black Diaspora in Britain: Afro-Caribbean students and the struggle for a political identity, 1900–1950', *Immigrants and Minorities*, 6, 2 (July 1987), pp. 151–73.
63 WASU, *The Truth about Aggrey House: Government Plan for Control of African Students* (London, WASU, March 1934).
64 MSS Brit. Emp. S23 HI/17, Note of proceeding of a joint conference between the Welfare of Africans in Europe War Fund (Surplus) Committee and the African Club Organising Committee, under the chairmanship of Dr Drummond Shields, held in the Colonial Office, Monday, 27 July 1931.
65 Garigue, *op. cit.*, p. 61 mentions this contact only in passing. Much of this account is derived from Dr R. B. Wellesley-Cole, 'Report on WASU hostel from data supplied by Mr Ladipo Solanke', SOR/168.
66 CO 847/5/11 L. Solanke to H. Vischer, 7 January 1936; H. Vischer memos 16 and 20 January 1936; MSS Brit. Emp. S23 HI/21, H. Vischer to J. Harris, 5 December 1935.
67 *Ibid.*, HI/28, H. Vischer to J. Harris, 28 July, 1, 4 and 6 August, 1939.
68 *Ibid.*, J. Harris to H. Vischer, 10 August 1939.
69 *Ibid.*, General Grey to Rt. Hon. Sir John Anderson, 10 July 1940.
70 *Ibid.*, H. Vischer to General Grey, 1 July 1940.
71 *Ibid.*, H. Vischer to C. W. W. Greenidge, 31 July 1941.
72 *Ibid.*, L. Solanke to H. Vischer, 18 August 1941.
73 SOR/168, L. Solanke to J. L. Keith, 28 April 1941.
74 *Ibid.*, L. Solanke to R. Sorensen, 12 May 1941.
75 CO 876/20, J. L. Keith, Minute, 24 October 1942.
76 CO 876/56, J. L. Keith, Minute, 19 June 1942.
77 *Ibid.*, J. L. Maloney, Minute, 9 October 1942.
78 CO 876/78, J. L. Keith, Minute, 30 June 1944; Garigue, *op. cit.*, pp. 63–4.
79 Speech of De Graf Johnson (Coloured People's Association, Edinburgh) in

George Padmore (ed.), *History of the Pan-African Congress*, 1st edn 1947 (London, Panaf Services, 1963), p. 29.

80 CO 876/157, J. Griffiths to R. Sorensen, 29 March 1951; L. Solanke to J. Griffiths, 18 April 1951.

81 D. A. Okusaga, 'Problems of indigenous West African students in Great Britain', *WASU Magazine*, 12, 6 (Spring 1949), p. 38.

82 SOR/174, Mildred Bailey to Canon J. M. Campbell, 29 November 1953.

83 SOR/168, R. Sorensen to Lord Milverton, 27 April 1950; Lord Milverton to R. Sorensen, 7 May 1950. See also Lord Milverton, 'Race relations in Africa', *The Sunday Times*, 13 March 1950. J. L. Keith noted that WASU was 'really doing good work in bringing West Indians over here together and in breaking down parochialism among them' (CO 876/155, J. L. Keith, Minute, 2 November 1950).

84 MSS Brit. Emp. S22 G501, C. M. McInnes to Col. E. W. Lennard (Royal Empire Society), 22 November 1943.

85 CO 876/10, J. L. Keith to Lionel Aird, 23 December 1941; Memorandum by J. L. Keith, 8 January 1941, entitled 'Notes on the Fund provided for the welfare of the colonial people in the United Kingdom'. In general the principle was to treat the colonials on the same basis as indigenous British people 'and we shall encourage colonials who have been absorbed in the general community to depend on the local welfare services, the Public Assistance Board and so forth, rather than look to the Colonial Office to special help'.

86 CO 876/238, J. L. Keith to Miss Parkin, 5 December 1949, pointed out that the Colonial Office Division of Colonial Scholars remained responsible to the Colonial Secretary.

87 PEP, *Colonial Students in Britain* (London, PEP, 1955), p. 4; CO 876/239, British Council Report of the working party for the Conference of Voluntary Societies on the Welfare of Students, 29 March 1950.

88 PEP, *Colonial Students in Britain*, pp. 158, 208.

89 *Ibid.*, p. 174. J. L. Keith wrote that many of the report's recommendations were 'entirely acceptable to us and indeed form part of our practice and that of Colonial Government in dealing with student affairs' (J. L. Keith to F. A. Norman, 23 April 1956, *Racial Unity Bulletin*, June 1956).

90 Mary Trevelyan, 'The African students at home', *United Empire*, 45, 5 (September–October 1956), p. 188; *Foreigners* (London, Edinburgh House Press, 1952).

91 See, for example, Krishnan Kumar, 'A child and a stranger: on growing out of English culture', in Bhikhu Parekh (ed.), *Colour, Culture and Consciousness* (London, Allen and Unwin, 1974), pp. 86–103, for the black student experience in Britain in the 1950s. See also G. K. Animashawrun, 'African students in Britain', *Race*, 5, 1 (July 1963), pp. 38–47.

92 Geiss, *The Pan-African Movement*, p. 408.

93 CO 876/15, L. Constantine to the regional controller, Min. of Lab. n.d. See also Arnold Watson, *West Indian Workers in Britain* (Liverpool, Hodder and Stoughton, 1942), p. 18; and Alex Watkinson, 'West Indian volunteer technicians', *Time and Tide*, 11 July 1942.

94 Learie Constantine, *Colour Bar* (London, Stanley Paul and Co., 1954), pp. 137–8. See also Smith, 'Jim Crow on the home front', p. 322. Constantine at that time was playing in an international cricket match at Lords. The manageress of the Imperial Hotel complained to Leatherbarrow, the manager of a recently concluded tour, with whom Constantine arrived: 'We will not

have niggers in the hotel because of the Americans. If they stay tonight, their luggage will be put out tomorrow and the doors locked' (p. 137). Constantine sued the hotel and damages were awarded against it. The discriminatory behaviour of hoteliers in London against blacks was a frequent cause of complaint. 'London is notoriously the only city in Britain', wrote one black man, H.W. Deer, 'where there is a colour bar. In Birmingham I could go into any hotel, but I cannot find within the directory an hotel in London which will admit me. If I walk in perhaps twelve millionaires will walk out and so I don't blame the proprietors' (CO 876/15, Notes by H.W. Deer, 2 Earls Gate, London, SW1, n.d.).

 95 See Cyril Erlich, 'Building and caretaking: economic policy in British tropical Africa, 1890–1960', *Economic History Review*, 26, 4 (1973), p. 651.
 96 CO 876/28, Ivor Cummings Report, 12 August 1942.
 97 *Ibid.*
 98 *Ibid.*, Ivor Cummings, Minute, 1 November 1942.
 99 See pp. 80–81, 145–150.
100 Erlich, *op. cit.*
101 CO 876/44, Ivor Cummings, Minute, 23 July 1942.
102 J. M. Lee, ' "Forward thinking" and war: the Colonial Office during the 1940s', *The Journal of Imperial and Commonwealth History*, 6, 1 (October 1977), p. 66.
103 Constantine, *op. cit.*, p. 100; The LCP tried to establish a branch in Liverpool in 1942 'for the purpose of intensive propaganda' and the establishment of a centre from which to operate. 'One of the main desires', it was asserted, 'is to tackle the problem of our children in Liverpool. This is essential, if we are to build up a new order for our people, and to make a positive contribution to the breakdown of the colour bar' (*LCP Newsletter*, 37 (October 1942), p. 2). The fortunes of the branch appear, though, to have been short-lived, though more detailed regional research is needed to confirm this.
104 LAB 26/226 CLWP(48)5, Colonial Office memo, 'Colonial Office experience of colonial workers in the United Kingdom', 23 October 1948, p. 2.
105 HO 213/714, S. E. Dudley, Minute, 28 May 1948. Clement Attlee tried to play down the issue by arguing that the 'Jamaican immigration' should not be taken 'too seriously' (*ibid.*, C. R. Attlee to J. D. Murray, 5 July 1948). See also *Reynolds News*, 11 July 1948.
106 CO 876/88, I. G. Cummings to H. L. Linden, 13 May 1948.
107 MT 9/5463, J. L. Keith to Under Secretary of State, HO, 3 September 1948.
108 LAB 20/218, Lord Listowel to Ness Edwards, 5 June 1948.
109 LAB 26/227 CLWP(48), 1st minutes, 6 October 1948, p. 2.
110 *Ibid.*, p. 4.
111 *Ibid.*, 2nd minutes, 27 October 1948, pp. 3, 5. Ivor Cummings pointed out that 16 men from the SS *Orbita* were working at Chippenham and were members of the Iron Foundry Workers' Union, but since this was categorised as skilled labour the meeting decided West Indian workers in general could not be placed in the foundries (p. 4).
112 LAB 26/226 and MT 9/5463, Notes of a conference held with representatives of the regions on Thursday, 20 January 1949, to discuss the placing of colonial negroes.
113 *Ibid.*
114 LAB 26/226 and MT 9/5463, Note of a meeting held at the Home Office on

18 Feburary 1949, to discuss problems of persons from the colonies and British protectorates, p. 4. See also CLWP(49), 3rd Minutes, 3rd March 1949, where the Home Office also sought the breaking-up of 'large aggregations of colonials', especially in London and Liverpool, as this was a 'law and order problem' (p. 4).

115 *Ibid.*, p. 2.
116 LAB 26/226, Minute by A.D.K. Davies, 8 February 1949. MT9/5463, W.H. Hardman to J.L. Keith, 22 June 1949, expressing opposition to the 'segregation of colonial workers from whites'.
117 MT 9/5463 CPUK(49), 3rd minutes, 6 July 1949, p. 3.
118 *Ibid.*, p. 3.
119 *Ibid.*, p. 2.
120 *Ibid.*, p. 2.
121 CO 876/255, K. Robinson to I. Cummings, 6 July 1950.
122 'We should consider', stated a Home Office memorandum, 'whether it is possible to make a more systematic study of the numbers, disposition, employment, etc., of the Coloured Community already here. There is no co-ordination of the information coming through various sources to Departments such as Home Office, Colonial Office, Ministry of Labour, Ministry of Transport and National Assistance Board' (MT 9/5463, Home Office Memorandum, 'Immigration of British subjects into the United Kingdom: further examination of certain methods of control', 31 July 1950, p. 4).
123 CAB 130/61 Gen. 324/1, Immigration of British subjects into the United Kingdom, Note by the Secretary of the Cabinet, 22 June 1950.
124 CAB 130/61, Minutes of a meeting of ministers held in the conference room 'A', Cabinet Office, 24 July 1950 and 11 January 1951.
125 CAB 130/61 Gen. 325/2, Memorandum by the Home Office, Ministry of Labour and National Service, Commonwealth Relations Office, Colonial Office and Ministry of Transport, 17 July 1950.
126 MT 9/5463, Immigration of British subjects into the United Kingdom, Notes of meeting held in the Home Office, 11 October 1950.
127 CO 876/234, Draft circular from the Secretary of State for the Colonies to colonial governors, 20 October 1950; Circular 'Warning to intending migrants from Jamaica to the United Kingdom', pointing out that 'The Colonial Office is not in a position to help migrants to find work or accommodation or to intervene in their domestic problems' (MT 9/5463, Home Office memorandum, dated 31 July 1950, detailing the successive administrative measures).
128 CO 876/231, Address by Lord Listowel to the London Council of Social Service, 6 July 1949; J. J. Nunn (HO), to E. G. Cass, 23 January 1950.
129 CO 876/231, J. L. Keith, 1 September 1950.
130 CO 876/231, Sir Charles Jeffries, Minute, 4 September 1950.
131 CO 876/231, N. D. Watson (PS Arthur Creech Jones) to E. G. Cass, 18 January 1950.
132 MT 9/5463, Welfare of Colonial People in the United Kingdom, Conference of non-official organisations at Church House, Westminster, Monday, 10 July 1950; CO 876/255, Minutes of the second meeting of the Inter-Departmental Committee on Colonial People in the United Kingdom, 19 July 1950, statement by chairman, J. L. Keith.
133 CO 876/232, Minutes of meeting of the Inter-Departmental Committee on Colonial People, 20 September 1951.

8. End of empire and rise of 'race relations'

1 A. Sivanandan, *Race and Resistance: the IRR Story* (London, IRR, 1974), pp. 1–2.
2 K. Little, *The Relations of White People and Coloured People in Great Britain* (Malvern, Le Play House Press, 1946), pp. 4, 8. Little tried to influence the Labour Party at this time via its Advisory Committee on Imperial Questions. See K. Little, 'The colour problem in Britain and its treatment', Labour Party, Advisory Committee on Imperial Questions, Memo No. 320, July 1948.
3 See, for example, Neil Wynn, *The Afro-American and the Second World War* (London, Paul Elek, 1976).
4 William Sumner, *Folkways*, 1st edn 1896 (New York, Dover Publications Inc., 1959); Harry Bell *et al.*, ' "Law and social change: Sumner reconsidered" ', *American Journal of Sociology*, 67, 5 (March 1962), pp. 532–40.
5 Gunnar Myrdal, *An American Dilemma*, Vol. 2 (New York, London, Harper and Brothers 1944), Appendix 1, p. 1032. For Sumner's sociology, see Robert Bannister, Jr., 'William Graham Sumner's Social Darwinism: a reconsideration', *History of Political Economy*, 5 (1973), pp. 89–109.
6 David Southern, *An American Dilemma* revisited: Myrdalism and white Southern liberals', *South Atlantic Quarterly*, 75, 2 (Spring 1976), pp. 182–97. For the debate on Myrdal's methods, see Ernest Kalser, 'Racial dialectics: the Aptheker–Myrdal school controversy', *Phylon*, 9, 4 (1948), pp. 195–302.
7 John Stanfield, 'Race relations research and black Americans between the two world wars', *Journal of Ethnic Studies*, 11, 3 (Fall 1983), pp. 61–93. See also Peter Rose, *The Subject is Race* (New York, Oxford University Press, 1968).
8 Robert Park, 'Our racial frontier on the Pacific', *Survey Graphic*, 9 (May 1926), p. 196, repr. in Robert Park, *Race and Culture* (New York, The Free Press, 1950), pp. 138–51; 'The nature of race relations', *ibid.*, pp. 81–116.
9 For Du Bois's role as a sociologist and his effective exclusion from the inner ranks of American sociology in the earlier years of the century, see Elliott Rudwick, 'W. E. B. Du Bois as sociologist', in James Blackwell and Morris Janowitz (eds.), *Black Sociologists: Historical and Contemporary Perspectives* (Chicago, University of Chicago Press, 1974), pp. 25–55. See also Dan Green and Edwin Driver (eds.) *W. E. B. Du Bois on Sociology and the Black Community* (Chicago and London, University of Chicago Press, 1978).
10 Louis Wirth, 'Problems and orientations of research in race relations in the United States', *British Journal of Sociology*, 1 (1950), p. 124.
11 *Lord Hailey Papers*, Edwin W. Smith, untitled memorandum, International African Institute, 2 April 1945, p. 1.
12 Bronislaw Malinowski, *The Dynamics of Culture Change* (New Haven and London, Yale University Press, 1945).
13 Audrey Richards, 'Tribal government in transition', *Journal of the Royal African Society*, suppl. to 34 (1935), pp. 1–26.
14 Malinowski, *op. cit.*, p. 145.
15 *Ibid.*, p. 161.

258 *Notes*

16 Hailey in Smith, *op. cit.*, p. 1.
17 Audrey Richards in Smith, *op. cit.*, p. 3.
18 Richard Brown, 'Anthropology and colonial rule: the case of Godfrey Wilson and the Rhodes–Livingstone Institute, Northern Rhodesia', in Talal Assad (ed.), *Anthropology and the Colonial Encounter* (London, Ithaca Press, 1973), pp. 173–97.
19 Max Gluckman and Fred Eggan, 'Introduction', in Michael Banton (ed.) *The Relevance of Models in Social Anthropology* (London, Tavistock, 1965), p. xi.
20 Brown, *op. cit.*, p. 197.
21 CO 926/61/28201, Minute by Andrew Cohen, 12 May 1947.
22 *Ibid.*, Minute by P. A. Wilson, 23 October 1947.
23 Douglas Johnson, 'Evans-Pritchard, the Nuer and the Sudan political services', *African Affairs*, 81, 322 (April 1982), pp. 231–46.
24 Peter Worsley, 'The analysis of rebellion and revolution in modern British social anthropology', *Science and Society*, 25 (1961), pp. 26–37.
25 Audrey Richards, 'The need for facts', *Spectator*, 4 February 1949.
26 Lord Hailey, 'Research in the colonies', *Spectator*, 4 March 1949.
27 'What is happening today in the British overseas territories', Sir Charles Jeffries wrote in 1956, 'can fairly be described as a social revolution . . . The crucial decision of 1939–40 was to intervene positively with the powerful tool of financial assistance on a significant scale. This made it possible to forestall discontent by keeping achievement in step with aspiration' (*The Colonial Office* (London, Allen and Unwin, 1956), p. 166).
28 Ronald Robinson, 'Andrew Cohen and the transfer of power in tropical Africa, 1940–51', in L. H. Morris-Jones and G. Fischer (eds.) *Decolonisation and Africa: the British and French Experience* (London, Frank Cass, 1980), p. 52.
29 Martin Channock, *Unconsummated Union, Britain, Rhodesia and South Africa, 1900–1945* (Manchester, Manchester University Press, 1977), pp. 259–60.
30 F. H. Soward, *The Adaptable Commonwealth* (London, RIIA, 1950), pp. 48–50.
31 Arthur Creech Jones, 'Black and white in Southern Africa', *Spectator*, 7 April 1950.
32 Lord Milverton, 'Race relations in Africa', *The Sunday Times*, 14 March 1950.
33 B. M. Osborne, *Colonial Affairs and the Public*, Report No. 171 (London, The Social Survey, Central Office of Information, 1956). On the issue of imperial propaganda, see John M. Mackenzie, *Propaganda and Empire* (Manchester, Manchester University Press, 1984).
34 Learie Constantine, *Colour Bar* (London, Stanley Paul and Co., 1954), p. 34.
35 Ian Fleming, 'Pleasant island', *Spectator*, 4 July 1952.
36 For Fleming's use of race in his fiction, see Margaret Marshment, 'Racist ideology and popular fiction', *Race and Class*, 19, 4 (1978), pp. 331–44. This was not true of all popular fiction at this time and the novels of Nevil Shute, especially, are significant for the manner in which they mark an erosion in the notion of a British imperial and civilising mission, whilst still maintaining the notion of the *separateness* of black and white races. See Donald Lammers, 'Nevil Shute and the decline of the "imperial idea" in literature', *Journal of*

British Studies, 16, 2 (Spring 1977), pp. 121–42.

37 This particularly meant depriving South Africa of its mandate over South West Africa (Namibia) and reviving the notion of 'international trusteeship'. C.W.W. Greenidge likened this to the earlier campaign to remove the Congo from King Leopold's control (MSS Brit. Emp. S 17 DIO/9f.1, C. W. W. Greenidge to David Astor, 17 December 1951).

38 *The Racial Relations Group*, leaflet of the Institute of Sociology (Malvern, Le Play House, 1938).

39 *J.D. Rheinallt-Jones Papers* C26/4, J.D. Rheinallt-Jones to Mrs John Jones, 11 March 1948; C26/5, E.J. Turner to J.D. Rheinallt-Jones, 9 June 1948; Mrs John Jones to J.D. Rheinallt-Jones, 24 April 1948.

40 *Ibid.*, C27/82a, H. S. L. Polak to J. D. Rheinallt-Jones, 30 March 1948.

41 *F. A. Norman Papers*, E. J. Turner, Memorandum, 2 February 1952; *The Annual Report of the Institute of Sociology for the Year 1948* (Malvern, Le Play House Press), p. 5.

42 Percy Black, 'Towards a systematic field of race relations', *Human Relations*, 4, 1 (February 1951), pp 95–102.

43 *F. A. Norman Papers*, E. J. Turner, Memorandum, 2 February 1952.

44 For the last phase of the Institute of Sociology, see Dorothea Farquharson, 'Dissolution of the Institute of Sociology', *Sociological Review*, 3, 2 (December 1955), pp. 165–73.

45 *F. A. Norman Papers*, Racial Unity, Minutes of meeting held at Denison House, Vauxhall Bridge Road, 14 January 1952.

46 *Ibid.*, Letter to the Rt. Hon. James Griffiths, 30 September 1951.

47 *Ibid.*, Minutes of Executive Committee, 4 July 1952; *The Friend*, 22 February 1952. The speakers included Krishna Menon, Dingle Foot and C.J.M. Alport, and Lord Hailsham presided.

48 *F. A. Norman Papers*, Racial Unity, Report on work up to March 1956, mimeo, n.d.

49 *Ibid.*, Minutes of meeting held at Denison House, 14 January 1952.

50 *F. A. Norman Papers*, Colin Turnbull to F. A. Norman, 20 December 1951. See also CO 876/272, M. Attlee to J. Griffiths, 15 August 1951.

51 *F. A. Norman Papers*, F. A. Norman, Memorandum entitled 'Racial relations', typescript, n.d., p. 2. See also CO 876/272, J. L. Keith, Minute, 3 October 1951. Ivor Cummings considered Racial Unity 'premature' (minute, n.d.).

52 *Ibid.*, p. 5.

53 *Ibid.*, pp. 8–9.

54 *Ibid.*, p. 9; Racial Unity, Minutes of meeting held at Denison House, 14 January 1952, note in margin in Norman's writing, p. 4.

55 *F. A. Norman Papers*, Racial Unity, Letter to Lennox-Boyd, 1 October 1954.

56 Anthony Richmond, *The Colour Problem*, 1st edn 1955 (Harmondsworth, Penguin, 1961), pp. 245–6. See also C. Senior and D. Manley, *A Report on Jamaican Immigration to Great Britain* (Kingston, Government Printer, Jamaica, 1955), pp. 23–4.

57 Senior and Manley, *op. cit.*, p. 51.

58 *F. A. Norman Papers*, Report to the second AGM of Racial Unity', 28 March 1955, p. 4.

59 Michael Banton, 'The influence of colonial status upon black–white relations

in England, 1948–58', unpublished paper, University of Bristol, 1983.
60 Mervyn Jones, 'A question of colour', *New Statesman*, 11 August 1951.
61 LAB 20/218, A. Richmond to Ministry of Labour, 10 April 1951.
62 *F. A. Norman Papers*, Racial Unity, 'Chairman's report for 1955', p. 5. The attendance for Cedric Dover's talks was described as 'disappointing'.
63 Rt. Hon. Lewis Silkin, 'Fostering communities', *Social Service*, 21, 2 (September–November 1947), pp. 101–2.
64 Nadine Peppard, 'Into the third decade', *New Community*, 1 (January 1972). Ivor Thompson, 'Welcome stranger', *Social Service*, 23 (January–August 1949), p. 38.
65 G.D.H. Cole, 'A retrospect of the history of voluntary social service', in A.F.C. Bourdillon (ed.) *Voluntary Social Services: Their Place in the Modern State* (London, Methuen, 1945), p. 25.
66 Leslie Banks, 'The growth of communities', *Social Service Quarterly*, 30, 2 (September–November 1956), p. 58.
67 *British Council of Churches Archive*, Box 13, Int. Dept., Race Rel. Group, 1950–2, Notes submitted by Rev. R. K. Orchard to the working party, 18 January 1950, pp. 1–2.
68 Michael Hill and Ruth Issacharof, *Community Action and Race Relations* (London, Oxford University Press, 1971), p. 5.
69 *Ibid.*, p. 7; *The Times*, 25 August 1956.
70 This first began to be systematically studied by J. Rex and R. Moore, *Race, Community and Conflict: a Study of Sparkbrook* (London, Oxford University Press for the Institute of Race Relations, 1967).
71 S. K. Ruck (ed.) *The West Indian comes to England* (London, Routledge and Kegan Paul, 1960), pp. 66–71; Hill and Issacharof, *op. cit.*, p. 8.
72 Ruck, *op. cit.*, p. 72.
73 Errol Lawrence, 'In the abundance of water the fool is thirsty: sociology and black "pathology" ', in Centre for Contemporary Cultural Studies, *The Empire Strikes Back* (London, Hutchinson, 1982), pp. 95–142.
74 John Rex and Robert Moore, *Race, Community and Conflict* (London, Oxford University Press, 1967).
75 Gordon Lewis, 'Fabian socialism: some aspects of theory and practice', *Journal of Politics*, 14, 3 (August 1952), p. 467. See also Elisabeth Littlejohn, 'The relations of community relations to community work', *New Community*, 1, 5 (Autumn 1972), especially pp. 100–01.
76 J. L. Keith to F. A. Norman, n.d. repro. in *Racial Unity Bulletin* (June 1956), pp. 1–2.
77 DCL 93/2a; Ivo de Souza *The British Caribbean Welfare Service*, July 1956, p. 2.
78 *Ibid.*, p. 3. See also *Beacon*, 26 May 1956.
79 London Council of Social Service, Conference on West Indian Migrants in London, 28 June 1956.
80 *Ibid.*, Brother Mark of Society of St Francis, Cable St.
81 *Ibid.*, Alfred Hyndman of the Family Welfare Association.
82 Ruth Glass, *Newcomers: the West Indian in London* (London, Allen and Unwin, 1960), pp. 147–51.
83 *Ibid.*, p. 143; *Time and Tide* noted that 'it was pure hooliganism with the Teddy Boy era arriving at its natural destination' (6 September 1958). See also Paul Rock and Stan Cohen, 'The teddy boy', in Vernon Bogdanor and Robert Skidelsky (eds.) *The Age of Affluence, 1951–1964* (London, Macmillan,

1970), pp. 288–320.
84 K. Little, 'Integration without tears', *New Statesman*, 20 September 1958.
85 Wallace Collins, *Jamaican Migrant* (London, Routledge and Kegan Paul, 1965), p. 116. The Council was described, though, as providing 'a unique achievement in London between the migrant and the English when they managed to get the full support of the borough officials and the Community as a whole' (p. 118). See also Hill and Issacharof, *op. cit.*, p. 9.
86 London Council of Social Service, *Report of a Conference on Racial Integration, St Edmund Hall, Oxford, 15–17 September 1960*, pp. 3–5. Jahoda began introducing these ideas in sociological circles in the early 1940s. See Dr Marie Jahoda, 'Some American investigations of race relations', *Le Play House Emergency Bulletin*, 1 (July 1943), pp. 1–2.
87 London Council of Social Service, *Report*, p. 7.
88 Ceri Peach, *West Indian Migration to Britain* (London, Oxford University Press, 1968), p. 56.
89 Nicholas Deakin, 'Harold Macmillan and the control of Commonwealth immigration', *New Community*, 4, 2 (Summer 1975), pp. 191–4.
90 Clarence Senior, 'Race relations and labor supply in Great Britain', *Social Problems*, 4, 4 (April 1957), p. 308.
91 Norman Manley, 'A challenge to Britain', *New Statesman*, 13 September 1958. See also Harold Chapman, 'Norman Manley', *Spectator*, 12 September 1958.
92 *Spectator*, 5 September 1958.
93 Esme Wynne-Tyson, 'Thoughts on the colour problem', *Contemporary Review* (January 1959), p. 43.
94 Nicholas Deakin, 'The politics of the Commonwealth Immigrants Bill', *Political Quarterly*, 39, 1 (1968), pp. 28–30.
95 Lord Butler, *The Art of the Possible* (Harmondsworth, Penguin, 1973), pp. 207–8.
96 For an explanation of this term, see Gerhard Lehmbruch, 'Consociational democracy, class conflict and the new corporatism', in Philipp Schmitter and Gerhard Lehmbruch (eds.) *Trends towards Corporatist Internationalism* (Beverley Hills and London, Sage Publications, 1979), pp. 53–61.
97 Butler, *op. cit.*, p. 208; Glass, *op. cit.*, pp. 142–3.
98 *Parlt. Deb.*, House of Commons, 649, 16 November 1961, col. 649.
99 *Ibid.*, col. 776.
100 *Report of the Commonwealth Immigrants Advisory Council*, Cmnd 2119 (London, HMSO, 1963), p. 1.
101 Hill and Issacharof, *op. cit.*, p. 12.
102 Bertram Doyle, *The Etiquette of Race Relations in the South: a Study in Social Control*, 1st edn 1937 (New York, Schocker Books, 1971).
103 K. Little, Memorandum entitled 'Colour bar legislation' submitted to the Commonwealth Subcommittee of the Labour Party National Executive Committee, p. 6. I am grateful to Professor Michael Banton for this document.
104 Keith Hindell, 'The genesis of the race relations bill', *Political Quarterly*, 36, 4 (October–December 1965), p. 391; Cedric Thornberry, 'Commitment or withdrawal? The place of law in race relations in Britain', *Race*, 1 (1969), pp. 76–7.
105 *Labour Party Archives*, Race Relations File, K. Little to H. Gaitskell, 4 September 1958; *Venture* (October 1958), pp. 1–2.
106 *V. Junod Correspondence*, V. Junod to K. Little, 23 July 1952; K. Little to V.

Junod, 28 July 1952.
107 Michael Banton, 'Negroes in Britain: the conceptualisation of culture contact', paper presented to a Conference on Race Relations, University of Edinburgh, 22 January 1952, p. 2.
108 Sydney Collins, 'Social processes integrating coloured people in Britain', *British Journal of Sociology*, 11, 1 (March 1952), p. 27.
109 Michael Banton, *The Coloured Quarter* (London, Jonathan Cape, 1955), pp. 214–15.
110 The London Labour Party, *Problems of Coloured People in London*, 27 September 1955, p. 2.
111 Interview with Professor K. Little, University of Edinburgh; Michael Banton, 'The changing position of the negro in Britain', *Phylon*, 14, 1 (1953), pp. 74–83.
112 *Labour Party Archives*, Race Relations File, James Cummings, Secretary, West Indian Workers and Students Association to the Secretary, Labour Party, 22 September 1958.
113 For an alternative account of the Institute's history based upon a more deterministic model of the IRR as a reflection of the interests of the British 'power elite', see C. P. Mullard, 'Power, Race and Resistance: a Study of the Institute of Race Relations, 1952–1972', Ph.D. thesis, University of Durham, 1980.
114 MSS Brit. Emp. S22 G512/513, K. Little to E. J. Turner, 22 April 1950. The welfare bodies by this time doubted their strength to establish an institute and the main objective was to establish a 'Welfare Institute' (*F. A. Norman Papers*, E. J. Turner, Memorandum for the Committee on the Establishment of an Institute of Race Relations, 30 November 1950).
115 *Ibid.*, Frank Lambert to C. W. W. Greenidge, 24 January 1949.
116 *Ibid.*, Committee on the Proposed Institute of Race Relations, Minutes of meeting held on 8 November 1950, pp. 2–3.
117 *W. M. Macmillan Papers*, H. V. Hodson to W. M. Macmillan, 27 October 1939.
118 H. V. Hodson, *Twentieth-Century Empire* (London, Faber and Faber, 1948), p. 177. See also Sir William Hailey to Lord Reith, 13 July 1952, in Charles Stuart (ed.), *The Reith Diaries* (London, Collins, 1975), p. 381.
119 H.V. Hodson, 'Race relations in the Commonwealth', *International Affairs*, 26 (July 1950), pp. 306–7.
120 *Ibid.*, pp. 313–15.
121 *F. A. Norman Papers*, Philip Eastman to F. A. Norman, 10 March 1952 encl. memorandum on proposals for 'A Board of Studies on Race Relations', n.d.; H. V. Hodson, 'The Institute of Race Relations', unpublished MS, 1976, University of York, pp. 5–6.
122 *Report of the Committee on the Provision for Economic and Social Research*, Cmnd. 6868 (London, HMSO, 1946), p. 12.
123 CO 876/244 H. V. Hodson to Secretary of State for the Colonies, 12 April 1951. For the research focus of the Institute, see Hugh Tinker, *Race Relations Roundabout*, unpublished MS, n.d., esp. Chapter 4. For the Institute's support for the partnership policy, see Philip Mason, 'Partnership in Central Africa', *International Affairs*, 33, 2 (April 1957), pp. 152–64, and 33, 3 (July 1957), pp. 310–18.
124 Mullard, *op. cit.*, p. 24; Tinker, *op. cit.*; H. V. Hodson, unpublished memoirs, University of York, 1976, pp. 6–10.

125 Philip Mason, 'Ten years of the Institute', *Race*, 10, 2 (1968), pp. 194–6.
126 Mullard, *op. cit.*, pp. 111–12.
127 See, for example, H. V. Hodson, 'The study of race relations', *Optima*, 6 (1956), pp. 52–4.
128 Nicholas Deakin, 'The Immigration Issue in British Politics, 1948–1964, Ph.D. thesis, University of Sussex, 1978, p. 45.
129 Paul Rich, *White Power and the Liberal Conscience, Racial Segregation and South African Liberalism, 1921–1960* (Manchester, Manchester University Press, 1984).
130 Political and Economic Planning, *British Immigration Policy*, 15, 268 (4 July 1947), p. 33. For the PEP role in the development of middle opinion on planning, see Arthur Marwick, 'Middle opinion and the thirties: planning, progress and political "Agreement" ', *English Historical Review*, 79 (April 1964), p. 295.
131 Philip Mason, 'What do we mean by integration?', *New Society*, 16 June 1965, p. 11.
132 Anthony Richmond, 'Applied social science and public policy concerning race relations in Britain', *Race*, 1, 1 (November 1959), pp. 14–26; Michael Banton, 'Sociology and race relations, *ibid.*, pp. 3–14.
133 See especially the writings of Friedrich Hertz, 'National character', *Le Play House Emergency Bulletin*, 11 (June 1944), pp. 1–2; *Nationally in History and Politics* (London, Routledge and Kegan Paul, 1944), esp. pp. 52–77.
134 See, for example, Maurice Broady, 'The social adjustment of Chinese immigration in Liverpool', *Sociological Review*, 3, 1 (July 1955), pp. 65–75.
135 Anthony Richmond, 'Immigration as a social process: the case of coloured colonials in the United Kingdom', *Social and Economic Studies*, 5, 2 (1956), p. 190; Norman Mackenzie, 'The West Indian in Britain', *New Statesman*, 17 September 1955.
136 CO 876/217, A Petition by the Community of Colonials in Manchester (under the Auspices of the African League M/C) to the Rt. Hon. James Griffiths, Secretary of State for the Colonies, on the occasion of his visit to Manchester, 10 February 1951.
137 Gordon K. Lewis, 'Protest among the immigrants: the dilemma of minority culture', *Political Quarterly*, 40, 4 (October–December 1969), p. 429.
138 See, for example, Donald Wood, 'Some considerations of Migration', *WISC Newsletter*, July 1961, pp. 2–3.
139 E. J. B. Rose *et al.*, *Colour and Citizenship* (London, Oxford University Press for the IRR, 1969), pp. 501–2.
140 NCCL 93/8, Claudia Jones, leaflet for the Seventh Afro-Asian-Caribbean Conference, 31 January 1962. See also Donald Hinds, *Journey to an Illusion* (London, Heinemann, 1966), p. 137; and Buzz Johnson, 'Claudia Jones: freedom fighter', *Dragons Teeth*, 16 (Winter 1983), pp. 8–10 and *'I Think of My Mother': Notes on the Life and Times of Claudia Jones* (London, Karia Press, 1985).
141 *Friend*, 10 and 24 Nobember 1961; Movement for Colonial Freedom leaflet 'Resolution on "No colour bar in immigration" ', 1 November 1961, St Pancras Town Hall.
142 Sheila Patterson, *Dark Strangers: a Study of West Indians in London* (Harmondsworth, Penguin, 1963), pp. 345–57.
143 Mullard, *op. cit.*, p. 182; Rose, *op. cit.*, pp. 511–32.

144 CARD leaflet 'A spur to racialism', 1965. For the development of CARD, see Benjamin Heinemann, *The Politics of the Powerless: a Study of the Campaign Against Racial Discrimination* (London, Oxford University Press for the IRR, 1972).
145 For the intellectual context of post-war race relations thinking in Britain, see Paul Rich, 'The politics of "race relations" in Britain, and the West', in Peter Jackson (ed.), *Race and Racism* (London, Allen and Unwin, 1987), pp. 95–114.
146 Guy Hunter (ed.), *Industrialisation and Race Relations* (London, OUP for the IRR, 1965).
147 Philip Mason, *Patterns of Dominance* (London, OUP, 1970). Mason was not keen on the director of the Institute's survey being a sociologist, for the important thing was to have 'someone who has both the sense that this is urgent and important and needs doing, and the objectivity to make a detached and rational job of it'. This might mean an 'organisation man' since 'so many scholars are specialists', *Margery Perham Papers*, Philip Mason to M. Perham, 1 and 21 March 1963.
148 See also V. G. Kiernan, 'Europe in the colonial mirror', *History of European Ideas*, 1 (1980), p. 60.
149 Tinker, *Race Relations Roundabout*, p. 139
150 Noel Annan, '"Our Age": reflections on three generations in England', *Daedalus*, 4 (Fall, 1978), pp. 100–1.
151 *Colour and Citizenship*, p. 31. For the gestation of the project see Philip Mason, 'The Institute's "Survey of Race Relations in Britain": a report on four years' progress', *Race*, 9, 4 (1968), pp. 511–20; 'Ten years of the Institute', *Race*, 10, 2 (1969), p. 193–202.
152 *Colour and Citizenship*, p. 553.
153 *Ibid.*, p. 676.
154 Robin Jenkins, 'The production of knowledge in the Institute of Race Relations', unpublished mimeo, Institute of Race Relations, 6 January 1971, p. 24.
155 Mullard, *Race, Power and Resistance*, pp. 128–32.
156 Tinker, *Race Relations Roundabout*, p. 156. 'June 1970 meant that the overall expectations of the Fabians that they could assist in planning an era of gradual improvements, at home and abroad, were now irrelevant. In race relations, the "softly softly" approach was now quite irrelevant. Things were going to get tougher, and a tough response was needed.'
157 *Race, Power and Resistance*, pp. 195–6.
158 *Race, Power and Resistance*.

Conclusion

1 George Watson, 'Race and empire', in *The English Ideology* (London, Allen Lane, 1973), p. 215.
2 Hans Kohn, 'The genesis and character of English nationalism', *Journal of the History of Ideas*, 1, 1 (January 1940), p. 92.
3 Gina Mitchell, 'A hierarchy of race: stereotypes in the popular fiction of England, 1880–1939', paper presented at the Conference on the History and Ideology of Anglo-Saxon Racial Attitudes, 1870–1970, Selly Oak, Birmingham, September 1982.

4 E. J. B. Rose, *Colour and Citizenship* (London, Oxford University Press for the IRR, 1969), p. 494.
5 John Darwin, 'Imperialism in decline? Tendencies in British imperial policy between the wars', *Historical Journal*, 23, 3 (1980), pp. 657–79.
6 *Record of the Proceedings of the First Universal Races Congress held at the University of London, 26–29 July 1911* (London, P. S. King and Son, 1911).
7 Martin Bulmer, 'Charles S. Johnson, Robert E. Park and the research methods of the Chicago Commission on Race Relations, 1919–22; an early experiment in applied social research', *Ethnic and Racial Studies*, 4, 3 (July 1981), pp. 289–306. See also Park Dixon Gois, 'City and "community", the urban theory of Robert Park', *American Quarterly*, 23, 1 (Spring 1971), pp. 46–59.
8 James Weldon Johnson, *Black Manhattan*, 1st edn 1930 (New York, Athenaeum, 1968) p. 231.
9 Lord Elton, *The Unarmed Invasion* (London, Geoffrey Bles, 1965), pp. 63–4.
10 See, for example, John Garrard, *The English and Immigration* (London, Oxford University Press, 1971); Colin Holmes, *Anti-Semitism in British Society 1876–1939* (London, Edward Arnold, 1979); Colin Holmes (ed.) *Immigrants and Minorities in British Society* (London, Edward Arnold, 1978); Kenneth Lunn, *Hosts, Immigrants and Minorities* (London, Dawson, 1980).
11 G. C. L. Bertram, *West Indian Immigration* (London, The Eugenics Society, 1958), p. 21.
12 See, for example, Ruth Benedict, *Race and Racism*, 1st edn 1942 (London, Routledge and Kegan Paul, 1983), esp. pp. 166–71.
13 Though Keith's ideas continued to guide sociobiology in the post-war period. See, for example, Richard Lynn, 'The sociobiology of nationalism', *New Society*, 1 July 1976, pp. 11–14.
14 Michael Howard, 'Empire, race and war in pre-1914 Britain', in Hugh Lloyd-Jones *et al.* (eds.), *History and Imagination* (London, Duckworth, 1981), p. 352.
15 George Watson, 'Race and the socialists', in *Politics and Literature in Modern Britain* (London, Macmillan, 1977), p. 121.
16 Anon. 'Social disintegration', *Macmillans Magazine*, May 1867, p. 31.
17 A. P. Thornton, *The Imperial Idea and its Enemies* (London, Macmillan, 1966), p. xi.
18 Bernard Porter, *The Lion's Share* (London and New York, Longman, 1975), p. 325. For a critical assessment of this thesis, see B. R. Tomlinson, 'The contraction of England: national decline and the loss of empire', *Journal of Imperial and Commonwealth History*, 11, 1 (October 1982), p. 61, who points out that the argument looks at developments within the imperial centre as opposed to nationalist movements in the colonial periphery, which may not, though, act on British power in any uniform manner.
19 'Although relationships between people of the white race and other races', declared Patrick Gordon Walker in the debate on the Commonwealth Immigrants Bill, 'is a world-wide problem, it is, in a special sense a peculiar Commonwealth problem' (*Parlt. Deb.*, House of Commons, 649, 16 November 1961, col. 712).
20 Derek Ingram, *Commonwealth for a Colour Blind World* (London, Allen and Unwin 1965), p. 27.

21 Bernard Porter, *Britain, Europe and the World, 1850–1982: Delusions of Grandeur* (London, Allen and Unwin, 1983), p. 111.
22 Dan Horowitz, 'The British Conservatives and the racial issue in the debate on decolonization', *Race*, 12, 2 (1970), pp. 169–87.
23 Lord Elton, *op. cit.*, pp. 19, 35.
24 Donald Horne, *God is an Englishman* (Harmondsworth, Penguin, 1965), p. 112.
25 Hannah Arendt, *The Origins of Totalitarianism*, 2nd edn (London, Allen and Unwin, 1958), p. 153.
26 Enoch Powell, *A Nation Not Afraid* (London, Hodder and Stoughton, 1965), p. 137.
27 *Ibid.*, pp. 140–3; 'The myth of empire: ce n'est que l'illusoire qui dure?', *Round Table*, 240 (November 1970), pp. 435–41.
28 Enoch Powell, *Freedom and Reality* (London, Batsford, 1969), p. 189.
29 Paul Foot, *The Rise of Enoch Powell* (London, Cornmarket Press, 1969). See also Paul Rich, 'Conservative ideology and race in modern British politics', in Zig Layton-Henry and Paul Rich (eds.), *Race, Government and Politics in Britain* (London, Macmillan, 1986), pp. 45–72.
30 Hugh Tinker, for example, wrote that 'insofar as we have an ideology about ourselves and our nation it is that the British are the British are the British . . . that is why Powell's message needs no elaboration or translation to his audience', 'Beyond Powell', *Race Today*, 3, 3 (March 1971), p. 103. Such a view failed to understand the cultural tradition from which this national ideology sprang.
31 Paul Rich, 'Patriotism and the idea of citizenship in post-war British politics', paper presented to the CCPR, Paris, April 1989.
32 Lord Scarman, *The Scarman Report: the Brixton Disorders, 10–12 April 1981* (Harmondsworth, Penguin, 1982), p. 175.
33 *Ibid.*, p. 160.
34 *Ibid.*, p. 210.
35 Department of the Environment, *Policy for the Inner Cities*, Cmnd 6845 (London, HMSO, 1977). See also John Rex, 'The 1981 urban riots in Britain', *International Journal of Urban and Regional Research*, 6, 1 (1982), p. 109.
36 John Holloway, 'The myth of England', *The Listener*, 15 May 1969, pp. 670–2; Martin Weiner, *English Culture and the Decline of the Industrial Spirit* (Cambridge, CUP, 1980).
37 Scarman, *op. cit.*, p. 168.

Bibliography

DOCUMENTARY SOURCES

Official

Files, reports and minutes from the following departments at the Public Record Office, Kew Gardens. The reference code follows in brackets:

The Cabinet Office (Cab)
The Colonial Office (CO)
The Home Office (HO)
Ministry of Information (Inf)
Ministry of Labour (LAB)
Ministry of Transport (MT)
Prime Minister's Office (PREM)

Organisations and societies

Anti-Slavery Society Papers, Rhodes House, Oxford (MSS Brit. Emp. S22)
British Council of Churches Archives, Selly Oak Colleges, Birmingham
British Museum Central Archives, British Museum
Central Board of Missionary Societies (CBMS), School of Oriental and African Studies, University of London
Fortnightly Club Papers, Church of the Province Archives, University of the Witwatersrand, Johannesburg
Institute of Sociology files, Keele University
Labour Party Archives, Walworth Road, London
London Group on African Affairs, Rhodes House, Oxford (MSS Brit. Emp. S1427)
Medical Research Council (MRC) – Anthropological Standards Committee, Medical Research Council
National Council of Civil Liberties (NCCL), University of Hull
Racial Unity files, in the private possession of Mr F. Norman-Smith
Round Table Papers, Bodleian Library, Oxford
Archives of the Royal Anthropological Institute (RAI), Royal Anthropological Institute
Scottish Anthropological Society (SAS), Edinburgh University
Society of Friends Archives, Friends Meeting House, Euston Road, London
South Place Ethical Society, files and minutes, South Place Ethical Society, Red Lion Square, London.

267

268   *Bibliography*

Individuals
Leonard Barnes collection, especially an unpublished autobiography, School of
    Oriental and African Studies
Victor Branford Papers (VB), Keele University
James Bryce Papers, Bodleian Library, Oxford
Reginald Coupland Papers, Rhodes House, Oxford
Lionel Curtis Papers, Bodleian Library, Oxford
Alexander Farquharson Papers (AF), Keele University
C. W. W. Greenidge Papers, Rhodes House, Oxford
A. C. Haddon Papers, Cambridge University
Malcolm Hailey Papers, Rhodes House, Oxford
A. L. Hammond Papers, Bodleian Library, Oxford
Winifred Holtby Papers, Hull Public Library
Lord Lothian Papers, Scottish Record Office, Edinburgh
W. M. Macmillan Papers, in the private possession of Mrs Mona Macmillan
E. D. Morel Papers, British Library of Economic and Political Science
Gilbert Murray Papers, Bodleian Library, Oxford
F. A. Norman Papers, in the private possession of Mr D. Norman-Smith
J.D. Rheinallt-Jones Papers, Church of the Province Archives, University of the
    Witwatersrand, Johannesburg
Margery Perham Papers, Rhodes House, Oxford
W. C. Scully Papers, Church of the Province Archives, University of the
Witwatersrand, Johannesburg
Reginald Sorensen Papers, House of Lords Library
Graham Wallas Collection, British Library of Political and Economic Science,
London
Alfred Zimmern Papers, Bodleian Library, Oxford

Newspapers, journals and magazines
African Telegraph
African Times and Orient Review
Daily Herald
Edinburgh Review
The Friend
Geographical Teacher
Illustrated London News
The Keys
Liverpool Review
Macmillans Magazine
Manchester Guardian
The Nation
News Chronicle
New Statesman
Nineteenth Century
Review of Reviews
Round Table
The Seaman
Social Service
Sociological Review
Spectator
Sunday Pictorial

Index

Abrahams, Peter, 87, 88
Africa Society, 36
Aggrey, Dr J.E.K., 67, 184
Aggrey House, 137, 143, 155-8, 161
Aggrey Housing Limited, 184
Ali, Duse Mohommed, 48
Allen, Grant, 52
Amery, Leo, 54, 57, 69, 76, 85, 146
Anglo-Saxonism, 1, 13-16, 24-6, 30, 51, 100-1, 212
Annan, Noel, 5
Anthropological Survey Committee, 109
anthropology, 18, 50, 80, 92-3, 96-7, 103, 106-9, 117-18, 171-3, 196, 209;
'culture contact' theory, 100, 172, 191;
see also Anthropological Survey Committee, Association of Social Anthropoligists, Edinburgh School of Anthropology, Imperial Bureau of Ethnology, Rhodes-Livingstone Institute, Royal Anthropological Institute, Scottish Anthropological Society 113-14
Anthropometric Standards Committee, 109
Anthropometric Survey, 103-4, 113
Anthropometry, 18, 51, 100-4, 110, 171, 209
Anti-Slavery Society, 37-8, 135, 137, 139, 142-4, 150, 156-8, 193; see also Welfare of Africans in Europe War Fund Committee
apartheid, 90
Archer, William, 52-3, 63, 66
Arendt, Hannah, 118, 211
Army Bureau of Current Affairs (ABCA), 153
Arnold, Matthew, 14, 21
Arnold, Thomas, 100
assimiliation, 10, 169-70, 184-5, 187, 192, 197-9
Association of Social Anthropologists, 173
Attlee, Clement, 157

Baldwin, Stanley, 65, 83
Banton, Michael, 181, 191-2, 198
Barker, Anthony, 4
Barnes, Leonard, 7, 70, 82-5, 87, 90, 207, 248 n. 80; *The Duty of Empire*, 84; *Empire or Democracy*, 84-5; *The New Boar War*, 83
Bateson, Gregory, 112, 241 n. 120
Beck, Maximilien, 100
Becker, Carl, 3
Beddoe, John, 20, 102
Beer, George Louis, 60
Benedict, Ruth, 2
Biddiss, Michael, 47
Brimingham Council of Social Service, 183
Bloch, Marc, 2-3
Blyden, Edward Wilmott, 29, 32-3, 48
Boas, Franz, 110, 118
Bolt, Christine, 3
Boxall, George E., 25
British Association for the Advancement of Science, 102-2, 107-8, 115-16
British Caribbean Welfare Service, 186-7
British Council of Churches, 168, 183
British Council for the Welfare of the Mercantile Marine, 138
British Nationality Act, 1948, 202
British Racial Relations Group, 176-9
British Sailors' Soceity, 141
British Social Hygiene Association, 138
British Sociological Association, 177
British Sociological Society, 23, 44, 94
Brockway, Fenner, 86-7, 90, 199, 204
Bryce, Jamesz, 20-4, 68, 71, 206
Buchan, John, 55-6
Burrow, John, 116
Butler, R.A.B., 189-90
Buxton, Charles Roden, 78

Campaign Against Racial Discrimination

269